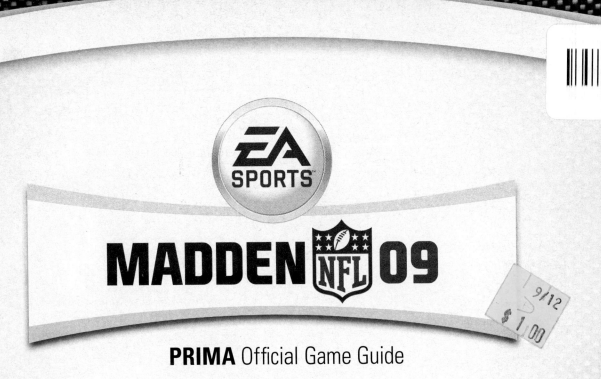

MADDEN NFL 09

PRIMA Official Game Guide

An Imprint of Random House, Inc.
3000 Lava Ridge Court, Suite 100
Roseville, CA 95661

NFL PLAYERS

Senior Product Manager: Donato Tica
Associate Product Manager: John Browning
Manufacturing: Suzanne Goodwin

Special thanks to: Brent Coyle, Anthony Stevenson, Chris Erb, Lorraine Honrada, Daniel Davis, Anthony White and Michelle Manahan.

Please be advised that the ESRB Ratings icons, "EC," "E," "E10+," "T," "M," "AO," and "RP" are trademarks owned by the Entertainment Software Association, and may only be used with their permission and authority. For information regarding whether a product has been rated by the ESRB, please visit www.esrb.org. For permission to use the Ratings icons, please contact the ESA at esrblicenseinfo.com.

ISBN: 978-0-7615-5923-8
Printed in the United States of America

08 09 10 11 GG 10 9 8 7 6 5 4 3 2 1

Written by **Mojo Media** and **VG Sports**

Editor: Joe Funk
Creative Director: Jason Hinman
Art Director: Daniel Tideman

VG Sports
President: Bert Ingley
Staff Writers: Paul Gleason, Bernie Hayes and Ron Jackson

CONTENTS

▲ *Virtual Trainer detail screen*

FEATURES

▲ *Virtual Trainer selections*

EA SPORTS has added some cool new features to *Madden NFL 09* with the goal being to help you learn the game at your own pace. *Madden NFL 09* comes with a built in Virtual Trainer to teach you the ropes. This Virtual Trainer tool will help you acquire the fundamental skills for playing football and using the controls in *Madden NFL 09*. You will get the most from the new trainer feature by playing through

all twelve tutorial drills. These drills are also the basis for the Madden Test, so if you want to increase your Madden IQ, practice the Virtual Trainer feature and then take or re-take the Madden Test.

The 12 new training games are broken into 4 main categories.

▲ *Virtual Trainer rushing options*

In the rushing Virtual Trainer you will learn how to rely less on outright speed, and instead learn to set up blockers to maximize the amount of yards you can gain. Setting up blocks

is just half of being a good back. This tutorial also lets you practice the agility moves you need to transform your back from being an average rusher to a feared one.

▲ *Offensive passing options*

The passing trainer is designed to get you comfortable with moving around in the pocket and being able to handle the pressure from rushing defenders. Quarterbacks who do this well give their receivers more time to get open and increase the chances of success on the play. The passing trainer also gets you used to reading the defense, finding the open receiver and putting the ball in a spot where only your receiver can catch it.

▲ *Rush defense options*

This set of drills is extremely helpful for all *Madden NFL 09* players. In order to make a tackle you have to be able to read the blockers, stay on a good

pursuit angle and then attack the runner. Once in position the drill calls on the multiple tackling options. There is one thing that is practiced every day on defense in football: tackling. This drill

▲ *Pass defense options*

will take care of that.

The NFL is a passing league and *Madden NFL 09*, like many of its predecessors, is still a passing game. The best way to have a dominant defense is by starting with defending the pass. In the Pass Defense drill, you have the opportunity to hone your pass rushing skills. Moving away from the D-Line and into the secondary, the pass coverage trainer drills your DB swat and coverage skills.

MADDEN NFL 09 CHALLENGE TIPS

Tendencies: To do well in the Madden Challenge you need to avoid showing tendencies, and work on picking up on other player's tendencies. Attack the weakness of others, but at the same time mix up your plays. Top players key in on this and make you pay when you go to the well one too many times.

▲ **Current My Skill level**

In *Madden NFL 09*, users will notice a change in the gamer levels. In past years there were only 4 gamer skill levels; Rookie, Pro, All-Pro and All-Madden. *Madden NFL 09* boasts two new skill levels: My Skill and Custom. These new levels are similar to sliders in a way, as they will make the game more specific to an individual's gaming experience.

▲ **My Skill level settings**

By default, *Madden NFL 09* starts of with a My Skill level equal to the All-Pro level. The skill level is also reflected in the individual's Madden IQ score. If you start off by not taking the Madden Test and get right to gaming then it may make your first few games a little lopsided, while the computer adjusts to your level of experience.

▲ **Skill results and new IQ rating**

At the end of every game of *Madden NFL 09* played on the My Skill level, the game will show how a user's skill level has progressed. It will also make training suggestions that can help the user become more proficient in weak areas of their game.

▲ **Post-game My Skill level**

After the My Skill level adjusts based on a user's performance, it goes into the next game with the new skill level settings. In short, this is how a user becomes better. *Madden NFL 09* is a game focused on enhancing the user's game skill so that they can continuously enjoy the game and get a somewhat new experience every time they play.

▲ **Beginner Game Style Playcall**

Not only will users have the ability to compete according to the My Skill level, but they will also be able to refine their level of play even more with the 4 different game style settings. For those playing in Beginner mode, you won't have to worry about picking a play at all. *Madden NFL 09* will call a play for you. The pre-play interface is condensed and only gives you the option of calling a play audible, making coverage audibles or cycling through players.

▲ **Intermediate Playcall screen**

Gamers who select the Intermediate game style will be given the option of selecting a play from the run, pass or special teams category. After selecting what play type they want, they will be able to choose from 4 possible plays.

In the Intermediate Game Style pre-play screen the user will have a few more controls than the beginner

level. They will be able to select a play audible, coverage audible, lineman audible, linebacker audible or cycle through the players.

▲ **Advanced Playcall screen**

The Advanced Game Style setting is the one that is commonly used among *Madden* players. This setting is for users with a keen sense of football knowledge who can scheme their offense and defense without any help.

▲ **Advanced Preplay controls menu**

In this Game Style when the offense or defense takes the field, the standard pre-play control screen appears. Advanced users have the added options of being able to call a Defensive Hot Route and use the Receiver Spotlight.

WHAT'S NEW

WHAT'S NEW

▲ *EA SPORTS BackTrack just before the analysis begins*

EA SPORTS BACKTRACK

▲ *EA SPORTS BackTrack Play call*

EA SPORTS BackTrack is an in-game learning tool that takes you through your last play and teaches you how to avoid the mistake that you made. You will feel like a real QB or Coordinator doing film study or looking at those old school NFL sideline pictures.

EA SPORTS BackTrack shows users what play was run for both the offense and defense, and gives them a success

▲ *Success percentage*

rate based on the two opposing play calls. This sort of detail is given when you play with the Advanced game style, and will teach you on the go.

After Cris Collinsworth comes on and starts to break the plays down, he will show the play art of the offense and the defense to paint a picture of the play.

This feature also encompasses the EA SPORTS Rewind feature. All you will have to do is press a button to rewind the play, and use your new found knowledge to make adjustments to your execution.

IN-GAME BUTTON HINTS

▲ *Take control of the wide receiver*

As you take the field and start to run your offense or defense, you will notice the new In-Game Button Hints feature. This feature will let you know what button options you have prior to the snap and while the play is in action. You will never have to guess what button to use, as this feature shows the best button to use based on the controlled player's strengths.

ENHANCED PLAY CALL

▲ *Enhanced Play Call Screen*

EA SPORTS has obviously been working hard to create the best possible play call screen for *Madden* fans young and old. In *Madden NFL 09* they have exceeded expectations. In the new Enhanced Play Call screen,

you will have the ability to view player stats, instant replays and get video tips on other aspects of the current game.

▲ *Bluff Mode*

Being able to hide your play calls in a head-to-head game is critical to enjoying this mode of play. All you need to do now is hold down the Bluff button to bring up a play selection menu that resembles the button options on the face of the controller. You don't need to worry about button spying or even picking a play before your live opponent anymore.

One of the coolest features in *Madden NFL 09* is the ability to sub players without leaving the play selection screen. All you have to do is press the sub button and then pick any of the available players to use in the play. This is not only great for offenses, but think of defenses like the NY Giants where you can have Strahan, Umenyiora and Tuck on the field at the same time. The offense should just come out in QB Kneel instead of making the quarterback take an unnecessary hit.

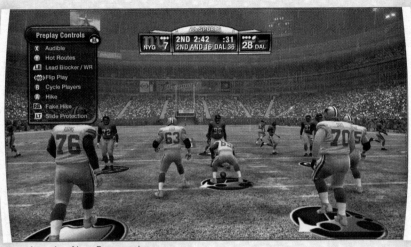

▲ *Amazing New Perspective*

ACTION CAMERA

▲ *See what Romo sees*

For years, gamers have been accustomed to a standard way of seeing the game of *Madden*. But in *Madden NFL 09*, EA SPORTS has brought a new Action Camera angle that will add variety and depth to the game presentation. This camera angle is on the line of the wire cam, or the eye in the sky cam (as it is called in several NFL broadcasts).

One of the main concerns of *Madden*

fans has been the desire to see the field from sideline to sideline, as a play is being run. The new Action Camera angle will help out with that. If the offensive player is rolling out to the right or left, the camera will follow him and present more of a view from that perspective. This will help prevent the blind throw back across the screen, as users will now be able to see pass options on the opposite side of the field.

At first glance, the Action Camera may seem better suited for the offense, but after some consideration, defenders will be able to see that they will have the same perspective and won't lose sight of any options that they may need to have covered.

RIVALRY GAMES

▲ *Manning surveys the defense*

Adding to the impressive gameplay in *Madden NFL 09* is the new rivalry aspect. Football has always been a game of rivalries. Whether it's the Browns vs. Bengals or Redskins vs. Cowboys, rivalries have fueled the love of the game for many years. EA SPORTS, in keeping with their "It's in the Game" motto, have added rivalries.

▲ *Brady calls for the ball*

One of the best current rivalries is between the Colts and Patriots. In rivalry games, the action is more intense than in non-rivalry games.

One aspect that users will notice is the responsiveness of the crowd. This is a little more subtle, but it does give the game a more exciting feel because of the increased movement around the screen. Fans seem to always be

▲ *Rivalry game crowds are hyped up*

standing when playing a rival, and the cameras don't stop flashing; these features all create a unique experience.

▲ *Celebration Time!*

MADDEN NFL 09 CHALLENGE TIPS

Stick work: You need to work on your stick skills. Don't depend on the CPU for anything. Manual players are the hardest players to beat. Learn how to take angles, focus on triggering certain animations, and make people miss.

WHAT'S NEW

7

WHAT'S NEW

TOTAL CONTROL ANIMATION

▲ *McFadden refuses to go down*

Many of the top-notch *Madden* players around the country, as well as the casual ones, have always wanted a little more in the area of animations. Too many times, players have felt that they were at the mercy of whatever animation started, because they could not break out of it. Things have changed; *Madden NFL 09* adds a new Total Control Animation system. We'll discuss what this means for the casual and hardcore *Madden* tournament player.

▲ *McFadden breaks away*

Users now have the chance to find the right button combinations to break away from tackle animations. Tapping the Spin button will let users spin and then spin in a different direction, helping to free their offensive player. One

of the most effective combos is to use a stiff arm followed by a spin while engaged. This will push the defender off the offensive player's body, and will provide enough room to let the spin move work.

With this type of feature, the possibilities of having a jaw-dropping run is greater and users will be looking for ways to break tackles and get those extra yards.

RETURN MISSED FIELD GOALS

▲ *Lining up for the field goal*

▲ *Looking the ball in*

Devin Hester came into the NFL and started to impact every aspect of the kicking game: kick returns, punt returns, and missed field goals. The mental wheels at EA SPORTS were turning and they have given users the ability to take advantage of missed

▲ *Give me a chance*

field goal attempts and try for a return. Right away, this will start to change the thinking behind attempting long field goals for fear of giving up an easy score to a speed burner.

▲ *Uh Oh!*

One thing that must be mentioned is that if a user is not in a punt return or field goal return play call, then they will not have an option of returning a missed field goal, unless it is caught. If the ball hits the ground there is no chance to return it. Fortunately, if the team has an athlete like Hester or Adam Jones, then users will be able to scheme regular defensive formations into their return game.

USER CELEBRATIONS

▲ *Jump Shot Celebration*

▲ *Doing the Moon walk*

Football is by far the most exciting game to watch and play. One way that EA SPORTS is trying ensure that players of *Madden NFL 09* are enjoying every aspect of the game is by giving users the ability to have some sort of control in celebrating after a score.

▲ *Can you believe these seats*

To access these celebrations, simply find the sweet spot in the end zone, normally around the helmet logo or right in front of the goal post, and then press the User Celebration button.

SLIDE PROTECTION

▲ *Slide Protection Options*

There are so many things that EA SPORTS has done to make the *Madden NFL 09* experience a great one for all that decide to play the game. They certainly did not ignore the passion of their dedicated fans who asked for certain aspects from the Legacy Gen versions to transition into the Next Gen game. One of the presents that EA SPORTS has packaged into *Madden NFL 09* is the Slide Protection blocking system. Users will be able to decide if they want their offensive linemen to step left, right, to the center, or away from the center. This will help level the playing field when facing a very aggressive defense.

▲ *Adjusting protection left*

When the offense comes to the line, if the quarterback reads an overload to one side of the defense or thinks the defense may be bringing

▲ *Wall of blockers*

heat from one side, they will now be able to adjust their blocking accordingly. All the user will need to do is press the Slide Protection button and then press the Left Thumbstick in the direction they want the protection.

▲ *Run Slide Protection*

Slide Protection is not limited to the passing game. Players that are ground pounders will also be able to adjust their run blocking in the same way as they would when passing the ball.

FORMATION AUDIBLES

▲ *Audible showing*

Not only has Slide Protection been

brought back, but so have Formation Audibles. Players will now have the added comfort of having four additional audibles for the formation that they are in. This feature is for both offense and defense. On offense, when you call for an audible, the Right Thumbstick will be used for the Formation Audible. Pressing up on the Right Thumbstick will call a quick pass, down will call a run, left will be a deep pass, and right will be a play action pass.

On the defensive side of the ball, if you call for an audible, the formation audibles will be up for man coverage, down for blitz, left for Cover 3, and right for Cover 2 zone. *Madden NFL 09* will surely reward good coaching and scheming.

BLUFF MODE

▲ *Actual play design*

With all of the enhancements to the play call screen (including formation audibles to help keep the defense on its toes), you will also have the ability to bluff your play art on the field.

You can show your actual play art by holding the Coach Cam button, and pressing up on the Right Thumbstick. To bluff your actual play call, press the Right Thumbstick right to show a run,

▲ *Bluff Run*

left to show pass, and down to bluff the current play call.

Smart Routes have made it to *Madden NFL 09* and users will enjoy having the chance to extend certain pass routes to make sure they aren't cut short of the first down marker.

▲ *Routes before adjustment*

Just press the Hot Route button, the receiver's icon whose route you want to extend, and then click the Right Thumbstick.

▲ *Adjusted route*

WHAT'S NEW

▲ *L.T. leaves defenders in his wake*

While the *Madden* franchise continues to evolve dramatically on Next Gen, *Madden NFL 09* on the Playstation 2 provides some new innovations of its own. There is still plenty of life and love left for the diehard PS2 gamers out there.

BALL CARRIER COMBO MOVES

The PS2 game has long been applauded for the responsiveness of the controls and the importance that stick control has in the game. EA SPORTS ups the ante yet again with Ball Carrier Combo Moves.

Simply put, these combo moves allow you to string movements together almost like you would in a fighting game. For example, you can start a spin move, then break out of it midstream, throw a stiff arm and then fire off a juke.

You'll be popping ankles and leaving defenders in the dust more than ever before. Doubling up on your jukes and spin moves is one of the most effective ways to utilize this feature.

FAMILY PLAY

▲ *Family Play makes playcalling easy*

Just like in *NCAA Football 09*, EA SPORTS has added Family Play to *Madden NFL 09* to make it more accessible to beginning players. Family Play allows you to modify the game to your level of play by streamlining controls and playcalling. You can of course still opt for the full advanced play call screens and myriad of control options.

The controls have been modified so that four buttons are all you need on offense and defense. Play art is streamlined where just the routes and important assignments are highlighted making it easy for beginners to get the gist of a play.

QB AVOIDANCE STICK

▲ *The QB Avoidance Stick in action*

The QB Avoidance Stick is a great tool that you can use to stay alive in the pocket and complete passes. Using the Right Thumbstick, you can have the QB make quick moves in the pocket to avoid the oncoming pressure from the defense.

Press up, down, left or right on the Thumbstick and your QB will slide in that direction to avoid the rush. This feature will take a little bit of practice to master, so go in practice mode and let the defense come after you until you get the timing down perfect.

CUSTOM PLAY MEMORY

This is our favorite new feature on the Legacy Gen consoles, and it is one that we hope makes its way to the Xbox 360 and Playstation 3 next season. With Custom Play Memory, you can save your most frequently called plays along with the adjustments that you made and access them again as an audible.

After you make your hot routes, press the audible button. Next click on the Right Thumbstick and push a Directional button to select an audible slot assignment. At any time in the future you can call this play with all the adjustments right from the audible menu.

▲ *Save your play adjustments*

The same holds true on the defensive side of the ball. You can make Individual Defensive Hot Route adjustments and save them to one of four audible slots. With this feature, you can speed up your ability to get your defense set up just the way you like it.

▲ *Basic Plays screen*

ALL PLAY

Madden NFL 09 on the Nintendo Wii brings accessibility to the whole family with enough depth to keep even the most serious football fan happy. All-Play mode streamlines the controls so that even Grandma can get on the sticks and compete. Passing, running and defensive controls have been condensed to just a few movements of the Wii Remote. Of course, you still have the option of standard mode with all the bells and whistles.

Calling plays has never been easier. You can let John Madden himself pick them for you, choose from a slimmed down set of choices, or access the full blown advanced play call screen. You can pick plays by type or by formation with this option.

Passing has been made more acces-

sible as well. On All-Play mode, you'll see an icon above each player once the ball is snapped. If it's red, then the receiver is covered and you need to look elsewhere. If the icon is green, he's open and you can feel safe firing in the pass.

CALL YOUR SHOTS

▲ *Draw up your own pass route*

Do you have fond memories of drawing up plays in the sand for your backyard football games? The Call Your Shots feature allows you to do

just that. Call a passing play as normal, and then press the Ⓐ button once you reach the line of scrimmage. You will now have the opportunity to "draw" the passing route that you want one of your receivers to run. You can pick up to three points in creating your route.

Experiment with all kinds of different routes in practice mode. One of our favorites is to add an angle route run by the Halfback. The angle route looks like a letter "V". It comes out of the backfield and then across the middle. This is a great route for getting your backs open against man coverage. Have fun! You are the coach and QB all rolled into one.

TELESTRATOR

▲ *The Telestrator in action*

The Telestrator feature is an enhanced version of Instant Reply Mode. Just like John Madden, you can draw right on the screen during an instant replay. This is a great teaching tool if you are trying to show a new player how to read coverages or find an open receiver. Better yet, you can show your friend exactly how you smoked his DB on the deep route. You'll just have to bring your own "Boom" sound effects.

5-ON-5

▲ *5-on-5 Playcalls*

This mode is a great pick up and go option when you have a buddy over to play. You'll play 5-on-5 with 5 TD's needed for the win. You get 4 downs to score just like you would in your neighborhood pick up game. You have the option of whether a "Mississippi" count is required before the pass rush, and you can turn Big Heads on or off.

The playcall options on offense are simple: short pass, medium pass, deep pass and run. Defense has: cover short, cover medium, cover deep and blitz. Be sure to use the Call Your Shots feature to change up the stock plays and get your favorite target open.

This may seem like a mode only for the younger *Madden* players, but it is great way to work on your stick skills and mastery of the Wii controls.

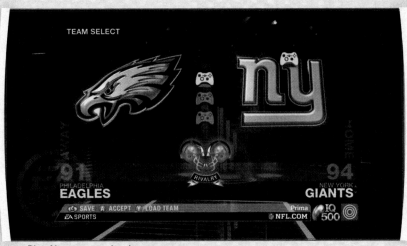

▲ *Play Now team selection screen*

PLAY NOW

If you're ready to get the virtual pads popping and want to get straight to the action, then Play Now is your gaming mode. Match your offensive and defensive mind against your friends, or see how well you can handle the always-learning computer AI. When you go into the Play Now mode you will be pitted against one of your rivals by default.

▲ *Advanced Play Now screen*

You have your choice of all 32 NFL Teams as well as the option of selecting the offensive and defensive playbooks that suit your gaming style. All you need to do is select the advanced options and choose 1 of the 38 offensive playbooks and 1 of the 37 defensive playbooks. This screen also lets you set the quarter length, time of day, stadium, weather and trophy options to play for. Simply put: Got Heart, Press Start.

Note: Advanced Gaming Settings

We've included some of the default settings for different types of events you might play in.

▶ Madden Challenge: All-Madden, 2 minute quarters, weather set to clear.

▶ Tournament Play: All-Madden, 3 minute quarters, weather set to clear.

▶ Online Sanctioned Leagues: All-Madden, 4-5 minute quarters, weather set to default, Game Style set to Hardcore.

▲ *Play Now skill level settings*

In the game settings screen you can adjust your skill level to Rookie, Pro, All-Pro, All-Madden, Custom, and My Skill. Each of the settings represents a growth in your gaming level and makes the computer AI a little tougher to deal with. The Custom and My Skill options are new to *Madden NFL 09*. The My Skill setting is your *Madden NFL 09* fingerprint. It sets the game's AI to match your unique skill level.

ONLINE PLAY

▲ *Online Lobby*

Playing *Madden NFL 09* against the computer or your local friends is great, but when you feel that you need to up your level of competition and see if you can whoop some virtual tail in other neighborhoods, then go online. You'll be able to test your skills against players all over the world.

▲ *Online Menu Options*

Once online you can head over to the Lobby area to find a game or hit the Quick Match option and be matched against a player similar to your current skill level. Many players want to play the best of the best, but the players that you see on *Madden Nation* or even in the Madden Challenge Finals often will not play online for fear of their schemes being copied. If you are lucky enough to get a game with a tournament player, *Madden Nation* participant or Madden Challenge Regional Champion then you will want to refer to the Advanced Gaming Settings above. They do not play ranked games because they only compete on the All-Madden gaming level. For more strategies and tips to help you survive and thrive online, see the Online Strategies section of the guide.

FRANCHISE MODE

▲ *Salary Cap and team weapons*

Franchise mode allows you to play the roles of Owner, GM, Coach and Player. It encompasses an NFL front office and lets you make those tough everyday off-season and regular season decisions. For example, you have a player that just signed a contract a year ago and now wants more money. What do you do? Cut him, trade him or redo his deal. The main concern at the Franchise start screen is the amount of cap room you have. This screen also lets you see your top two weapons.

▲ *Setting your Franchise options*

After you have selected a team to start a franchise with, you will be taken to the Franchise Setup Options screen. This screen allows you to set the options for how you will play your franchise. Some of the main decisions are: Sim Injuries, Salary Cap,

Trade Deadline, Re-Sign Players, Free Agent Wire and Sign Draft Picks. Even though *Madden NFL 09* defaults to the computer re-signing players, draft picks and working the free agent wire, most die hard franchise players want total control of these options.

▲ *Train your players for a game*

As you progress through the pre-season you will be able to train your team for this week's opponent. The computer will show you some suggestions for what positions to drill for this week's opponent. This is where those Monday morning quarterback, GM or Coach skills come in to play and you can see if you're on the right path to a Dynasty.

SUPERSTAR MODE

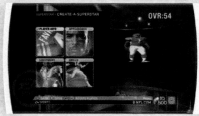

▲ *Creating a Superstar*

Every football fan grows up dreaming of playing football in the NFL one

day. This is where you can see how you would have done if you made it to that level (okay, maybe not, but it's still fun to imagine). Superstar mode lets you create a player and then put him through his paces on the way to the NFL Combine, Draft, Training Camp and Regular Season.

The fun begins in this mode after you are drafted. You will send your player through the different tests in training camp and work to improve your skills. This mode is also played in a first person perspective.

VIRTUAL TRAINER

▲ *Virtual trainer setup*

▲ *Virtual trainer details*

The Virtual Trainer mode brings you some of the best practice tools from the PS2/XBOX and gives them a Next Gen flare. In this mode you will be tested in 12 new drills that will

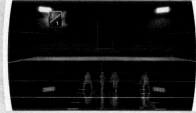

▲ *Working the pocket*

teach you the game while sharpening your skills.

One of the most useful trainers is the Pocket Presence/Throwing to Receivers. This drill will be a key foundation piece in building your comfort in the pocket, while teaching you to make good decisions as defenders are rushing you.

▲ *Hard passing level*

At the highest level of this drill, the offense will face 8 defenders. You will have to read your pass blocks and also determine the open receiver without the comfort of seeing the pass routes before the play starts.

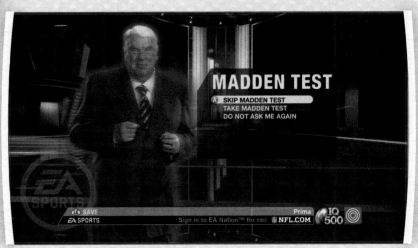

▲ *Welcome to the Madden Test*

MADDEN TEST

▲ *Madden Test details*

The Madden Test is the first gaming mode that you see as soon as you load up *Madden NFL 09*. This gaming mode combines the Virtual Trainer and the "My Skills" feature to compute your skill level, IQ, and tailor the game to your strengths and weaknesses. The default Madden IQ is 500.

After every series of tests you will be given a setting based on how you performed. The better you do, the

closer to All-Madden your skill level will be. If you believe you can do better, and want to retake the previous series of tests, then select retake test and try again. Not only will you get an immediate view of your skill level, but you will also see that your IQ has started to grow.

▲ *Madden Test results*

When the testing has been completed, the computer will show the skill level for each of the 4 main categories, as well as your current IQ. This screen

still allows you to retake a test if you believe you can do better. If you are satisfied, then select the Finalize option. Even though you have finalized your Skill level and IQ that does not mean it is set in stone. Every single player game of *Madden NFL 09* that you play will update your "My Skill" level and IQ.

MADDEN MOMENTS

▲ *Madden Moment selections*

Feel like reliving one of the most exciting games from the 2007 NFL Season? If so, then head on over to the Madden Moments game mode and play your way through real life situations from the 2007 season.

Once you have selected one of the game situations to replay, you will be taken to the Madden Moments detail screen. Here you will receive instructions on what is needed to complete the Madden Moment successfully. Pay

▲ *Madden Moment details*

▲ *Nothing is better then Success*

close attention to the details as the only way to advance is to complete the task exactly as instructed.

Each completion of a task is rewarded with a Success stamp. You have the option of playing the Madden Moment again or returning to the Madden Moments selection screen. Once you have completed a task once, you do not have to worry about not completing it in the future.

In order to progress through the

▲ *Unlocked Madden Moments*

Madden Moments and unlock other options, you must first complete the initial five. Once completed, five more moments are unlocked. The same process is continued until you reach the most memorable moment of the 2007 NFL season; the Giants upset win over the Patriots in Super Bowl XLII.

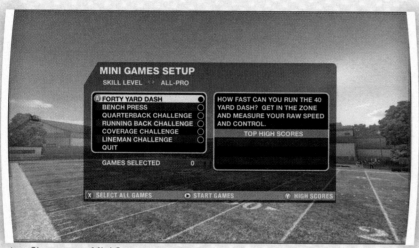

▲ Choose your Mini Game

MINI GAMES

▲ Reading the defenders

The Mini Games mode consists of a series of different skill competitions designed to work on all areas of your game. If you are looking for some fun, the 40-yard dash and bench press challenge are the perfect tools for a quick game. Get together with your close friends to see who can post the lowest 40-yard dash time or crank out the most bench press reps.

One of the most helpful Mini Games

▲ Running Back/Defensive Pursuit drill

is the Running Back Challenge. This challenge will help you develop into a serious runner and make sure you get comfortable with all the running tools that Madden NFL 09 offers. Not only

▲ Working on Receiver control

▲ Ring progress after mini games drills

will your running skills get sharpened, but you will also perfect your defensive pursuit angles and the different tackle options that you have at your disposal.

The Coverage Challenge is sure to help you prepare your offense for making correct decisions under pressure. Another reason for using this drill is to work on taking control of your cornerback and playing one-on-one defense. If you hold the press coverage button, then your defender will attempt to jam the receiver in front of him.

Progress made while in the Mini Games will be added to your Ring progress points. These points not only help move your gamer levels along, but they can also be used online at the EA SPORTS World site.

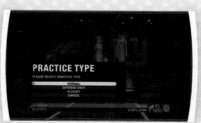

▲ Practice selection menu

Perfect practice makes perfect. That has become more evident this year, as EA SPORTS has added a ton of features to Madden NFL 09 to help you get a better understanding of the game of football. With features like the EA SPORTS BackTrack, you can now see your mistakes in detail. After the game you can hit the practice field, and work on what you learned from Cris Collingsworth. In order to be a top-notch player, you have to dedicate some time to practice mode and work on every aspect of your game. Here is a simple daily practice plan that will keep your skills sharp:

Passing Game: Work on reading the safeties in zone coverage, and find motion that beats man coverage.

Running Game: Practice dive, slam, trap, stretch and toss plays against overloads to the play side.

Defense: Know how to stop your Offense, so when someone runs it against you, you're not at a disadvantage. Scheme ways to make man and zone look alike.

Kicking Game: Start at the 20 and kick field goals. Back up 5 yards after each made field goal. Be sure to practice kicking from both hash marks.

GETTING STARTED

Establishing the run game is very important if you plan on keeping the defense honest. Before you can establish the run game, however, you need to learn the basic running moves in *Madden NFL 09*.

COVER UP

▲ *Peterson covers up the ball*

Use the cover up button to prevent the ball carrier from putting the ball on the ground as he is being tackled. Another advantage of using the cover up button is that there is a good chance the ball carrier will run the defender over. It's not as effective as the highlight stick, but there is less chance of him fumbling the ball.

HIGHLIGHT STICK

▲ *Reggie Bush avoids being tackled*

One of the better additions to run-

ning game over the years has been the Highlight Stick. By pressing up on the Right Thumbstick when in control of a big bruising running back, he will run defenders over. If the running back is smaller, he will try to avoid the tackler by going around him with a variety of moves. Have a running back who can run over or go around defenders makes using the Highlight stick that much more effective.

JUKE MOVE

▲ *Juke move evades the tackle*

The juke move allows you to fake a defender right out of his shoes. The key to pulling off a juke move is to get the defender at a bad angle and at full speed. Once the ball carrier pulls off the juke move, get going moving forward as fast as possible. More often than not, players who first pick up the controller will get carried away with

the juke move. It is good to use it, but make sure you learn to use it at the right time.

SPRINT BUTTON

▲ *Reggie Bush turns on the jets*

The Sprint button is the one used most commonly in *Madden NFL 09*. The key to using it is not to use it too early. When running inside, most top players won't use it until they get to the line of scrimmage. When running outside, they let the run blockers set up their blocks before using the Sprint button. They do this so they don't outrun their blockers.

SPIN MOVE

▲ *Peterson spins out of the tackle*

The Spin move is one of the most effective moves when it comes to running the ball. It can turn what

should have been a short gain into something special.

When using the Spin move, timing is everything. Just as the defender is about to make the tackle, use the Spin move to get away from the defender.

Another reason to use the Spin move is to get a run blocker out in front to engage a defender. Often when the Spin move is used, the defender will take a different angle. If a run blocker is out in front of you, use the Spin move so that the defender will run right into him.

STIFF ARM

▲ *L.T. is great for the stiff arm*

Use the Stiff Arm button when you are just about to be tackled. Having a strong back who is able to break tackles is a plus when using a stiff arm. Frequently the back will shed the defender and knock him to the ground. Smaller backs will have a harder time knocking defenders out of the way when using the stiff arm.

LEAD BLOCKING CONTROL

Lead Blocking Control gives you the option of taking control of a blocker while the CPU controls your running back. Once you have engaged with a defender, control changes back to your running back so you can attack the space cleared by your blocker.

LEAD BLOCKING

▲ *Lead Block Control for the LT*

After calling your play, you can cycle through the available backers with the select player button. You can select a blocking back, lineman, tight end or even wide receiver. Once you have the correct player selected, you can activate Lead Blocking Control.

Once the ball is snapped, you have two options when it comes to blocking. By flicking up on the Right Thumbstick, you can attempt a pancake block. Size is very important here. Don't expect to flatten a defensive end

▲ *Our TE drops the hammer*

with your wide receiver.

In cases where you are over-matched size wise, you will want to go for a cut block there. By flicking down on the Right Thumbstick, you can attempt a cut block. On a cut block, your blocker will go low and attempt to knock the legs out from under the defender. However, if you are controlling a burly offensive lineman go for the pancake block.

Once you attempt to cut block a defender, your blocker is pretty much out of the play. If you are successful with a pancake block, your blocker is still alive to make another block on a defender.

I-FORM PRO ISO

▲ *With run direction flipped*

This is a great play choice to use as you are learning to master Lead Blocking Control. One of our favorite ways to use this feature is to look for

a defensive end that is slightly offset from our tackle.

In this instance, we flip the run at the line of scrimmage so that the play is going to the left side. We are going to take control of the Left Tackle and attempt to cut block the Right Defensive End. If you can make this block and take him out of the play, you'll have plenty of room to run.

▲ *The LT blows up the Defensive End*

After a successful block, Adrian Peterson has plenty of space to run for daylight. If we can make a second level defender miss, then getting into the endzone is a good possibility.

I-FORM PRO TWINS POWER O

▲ *I-Form Pro Twins Power O*

Power O plays have a pulling guard and plenty of lead blockers out in front

of the runner. On sweeps and tosses we like to take control of the fullback so we can get out in front and wreak havoc on the defense.

▲ *We lead out with Fullback #44*

On this play, we take the Fullback (#44) and get out in front of Adrian Peterson as quickly as possible. The Defensive End is scraping off his blocker and will shut down this play if we don't do something about it.

▲ *A perfect cut block*

We use a cut block to take down the Defensive End and spring Peterson for a big gain.

Lead Blocking Control takes some practice to master. Once you get the hang of it, you can take advantage of mismatches or weaknesses in the defensive fronts for huge gains.

OFFENSIVE STRATEGY

OFFENSIVE STRATEGY

"Why should I run inside?" is a question that is frequently asked. Why not just pass the ball? Facing a strong inside running game is one of the most demoralizing experiences a player on defense can have. It changes the whole way that the defensive game plan is called. If you are the one dishing out the pain, it is one of the most satisfying experiences you will have with *Madden*.

The inside running game may not be the glamorous part of playing football, but is certainly one of most important parts. If you are able to pound the ball, you can control the clock and keep the ball out the opposition's hands. The longer you pound the ball, the weaker the defense becomes. By the fourth quarter, you will be busting loose for hefty gains. If you control the ball with the inside game, you can set up the defense for a play action pass that may result in a huge play downfield.

There are a wide variety of inside run plays in *Madden NFL 09*. We will take a look at a few of the more commonly-used ones.

I-FORM PRO ISO

▲ *Receivers on the outside run block*

The I-Form Pro Iso is the simplest form of an inside run play that you will find in the game. The fullback will lead block for the halfback between the center and right guard.

As soon as the halfback takes the handoff, he will look to run between the center and guard. It depends on the run play being called.

▲ *FB blocks the linebacker*

Once through to the line of scrimmage, press down on the speed burst button and pick up what you can.

▲ *Marion Barber finds daylight*

We pick up 7 yards before being brought down.

I-FORM PRO FB DIVE

▲ *Motion the HB as a decoy*

If you ask any top player what the most consistent run play in the game is, they will tell you the fullback dive. This is because it's a quick-hitting run play that almost always picks up positive yardage. The most common FB Dive play in the game is the I-Form Pro FB Dive.

This play has the fullback taking a quick hand off from the quarterback and running between the center and right guard.

▲ *Don't get fancy with the fullback*

▲ *Package in a second HB*

Once through the hole, there is usu-ally some wiggle room to pick up solid run yardage.

SINGLEBACK ACE HB DIVE

There are several types of HB Dive plays in *Madden NFL 09*. One of the more frequently-used ones is the Singleback Ace HB Dive. This play does not have a lead blocker for the halfback to run behind.

▲ *Run between the C and RG*

As the ball is being handed off to the halfback, look for running lanes to open up. Sometimes the primary may not be open, as shown in the screenshot.

▲ *See if they can hold their blocks*

If another opens up, be prepared to switch directions.

We press down on the speed burst button, and run between the center and left guard for a pick-up on the ground.

WEAK PRO HB GUT

▲ *Bounce it outside*

The Weak Pro HB Gut is a weak inside run play that has the fullback leading blocking to the opposite of the tight end. The halfback looks to run between the center and left guard.

The fullback will look to block any defender run blitzing from the outside on the left side of the offensive line.

▲ *It's tough going to the weak side*

We run between the center and left guard to pick up 4 yards before being brought down.

▲ *Follow your blockers*

Use the highlight stick to run over

defenders. Be sure to follow your blockers on inside running plays like the HB Gut.

GUN SPLIT SLOT FB INSIDE

Not all inside run plays have to be run from under the center. There are a few inside run plays from the Gun in *Madden NFL 09* that we feel are actually fairly effective. One of those inside run plays is the Gun Split Slot FB Inside. This play has the fullback running inside between the center and left guard. The halfback reverses rolls and becomes the lead blocker.

▲ *Slot receiver opens up the inside*

Once the fullback has the ball, look to follow the halfback.

▲ *Use the RB Swap package*

We pick up 8 yards before being wrestled to the ground.

▲ *Use Gun inside run plays*

MORE QUICK INSIDE RUNNING TIPS

▶ Find inside run plays that get the ball carrier to and through the line of scrimmage quickly. Avoid inside run plays where it takes time to develop.

▶ The higher the running back's break tackle ratings, the better chance he has of breaking a few tackles as he pounds his way through the line of scrimmage.

▶ Decide if you like to run the ball inside with or without a fullback. Some players prefer to have a lead blocker, and others prefer not to have a lead blocker. Both have their pros and cons, you just need to decide which suits your style.

MADDEN NFL 09 CHALLENGE TIPS

Adjustments: *The number one reason that most players lose is because they fail to adjust. You need to make quick adjustments on both sides of the ball. If they're killing your zone, go to man. If they are killing your run, pass the ball. If they are running on you then force them to pass. If they are going to one person or side, shut it down. In most games one turnover is all you need.*

Basic offense: *The past few Madden Challenge winners had basic offensive and defensive schemes. Keep it simple and move the chains. You want plays that give you multiple options and easy reads.*

Execution: *This is what makes a player Elite. It's not about the plays you use; it's about how you run them. Making the right reads and completing the play is what wins the tourneys.*

OFFENSIVE STRATEGY

Running the ball inside is all well and good, but being able to run to the outside and making a spectacular dash to the end zone is what makes the highlights. To get to the outside, running backs need high speed and acceleration ratings. Fortunately, there are many running backs in *Madden NFL 09* that have the speed, agility, and acceleration to get to the corner, and then turn on the jets to get up the field quickly.

In this section of the guide, we break down some outside runs and provide some tips on how to make the most of your outside rushing attack.

who is running horizontally behind the offensive line.

Once the halfback gets the ball, he can go outside or cut back inside depending on what opens up.

PITCH

▲ *The receivers are lined up tight*

The Pitch can be run from one or two back sets. The one we use is from the Singleback Ace HB Pitch. The right tackle pulls outside to the right to be the halfback's lead blocker.

The quarterback takes the snap and pitches the rock to the halfback,

▲ *Watch for blitzing linebackers*

▲ *Don't outrun your blockers*

Usually there is at least one offensive lineman pulling in the same direction to escort the HB down the field.

▲ *Willie Parker is a tricky back*

STRETCH

One of the more popular outside running zone plays over the last few years is the stretch. In *Madden*, many top players like this run play because of its versatility. If nothing opens up out wide, there is usually a hole to cut back inside to pick up positive yardage. Throw in the play action pass, and the stretch play can be hard to defend. One of the stretch plays we like to run is the Singleback Jumbo HB Stretch out of the Steelers' playbook.

▲ *Works best against man coverage*

The quarterback runs at an angle towards the running back before handing the ball off.

▲ *Pair the PA Roll Lt and HB Stretch*

The idea behind the stretch is to get outside quickly. The offensive linemen must seal the defenders off for the stretch play to be successful.

▲ *If nothing opens up, cut inside*

Once to the outside, press down on the sprint button and pick up yardage.

▲ *There are lots of stretch plays*

STRONG TOSS

The HB Toss is the bread and butter play that teams run the most if they are going east-west rather than north-south. The Strong Tight Pair Strong Toss is one of our favorite outside run plays in the game because the right guard and right tackle lead the halfback to the exterior part of the field. Throw in the fact that both tight ends line up on the same side we are running to, and this toss play is very explosive.

▲ *Flip the play vs. overloads*

▲ *The FB helps with the blocking*

The right guard and right tackle pull to the right and take out any would-be tacklers.

Once they do their part, lay the hammer down on the speed burst and take off down the sideline.

SWEEP

▲ *Twins sets are easiest to run sweeps*

Another standard run play to the outside that you will find in every team's playbook is the Sweep. It might show up in I-Form Pro, Singleback Bunch, or other formations, but you can bet it's somewhere in your team's playbook. For this example, we use the I-Form Tight Pair HB Sweep.

The HB Sweep is somewhat different than the HB Toss play because the HB takes a wider angle towards the corner. However, just like the Toss, the Sweep always has at least one offensive lineman pulling to the outside and leading the ball carrier around the corner.

▲ *The RG and RT lead the way*

The play is drawn up to attack the outside. Offensive coordinators choose to run at defenders who have a hard time stopping the run.

▲ *Blockers seal off the defenders*

If there is a less skilled defensive end on one side of the line flanked by a suspect outside linebacker, you can bet they will see a lot of sweeps come their way.

▲ *Sprint once you get outside*

QUICK OUTSIDE RUNNING TIPS

▶ Having receivers who are willing to run block really makes a huge impact on how well a team can run to the outside. Look for receivers with high run blocking attributes to improve your outside run game.

▶ If the defense is playing man coverage in I-Form Pro, send the flanker in motion all the way to the other side. This will clear out that side of the field and give the HB plenty of room to make his way down the field.

▶ If the defense loads the box with 8 and 9 defenders, call outside run plays. It will force them to not crowd the box.

▶ Try to have at least one outside run play set in your audibles.

MADDEN NFL 09 CHALLENGE TIPS

Know you will win: *A great tourney player told me that he expects to win every tourney he gets into. If you don't have faith in your ability you have lost before you even pick up the sticks.*

Use a team that can help you win: *Many people play with their favorite team. Forget that idea. You need to examine the game and see what the game is giving you. Get the team that fits your skills and gives you the best chance to win. This is why you see so many people playing with the same couple of teams.*

Focus: *You will have guys yelling in your ear, and you will have all kinds of pressure. Focus on the task at hand. Save the trash talk and block out bad plays. Your goal is the Championship. Let your skills do the talking.*

OFFENSIVE STRATEGY

There are a few plays in the game that can fool the defense into going one way, while you take control of the ball carrier to go the other way. These types of plays normally take a little more time to develop and don't always work. But when they do, they can really throw a monkey wrench into the opposing defense's defensive scheme.

ZONE READ

▲ *Receivers fake the streak route*

In some of the Gun formations in the game, there is a play named Zone Read. This play is a very effective run play because, based on what the defense does before the snap, this will determine what you do with the ball shortly after it's snapped. The Zone Read play we use for this example is the Gun Split Slot Zone Read.

If the defense looks to shift the defensive line to the weak side (same side as the halfback) we like to hand off to the halfback. This allows us to run to the strong side (same side as the fullback).

The fullback becomes the lead blocker. We can follow him inside or bounce the rock outside.

If the defense shifts the defensive line to the strong side, we then like to have our quarterback keep the ball.

▲ *Package in a TE*

Notice the running room that opens between the left guard and left tackle.

COUNTERS

▲ *This play uses auto motion*

There are several types of counter plays throughout all the playbooks in *Madden NFL 09.* Some players like them and others hate them. The ones that like to run them feel like they can get to the outside and pick up yardage by getting the defense going in the wrong direction. The ones that don't like them are worried that defenders will shoot through the gaps and blow up the running back before he ever gets going. The play we use for the example is the Singleback Bunch HB Counter.

The running back's initial movement right after the snap indicates he is going to run to the right side. It's at this point that the defense will go towards him.

▲ *Watch for defenders in the gaps*

The running back then heads back towards the left. The quarterback hands the ball off.

▲ *Watch for blitzing defenders*

If the defense does go in the wrong direction, the running back should have a few extra steps to get outside (as we have shown in the screenshot).

DRAWS/DELAY

Over the last few editions of *Madden,* draws and delays have actually become very effective when called against the right defense. The

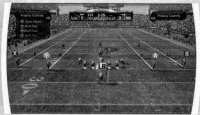

▲ *All receivers run fake pass routes*

draw/delay throws the defense off by delaying the movement towards the line of scrimmage. Draws and delays work best when the offense spreads the defense out. This helps create open lanes for the running back to run through. The Singleback Spread HB Draw is a good example of this.

▲ *Draws are hit or miss runs*

Once the ball is snapped, the quarterback will drop back as if he is going to pass. The offensive line will act as if they are going to pass block.

The quarterback will then place the football in the running back's gut.

If the offensive line is able to hold their blocks long enough, there will be plenty of running lanes to run through.

ADVANCED RUNNING TIPS

▲ Don't get too crazy with the spin move

Let the hole develop: Don't get in a hurry to run into the line, but calmly allow for the big guys up front to create running lanes for you to run the HB through. Once it opens though, RUMBLE through it. When you see the hole speed burst through it, allowing your back to hit the hole hard and break through the first tackle.

Spin move: Gains an extra yard or two when running inside, that's about all it is good for when pounding the ball.

Use your juke effectively: The juke move does have its uses in the inside running game. If the daylight is closing on your hole, you can often juke through at an angle and pick up an extra yard or two. Once you burst through the line, quickly juke to avoid the linebackers plugging the hole. The

juke often also serves to lower your shoulder into the defender and get those couple of extra yards.

Dive, dive, dive: As the hole is closing up hit your dive button and get that last extra yard. This is especially effective in short yardage situations. Find the hole and dive on through.

Bounce it outside: If the line is closed up, cut back against the grain, or take the ball outside. You may have to use your juke move to get unstuck from the line. Break it out a couple of times and you'll have a very frustrated defense.

Use the fullback: Reward the big guy who's been lead blocking for you every play. Down inside the red zone, the Goal Line FB Dive is a bread and butter play. Give him a quick handoff and let

him pound it into the line. Look to dive at the end of the play if you do not think the FB will make it. Don't use special runs with the FB; most of them just don't have the agility to pull moves, and you would be better off to just pound him straight ahead.

Use motion to add an extra run blocker: By using motion, you can add an extra run blocker in the hole you plan on running through. Many top players will package in a tight end in the slot and then motion them. Once the tight end gets near the designated running hole, they will snap the ball. This adds an instant run blocker into the mix.

▲ Motion the TE as an extra blocker

Use motion to open the outside running game: If the defense likes a lot of man coverage, use motion to open holes for the outside run game. For instance, call an outside run play right out of the I-Form Pro and then motion the flanker to the left. This will create a huge void to run the ball outside on the right.

Speed is the most important attribute for the outside running game: If your running back doesn't have the speed to get outside, chances are he

won't find much success. Look for running backs with 93 plus speed.

There are designed quarterback runs: If you have a mobile quarterback, there are plenty of designed quarterback runs in the game to make the defense respect the quarterback taking off and running the ball.

Mobile quarterbacks add another element to the run game: If no receiver is open down the field, take off and run with a mobile quarterback. Another way players will use the mobile quarterback is to hot route all their receivers on streaks. Once the ball is snapped, they'll wait a few seconds and run with no intention to throw the ball.

▲ Some consider QB runs cheesy

Highlight stick use: The highlight stick is the most effective running move in the game. Big backs will run defenders over. Smaller backs will go around defenders. Running backs that can run over and go around defenders are tough to stop.

Learn run combos: This year use chain running moves to have the running back break out of one animation into another, all in the blink of an eye.

OFFENSIVE STRATEGY

OFFENSIVE STRATEGY

If you are to be a successful virtual quarterback, then you need to master the passing controls in the game. Players that are new to the *Madden* series will want to read this page to get familiar with how each control works before getting too involved in a real game.

PLAY ART

▲ *Play Art view*

Before the ball is snapped, you may want to take one last look at the pass routes before snapping the ball. Not only can you see each receiver's pass routes, but you also can view each receiver's pass icon. You also want to take a look at the overall defensive coverage to see if you can find a gap to exploit.

MOTION

Although motion is not technically a quarterback control, motion can be used to help determine the pass coverage before the snap. In most cases when a receiver is sent in motion and his defender follows, you can be sure it's man coverage. If the defender does not follow the receiver, then it's typically zone coverage. To send a receiver in motion, use the Switch player button to cycle through the receivers. Once the receiver is selected, press left or right on the Left Thumbstick to send him in motion.

PUMP FAKE

▲ *Pump fake gets linemen in the air*

Once the ball is snapped, try using a pump fake to draw the safeties away from where you actually want to throw the ball. The quarterback will start to throw the ball, and then at the last second he will pull it back down.

PASS ICONS

When you find a receiver open and are ready to throw to him, press the button corresponding to the receiver's icon. If you press hard on the receiver's pass icon button, he will throw a bullet pass. If you tap the receiver's pass icon button, he will throw a lob pass. You will need to practice both types of throws in practice mode to learn how to use them effectively.

PASS LEAD

▲ *The receiver jumps to make the catch*

You can lead the receiver by pressing one of four directions on the Left Thumbstick. Different types of passes will be thrown based on your direction.

Pressing up on the Left Thumbstick will cause the quarterback to throw a high pass to the receiver.

Pressing down on the Left Thumbstick will cause the quarterback to throw a low pass to the receiver.

Pressing left/right on the Left Thumbstick will cause the quarterback to pass to the inside or outside.

▲ *Making a shoe string catch*

SPRINT

If nothing is open down the field, you can use the Sprint button to pick up yardage on the ground. Make sure to use the Slide button before being tackled. A big hit by a defender can often lead to the ball being knocked out of the quarterback's hands or even cause injury.

THROW PASS AWAY

▲ *Throw away the pass or get sacked*

You have two major mistakes that you want to avoid as a quarterback. You don't want to take a sack, and you don't want to throw the ball into coverage. If you don't see any of your receivers open, get outside of the tackle box and throw the ball away. Obviously, if you have room, then take off with the QB. If you are being pursued and can't escape, then throw it away.

HOT ROUTES

Hot routes are a big part of most top player's offensive schemes. Regardless of whether you play against the CPU or another person, hot routes should be implemented into your passing game. You can run a complete offensive scheme based on hot routes if you understand how each one works. In this section of the guide we are going to cover all the hot routes in the game, plus let you know how best to use them.

STREAK

▲ *The Streak has big play potential*

Use the streak when a receiver is matched with a slower defender and there are no safeties playing deep. Throw the ball once the receiver gets a few steps on the defender. Another common use of the streak is to draw defenders away from a pass route that is running underneath.

CURL

The curl works best when the defense has called man coverage. Wait for the receiver to curl back towards the quarterback and then make the throw. Curls can also be effective against zone coverage when another receiver runs a flat route. Often the defender covering the flat area will pick up the receiver running his way, leaving the receiver running the curl route wide open.

OUT/IN ROUTE

▲ *Outs work against soft zone coverage*

Out and in routes both work well against man coverage. If the receiver is running an out route, wait for him to make his cut to the outside. Once he does, lead him to the outside by pushing the Left Thumb Stick in that direction as you throw. If the receiver is running an in route, wait for him to cut inside. Once he does, lead him to the inside. Make sure no defenders are playing over the middle of the field when making the throw.

FADE

Use the fade route to get the receiver off the line of scrimmage quicker against bump-n-run man coverage. Fade routes can also be used against zone coverages such as Cover 2. Once the receiver gets past the initial jam he will have more room between the cornerback and safety to make the catch.

DRAG/FLAT

Whether you motion the receiver or not will determine if the route is a drag or flat route. If the receiver is not sent in motion, he will be running a drag route. This route is best if you are planning on utilizing the short passing game. It works well against man and zone coverage. If the receiver is hot routed on a drag and then motioned to the other side of the field, he will run a flat route. Against Cover 4, the receiver will be open in the flat.

SLANT IN/OUT

There are two types of slant routes you will find in the game. One will have the receiver run a slant route to the inside. This route works very well against normal man and press man coverage. The slant out is another hot route many top players will use to get the receiver open. When running this route against man coverage, the ball needs to be thrown over the top of the defender. Some players will throw a lob pass. If you throw it right, it is very hard to defend.

PASS BLOCK

▲ *Use motion with hot routes*

Leaving in running backs, tight ends and even receivers in some cases to pass block can mean the difference between being sacked and getting the ball off. Many players will leave up to two extra players in to pass block to give them enough time in the pocket to find the open receiver down the field.

HOT ROUTES TIPS

Use hot routes to set up different route combinations. For instance if the slot receiver is running a corner route, and the split end is running a curl, try hot routing the split end on a streak. Against Cover 3 zone, the slot receiver will be open once he breaks to the corner because the split end will draw the right cornerback deep.

Many top players use hot routes as one of their primary means to attack through the air. Learn how to use them effectively. It will help make your passing offense much more potent.

OFFENSIVE STRATEGY

The West Coast Offense (WCO) was the brainchild of Bill Walsh while an assistant coach to Paul Brown in the late '60s. Cincinnati was an expansion team that year and did not have the same levels of athletic talent as the rest of the league. Coach Brown wanted an offense that could keep control of the ball and keep their weaker defense off the field. He felt they needed to make 25 or more first downs each game in order to stay competitive due to the lack of personnel needed for an aggressive ball control running game.

Head Coach La Vell Edwards of Brigham Young University (BYU) also used the West Coast Offense and won the 1984 NCAA Championship by beating Michigan in the Holiday Bowl 24-17. Many college football observers began to take notice and started to incorporate the West Coast Offense in their playbooks. Unlike previous air attacks from pass-minded coaches such as Sid Gillam and Don Coryell which were about passing the ball deep, the West Coast Offensive System used short, high percentage passes. This type of scheme would allow teams to control the clock without having to run the ball as much. Today, the NFL is full of teams running some version of the West Coast Offense.

PHILOSOPHIES OF THE WEST COAST OFFENSE

▶ Spreads the defensive coverage over a much bigger area of the field, both horizontally and vertically.
▶ Creates mismatches in the speed, size, or number of receivers the defense tries to cover.
▶ The West Coast Offense can be executed on any down or distance. This keeps the defense from picking up tendencies that the defenders can key in on.
▶ Maintains ball control through the air, whereas other teams try to gain ball control on the ground.
▶ Having a good quarterback is necessary to run the West Coast Offense. He does not need the strongest arm to succeed, but he must be able to make quick reads to beat the defense.
▶ The receivers must run precise routes since the West Coast Offense is about timing and precision.
▶ Use of a running back coming out of the backfield is a must in the West Coast Offense. A running back with good hands should become the focal point of the West Coast Offense.
▶ Use of the tight end is another must if you are to run the West Coast Offense successfully. When the offense gets in the Red Zone, the use of the tight end becomes most effective.
▶ Even though the West Coast Offense is about short passing, do not forget to run the ball. You still need to have some pass-run balance.

PRACTICING THE SHORT PASS OFFENSE

Timing is everything in this offense. Get into practice mode and work on curls, hitches, and hooks. You will need to learn to hit your receivers right as they cut to get the most yards on any given play. Work on your drag routes over the middle. Practice cutting downfield as soon as you get the ball. The quicker you get moving North and South, the more yards you can squeeze out of each play. Passing to the backs takes a little touch as well. You don't want to throw a bullet, as they are too close and don't usually have as good a catch rating as your WRs. However, throwing too much of a lob gives the LBs the opportunity to break on the pass and intercept, or leaves your back hung out to dry on a big hit.

COMMON SHORT PASS ROUTES

There are several short pass routes that can be found in *Madden NFL 09*. We look at a few of the more common ones that players who like the short passing game tend to use.

CURL

Good pass route to beat man and zone coverage. The receiver runs straight up about 6-8 yards and then comes back towards the quarterback. Once the receiver shows his numbers, throw him a bullet pass.

If bump-n-run man coverage is called, the receiver will run his curl route a little further down the field. This means the pass protection must hold up until the receiver curls back to the quarterback.

Once the receiver curls back, throw him a bullet pass. In years past, top

players have thrown a high bullet pass to get the receiver up in the air. This makes it very hard for the defender to make any play on the ball. About the only thing the defender can do is try to jar the pass out of the receiver's hands.

We make the catch for a 10-yard pick-up before being tackled.

DRAG

Of all the short pass routes in the game, the drag route may be the most versatile. This is because it can beat just about any pass coverage in the game. The receiver runs 2-3 yards up the field and then cuts across the

middle of the field, looking for the ball.

If the defense brings pressure and you don't have much time to wait for the deep routes to get open, look for the receiver running a drag route underneath. That is why several top players almost always have one

receiver running a drag route, regardless of the play they called.

Once you decide to make the throw to the receiver running the drag route, throw him a bullet pass.

Once the catch is made, expect to pick up a minimum of 3-5 yards.

FLAT

Another route that top players use to beat man coverage is the flat route, especially to the running back out of the backfield. If your opponent keeps bringing the heat, use this route to make him pay.

Watch for the defenders playing the

flat. That's the best way to counter a player who bases his offensive scheme on attacking the flats.

Throw a bullet pass towards the running back. You don't want to lob him a pass. It gives the defense too much time to react.

Once the catch is made, turn up the field. Running backs with high trucking or elusiveness ratings can often run over defenders to pick up extra yardage once the catch is made.

SHORT SLANT

The Short Slant is a good pass route to beat the blitz, and if timed right, it's

almost impossible to stop as long you read the pass coverage. If a speedy receiver makes the catch, there is always a chance for a big play. The receiver runs straight up for about 3-5 yards and then slants 45-degrees towards the middle of the field.

We throw to the receiver running slant route. Watch to see if any defender drops into the area in which the slant is being run.

Once you spot the open receiver, throw him a bullet pass to get the ball to him quickly.

Ideally you want to have the receiver make the catch on the run, so he is at full speed to pick up yards after the catch.

OFFENSIVE STRATEGY

Of the three phases of the passing game, the one that is most overlooked is the intermediate pass routes. Most players either run some type of dink and dunk, or chuck it up deep offense. However, there are several intermediate pass routes in *Madden NFL 09*.

Intermediate passing routes take a little longer to develop, so the pass protection schemes must hold up long enough for the receivers to run their pass routes.

In order to succeed in the medium to long passing game, you must have good pocket presence. In *Madden NFL 09*, the defensive line can create a pass rush all by themselves. This really punishes players that like to take deep drops. Practice forming a pocket, taking crisp drops, and delivering the ball within 3-5 seconds. You may even need to step up in the pocket to make the throw to avoid the outside pass rush by the defensive ends.

CROSS

Of all intermediate pass routes in the game, the one used the most is the crossing route. This route is deadly against both man and zone coverage. Most players that use this route will roll the quarterback out to the same side that the receiver is running the crossing route. To make it even more difficult to defend, they will have two slot receivers running crossing routes from both sides of the field. At some point during the play, they will cross each other.

Having a fast receiver running the crossing route makes it that much easier to complete the pass.

Notice that we slide the quarterback to the right and then step in to make the pass. When throwing to the receiver running the crossing route, make sure he has a few steps on the defender in coverage.

We make the catch on the run for a 15-yard pick-up.

DIG

Another intermediate pass route that is often used is the dig route. This route works best when a receiver isolated on the backside is matched up one-on-one with a defender. Once the receiver breaks over the middle of the field, the ball is thrown.

Notice that the receiver takes an inside release and then runs straight up the field about 7-10 yards. At this time, you may be able to throw him a hard bullet pass. Make sure you lead the pass to the inside.

If you don't make the pass while he is running straight up the field, then wait until he cuts towards the middle before making the throw.

Before making the throw, make sure

he has inside position on the defender if man coverage has been called.

We make the catch for a 12-yard pick-up.

HITCH

The hitch route is often forgotten because many players would rather run curl routes. Against man coverage they are fairly effective, as long as there is enough time for the receiver to run his route.

The receiver runs straight up the field about 8-12 yards.

OFFENSIVE STRATEGY

He then pivots towards the sideline. Now the ball must be thrown with a hard bullet pass.

Notice as we make the catch how far off the defender is. We are able to avoid the tackle, and may turn a simple pass route into a big gain.

OUT

Over the years, the out route has been known as a man beater by the hardcore *Madden* community. In *Madden NFL 09,* it's as effective as ever. It's also an effective pass route to run against soft zone coverage.

The receiver runs about 8-12 yards straight up the field.

He then cuts hard towards the side.

As soon as he cuts, a hard bullet pass needs to be thrown. Use the pass lead feature to make sure the defender has no chance to jump the pass route.

We make the catch near the sideline for a 12-yard pick-up.

POST

There are two different types of post routes in the game: intermediate post and deep post. The intermediate post has the receiver breaking towards the post about 5-7 yards earlier than the deep post. Against Cover 2 man, this route is very effective.

The receiver runs straight up the field about 7-9 yards.

He then breaks towards the post. He

will then establish inside position on the defender in pass coverage.

Once you see that he has established position, throw him a high bullet pass.

We make the catch for a 12-yard gain.

PATTERN COMBINATIONS

Route combinations are the foundation of a solid passing game. Without route combinations, the defense would be able to shut down most passing attacks. That is why it is so important to know which pass route combinations are effective against different pass coverages.

WHAT ARE PATTERN COMBINATIONS?

Pattern combinations are based on a passing tree that all offensive coordinators have in their playbooks. All of the trees use the same basic numbering system; even-numbered routes are directed toward the middle of the field, while odd-numbered routes head for the sidelines. The tree allows the offensive coordinator and quarterback to communicate pass plays to the rest of the skills position players. Without the tree, there would be communication problems.

PASSING TREE ROUTE NAMES

NUMBER	ROUTE NAME
1	Quick Out
2	Slant Route
3	Deep Out
4	Drag Route
5	Flag Route
6	Curl Route
7	Shoot Route
8	Post Route
9	Streak Route

☐ Odd ☐ Even

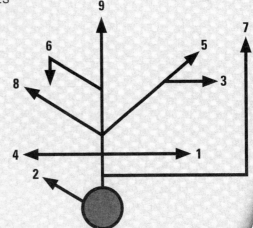

OFFENSIVE STRATEGY

Throughout NFL history, the vertical passing game has given rise to some of the best highlight plays ever. There is the one-handed, tipped by the DB pass that Lynn Swan caught while falling down in the Super Bowl. And of course there are the mighty receiving corps of the Redskins Posse, and the Denver Broncos Three Amigos, led by Vance Johnson. In more recent history, we have seen the emergence of the vertical game through the plays of the St. Louis Rams. The NFL has turned predominately to the West Coast Offense, with not many teams just airing it out.

The vertical passing game is the second part of the passing attack and is the most feared by the defense. A defense believes that the longer the offense is on the field, the better their chance is of making a mistake that will benefit the defense. A good balance of the medium passing game with the explosiveness of the vertical passing game is a guaranteed headache for any defense.

The primary job of the vertical passing game is to stretch the defense. This can be done vertically by going deep against the defense, or this can be combined with stretching the defense horizontally by using the Shotgun, Singleback 4WR, and 5 Wide sets. Each of these formations spreads the defense and forces them to protect the boundary as well as the deep route. The key to this offense is to make sure that you have established the medium passing game. The vertical game can work by itself on occasion, but with the proper mix, you will have consistent results when throwing the deep routes.

To make sure that the offense is prepared to use this type of attack, the quarterback must be able to read the coverage of the safeties. Each type of coverage has a different area of attack. Through constant practice and repetition, the quarterback will see the drop of the safety and be able to determine the type of coverage being played.

COMMON VERTICAL PASSING ROUTES

There are several types of vertical passing routes that can be found in *Madden NFL 09*. We take a look at a few of the ones that players commonly like to incorporate in their offensive passing attack. It is effective against Cover 0, Cover 1, Cover 2 zone, and some Cover 3 coverage.

CORNER

The corner route has remained one of the most frequently used deep pass routes in *Madden* over the years.

The receiver will run straight up the field about 8-10 yards.

He will break towards the sideline. Then, the pass should be thrown. Watch to see what the safeties do. If Cover 2 man or Cover 4 is called, the corner route can be difficult to complete. There are also a few Cover 3 coverages that shut down corners, primarily ones that have defenders dropping in buzz zones.

We take control of the receiver and make the catch for a big gain down field.

FADE

The fade route, in our opinion, is the easiest to use to learn to user catch with. It's one of few pass routes in the game that can be run against just about any pass coverage and still be effective. Having tall receivers run this route can make it that much more effective if you are able to user catch.

The receiver starts towards the sideline at an angle.

He then turns straight up the field. If zone coverage is called, wait for him to clear the underneath pass coverage.

Once he does, throw him the ball. While the ball is in the air, take control of him and try to undercut the defender in pass coverage.

Use the Catch button to grab the pass. If done correctly, you will pick up yardage deep down the field.

DEEP POST

The best way to attack most Cover 2 coverage is with a receiver running a deep post route. With the safeties splitting out wide, there will be a huge void over the deep middle of the field.

The receiver will first run straight up

the field.

Once he gets about 8-12 yards, he will cut towards the post.

Watch the safeties. If they both split out wide like in the screenshot, throw him a high bullet pass. Take control of the receiver and press the Catch button to make the grab. Watch for the middle linebacker dropping over the deep middle. Cover 2 Buc is good example of a defense in which the safeties split out wide, but the middle linebacker drops back over the middle to fill the deep middle void.

STREAK (GO)

The streak route is the most commonly used deep pass route in the game. Just like the fade route, it's a very easy pass route to learn to user catch with. Ideally, you want to have a fast receiver running the streak to blow by defenders, but tall receivers also can be effective if you are able to take control of them and undercut the defenders to make the catch.

There is nothing fancy about the streak. The receiver runs as fast as he can in a straight line down the field.

If the defensive coverage doesn't have a safety playing over the top of the receiver, it is time to let the ball fly. Make sure the receiver has a couple of steps on the defender in coverage.

Once the ball is up in the air, take control of the receiver and press the sprint button to get some extra separation from the defender. Hold down the catch button to make the grab.

MADDEN NFL 09 CHALLENGE TIPS

Script plays: This helps you to get into a flow and see how the person you're playing is going to adjust to you. From these plays you can see what they are weak in and expose them. This goes for defense as well as offense.

OFFENSIVE STRATEGY

For those of you who don't know what a passing concept is, let us educate you. Think of a football field as a flat, two-dimensional plane. The offense attacks the defense horizontally and vertically with different types of passing concepts.

Passing concepts, in some cases, help simplify the reads for the quarterback. The reason that many players struggle in the passing game is that they don't understand how passing plays work. By understanding pass concepts, it will help make the learning curve less complicated, and ultimately improve the passing game.

Four of the more common types of passing concepts that are found in *Madden NFL 09* are as follows:

HORIZONTAL PASSING CONCEPTS

Passing concepts that stretch the field are considered horizontal passing concepts. By stretching defenders underneath zone coverage with multiple receivers running horizontal routes, it makes it very difficult for those defenders to cover. In the screenshot above, notice that we have five receivers running underneath routes. On the left,

we have the split end and slot running a hi lo pass combo. On the right, we have the same hi lo combo between the flanker and the inside receiver. The slot receiver lined up next to the flanker is running a drag. This horizontal passing concept can be run against zone coverage with a high rate of success.

We first look to the right side; there are three receivers and two defenders. Conventional wisdom says we should look to one of those receivers. The receiver running the drag route is the best option.

For this example, we are going to continue through our read progression on the left side to see what the coverage looks like. Notice that there are two defenders covering the two receivers on the left. The right cornerback is dropping back to cover 1/3 of the left side of the field. The dimeback on the left covers the flat.

Since the slot receiver is covered in the flat, we look to throw to the split

end running the curl. We throw him a bullet pass.

The catch is made for an 11-yard gain.

VERTICAL PASSING CONCEPTS

Passing concepts that stretch the field vertically with multiple receivers are considered vertical passing concepts. For instance, if a play is called All Vertical or 4 Verticals, this would be considered a vertical passing concept. By sending more receivers deep than what the defense has playing, in theory at least one of those receivers

will become open. In the screenshot we have four receivers running vertical routes. The two outside receivers run fades, while the two inside receivers run seam routes. This passing concept is known as 4 Verticals.

If the defense plays some type of Cover 3 coverage, the three defenders playing deep will be out-numbered by the four receivers. At least one of them will be open at some point of the play. It's just a matter of finding him.

The free safety rotates over the middle, while the strong safety plays a hook zone.

This tells us to look to throw to the slot receiver running the seam route on the right.

The passing window is not very big, but with Tom Brady, this is a pretty simple pitch and catch.

HORIZONTAL/ VERTICAL PASSING CONCEPTS

Plays drawn up that implement both horizontal and vertical passing concepts are very effective because the defense has to cover more space on the field. One of our favorite horizontal/ vertical passing concepts is to send three receivers deep and have two receivers running underneath pass routes. For this example, the outside receiver on the left runs a fade, the slot receiver lined up inside runs a seam, and the tight end runs a corner. This gives the play three vertical routes. The slot receiver lined up next to the split end runs a drag route, while the running back runs a swing. This gives the play two horizontal pass routes. We like to call this passing concept 3 Verts/2 Under.

Once the ball is snapped, we read the pass coverage. If three defenders are dropping back, we can tell it's Cover 3.

The split end and the inside slot receiver attack the right cornerback deep. Normally, we look to throw to the split end on the fade route. However, for this example, we will look to throw underneath. Notice that the slot receiver running the drag route is open.

As we have already mentioned, the drag route is one of the most effective routes in the game. We throw him a hard bullet.

We make the catch for a 7-yard pick-up before being tackled.

OBJECTIVE RECEIVER CONCEPTS

Passing concepts that have one primary (specific) receiver that the play is designed to get open are considered objective receiver concepts. For quarterbacks that have a hard time reading the passing coverage, this is the easiest passing concept to learn. When running objective receiver concepts, we like to isolate the intended receiver. At this point, we plan on throwing to the flanker running the quick slant on the right, but we don't have him isolated.

To get him isolated, we take control of the right slot receiver and motion him to the left.

We now have the flanker isolated on the left cornerback.

Once the ball is snapped, we look to make sure no defender drops any-where in the area in which the flanker

is running his quick slant.

If no other defender besides the defender covering the flanker drops into the area, we know where to throw the ball.

We throw a hard bullet pass as the flanker cuts towards the middle.

We make the catch on the run and pick up 12 yards before being brought down.

OFFENSIVE STRATEGY

There are four basic coverages in *Madden NFL 09*. Each one needs to be attacked differently to maximize the passing game.

COVER 1 (MAN FREE)

In a Cover 1 defense, one of the safeties will drop to the deep middle of the field after the ball is snapped. His coverage responsibility is to prevent any receivers from getting over the deep middle. He also needs to have the speed to provide assistance to the corners on deep sideline routes, which is a weak spot in the Cover 1 coverage. In most Cover 1 defenses there is at least one extra pass rusher that goes after the quarterback. The rest of the defenders play man coverage.

▲ *The FS rotates over the middle*　　▲ *Look to attack the sidelines*

STRENGTHS With man-to-man coverage all around, Cover 1 provides adequate coverage deep down the field with a safety over the top. The other safety is free to cheat up to help with run support or blitz. In most Cover 1 defenses one of the linebackers will blitz to create a four or five man rush.

WEAKNESSES There is very little underneath help, so crossing routes and pick routes can be very effective against this scheme. This is especially true when matched up against a faster receiver. The deep safety must be disciplined and not bite on play action. If he does there is potential for a big play by the offense. The corners get very little help on deep sideline routes such as corner and post corner routes.

READING COVER 1 The key to reading the Cover 1 defense is to read the safeties after the snap of the ball. If one of them goes to the deep middle and the other plays man, then the pass coverage is Cover 1. Another name you may hear thrown out is Man Free, which is just another designation for Cover 1.

COVER 2

You will see both safeties dropping deep and to the outside. Whether Cover 2 Man or Cover 2 zone coverage is called will determine what the coverage underneath looks like. If man coverage is called, typically five defenders will cover the receivers in one-on-one coverage. If zone coverage is called, the five defenders will usually drop back in zone coverages. Normally three defenders play hook zones, while the two cornerbacks cover the flats. There are some Cover 2 man and zone defenses where a defender may blitz or play QB Spy.

▲ *Both safeties are split wide*　　▲ *Post routes can destroy Cover 2*

STRENGTHS This coverage scheme is strong against the short passing game with up to five defenders playing zone coverage. The cornerbacks jam the receivers at the line to disrupt the timing of the play. Once the corners release the receivers, they play the flats. This makes Cover 2 zone defense very effective against players who like to attack the flats. Cover 2 man's strength is that no receiver is left uncovered underneath since all five defenders are playing man coverage.

WEAKNESSES Both Cover 2 coverages can be vulnerable to fades and deep middle routes. A post corner route can also cause trouble for both of these pass coverages. Strong side run support is weaker than in Cover 1 as the SS must play the pass first. There are two other areas we consider weak, although they are not as big as the three deep areas of the field. There is a small window between the linebackers. This window can be wider based on what defensive formation the defense comes out in. Cover 2 zone needs the front four to get pressure on the quarterback. If the defensive line is unable to do that, the Cover 2 zone scheme can easily be exploited.

READING COVER 2 Once the ball is snapped, watch to see if the safeties split out wide. If they do, then it's some type of Cover 2 coverage. Next, look at the defenders playing underneath. If they go cover receivers, then it's Cover 2 Man. If they drop back, it's Cover 2 Zone.

COVER 3

Of all the zone coverage types found in *Madden NFL 09,* Cover 3 is by far the most used by top players. There are very few vulnerable spots on the field to attack. Also multiple zone blitz schemes can be created in Cover 3 to bring pressure on the quarterback.

▲ *Three defenders in deep coverage*

▲ *Flood the zone vs. Cover 3*

STRENGTHS Because there so many types of Cover 3 coverage, the quarterback may have a hard time reading the defense and knowing where to go with the ball. Many schemes can be created with different blitz assignments to confuse the quarterback. With the ability to rush either a safety or cornerback, the quarterback may not see the defender coming before it's too late.

WEAKNESSES Flooding the zones to either side makes it tough for Cover 3. If the offense attacks with 4 players vertically, the three defenders deep will be out manned at the point of attack. The flat areas can be vulnerable to attack depending on which Cover 3 coverage has been called.

READING COVER 3 You will see three defenders dropping deep into zone coverage. This can be two safeties and a corner, or both corners and one safety. The three men in deep zones help cover the entire width of the field.

COVER 4

Most players call Cover 4 to prevent the deep pass. They would rather force the opposing offense to throw underneath than give up the big play deep. This is often referred to as a "Bend But Don't Break" style of defense. Most of the Cover 2 zone and Cover 3 defenses also fit into this philosophy.

▲ *Four defenders drop back*

▲ *Attack Cover 4 with running backs*

STRENGTHS This defense provides excellent deep coverage with four defenders playing across the back. Against base sets, the safeties can provide double coverage on the deep routes.

WEAKNESSES The flat areas to either side are vulnerable in this scheme. Safeties must be disciplined and not be fooled by play action. If they do fall for the play, it may cause a break down deep. Flooding receivers horizontally to one side is the common passing concept used to attack Cover 4 coverage.

READING COVER 4 You will see four defenders dropping deep into coverage. The corners and safeties will each cover a quarter of the field deep. The pass coverage underneath is either pure zone or a man/zone combination.

Note: Reading Pass Coverages

There are other types of pass coverages in the game, such as Cover 0 (no safeties deep) and prevent (all defensive backs deep). We won't be breaking them down in this section of the guide, but know they are in the game.

OFFENSIVE STRATEGY

Pass Route Combinations are very important to learn if you plan on moving the ball against zone coverage. Pass route combinations can consist of two or more pass routes that work together to get a receiver open against different types of zone coverages.

In this section of the book, we are going to show one of the more common pass route combinations that we like to use to beat various types of zone coverages in *Madden NFL 09*.

CURL FLAT COMBO

Of all the pass route combinations in the game, the most common one is the Curl Flat combo. This route pass combo has two receivers line up on the same side. The outside receiver runs a curl route, while the inside receiver runs a flat. The idea is to force the defender (typically a cornerback) playing the flat to either cover the curl or flat receiver. He can't cover both because the receivers are spaced apart just enough. Once the defender determines who he is going to cover, the ball is thrown to the receiver that is left uncovered.

GUN DOUBLE CURL FLATS

The Gun Double Curl Flats is a good example of how the Curl Flat combo works. Notice this play has a curl flat combo mirrored on both sides of the field. The flanker and split end run curls,

▲ *Find other curl flat combos*

while the slot receivers run flat routes.

For this example, we are going to focus on the left side of the field. Once the ball is snapped, we notice that the left cornerback bumps the split end. Generally this is a clear indication that the defense is playing some type of Cover 2 scheme.

▲ *The receivers get jammed*

Once the slot receiver runs toward the flat, the right cornerback will release the split end.

Notice the slot receiver is now covered in the flat by the right cornerback. This leaves the split end open once

▲ *Motion gets the receiver open quicker*

he curls back. Before making the throw, we look to see if any defender drops near the split end. We see that the split end is open, so we throw him a hard bullet pass.

▲ *Work it to the outside*

We make the catch for a 10-yard pick-up.

▲ *Always expect to break a tackle*

QUICK PASS ROUTE COMBINATION TIPS

In this year's game you must really pay attention, because defenders tend to react differently on each play. For instance, say the same pass route curl flat combination is called against the same zone defense. The first time we run the curl flat combo, the receiver running the curl route is open. The next time we run the same pass route combo, a defender drops back in the same area.

There are different types of Cover 2 zone coverages. There is normal Cover 2 zone and Cover 2 Sink. If normal Cover 2 zone is called, the curl route is normally going to be open because the cornerback will cover the receiver in the flat. If Cover 2 Sink is called, the cornerback will sink and take away the curl route, leaving the flat route open.

Spend a lot of time learning different pass route combinations in practice mode. Learn to see how they work against different types of pass coverages. Once you learn how each one works, you will become that much better of a passer.

ATTACKING BUMP-N-RUN COVERAGE

One of the first things top players will do as soon as they get their hands on *Madden* is to look for bump-n-run man beaters. This is because most players on defense will call a good amount of bump-n-run man coverage during the course of the game. If you can't beat this type of coverage, your opponent will likely keep calling it.

In this section of the book, we show two bump-n-run man beating pass plays that will give you an advantage as soon as you play your first real game against a human opponent.

SPLIT SLOT QUICK BURST

▲ *Flat routes are very effective*

One of the most common ways to beat bump-n-run man coverage is to select pass plays where the halfback runs a flat route, such as the Split Slot Quick Burst. Notice the halfback running the flat route to the left side of the field. His route obviously can't be jammed at the line of scrimmage since he is coming out of the backfield. However, the defender guarding him will still cover him tightly.

We take control of the halfback and

motion him out to the left.

▲ *Motion is key to beating bump-n-run*

▲ *Read your league rules on motion*

Before he sets, we snap the ball. This allows him to get off the line of scrimmage without being jammed, and it allows him to run his flat route already at full speed.

The defender in coverage is a few steps behind the halfback.

Once the catch is made, we turn up the field and pick up 7 yards.

SINGLEBACK BUNCH Z SPOT

▲ *Get the TE open in the flat*

Another common way to attack bump-n-run man coverage is to find plays out of compressed sets such as Bunch and Snugs, in which a receiver is running a flat route. What makes these types of plays so effective is that the receiver running the flat runs his pass route behind another receiver. This allows him to get a clean release since he cannot be jammed at the line of scrimmage.

The way we like to run this play is to take control of the flanker and motion him to the left. This ensures that the defender covering the flanker doesn't switch with the defender covering the tight end once the ball is snapped.

▲ *Motion keeps them off balance*

After the snap, the tight end will run his flat route underneath the slot receiver.

The defender covering the tight end is too far off to defend a quick pass from our quarterback.

▲ *Use a fast receiver if the TE is slow*

We make the catch and turn up the field for a 6-yard pick-up.

QUICK TIPS FOR ATTACKING BUMP-N-RUN MAN COVERAGE

▶ Spend some time in practice mode learning to beat bump-n-run man coverage. You can bet you will see a heavy dose of it when playing against humans.

▶ Most players that call bump-n-run man coverage normally call some type of blitz. Look for quick passing plays that get the ball out of the quarterback's hands and into a receiver's hands.

▶ Slants, drags, and quick pass routes work well against bump-n-run man coverage, even though the receiver will get jammed at the line of scrimmage.

▶ Use motion to get receivers off the line of scrimmage without being jammed.

DEFENSIVE STRATEGY

Madden NFL 09 is packed with defensive moves to help you get a pass rush on the quarterback, tackle ball carriers, and intercept passes. In this section of the guide, we are going to show how each one of the defensive moves work.

PRE-SNAP DEFENSIVE CONTROLS

AUDIBLE

Use the audible button to select one of five defensive audibles. You can set these at any point during the game, or adjust them in the user settings menu. Each audible corresponds to one of five buttons. You can also choose between one of four pre-set formation audibles by pressing the Right Thumbstick up/down or left/right.

COVERAGE AUDIBLE

Coverage audibles are used to change the way defensive backs cover the field once the ball is snapped.

Note: *See the Defensive Back Shifts section for more details.*

DEFENSIVE PLAYMAKER

Defensive playmaker gives the defense options for making adjustments to each defender on the field.

Note: *See the Individual Defensive Hot Routes section for more details.*

DEFENSIVE LINE AUDIBLES

▲ *Create enhanced blitz set ups*

Defensive line audibles are used to change the way the defensive linemen line up, and the way they attack when the ball is snapped.

Note: *See the Defensive Line Shifts section for more details.*

LINEBACKER AUDIBLES

Use the Linebacker Audible to change the way linebackers line up before the snap, or the way they play coverage.

Note: *See the Linebacker Shifts section for more details.*

COACH CAM

Use the Coach Cam to get a full field view of the offensive and defensive formations.

PUMP UP THE CROWD

Use the Pump Up the Crowd button to get the fans involved in the game. The more you pump the crowd up, the louder they get.

SWITCH PLAYER

▲ *Switch players for total control*

There are two ways to switch players in *Madden NFL 09*. The most common way is to keeping pressing the Switch Player button until you cycle through to the defender you want to use for the play. The other method is to hold down the Switch Player button and then press the Left Thumbstick up/down or left/right until you highlight the defender you want.

DEFENSIVE LINE MOVES

POWER MOVE

The Power move's effectiveness is dependant on the player's strength rating. The higher his strength rating, the better the chance he will be able to bull rush the defender. Once the defender is engaged with a blocker, press the Power Move button repeatedly to

▲ *Power move blockers to the ground*

knock the blocker out of the way. Defensive linemen with the Power Move weapon are very effective at getting to the quarterback or disrupting the run game.

SPIN MOVE

▲ *Seymour blows by the left tackle*

Use the Spin move when you are engaged with a blocker. Once executed, the defender will try to spin out of the block. This move is effective when a defensive lineman has the finesse weapon. There are a few defensive ends in the game that have the finesse weapon and the speed to spin around offensive tackles, and go straight after the quarterback.

HANDS UP/BAT

If you are in control of a defensive lineman and are unable to get to the quarterback, use the hands up/bat button to knock the pass down. Timing and position are very important when you try to knock the pass down before it crosses the line of scrimmage. Obviously taller defensive linemen have a better chance of batting the ball down while it's in the air.

DEFENSIVE PURSUIT

DIVE

▲ Making a user tackle

Use the Dive button to make a tackle on the ball carrier. Learning to make user tackles takes some practice to get down. Master them, and you'll be making tackles all over the field.

HIT STICK

▲ Harrison tackles the ball carrier

By pressing the Right Thumbstick down, you can deliver crushing hits to

tackle the ball carrier. Defenders with the Brick Wall weapon can devastate ball carriers and cause fumbles more often.

SPRINT

▲ Putting pressure on the QB

The Sprint button gives your defender an extra speed boost to chase down ball carriers.

STRAFE

▲ Square up on the ball carrier

Use the Strafe button to get your defender squared up with the ball carrier.

STRIP BALL

When the ball carrier is close try using the Strip Ball button to knock the ball out. This takes some timing and a little luck. The downside of using the strip ball button is if you don't strip the ball, you may miss the tackle. We rec-

ommend using this control when you have other defenders around the play.

SWITCH PLAYER

At any point once the ball is snapped you can switch to another defender. When the Switch Player button is pressed you will take control of the closest defender to the ball.

BALL IN AIR/LOOSE BALL

CATCH

Use the Catch button to intercept the pass. The best way to use the Catch button is to use the strafe and catch button together. If you can get the timing down, you'll be snagging passes out of the air in no time.

DIVE

If the receiver is too far away to pick off or swat the pass, trying using the dive button. It is possible that you will be able to knock the ball out of the receiver's hands or bat the pass away.

HIT STICK

Most top players will use the Hit Stick to jar the ball loose from the receiver. Make sure you only try this when you have help. If you miss, the receiver may take the rock to the house for 6 points. Spend some time

in practice mode timing your hits. If you get good at it, you can really make life a pain for players that like to lob the ball deep. Defenders with the Big Hit weapon really can take advantage of this control.

SWAT

▲ The swat button is a useful tool

Use the Swat button to knock the ball away from the receiver. Spend a lot of time in the lab until you feel comfortable with taking control of defenders when trying to defend the pass. Try practicing against the Hail Mary Pass in practice mode to get the hang of it.

MADDEN NFL 09 CHALLENGE TIPS

Practice different playbooks and routes: *This way when someone uses a certain playbook you have an idea of what it contains and how to defend the plays or beat the coverage. You must also practice how to stop certain routes using defensive hot routes or manually moving players*

DEFENSIVE STRATEGY

Being able to control the line of scrimmage on the defensive side of the ball starts with the defensive linemen. In *Madden NFL 09,* you have a variety of shifts and pass rush alignment adjustments to stop the run, and get pressure on the quarterback.

DEFENSIVE STRATEGY

Spread Defensive Line

Press the Line Audible button, then push the Left Thumbstick up to spread the defensive line.

Strengths
▶ Puts the defensive ends in better position to defend run plays to the outside.
▶ With the defensive ends spread out, they get a better angle for putting pressure on the quarterback from the outside.
▶ If the defensive ends are in QB Contain, they do a good job at forcing the mobile quarterback to stay in the pocket.

Weaknesses
▶ Having the defensive linemen spread out weakens inside run support.
▶ Defensive ends need to have speed to be effective pass rushers from the outside when the defensive line is spread out.

Pinch Defensive Line

Press the Line Audible button, then push the Left Thumbstick down to pinch the defensive line.

Strengths
▶ Creates pressure up the gut.
▶ Improves run support against the inside run.
▶ Frees up linebackers to shoot though the A and B gaps to either make tackles on the ball carrier in the backfield or sack the quarterback.

Weaknesses
▶ Outside pressure from the defensive ends is non existent.
▶ Outside runs are hard to defend because the defensive linemen are lined up closer inside.
▶ Mobile quarterbacks can get outside of the pocket because the defensive linemen pinch in.

Shift Defensive Line Left

Press the Line Audible button, then push the Left Thumbstick left to shift the defensive line.

Strengths
▶ Creates pressure from the weak side by overloading the offensive line.
▶ Puts the defensive linemen in better position to defend against weak side runs.
▶ Decent against the inside run.

Weaknesses
▶ Pressure from the strong side is not as intense.
▶ Defensive linemen are not in good position to defend against strong side runs.

Shift Defensive Line Right

Press the Line Audible button, and then push the Left Thumbstick right to shift the defensive line.

Strengths
▶ Creates pressure from the strong side by overloading the offensive line.
▶ Puts defensive linemen in better position to defend against strong side runs.

Weaknesses
▶ Pressure from the opposite side is not as effective.
▶ Defensive linemen are not in good position to defend against weak side runs.

Crash Out

To have the defensive line crash out, press the Defensive Line Audible button, then press up on the Right Thumbstick.

When to Use: To pressure the quarterback from the outside or to defend outside runs.

Crash In

To have the defensive line crash in, press the Defensive Line Audible button, then press down on the Right Thumbstick.

When to Use: To pressure up the gut or to shut down the inside run game.

Crash Left

To have the defensive line crash left, press the Defensive Line Audible button, then press left on the Right Thumbstick.

When to Use: To overload the left side of the offensive line or to stop runs to the left.

Crash Right

To have the defensive line crash right, press the Defensive Line Audible button, then press right on the Right Thumbstick.

When to Use: To overload the right side of the offensive line or stop runs to the right.

LINEBACKER AUDIBLE SHIFTS

Linebacker shifts allow you to create pressure on the quarterback from the inside and outside. You can use defensive linemen and linebacker shifts together to create some nice run and pass schemes to shutdown the opposing offense's game plan.

Spread Linebackers Out

Press the Linebacker Audible button, then press up on the Left Thumbstick to spread the linebackers out.

Strengths

- By spreading the outside linebackers out you have better pass rush angles for getting pressure on the quarterback.
- The outside linebackers take better angles at stopping the outside run.
- Spreading the linebackers out puts them closer to cover the slot receiver.
- It helps prevent the athletic quarterback from rolling out of the pocket if the linebackers are in QB Contain.

Weaknesses

- Makes it harder for the outside linebackers to defend the inside run since they have more ground to cover.

Pinch Linebackers In

Press the Linebacker Audible button, then press the Left Thumbstick down to pinch the linebackers in.

Strengths

- Puts linebackers in a better position to be able to stop the inside run.
- By pinching the linebackers in, you are now in better position to put pressure on the quarterback up the middle if you blitz them.

Weaknesses

- Linebackers do not defend against the outside run as well because they often will get blocked before having a chance to get outside to make a tackle on the ball carrier.
- Linebackers are not in position to defend multiple receiver sets since they line up further inside.

Shift Linebackers Left

Press the Linebacker Audible button, then press the Left Thumbstick left to shift the linebackers left.

Strengths

- The right outside linebacker has an improved pass rush angle to put pressure on the quarterback.
- Good for stopping weak side toss and pitch plays.
- Does a decent job against inside runs.

Weaknesses

- The left outside linebacker's pass rush angle is somewhat sacrificed.
- Weak at containing athletic quarterbacks to the strong side.

Shift Linebackers Right

Press the Linebacker Audible button, then press the Left Thumbstick right to shift the linebackers to the right.

Strengths

- The left outside linebacker has an improved pass rush angle to the quarterback.
- Good at stopping the strong side toss.
- Does a decent job against inside runs.

Weaknesses

- The right outside linebacker's pass rush angle is somewhat sacrificed.
- Weak at containing athletic quarterbacks to the weak side.

All LBs in Hook Zones

Press the Linebacker Audible button, then press the Right Thumbstick up.

When to Use: During attacks on your defense with short pass routes over the middle, drop the linebackers in hook zones.

All Linebackers Blitz

Press the Linebacker Audible button, then press the Right Thumbstick down.

When to Use: Sending all the LBs in on a blitz makes it harder for the offensive linemen to pick up all the pass rushers.

Right Outside LB Blitz

Press the Linebacker Audible button, then press the Right Thumbstick right.

When to Use: Pressures the quarterback from his blind side. A fast right outside LB will enhance the pressure on the QB.

Left Outside LB Blitz

Press the Linebacker Audible button, then press the Right Thumbstick left.

When to Use: To defend strong side running plays. The left outside LB will be more aggressive at defending the run.

DEFENSIVE STRATEGY

There are several ways to disguise your pass coverages. This is more important when you are playing a human opponent than playing against the CPU. Below we show you how each one works along with their strengths and weaknesses.

DEFENSIVE STRATEGY

Back Off Coverage

Press the Coverage Audible button and then press up on the Left Thumbstick.

Strengths
- The cornerbacks and safeties drop back in a deeper alignment before the snap. This puts them in better position to defend the deep pass.
- Cornerbacks that play loose coverage are less likely to be blocked on outside runs.

Weaknesses
- Short pass routes to the sidelines can exploit this type of pass coverage, unless the cornerbacks are playing the flats.

Press Coverage

Press the Coverage Audible button and then press down on the Left Thumbstick.

Strengths
- The defensive backs jam the receivers at the line of scrimmage. This will throw the timing off between the quarterback and receiver on routes such as slants, drags, and quick outs.
- Press coverage forces the offense to adjust their playcalling.

Weaknesses
- You must have defensive backs that have high Press ratings for it to be effective. If not, receivers can easily get off the line of scrimmage, and will easily get open.
- Press coverage is not very good against the run because receivers tend to lock on to the cornerbacks longer.

Show Blitz

Press the Coverage Audible button and then press left on the Left Thumbstick.

Strengths
- Enhances inside run support.
- Provides opportunities for safeties to put pressure on the quarterback by shooting through the gaps.

Weaknesses
- Weak against outside runs.
- Safeties are suspect against the deep pass.
- Safeties tend to bite on play action more often than if in normal or loose coverage.

Man Align

Press the Coverage Audible button and then press right on the Left Thumbstick.

Strengths
- Puts the defenders in better position to cover receivers in the man coverage.
- Quicker to use than manually moving defenders into place before the snap.

Weaknesses
- Easy for a good player on offense to recognize the pass coverage assignments based on how defenders line up before the snap.

Zones to Sideline

Press the Coverage Audible button and then press up on the Right Thumbstick.

When to Use: Works best against streaks, fades, post corners and corner routes. Leaves the middle vulnerable to posts and seam routes.

Zones to Middle

Press the Coverage Audible button and then press down on the Right Thumbstick.

When to Use: Takes away deep post routes, but leaves fades and streaks to the sidelines open.

Zones to Left/Right

Press the Coverage Audible button and then press left/right on the Right Thumbstick.

When to Use: This coverage audible well help defend the deep ball to the side the zone is shifted to. As a result, passes to the opposite side are weakened.

INDIVIDUAL DEFENSIVE HOT ROUTES

One the most popular features ever added to the *Madden NFL* franchise over the years is the Individual Defensive Hot Route. Top players around the country like to use them because they are able make defensive adjustments on the fly to counter just about anything the opposing player on offense can throw at them.

For example, many players like to use a base 2 Man Under defense. They will make adjustments on the fly based on the types of plays their opponents run. Another reason why top players like Individual Defensive Hot Routes is they can set up enhanced blitz schemes that quickly get to the quarterback. The bottom line is having Individual Defensive Hot Routes allows players to be creative and makes playing defense fun.

HOW DEFENSIVE HOT ROUTES WORK

To call a defensive hot route, tap the switch player button or hold the switch play button. Press the Left Thumbstick up/down or left/right until your desired defender is selected, press the **A** button (Xbox 360), or ✖ button (PS3) to activate the Defensive Hot Routes, then use one of the following options:

Hook Zone (yellow circle)
Press up on the Left Thumbstick

The defender will drop back in a hook zone. This coverage is good at defending short passes over the middle of the field. If your opponent is beating you

▲ *Hook Zone*

with drags, slants, crosses, or circle routes, this is a good coverage to call.

▲ *QB Curtain*

QB Contain (black arrow)
Press down on the Left Thumbstick

When playing against a quarterback who has the ability to scramble, consider putting a defender or two in QB Curtain. This forces the QB to stay in the pocket.

Man Coverage (red line)
Press the receiver's icon, then left on the Left Thumbstick

There are some receivers in the game that may need some extra attention to prevent them from getting the ball. This call can be made from man and zone defenses.

Curl to Flat (purple circle)
Press right on the Left Thumbstick

▲ *Curl to Flat*

Most players that use Curl to Flat use them to defend against corner routes. They also can be used to defend the flats, since the defenders play near the sideline.

Deep 2A/2B (blue)
Press up on the Right Thumbstick

▲ *Deep 2A/2B*

Deep 2A/2B hot routes are used to take away the deep pass. If your opponent likes to throw bombs, you may consider dropping a few extra defenders deep to take away his bread and butter.

Blitz (orange arrow)
Press down on the Right Thumbstick

▲ *Blitz*

Assigning defenders to blitz can help you create schemes on the fly against the run and pass. Just remember that this will leave holes in the pass coverage. To send a defender on a blitz, press down on the Right Thumbstick.

QB Spy (orange circle)
Press left on the Right Thumbstick

This is another defensive hot route that can be used to counter a quarterback that likes to take off and run. The QB Spy hot route can also be used to defend short passes over the middle of the field.

Flat Zone (dark blue)
Press right on the Right Thumbstick

If the offense is attacking the flat areas, consider hot routing a defender into the flat area in question. Flat zones can also be used to defend screens or prevent the quarterback from taking off.

DEFENSIVE STRATEGY

DEFENSIVE STRATEGY

Bringing heat is a game of cat and mouse, and has high risks and high rewards. When the defense decides to blitz, it is purely to disrupt the timing of the pass and force a throw into coverage or generate a sack from the pressure. Mixed with different coverages and fronts, the blitz can cause fits for the offense.

There are a few ways to blitz. You can call a play designed to blitz and run the play according to the design, or run a play where you pull a player that's not designed to blitz and manually blitz them. Players will also overload one side of the offensive line to bring more blitzers than there are blockers, so that one defender will get through to make the sack on the quarterback. These types of blitzes all require some type of coverage to support them. The most aggressive blitz is the Cover 0 blitz, in which there is no deep zone. Usually at least seven defenders blitz with coverage behind them in order to protect the defense in case the offense gets off a pass. Most good players will blitz with coverage in order to force the throw to a covered area if they don't sack the quarterback. You can use the playmaker to assign different players to blitz, but make sure that you don't leave big holes for the offense to exploit.

INSIDE BLITZ

The quickest way to bring heat on the quarterback is to create blitz schemes that bring A and B Gap heat.

For those that don't know what A and B Gaps are, let us educate you quickly. The A Gap is between the center and guards on both sides of the ball. The B Gap is between the guards and tackles on both sides of the ball. By creating A and B Gap pressure, you can really throw off the quarterback's ability to step up in the box.

One of our favorite A Gap blitz schemes is the 3-4 Solid Gap Press. With just a few pre-snap defensive adjustments, we can get instant pressure from the right inside linebacker.

▲ *No safeties play deep*

To set up the blitz scheme, we first show fake blitz.

Next, we take control of the right inside linebacker and hot route him to blitz. He should be lined up between the center and left guard.

Once the ball is snapped, the left

▲ *The RILB is in the A Gap*

guard will block the right end, while the center blocks the nose tackle.

▲ *Speed rules in Madden NFL 09*

This creates a gap between the center and left guard for the right inside linebacker to shoot through.

▲ *The quarterback is in trouble*

▲ *Nothing better than an instant sack*

The quarterback is dropped to the ground for a sack.

OVERLOAD BLITZ

This is another common blitz scheme that is used to overload one side of the offensive line with multiple pass rushers. The idea behind this scheme is to send more defenders in on a blitz than the offensive line can block.

The Dollar Normal SS Zone Blitz is a good example of an overload blitz scheme that creates pressure from the right side of the offensive line.

▲ *Three defenders drop deep*

To set up the overload blitz scheme, we take control of the strong safety and move him just outside of the right end.

▲ *We have created an overload*

There are only two pass blockers versus three pass rushers on the right side.

▲ *The RT must make a quick decision*

The right tackle slide is to block the left linebacker. The right guard blocks the right defensive end.

▲ *The pass protection isn't holding up*

There is no one to account for the strong safety.

▲ *Not much time in the pocket*

The result is quick pressure and a sack on the quarterback.

QUICK BLITZ TIPS

▶ For best results, put your fastest defensive personnel out on the field when blitzing the quarterback. The more speed the defender has, the quicker he will get to the quarterback.

▶ Test blitz packages in practice mode. A blitz that works in practice mode may not always work the same way in the regular game mode. Once you feel your blitz schemes will work, try them in a real game situation.

▶ Put one controller on your team and the other controller on the other. Once on the field, set up the defense and then run the play to see if it works. If it does, then you know you can run it against a human opponent online or offline.

▶ Learn to manually blitz a defender if he is playing zone or man coverage. We like to call these defenders "flex defenders."

▶ Hot route defenders to blitz to create different blitz schemes in *Madden NFL 09*.

▶ Use defensive line shifts and linebacker shifts to create blitz schemes.

▶ Manually move defenders in different places to generate different types of pressure.

▶ Test your blitz schemes against different types of slide protection and pass blocking schemes. One that works against one type of slide protection may not always work against other types of slide protection.

▶ Use instant replay to see how your blitz schemes work or even how the CPU schemes work.

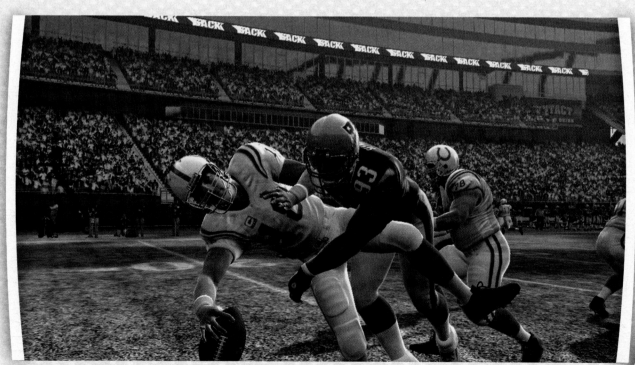

▲ *The perfect blitz scheme results in a QB sack*

DEFENSIVE STRATEGY

Playing good inside run defense requires the attitude to destroy your opponent. It is not good enough just to contain a play; you have to create a defensive scheme that totally shuts down a play. Doing this allows you to protect your weak areas on defense and dictate the flow of the game to the offense.

When it comes to playing *Madden*, the first thing you need to focus on is developing a good inside run defense. The passing game in football generally takes time for most players to become successful, so players will gravitate to the run first because it is slightly easier. Get your cleats tied up and your helmet and shoulder pads on, and meet us on the field for some inside run defense training.

LOAD UP THE BOX

▲ *The pass coverage is weak*

If you are unable to stop the inside run with 7 defenders, the best way is to load up the box with as many defenders as you can. Some players like to load up 8, and some will even go so far as loading the box with 9 defenders. We are going to show how some top players will load the box up to stop

the inside run by putting 9 defenders in the box.

The 4-3 Normal Thunder Smoke sends all three linebackers in on a blitz. The free safety plays the deep middle, while the two cornerbacks and strong safety play man coverage.

What we like to do is show fake blitz. This brings the strong safety down closer to the line of scrimmage.

▲ *Eight defenders in the box*

Next, we take control of the free safety and bring him down near the center.

▲ *Nine defenders in the box*

Once the ball is snapped, we stay in control of the free safety. If an offensive lineman (normally the center) doesn't block our free safety, the fullback will. With the fullback out of the picture, there is no one to lead block for the halfback.

▲ *Drop the free safety back*

The right outside linebacker and strong safety have clear paths at making the tackle on the halfback before he ever gets going.

INSIDE RUN BASE DEFENSIVE SETS

There are three inside run base defensive sets in *Madden NFL 09*. Here is quick overview of how each works against the inside run game.

3-4 Defense This defense should only be used if you have a solid core of linebackers and a big defensive line. Attacking the run in this defense normally prevents the outside run because the added linebacker puts more speed on the edge and can string the play out sideline to sideline. The disadvantage of this scheme is a lot of teams will run inside on you and the offensive

lineman will get on the linebackers, causing a mismatch in favor of the offense. The 3-4 sets are the weakest of the three base defensive sets.

4-3 Defense This defense uses a four man front with three linebackers. It is normally run by teams with better pass rushing linemen than the 3-4. The 4-3 provides good run support to the weak, middle, or strong side and is the most common of the three base defensive sets used to stop the inside run. It is helpful for beginners who are not sure what each defensive set does. If you are not sure what the defenders are supposed to do, we suggest learning by running the 4-3 Normal defense. The flaw to this defensive set is that you can't really change the look of the defense because it is a base formation.

46 Defense This defense is a variation of the 4-3 defense, but it brings the strong safety down in the box just outside of the left defensive end. Of the three base defensive sets, the 46 is the best at defending the inside run. It was designed to stop offenses with conventional formations, such as the I-Form Normal, Strong I, or Weak I sets. This defense has worked the best when stopping the run in *Madden*, but you must back out of it when the offense goes to a spread receiver set. If the offense gets you in a mismatch based on formation, then make sure the pressure gets to the quarterback before the pass gets off. Against the run, you will love this set.

OUTSIDE RUN DEFENSE

The key to playing solid outside run defense is keeping the running back from getting outside, or if he does get outside, forcing him back inside where defenders can converge on him.

With the amount of fast running backs in the game, plus the well-designed outside plays, stopping them is easier said than done. The only way to become good at playing outside run defense is through repetition. The more you do it, the more it becomes second nature. That's why coaches preach, "Perfect practice makes perfect." By practicing over and over again it's possible to turn great fundamentals into natural habits, and ultimately improve your outside run defense.

DE CONTAIN

▲ Both DEs are in QB Contain

This may sound crazy, but DE Contain plays are quite effective at defending outside run plays. As you know, DE Contain plays are normally used to keep the quarterback from rolling out of the pocket. DE Contain plays can also be used to force the running back inside, or, even better, to stop the running back before he ever gets outside.

The 4-3 Normal DE Contain has both defensive ends in DE Contain, while the middle linebacker plays QB Spy. The outside linebackers and cornerbacks are in man coverage. The two safeties play the deep halves of the field.

We take control of the cornerbacks and move them inside just a tad. This will keep them from being blocked by the outside receivers. Don't worry if a pass is called, they will still be in position to defend their men.

▲ The CBs are moved inside 2 yards

Once the ball is snapped, the defensive ends will shoot outside. Most of the time, they will be able to avoid being blocked.

▲ The LE fights off the blocked

This allows them to quickly pursue the running back before he ever gets going.

▲ The LE closes in to make the tackle

The left end tackles the running back in the backfield for a loss.

▲ Even Peterson can't avoid the tackle

OUTSIDE RUN BASE DEFENSIVE SETS

3-4 Defense The 3-4 defensive set is by far the best of the three defensive sets to use to stop the run. With the outside linebackers playing further out wide, they are in a much better position to defend the outside run. Throw in the fact that most teams play the 3-4 base scheme and have outside linebackers that are pretty fast.

4-3 Defense The 4-3 defensive sets are decent against the outside run, provided that the linebackers have the speed to chase down ball carriers. Also, having fast defensive ends comes into play if they are able to shed off blocks. One way to increase the effectiveness of the 4-3 defensive sets is to spread the linebackers out. This puts them in better position to defend against outside runs.

46 Defense The 46 defensive sets are the weakest of the three base defensive sets, despite the safety playing in the box. This is because a run blocker often engulfs him. Another reason is that the linebackers are compressed inside the tackles and can't get outside as quickly to defend the outside run.

QUICK RUNNING DEFENSE TIPS

When pursuing the run, while in front of the halfback, make sure to use the strafe. This keeps you in a good defensive position and allow you to attack whichever hole the halfback chooses.

Only dive when it is the last option. Leaving your feet against a player with good stick control will cost you big time, and if you like diving this will become a hard habit to break.

Another tactic that many *Madden* players use when defending the run, more so in the open field, is the click on-click off technique. First, get the defender in the best possible position to make the tackle, and then click off to let the computer make the tackle.

DEFENSIVE STRATEGY

▲ Cover 2 Buc is a solid zone defense

One of things we have noticed this year is that underneath zone coverage has been tightened up substantially from previous versions of *Madden*. What this means for the defensive side of the ball is that defenders will be where they are supposed to be, provided that the right pass coverage has been called.

DEFENDING QUICK SLANTS

One of the most common short pass routes you can expect to see is the slant route. Against man coverage, they can be completed at a very high rate. Against zone coverage, they don't have such a high rate of completion, provided that the right zone defense has been called.

One defense we like to use to defend quick slants is 4-3 Normal Cover 2 Buc with a few pre-snap adjustments.

Notice that the middle linebacker drops back over the deep middle. His coverage assignment does well at defending the deep post, which is a weakness in the Cover 2 zone scheme. By his dropping into this area of the field, it leaves

▲ Cover 2 Buc is a solid zone defense

the short middle of the field open.

We hot route him into a hook zone. Keep this in mind: this leaves the deep middle of the field vulnerable to the deep post.

▲ Three linebackers are in hook zones

Next, we spread the linebackers out.

▲ Puts OLBs outside the DEs

Once the ball is snapped, the two cornerbacks will jam the outside receivers running quick slants. This will slow them down as they get into their pass patterns.

Notice as both outside linebackers drop in hook zones and take any

▲ Press coverage ratings are critical

chance of the quarterback throwing to them.

▲ The quarterback scans the field

If the middle linebacker were to drop back over the deep middle like he was supposed to in the Cover 2 Buc scheme, one of the receivers would have been open. However, since the middle linebacker has been hot routed into a hook zone, he is in position to take away any quick pass in his area.

▲ The QB has no open receiver

The quarterback has no open receiver and the result is a coverage sack.

DEFENDING THE CURL FLAT COMBO

One of the hardest pass route combos to defend in football is the Curl Flat combo. This is because one of two receivers running the curl flat combo is almost always open at some point against man or zone coverage. It's just a matter of the quarterback making the right read and throwing to the correct receiver.

The 3-3-5 Cover 2 by default doesn't do a good enough job of covering the curl flat combo. Usually, the receiver running the curl route is wide open. We make a few pre-snap adjustments to make sure that neither of them is a target.

First, we drop the left end into a hook zone. We do this to take away any short pass in his area.

Next, we take control of the middle linebacker and have him play buzz zone.

▲ Cover 2 Buc is a solid zone defense

▲ Two defenders drop in buzz zones

With our defensive scheme now in place, the quarterback has no open receiver on the right side of the field.

▲ The QB looks over the defense

MORE TIPS FOR DEFENDING THE SHORT PASS

If your opponent likes to throw a lot of short passes, there is really no point in blitzing, especially if he is a well-seasoned veteran of the game. He will just pick your defensive blitz schemes apart. You are better off rushing two or three pass rushers and dropping everyone else back in pass coverage to take away the underneath throwing lanes. Having five, six, or even seven defenders playing underneath zone coverage will make it very difficult to get the short passing game going, even for high level players.

If your opponent is inside your 10-yard line and it's third down, consider dropping all your defenders back in pass coverage. A typical all coverage defense may consist of two defenders in QB spy, two defenders covering the flats, two defenders covering buzz zones, three defenders in hook zones, and two players playing the back area of the end zone.

▲ Not a lot is going to be open

Use bump-n-run and press coverage to delay the receivers from getting off the line and into their short pass patterns. This helps throw the timing off for the quarterback, and gives the defensive line more time to get pressure and hopefully sack the quarterback.

Defenders with high zone coverage and awareness ratings tend to make more plays on pass routes underneath. Often they are in better position to pick the pass off, knock the pass away, or make the tackle as soon as the receiver makes the catch.

Learn to be quick at making hot route adjustments on the fly. They can be a lifesaver in defending even the most potent offenses in the game.

Watch for wide receiver screen routes. This year, wide receiver screen routes are very effective against zone coverage. The best way to defend them is to call bump-n-run man coverage. If you have a lock down cornerback, he may even pick off a few.

▲ Solid coverage over the middle

If your opponent likes to run drag routes, try putting defenders in hook zones, QB spy, or a combination of both to take away these types of passes.

DEFENSIVE STRATEGY

▲ *Not a lot of pressure from 9 Velcro*

Of the three areas of the field (short, intermediate, and deep), the area thrown to the least is probably intermediate. Outside of the crossing route, most players would rather throw short routes underneath such as drags, slants, and flats, or throw deep routes such as streaks, posts, and corners. Regardless, you still need to know how to defend intermediate pass routes.

In this section of the book, we are going to take a look at three of the more common intermediate pass routes that you will see in *Madden NFL 09*.

CROSS

From what we have seen so far, zone coverage works much better at defending intermediate pass routes than man coverage. This holds especially true when it comes to defending crossing routes. If man coverage is called,

receivers tend to get separation from the defenders in coverage. In zone coverage, on the other hand, the defenders do an excellent job of defending the receiver running the crossing route all the way across the field.

The Nickel Normal 9 Velcro is a good example of a defense that can be used to defend pretty much the entire field, except maybe some types of corner routes. The nickelback and right end drop in the flats. The left end and both linebackers drop in hook zones. The

two cornerbacks and safeties drop back in 4 deep coverage. The only two defenders that rush the quarterback are the defensive tackles. With this many defenders dropping back in underneath pass coverage, it is very hard to complete a pass to a receiver running a crossing route.

▲ *Not a lot of pressure from 9 Velcro*

Notice that the receiver lined up in the slot on the left is running a crossing route. He will be the receiver we focus on.

▲ *Steve Smith is lined up in the slot*

▲ *Five defenders play under coverage*

Once the ball is snapped, notice

how he is covered. Each defender dropping back underneath zone coverage will cover the slot receiver as he works across the field.

▲ *Five defenders play under coverage*

At no point will he be open where the quarterback can make a throw to him.

CURL

The curl route can be run short, intermediate, or deep. Just like most underneath pass routes, we find that zone coverage is the best way to defend the curl route. If man coverage is called, the receiver running the curl is generally open once he curls back towards the quarterback. That's why we believe that zone coverage works better.

The Dollar Normal Cover 2 Sink does a good job of covering most underneath pass routes. Notice that the cornerbacks drop back in hook zones rather than play the flats as in most traditional Cover 2 coverages. Because of the way they drop, they are in better position to defend the curl. If a curl flat combo is called, they will cover the curl route instead of the receiver in the flat. The split end lined up on the left is running a curl route. He will be the

▲ *The ROLB is sent in on a blitz*

receiver we focus on.

Notice how the right cornerback sinks back into a hook zone.

▲ *There is a four man pass rush*

Even if the quarterback makes the throw to the running back in the flat, the cornerback will react quick enough to make the tackle for a minimal gain.

▲ *The quarterback looks left*

Once the split end curls back, there is no chance that the split end is going to be open.

▲ *Five defenders play underneath*

DIG

The last intermediate pass route we want to discuss is the dig route. This route is also very hard to defend when man coverage is called. Often the receiver running the route will get separation once he breaks over the middle. That's why when our opponent likes to run these types of pass routes we like to call some type of zone coverage.

The defense we use is the Dollar Normal Cover 3. This defense drops five defenders in underneath pass coverage. The two inside defensive backs drop into the flats. The two linebackers and strong safety play hook zones. The two cornerbacks and free safety play 3 deep. There is only a 3 man pass rush. The only real weaknesses of this pass coverage are corner routes or vertical stretch passing concepts.

The split end running the dig route is the receiver we will focus on.

At this point, the split end is covered by the inside defensive back underneath and right cornerback over the top.

▲ *The SE runs a backside dig*

Once the split end breaks over the middle, there is a small passing window for the quarterback to make the throw. If the pass were to be thrown, the right outside linebacker, who is dropping back in a hook zone, would be in position to knock it down or pick the pass off.

MORE TIPS FOR DEFENDING THE INTERMEDIATE PASS

As we have already mentioned, playing man coverage is not a good idea against players who like to run intermediate pass routes. This advice especially holds true when a faster receiver is matched up with a slower defender. If you call man coverage and you notice a match-up that favors the offense, consider audibling into a zone defense.

If you plan on running man coverage, consider running man/zone combo covers. For instance, have the cornerbacks play man coverage, while the linebackers drop in zones.

Intermediate pass routes take longer to develop, so blitzing the quarterback is another option to consider.

EA SPORTS **MADDEN NFL 09 CHALLENGE TIPS**

Avoid the user-controlled defender. *Why test someone's stick skills if you don't have to? Stay away from that side or person. Most people control a person that they can make plays with.*

DEFENSIVE STRATEGY

DEFENSIVE STRATEGY

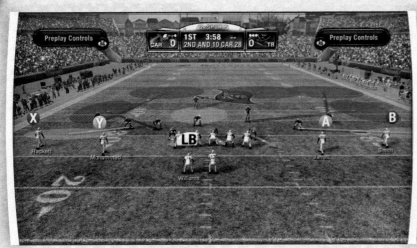

▲ *Defenders drop back in coverage*

Between players on offense being able to take control of receivers and make amazing user catches and sometimes shady defensive AI, defending the deep pass over the years in *Madden* has been a difficult task for even the best players. In this year's game, EA SPORTS went to great lengths to even the playing field, so that players on defense would have a chance at defending the long ball. So far from what we have seen, they have done an outstanding job at making defending the deep pass more balanced.

In this section of the book, we discuss some different types of coverage that can be used to defend two of the more common deep passing routes found in the game.

CORNER

The corner route has been a thorn in many cyber defensive coordinators' sides over the years. There are different types of corner routes in the game and each can be hard to defend. The most common is the corner route run by the slot receiver. Normally, most players on offense will have the outside receiver run a streak, while the slot runs the corner. This route combination can be very deadly against just about any pass coverage in the game. Another corner route used by many is the post corner route. Players will have the slot receiver run a streak, while the outside receiver runs the post corner. This route, like the streak corner combo is also hard to defend.

One last corner route is one in which the receiver takes an inside release, and then breaks up the field, before breaking towards the corner. Some of you who are in the *Madden* community may have heard this route called the backwards C route. The way most players run this route is to have a slot receiver run a streak and the outside receiver run the backwards C route. Just like the other two corner routes we have mentioned, this one is effective against most coverages.

The best way to defend these types of corner routes is to call some type of defense where the defenders drop back in buzz zones. Once such defense is the Nickel 3-3-5 Cover 3. The right outside linebacker and strong safety both play hook zones, while the nickelback and left outside linebacker cover the flats. The right cornerback, free safety, and left cornerback drop back in three deep coverage.

Notice that the offensive play we have shown has the two outside receivers running inside release corner routes.

▲ *The FL is the primary receiver*

Once the ball is snapped, the flanker takes an inside release, and then breaks straight up the field.

▲ *Seam routes can be effective*

The flanker then breaks to corner. Notice the left outside linebacker drops back to help defend the corner route.

▲ *The QB is ready to launch the pass*

The ball is thrown. The left outside linebacker and left cornerback converge on the flanker.

▲ *Not much of a passing window*

We take control of the left cornerback and step in front of the pass to knock it away.

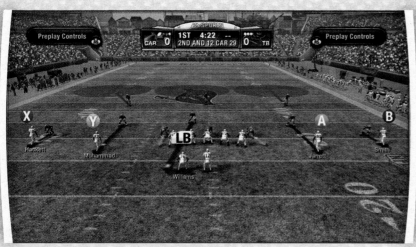

▲ *Watch for inside runs*

STREAK

The most common deep route you must learn to defend is the streak. You can bet that human opponents will look to throw plenty of deep balls to players running streaks. If you are playing against a team with a fast receiver such as Carolina Panthers' Steve Smith (97 speed), you really don't want to leave him in one-on-one coverage. It's best to leave at least one extra defender over the top.

The Quarter Combo 3 Deep Press has the three safeties playing deep coverage. The free safety 1 plays the deep left, the free safety 2 plays the deep middle, and the strong safety plays the deep right. This makes for very stout deep defensive pass coverage. On top of those three playing deep, there is man coverage under-

neath and the cornerbacks are in press (bump-n-run) coverage.

We have hot routed Steve Smith on a streak on the right side of the field.

▲ *The FL is the primary receiver*

▲ *Jam the receivers to slow them down*

At the snap, the left cornerback will jam him at the line of scrimmage.

Notice how the strong safety plays over the top. This makes it quite dif-

▲ *The QB looks to throw deep*

ficult for the quarterback to throw a deep pass to Smith.

▲ *Not much air on the throw*

The quarterback decides to make the throw anyway.

▲ *We pick the ball off*

This is a mistake, and the pass is picked off.

MORE TIPS FOR DEFENDING THE DEEP PASS

Check your cornerbacks' and your opponent's receiver ratings. If any of your cornerbacks are slower than the receivers they are covering, try not to leave them in one-on-one coverage. In this year's game, the deep bomb is there if the receiver has more speed than the cornerback in coverage. We can't tell you how many times we have burned our opponent by going up top when our fast receiver is able to blow past the cornerback in coverage. Make sure you have a safety playing over the top.

Most top players like to control safeties before the snap. One of the key reasons they do this is to make sure that if their opponent uses the pump fake, their safeties don't bite on it. Normally, players will take control of the safeties with lowest awareness rating. That way, he won't be susceptible to the pump fake.

Top players may also take control of the fastest safety on the field or even sub in a fast cornerback at safety. The reason they do this is so they cover ground quickly when the ball is in the air. Top players usually have great stick control and can pick the pass off or at least knock the pass down while in control of a fast safety.

DEFENSIVE STRATEGY

53

In *Madden NFL 09,* each team has its own specific defensive playbook. Most teams in the NFL primarily run a 4 down linemen scheme; however, there are more and more teams making the switch to the 3 down linemen scheme. We take a look at each of the defensive sets and formations in the game.

4-3 SET

The basic 4-3 defense is good against the inside running game and gives you a good pass rush from your four down linemen. The ROLB (Willy) is generally the team's fastest linebacker. He should be able to blitz from his side and put heat on the QB. The MLB (Mike) is normally the defensive team's quarterback. He should be able to make all the adjustments and let his teammates know what is going on. Look for your MLB to have a high awareness rating. The higher it is, the better chance he will be in position to stop the inside run. The LOLB (on the TE) can cover the TE, blitz, or cover any of the short zones to that side or the hook zone over the middle. The CBs can blitz with the safety(s), assuming the corner's responsibilities. Or a corner can drop back in deep coverage allowing a safety blitz.

4-3 Formations

  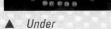

▲ *Normal*　　　▲ *Under*　　　▲ *Over*

3-4 SET

The 3-4 is a defense that has three DLs, four LBs, and four DBs. The 3-4 is helpful if you have a better set of LBs than D-Linemen. The reason for having four LBs is to have more speed on defense. The three defensive linemen's purpose is to keep the offensive line off the LBs, so they can make the plays. The strength of the 3-4 is in stopping the outside run. You will also get good coverage in short passes with the extra LB. The weakness of the 3-4 is that it struggles against the inside run, and you will not get a lot of pressure from your defensive line. You will want to blitz more to add pressure if you decide to use the 3-4. You will find a variety of Cover 1, 2, 3, and 4 type coverages in *Madden NFL 09* from the 3-4 formations.

3-4 Formations

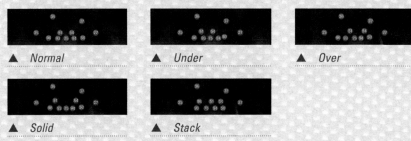

▲ *Normal*　　　▲ *Under*　　　▲ *Over*

▲ *Solid*　　　▲ *Stack*

46 SET

The 46 Normal defense can wreak havoc on the opposing team's passing game with multiple defenders blitzing from all directions. The 46 Normal defense can cause turnovers in a hurry. It's also a great run defense to call because it places 8 men in the box.

46 Formations

▲ *Normal*　　　▲ *Bear*

NICKEL SET

The Nickel defense traditionally has four D-Linemen, but in *Madden NFL 09,* there are formations that have one, two, and three down linemen. This set is primarily used for pass defense, but the two linebackers still provide decent run support. You will want your four best pass rushers on the defensive line. Your two best cover LBs should be in the nickel as well. The fifth DB (Nickelback) you bring in should be your third best cover back. The object of the nickel defense is to get enough defenders to cover the offense's multiple receivers. When you see the offense using 3 WR, 4 WR, and 5 WR sets you will want to call the Nickel defense.

Nickel Formations

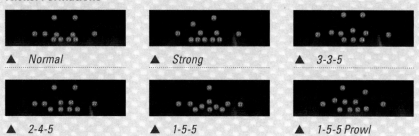

▲ *Normal*   ▲ *Strong*   ▲ *3-3-5*

▲ *2-4-5*   ▲ *1-5-5*   ▲ *1-5-5 Prowl*

DIME SET

The Dime defense brings in a sixth DB, plus four D-Linemen and one LB. This gives the defense six DBs to defend the pass. It is mostly used against 4WR and 5WR sets when you know the offense is going to pass. When using the Dime defense, you are sacrificing the run defense to be able to stop the pass.

Dime Formations

▲ *Normal*   ▲ *Flat*

DOLLAR SET

The Dollar set only has one formation—Normal. It's very similar to the Dime in the sense that it has six DBs. However, an extra linebacker is added, replacing the WDT. This gives the Dollar defense a little more speed to defend against the pass.

Dollar Formations

▲ *Normal*

QUARTER SET

The Quarter Defense is used to counter multiple receiver sets like the Shotgun 5 Wide. The defense consists of three down linemen, one linebacker, and seven defensive backs. This allows the Quarter defense to clog up the passing lanes. If you plan on using this defense as a run defense, forget about it. It is not designed to stop the run.

Quarter Formations

▲ *Combo*

GOAL LINE

Goal Line is primarily used when the offense is near your end zone or in short yardage situations. There are five defensive linemen on the line of scrimmage along with two linebackers. Another linebacker and safety play just behind the interior defensive linemen. The right and left cornerback line up outside.

Goal Line Formations

   ◄ *Goal Line*

DEFENSIVE STRATEGY

CHICAGO BEARS

| ▶ **Division** NFC North | ▶ **Stadium** Bears Field | ▶ **Type** Open | ▶ **Capacity** 61,500 | ▶ **Surface** Grass |

TEAM STRATEGY

FRANCHISE MODE STRATEGY

Grabbing an experienced receiver through a trade or free agency will give Grossman or Orton another target. Defensively, the Bears are in good shape; look to build depth at linebacker through the draft.

KEY FRANCHISE INFORMATION

Cap Room: $15.8M
Key Rivals:
- Lions, Packers, Vikings

Philosophy:
- Offense: Run with Play Action
- Defense: 4-3, Cover 2

Highest Paid Players:
- C. Tillman
- C. Benson

Team Weapons:
- B. Urlacher – Smart Linebacker
- L. Briggs – Brick Wall Defender

Best Young Players:
- T. Harris
- G. Olsen

2007 STANDINGS

Wins	Loses	Ties	PF	PA	Home	Road	vs. AFC	vs. NFC	vs. Div
7	9	0	334	348	4-4	3-5	3-1	4-8	2-4

TEAM OVERVIEW

It's hard to believe that the Bears went to the Super Bowl only two years ago. Listed as 5th overall in 2006, the Bears' defense went to 28th in the NFL last season. Offensively, the Bears have taken big hits from losing key players, and are still having problems at the quarterback spot. They took a major hit at wideout, losing Berrian and Muhammad. The running back situation is also not looking great, with Benson never living up to his ability. He averaged 3.4 yards a carry and ran for 674 yards. The bright spots for the Bears are that they still have a decent group of players on defense, and that Hester is a threat to score at any time.

OFF-SEASON UPGRADES

TYPE	ROUND	FIRST NAME	LAST NAME	SCHOOL/TEAM	POSITION
Free Agent	N/A	Marty	Booker	Dolphins	WR
Free Agent	N/A	Brandon	Lloyd	Redskins	WR
Draft	1	Chris	Williams	Vanderbilt	T
Draft	2	Matt	Forté	Tulane	RB
Draft	3	Earl	Bennett	Vanderbilt	WR

SCOUTING REPORT

	DESCRIPTION	MAXIMIZING POTENTIAL	TIPS FOR OPPONENTS
STRENGTHS	Devin Hester is a human highlight reel. Get the ball in his hands.	Put Hester in at wideout and use him on special teams.	On special teams, kick away from him; on offense, double team him.
	Brian Urlacher is a Pro Bowl middle linebacker who's the heart of the defense.	Use him to roam the field and manually rush at times.	Give him something to do. Flood the area with routes and use motion with run.
WEAKNESSES	The Bears' passing attack is not the strongest facet of their offensive attack.	Be conservative and throw to Olsen and Clark (your tight ends) often.	Load the box and send heat until they show you they can establish the pass.
	The Bears' secondary was ranked 27th and gave up 231 yards a game.	You need to use zone blitzing to defend against the passing attack.	Use route combinations and overloading formations (spread/compressed) to expose secondary. Hit uncovered wideouts.

80	74	82
OVERALL	OFFENSE	DEFENSE

▼ ROSTER AND **PACKAGE TIPS**

KEY PLAYER SUBSTITUTIONS

Position: TE
Substitution: Greg Olsen
When: Global
Advantage: Desmond Clark is a rock-solid tight end, there is no question about that. However, Greg Olsen has more speed. With the Bears not having a top receiver lined up outside, whoever the quarterback is, he can use any help he can get.

Position: RE
Substitution: Mark Anderson
When: Global
Advantage: Mark Anderson has a higher speed rating than Alex Brown. Having that extra speed will allow him to get to the quarterback a little quicker than Brown. You can always move Brown to WDT in passing situations.

Position: 3DRB
Substitution: Matt Forte
When: Global
Advantage: With a 99 overall rating, it just makes sense to move Forte up the depth chart as the Bears' third down running back. Throw in the fact that he is the team's best pass catcher out of the backfield, and it's a move that needs to be made.

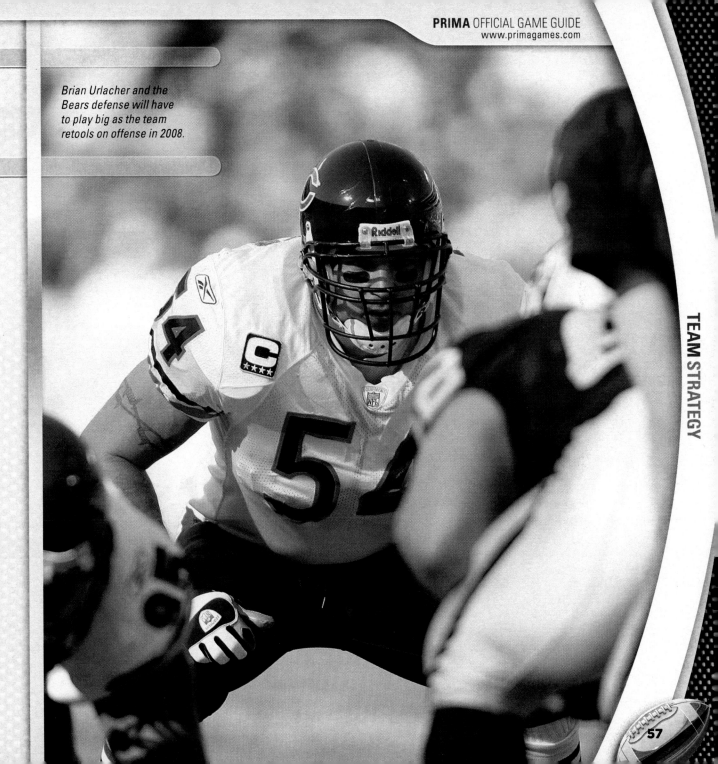

Brian Urlacher and the Bears defense will have to play big as the team retools on offense in 2008.

TEAM STRATEGY

TEAM STRATEGY

#57 Olin Kreutz *Center (C)*

▼ OFFENSIVE **STAR PLAYER**

Krutz is as solid as they come. He hasn't missed a game since 2000, and is an excellent pass protector and blocker for the run. He gives up fewer sacks than any other center in the league. Krutz has been an anchor for the Bears for over 10 years.

Run Block Strength	90
Run Block Footwork	90
Pass Block Strength	92
Pass Block Footwork	92

Player Weapon: None

#23 Devin Hester *Wide Receiver (WR)*

▼ OFFENSIVE **STAR PLAYER**

This guy is always only a snap away from being in the top 10 plays on ESPN. No one has dominated the game and brought fear to special teams like Hester has. He has speed, agility, and reads his blocks very well. When you need a big play, no one is better.

Speed	100
Catch	83
Catch Traffic	70
Route Run	80

Player Weapon: Speed

#88 Desmond Clark *Tight End (TE)*

▼ OFFENSIVE **STAR PLAYER**

Desmond Clark is a sure-handed tight end with deceptive speed. He's been a quality addition to the Bears and part of their passing attack. He will most likely platoon with Greg Olsen this season. Consider running double tight end sets so you can get both guys on the field.

Speed	79
Catch	86
Run Block	60
Pass Block	55

Player Weapon: None

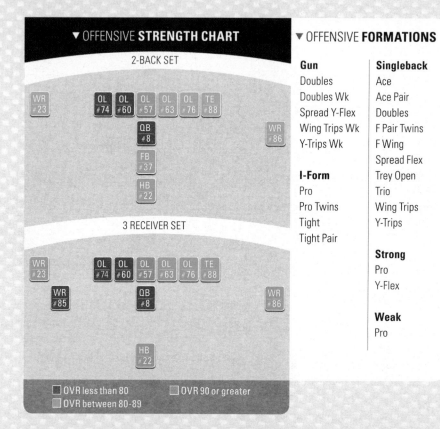

▼ OFFENSIVE **STRENGTH CHART**

2-BACK SET

WR #23 — OL #74 — OL #60 — OL #57 — OL #63 — OL #76 — TE #88 — WR #86 — QB #8 — FB #37 — HB #22

3 RECEIVER SET

WR #23 — OL #74 — OL #60 — OL #57 — OL #63 — OL #76 — TE #88 — WR #85 — QB #8 — WR #86 — HB #22

☐ OVR less than 80   ☐ OVR 90 or greater
☐ OVR between 80-89

▼ OFFENSIVE **FORMATIONS**

Gun	Singleback
Doubles	Ace
Doubles Wk	Ace Pair
Spread Y-Flex	Doubles
Wing Trips Wk	F Pair Twins
Y-Trips Wk	F Wing
	Spread Flex
I-Form	Trey Open
Pro	Trio
Pro Twins	Wing Trips
Tight	Y-Trips
Tight Pair	
	Strong
	Pro
	Y-Flex
Weak	
Pro	

▼ RECOMMENDED OFFENSIVE **AUDIBLE PACKAGES**

I-Form	Singleback	Weak	Singleback	Gun
Power O	Inside Cross	HB Gut	Short Ins N Outs	X Follow

▼ OFFENSIVE **PLAYCOUNTS**

Quick Pass:	22	Screen Pass:	15	Pitch:	10
Standard Pass:	89	Hail Mary:	1	Counter:	9
Shotgun Pass:	41	Inside Handoff:	34	Draw:	3
Play Action Pass:	63	Outside Handoff:	16		

OFFENSE **KEY OFFENSIVE PLAYS**

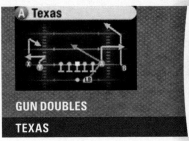

A Texas

GUN DOUBLES

TEXAS

The origin of the Texas play has its roots in the West Coast offense. The tight end and flanker will work to get the halfback open for an easy catch across the middle.

To enhance the effectiveness of this play, motion the slot receiver to the right. Hike the ball when he passes the tight end.

Adding the slot's whip route to the strong side gives the offense multiple open routes.

Get the ball to the tight end on the right for an easy gain versus man coverage.

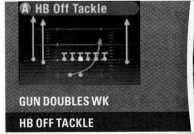

A HB Off Tackle

GUN DOUBLES WK

HB OFF TACKLE

Sitting in the Gun can leave an offense susceptible to the blitz. The HB Off Tackle is a great way to slow down an aggressive pass rush.

The run is designed to flow to the right, but versus an unsuspecting defense we have our choice.

Solid blocking up front creates a nice running lane for the half back to exploit.

The defense will have to respect the threat of giving up a 5-yard run if they overplay the pass.

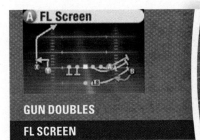

A FL Screen

GUN DOUBLES

FL SCREEN

Devin Hester's speed is an asset that must be used on offense. Use the WR Swap package to get him in position for the FL Screen.

As soon as the ball is hiked, wait a second and then hit Hester with the Screen Pass.

When the timing is right, there will be a wall of blockers at his disposal.

Now that the ball is in his hands, hit the speed burst and take advantage of his blazing speed.

TEAM STRATEGY

 **CHICAGO BEARS**

DEFENSE

TEAM STRATEGY

#54 Brian Urlacher *Linebacker (MLB)*

▼ DEFENSIVE **STAR PLAYER**

Clearly one of the best middle linebackers in the NFL, Brian Urlacher plays the run and the pass extremely well. He creates turnovers and is the backbone of the Bears' defense. This future Hall of Fame player wreaks havoc as a pass rusher and sets the tone for the Bears' defense.

Speed	88
Tackling	93
Pursuit	97
Play Recog.	95

Player Weapons: Big Hitter, Brick Wall Defender, Smart Linebacker

#55 Lance Briggs *Linebacker (ROLB)*

▼ DEFENSIVE **STAR PLAYER**

Briggs is also one of the defensive playmakers for the Bears' defense. He is as solid as they come. This OLB has made well over 100 solo tackles with 1.5 sacks in four out of his five seasons with the Bears. This is why he was given the franchise tag in 2006.

Speed	80
Tackling	92
Pursuit	94
Play Recog.	85

Player Weapons: Big Hitter, Brick Wall Defender

#91 Tommie Harris *Defensive Tackle (DT)*

▼ DEFENSIVE **STAR PLAYER**

When you want a solid defensive line, you need someone that plugs the middle and generates a pass rush. Tommie Harris is skilled at doing just that; he got 8 sacks last season and gave up nothing up the middle on the ground. He is an offensive lineman's nightmare.

Speed	77
Strength	90
Power Moves	93
Finesse Moves	93

Player Weapons: Finesse Move D-Lineman, Power Move D-Lineman

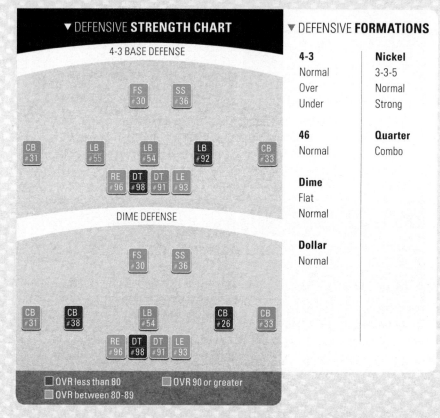

▼ DEFENSIVE **STRENGTH CHART**

4-3 BASE DEFENSE

FS #30 SS #36

CB #31 LB #55 LB #54 LB #92 CB #33

RE #96 DT #98 DT #91 LE #93

DIME DEFENSE

FS #30 SS #36

CB #31 CB #38 LB #54 CB #26 CB #33

RE #96 DT #98 DT #91 LE #93

☐ OVR less than 80   ☐ OVR 90 or greater
☐ OVR between 80-89

▼ DEFENSIVE **FORMATIONS**

4-3	Nickel
Normal	3-3-5
Over	Normal
Under	Strong
46	**Quarter**
Normal	Combo
Dime	
Flat	
Normal	
Dollar	
Normal	

▼ RECOMMENDED DEFENSIVE **AUDIBLE PACKAGES**

4-3	4-3	Nickel	Dime	Quarter
2 Man Under	Free Fire	Cover 3	Cover 2	Man Up 3 Deep

▼ DEFENSIVE **PLAYCOUNTS**

Man Coverage:	43	Cover 2 Zone:	15	Man Blitz:	57
Man Zone:	37	Cover 3 Zone:	26	Zone Blitz:	63
Combo Coverage:	8	Deep Zone:	18	Combo Blitz:	17

DEFENSE **KEY DEFENSIVE PLAYS**

Ⓐ Free Fire

4-3 NORMAL

FREE FIRE

1

2

3

The Bears have two of the best linebackers in football. The Free Fire will let the defense put Briggs and Urlacher in position to disrupt any offense.

Shift the defensive line left and have Urlacher and Briggs crowd the left A gap.

Take control of the left defensive end and manually rush him toward the right guard.

This simple blitz setup will have the opposing quarterback running for his virtual life.

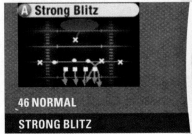

Ⓐ Strong Blitz

46 NORMAL

STRONG BLITZ

1

2

3

The Strong Blitz is a solid pass defense that gives the Bears 5 men in man coverage with the strong safety and outside linebacker blitzing.

Call press coverage and pinch the linebackers. This will help keep the QB in the pocket.

The quarterback will try to avoid Urlacher and move directly in the path of our end.

Great coverage in the secondary and a good pass rush leads to an easy sack.

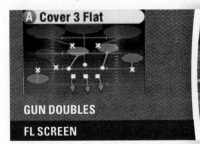

Ⓐ Cover 3 Flat

GUN DOUBLES

FL SCREEN

1

2

3

When facing a pass threat that likes to attack the sideline both vertically or with flood routes, the Nickel 3-3-5 Cover 3 Flat gets the job done.

Both the outside corner and nickel back jam their receivers to help prevent a clean release off the line.

Some teams are in love with throwing down field and will still try to fit the pass in between the coverage.

They will find that completing a pass to the sideline is a no go versus this defense.

TEAM STRATEGY

CINCINNATI BENGALS

▶ **Division** AFC North ▶ **Stadium** Paul Brown Stadium ▶ **Type** Open ▶ **Capacity** 65,535 ▶ **Surface** Grass

▼ 2007 STANDINGS

Wins	Loses	Ties	PF	PA	Home	Road	vs. AFC	vs. NFC	vs. Div
7	9	0	380	385	5-3	2-6	6-6	1-3	3-3

▼ TEAM OVERVIEW

The Bengals underachieved last season after having a strong showing in 2006. The Bengals' offense is balanced and can be a handful, thanks to gunslinger Palmer and the passing duo of T.J. and Chad Johnson that hooked up for 4131 passing yards and 26 touchdowns last season. The running game suffered a bit because of injuries to Rudi Johnson. The main problem for the Bengals is defense. The defense gave up 5580 yards last season, but the team made some moves in the draft to help address this issue. They picked up Keith Rivers (LB) in the first round, Pat Sims (DT) in the third, Corey Lynch (FS) in the fifth, and Angelo Craig (DE) in the seventh. The Bengals attempted to use the draft to fix the defense and keep the high-powered offense intact.

▼ OFF-SEASON UPGRADES

TYPE	ROUND	FIRST NAME	LAST NAME	SCHOOL/TEAM	POSITION
Free Agent	N/A	Antwan	Odem	Titans	DE
Draft	1	Keith	Rivers	USC	LB
Draft	2	Jerome	Simpson	Coastal Carolina	WR
Draft	3	Pat	Sims	Auburn	DT
Draft	3	Andre	Caldwell	Florida	WR

▼ SCOUTING REPORT

	DESCRIPTION	MAXIMIZING POTENTIAL	TIPS FOR OPPONENTS
STRENGTHS	The Bengals have one of the best passing attacks in the league, hands down.	Use your passing attack to open up the run game.	Mix your passing coverages. Blitz and double up Chad Johnson and T.J.
	Deltha O'Neal is the best defensive back they have. Use him in multiple packages.	Move him around and also use him in blitzing packages.	Be aware of where he is lining up and expose the weaker corner.
WEAKNESSES	The ground attack of the Bengals needs to improve to support the passing attack.	Use running back by committee to keep Johnson and the crew fresh.	Use more 4 man fronts that allow you to defend the pass and for run support.
	The Bengals' defense was listed 26th defending the pass and 21st against the run.	You need to blitz more to help against the run and pass.	Run a balanced attack using the run. Then attack with PA for big plays.

TEAM STRATEGY

FRANCHISE MODE STRATEGY

With the departure of Chris Henry, the Bengals need a third receiver that can vertically stretch the defense. Use the draft and free agency to shore up the Bengals' linebacking corps.

KEY FRANCHISE INFORMATION

Cap Room: $17.96M
Key Rivals:
- Browns, Ravens, Steelers

Philosophy:
- Offense: West Coast
- Defense: 4-3

Highest Paid Players:
- C. Palmer
- C. Johnson

Team Weapons:
- C. Johnson – Quick Receiver
- C. Palmer – Cannon Arm QB

Best Young Players:
- J. Joseph
- D. Peko

80	**85**	**76**
OVERALL	OFFENSE	DEFENSE

▼ ROSTER AND **PACKAGE TIPS**

KEY PLAYER SUBSTITUTIONS

Position: HB
Substitution: Kenny Watson
When: Passing Situation
Advantage: Kenny Watson is faster and has better hands than Rudi Johnson. Regardless of whether it is first, second, or third down, Watson should be packaged or subbed in.

Position: LG
Substitution: Stacy Andrews
When: Global
Advantage: There is not much of a difference between left guards Andrew Whitworth and Stacy Andrews. The reason we make this sub is because his speed rating is a few points higher. This allows us to run plays that have the left guard pulling more effectively.

Position: CB2
Substitution: Deltha O'Neal
When: Global
Advantage: We recommend moving Deltha O'Neal up to the number two cornerback position on the depth chart. O'Neal is a slightly better overall corner than Leon Hall.

Caron Palmer passed for more than 4,000 yards the last two seasons. If he can do it again in 2008, the Bengals will compete for the playoffs.

TEAM STRATEGY

TEAM STRATEGY

#85 Chad Johnson *Wide Receiver (WR)*

▼ OFFENSIVE **STAR PLAYER**

Clearly one of the best wideouts, Johnson caught 93 passes for 1,440 and scored 8 touchdowns. He has also averaged over 1,000 yards a season after his rookie season. Johnson destroys coverages with his powerful route running, speed, and hands.

Speed	96
Catch	94
Catch Traffic	90
Route Run	97

Player Weapons: Quick Receiver, Possession Receiver, Spec Catch Receiver, Hands, Speed

#84 T.J. Houshmandzadeh *Wide Receiver (WR)*

▼ OFFENSIVE **STAR PLAYER**

Guess who led the team in receptions? It wasn't number 85; it was T.J. He led the team with 112 receptions, 1143 yards, and 12 touchdowns. He had a monster season last year, and is expected to have a repeat performance this year. His speed and size make him an excellent target.

Speed	90
Catch	98
Catch Traffic	99
Route Run	95

Player Weapons: Quick Receiver, Possession Receiver, Hands

#9 Carson Palmer *Quarterback (QB)*

▼ OFFENSIVE **STAR PLAYER**

This guy is a pure passer. He has accuracy, throwing power, and outstanding touch with the deep ball. When Palmer has a solid running game, it is quite difficult to stop his passing attack. Carson has averaged 4,000 yards for the past 3 seasons. When he is healthy, Palmer is a top 5 passer.

Speed	54
Awareness	93
Throwing Power	97
Throwing Accuracy	95

Player Weapons: Smart Quarterback, Accurate Quarterback, Cannon Arm Quarterback

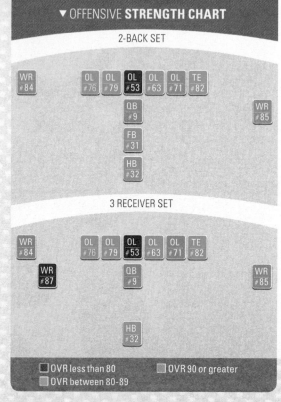

▼ OFFENSIVE **STRENGTH CHART**

2-BACK SET

WR #84 · OL #76 · OL #79 · OL #53 · OL #63 · OL #71 · TE #82 · WR #85
QB #9
FB #31
HB #32

3 RECEIVER SET

WR #84 · OL #76 · OL #79 · OL #53 · OL #63 · OL #71 · TE #82
WR #87 · QB #9 · WR #85
HB #32

☐ OVR less than 80 ☐ OVR 90 or greater
☐ OVR between 80-89

▼ OFFENSIVE **FORMATIONS**

Gun	Singleback
Bunch TE	Ace
Double Flex	Ace Pair
Doubles On	Bunch
Split Slot	Doubles
Wing Trio Wk	Flex
	Snugs
I-Form	Trey Open
Close	Y-Trips
H Slot Flex	
Pro	**Strong**
Pro Twins	H Slot
Tight Pair	Pro
	Weak
	H Slot
	Pro

▼ RECOMMENDED OFFENSIVE **AUDIBLE PACKAGES**

Singleback	Singleback	I-Form	Singleback	Gun
HB Dive	Quick Slants	Power O	Shallow Cross	Corner Strike

▼ OFFENSIVE **PLAYCOUNTS**

Quick Pass:	21	Screen Pass:	10	Counter:	12
Standard Pass:	97	Inside Handoff:	35	Draw:	12
Shotgun Pass:	41	Outside Handoff:	11	FB Run:	7
Play Action Pass:	55	Pitch:	9		

OFFENSE **KEY OFFENSIVE PLAYS**

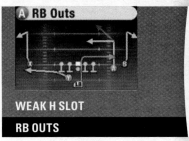

Ⓐ RB Outs

WEAK H SLOT

RB OUTS

The Bengals' offense has some of the most talented wide receivers in the NFL. The RB Outs puts 3 of those receivers on the field and showcases their skills.

When facing an aggressive defense, knowing our options at receiver provides an uncanny calm.

The primary read on this play when facing the blitz will be the route of the running back.

Anticipate the slot receiver being open as soon as the running back cuts outside. Hit him here for a big gain.

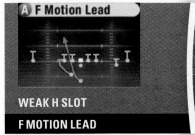

Ⓐ F Motion Lead

WEAK H SLOT

F MOTION LEAD

Every offense can benefit from a balanced attack. Use the threat of a 3 receiver set to help open running lanes for the F Motion Lead.

The auto motion by the FB gives the half back a chance to pre-read where he can take the run.

The back has a choice of taking the ball through the interior of the defense or bouncing it outside.

He bounces the run outside and takes advantage of the blocking, and picks up a gain of 6 yards on the play.

Ⓐ Strong Flood

GUN WING TRIO WK

STRONG FLOOD

The Trio Strong Flood is designed to use the flood routes to make the defense think shallow and then hit them for the bomb over the top.

Flood plays are great because they give the offense a chance to beat the defense when in man or zone.

The defense is in man, so the tight end or slot receiver will be open as they break outside.

The pass is thrown to the tight end in the flat. He tight ropes the sideline and gains a first down.

TEAM STRATEGY

TEAM STRATEGY

#98 Antwan Odom *Defensive End (LE)*

▼ DEFENSIVE STAR PLAYER

Odom had a career high in sacks last season with 8. He also logged 21 tackles and a forced fumble. The Bengals need him to improve on his production from last season. He uses his strength and leverage through stunts to pressure the quarterback from the edge.

Speed	75
Strength	78
Power Moves	83
Finesse Moves	83

Player Weapon: None

#58 Keith Rivers *Linebacker (ROLB)*

▼ DEFENSIVE STAR PLAYER

After losing Thurman Odell due to off the field problems, the Bengals needed to fill a void. In the first round, they drafted Keith Rivers, the talented MLB from USC. He moves well from sideline to sideline. He will also be relied on as a pass rusher.

Speed	88
Tackling	84
Pursuit	88
Play Recog.	66

Player Weapon: None

#24 Deltha O'Neal *Cornerback (CB)*

▼ DEFENSIVE STAR PLAYER

O'Neal is the Bengals' best corner. His speed and agility allows him to be in every play. He is also a special teams player who, when he finds a crease, can help the team get decent field position. O'Neal had only one interception last season.

Speed	84
Man Cover	82
Zone Cover	85
Press	72

Player Weapon: None

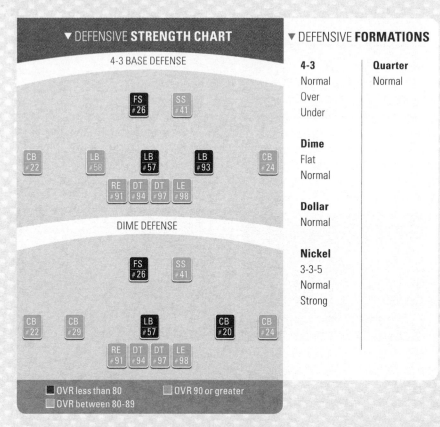

▼ DEFENSIVE STRENGTH CHART

4-3 BASE DEFENSE

FS #26 SS #41

CB #22 LB #58 LB #57 LB #93 CB #24

RE #91 DT #94 DT #97 LE #98

DIME DEFENSE

FS #26 SS #41

CB #22 CB #29 LB #57 CB #20 CB #24

RE #91 DT #94 DT #97 LE #98

- ■ OVR less than 80
- ■ OVR between 80-89
- □ OVR 90 or greater

▼ DEFENSIVE FORMATIONS

4-3	Quarter
Normal	Normal
Over	
Under	

Dime
Flat
Normal

Dollar
Normal

Nickel
3-3-5
Normal
Strong

▼ RECOMMENDED DEFENSIVE AUDIBLE PACKAGES

4-3	4-3	Nickel	Dime	Quarter
2 Man Under	Free Fire	Cover 2	Cover 1 Press	3 Deep Man

▼ DEFENSIVE PLAYCOUNTS

Man Coverage:	45	Cover 2 Zone:	14	Man Blitz:	53
Man Zone:	35	Cover 3 Zone:	26	Zone Blitz:	63
Combo Coverage:	6	Deep Zone:	18	Combo Blitz:	12

DEFENSE **KEY DEFENSIVE PLAYS**

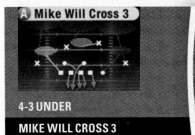

4-3 UNDER

MIKE WILL CROSS 3

Stopping the pass can be a task in and of itself, but a strong defensive play will prevent the pass as well as the run.

Shift the defensive line right to help enhance the line stunt versus 2 back running formations.

This one adjustment will put the defense in great position to make a play on outside runs.

The defense swarms the ball carrier and sets the tone early that every yard will be tough.

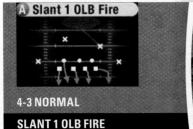

4-3 NORMAL

SLANT 1 OLB FIRE

Paying attention to positioning on the field can help strengthen a defense. Look to use this play with the man coverage linebacker closer to the sideline.

When an offense tries to use combo routes to create openings, this man defense proves that it will remain solid.

By having the man coverage linebacker toward the sideline, he can easily defend a more athletic receiver.

Coaching is about putting players in the best position for success. The linebacker has prevented the pass completetion.

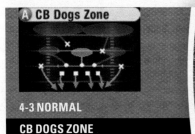

4-3 NORMAL

CB DOGS ZONE

All blitzes are meant to pressure the quarterback, but some are less likely to reach him. Use this blitz to show pressure but benefit from the zone behind it.

As soon as the play starts, both outside cornerbacks will explode inside to get the quarterback.

The quarterback will have to make a good read and throw without leaving the pocket.

Quarterbacks are taught to throw to the vacated area, and when he does that, he finds out that the defense was prepared.

BUFFALO BILLS

▶ **Division** AFC East ▶ **Stadium** Ralph Wilson Stadium ▶ **Type** Open ▶ **Capacity** 73,967 ▶ **Surface** Field Turf

▼ 2007 STANDINGS

Wins	Loses	Ties	PF	PA	Home	Road	vs. AFC	vs. NFC	vs. Div
7	9	0	252	354	4-4	3-5	6-6	1-3	4-2

▼ TEAM OVERVIEW

The Bills are rebuilding. They have an excellent back in Lynch and a wideout in Evans that can stretch the field. Losman is beginning to settle in at QB. The problem is that the Bills gave up 22.1 points a game. Additionally, they were ranked 31st in the league on yards given up per game. They gave up 285 yards in the air and 124 yards on the ground. They were listed 30th in passing yards per game with 164 yards, and 15th in rushing yards with 112 yards per game. The numbers from last year are not great, but the Bills play hard. Five of the games were lost by 6 points or less.

▼ OFF-SEASON UPGRADES

TYPE	ROUND	FIRST NAME	LAST NAME	SCHOOL/TEAM	POSITION
Trade	N/A	Marcus	Stroud	Jaguars	DT
Free Agent	N/A	Kawika	Mitchell	Giants	LB
Free Agent	N/A	Spencer	Johnson	Vikings	DT
Draft	1	Leodis	McKelvin	Troy	CB
Draft	2	James	Hardy	Indiana	WR

▼ SCOUTING REPORT

	DESCRIPTION	MAXIMIZING POTENTIAL	TIPS FOR OPPONENTS
STRENGTHS	Marshawn Lynch is an up and coming running back. Feed him to establish the pass.	He's well balanced for rushing/receiving. Use him to set up Evans.	Double Evans and load the box to defend against the rushing attack of Marshawn Lynch.
	Stroud and Shobel will make some noise this season. They will establish your line.	Get pressure from the opposite side to improve the pass rush.	Run on the other side of Stroud/Shobel. Then have proper protection on their side.
WEAKNESSES	Losman struggled last season. The Bills passing attack was 30th in the NFL.	Use a West Coast passing attack with short passes.	Double Evans, load the box, and send heat. Make them show you they can pass.
	The Buffalo Bills' secondary can be exposed. They gave up 285 yards per game in 2007.	Double playmakers, mix coverages, and use zone blitzing to keep them off-balance.	Air them out and then use the run, screens, and play action when they adjust.

TEAM STRATEGY

FRANCHISE MODE STRATEGY

The Bills still don't have a QB that you can bet the franchise on. Make this and more receivers the focus of your offseason moves. The Bills' defense is pretty solid, so spend your time and effort improving the offense.

KEY FRANCHISE INFORMATION

Cap Room: $27.34M

Key Rivals:
• Dolphins, Jets, Patriots

Philosophy:
• Offense: Quick Passing
• Defense: 4-3

Highest Paid Players:
• A. Schobel
• D. Dockery

Team Weapons:
• J. Peters – Pass Blocker
• M. Stroud – Power Move D-Lineman

Best Young Players:
• D. Whitner
• M. Lynch

82 OVERALL | 78 OFFENSE | 85 DEFENSE

Marshawn Lynch leads a gritty Bills team that should remain competitive in 2008—if they can shore-up their defense.

▼ ROSTER AND **PACKAGE TIPS**

KEY PLAYER SUBSTITUTIONS

Position: QB

Substitution: J.P. Losman

When: Global

Advantage: This substitution really depends on your style of play. Trent Edwards is a better passer than J.P. Losman. However, Edwards lacks the mobility to avoid the pass rush, making Losman more of a threat to take off and run if nothing down the field opens up.

Position: Slot

Substitution: Robert Royal

When: Running situations

Advantage: This move is not one you will want to make all the time, but if you plan on running the ball inside, consider pack-aging Royal into the slot. Before the ball is snapped, motion him inside and snap the ball when he gets in the gap where the run is designed to go.

Position: DT2

Substitution: John McCargo

When: Global

Advantage: John McCargo is a better pass rusher than Kyle Williams. If you don't want to make him the permanent starter at the weak defensive tackle posi-tion, at least sub him in during obvious passing situations.

TEAM STRATEGY

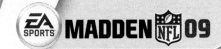 
TEAM STRATEGY

#71 Jason Peters *Tackle (LT)*

▼ OFFENSIVE **STAR PLAYER**

One of last season's problems with the Bills was pass protection. Peters is one of the better pass protectors and run blockers on the line. In order to improve their pass percentage, the Bills need Peters and the line to step it up.

Run Block Strength	92
Run Block Footwork	89
Pass Block Strength	97
Pass Block Footwork	96

Player Weapon: Pass Blocker

#83 Lee Evans *Wide Receiver (WR)*

▼ OFFENSIVE **STAR PLAYER**

Lee Evans has outstanding speed and is the go-to wideout on this squad. He has averaged over 800 yards and 6 touchdowns a season. In order to make a statement, the Bills need Evans to reproduce his 2006 numbers of 1,292 yards and 8 touchdowns; this will open up the running game.

Speed	98
Catch	88
Catch Traffic	85
Route Run	88

Player Weapon: Speed

#23 Marshawn Lynch *Halfback (HB)*

▼ OFFENSIVE **STAR PLAYER**

While everyone was looking at LT and Peterson, Marshawn Lynch had a fine season last year for the Bills. Lynch put up 1,115 yards, 7 touchdowns, and 280 carries. He also had a rushing average of 4 yards a carry. Lynch has excellent hands and is a solid pass protector.

Speed	93
Agility	93
Trucking	95
Elusiveness	86

Player Weapon: Power Back

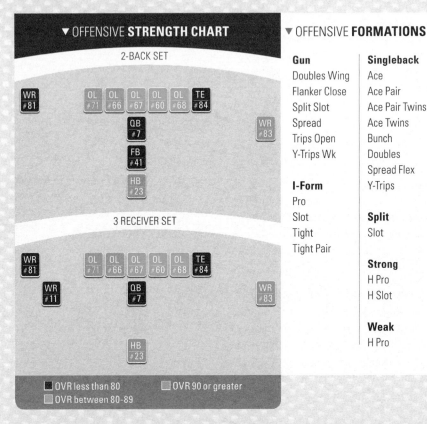

▼ OFFENSIVE **STRENGTH CHART**

2-BACK SET

3 RECEIVER SET

- ■ OVR less than 80
- □ OVR between 80-89
- □ OVR 90 or greater

▼ OFFENSIVE **FORMATIONS**

Gun	Singleback
Doubles Wing	Ace
Flanker Close	Ace Pair
Split Slot	Ace Pair Twins
Spread	Ace Twins
Trips Open	Bunch
Y-Trips Wk	Doubles
	Spread Flex
I-Form	Y-Trips
Pro	
Slot	**Split**
Tight	Slot
Tight Pair	
	Strong
	H Pro
	H Slot
	Weak
	H Pro

▼ RECOMMENDED OFFENSIVE **AUDIBLE PACKAGES**

Singleback	Singleback	Weak	Singleback	Gun
HB Dive	Cross In	HB Gut	Slot Pivot	Corner Strike

▼ OFFENSIVE **PLAYCOUNTS**

Quick Pass:	22	Screen Pass:	12	Pitch:	9
Standard Pass:	87	Hail Mary:	2	Counter:	11
Shotgun Pass:	48	Inside Handoff:	30	Draw:	12
Play Action Pass:	56	Outside Handoff:	14		

OFFENSE **KEY OFFENSIVE PLAYS**

TEAM STRATEGY

A HB Power O

SINGLEBACK ACE PAIR TWINS
HB POWER O

In recent years, the Buffalo Bills have had the luxury of highly-skilled running backs. Marshawn Lynch is a back that can take this power run and churn out some good yards.

An added advantage to this play is the auto motion. It adds extra run blocking for Lynch.

With the ball in his hands and that extra blocker, the field looks like there is plenty of daylight.

Lynch sees what he wants and hits the hole for a 6-yard gain on the play.

A PA Boot Lt

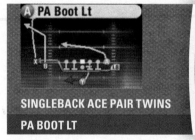

SINGLEBACK ACE PAIR TWINS
PA BOOT LT

Play action always works well when the offense has established the run. Use the PA Boot Lt to beat a run-suspecting defense.

Because of the success in the run game, Losman benefits from the run fake to Lynch.

While rolling out on the bootleg, Losman spots the wide open tight end running a crossing route.

The pass to the tight end results in an easy catch and gain of 15 yards on the play.

A Slot Wheel

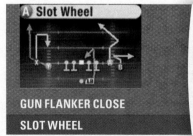

GUN FLANKER CLOSE
SLOT WHEEL

There are many ways to help get certain pass routes open. The Slot Wheel uses a combo route to free up the sideline for the slot receiver.

As the split end starts up the field on his route, he is pulling the defender with him.

As soon as he breaks inside, the quarterback has great spacing to fit the pass in on the sideline.

The ball is thrown perfectly to the slot receiver on the wheel route for a first down.

TEAM STRATEGY

#99 Marcus Stroud *Defensive Tackle (DT)*

▼ DEFENSIVE **STAR PLAYER**

The Bills needed help up front, and got it with Stroud. This Pro Bowler plugs the middle and generates a good rush in the middle. There aren't many tackles that pass rush and play the run well. Stroud is one of the few that will improve the Bills' line.

Speed	61
Strength	95
Power Moves	97
Finesse Moves	80

Player Weapon: Power Move D-Lineman

#94 Aaron Schoebel *Defensive End (RE)*

▼ DEFENSIVE **STAR PLAYER**

There are players that are strictly business, and deliver day in and day out. This is the kind of player that Schoebel is. He is a pass rusher that stuffs the run and generates pressure, and hasn't even missed a game.

Speed	74
Strength	82
Power Moves	92
Finesse Moves	80

Player Weapon: Power Move D-Lineman

#55 Angelo Crowell *Linebacker (LOLB)*

▼ DEFENSIVE **STAR PLAYER**

Crowell is a solid player, logging 126 tackles last season with 2 sacks and an interception. Crowell is a balanced player that can bring pressure and cover. He had a great season last year and needs to build on that this season to help improve the Bills' defense.

Speed	82
Tackling	92
Pursuit	92
Play Recog.	85

Player Weapon: Brick Wall Defender

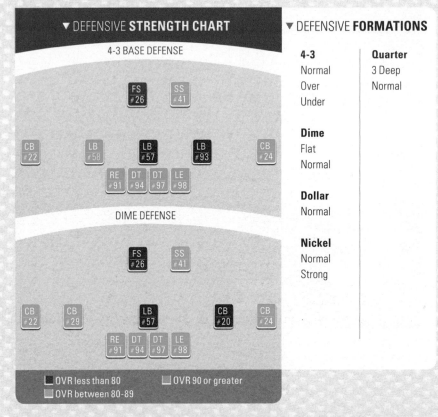

▼ DEFENSIVE **STRENGTH CHART**

4-3 BASE DEFENSE

FS #26   SS #41

CB #22   LB #58   LB #57   LB #93   CB #24

RE #91   DT #94   DT #97   LE #98

DIME DEFENSE

FS #26   SS #41

CB #22   CB #29   LB #57   CB #20   CB #24

RE #91   DT #94   DT #97   LE #98

■ OVR less than 80   ☐ OVR 90 or greater
☐ OVR between 80–89

▼ DEFENSIVE **FORMATIONS**

4-3	Quarter
Normal	3 Deep
Over	Normal
Under	
Dime	
Flat	
Normal	
Dollar	
Normal	
Nickel	
Normal	
Strong	

▼ RECOMMENDED DEFENSIVE **AUDIBLE PACKAGES**

4-3	4-3	Nickel	Dime	Quarter
2 Man Under	OLB Fire Man	Cover 3	Cover 2	Man Up 3 Deep

▼ DEFENSIVE **PLAYCOUNTS**

Man Coverage:	43	Cover 2 Zone:	13	Man Blitz:	54
Man Zone:	39	Cover 3 Zone:	26	Zone Blitz:	61
Combo Coverage:	8	Deep Zone:	21	Combo Blitz:	15

DEFENSE **KEY DEFENSIVE PLAYS**

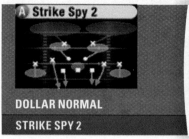

DOLLAR NORMAL

STRIKE SPY 2

Zone blitzing has always been problematic for offenses. The Strike Spy 2 is a Cover 2 Zone blitz that brings good pressure but doesn't sacrifice much in coverage.

The quarterback surveys the field and sees the outside pressure and our d-tackle taking away the shallow route.

The flat looks open because the corner is pressing the vertical receiver. Will the quarterback test us?

The quarterback throws to the flat. The corner releases the vertical receiver and intercepts the pass for a touchdown.

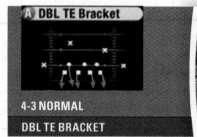

4-3 NORMAL

DBL TE BRACKET

Teams that can't defend the run are tortured on the field. The DBL TE Bracket puts players in position to stuff the run.

The Bills get a great push up front from their d-tackles. No inside run is safe for opposing teams.

When the back takes the hand-off, he is already contained by the pursuit of the defense.

The defensive tackle sheds the block of the guard and stops the back from gaining a yard on the play.

NICKEL STRONG

NB BLITZ

The Nickel Strong is a formation that puts the nickelback up on the line of scrimmage. To take advantage of this alignment, we send the nickel back on a blitz.

At the snap, the nickelback will charge around the edge and into the backfield.

The quarterback has no option to roll out, as both the nickelback and d-end are closing in.

He is taken down for a sack and the defense celebrates a loss of 6 yards on the play.

TEAM STRATEGY

DENVER BRONCOS

> **Division** AFC West | > **Stadium** Invesco Field at Mile High | > **Type** Open | > **Capacity** 76,125 | > **Surface** Grass

2007 STANDINGS

Wins	Loses	Ties	PF	PA	Home	Road	vs. AFC	vs. NFC	vs. Div
7	9	0	320	409	5-3	2-6	6-6	1-3	3-3

TEAM OVERVIEW

The Broncos are going through a transition period of rebuilding. They were once a threat to make it to the Super Bowl every season. Now they have to fight to win every game. Defensively, the Broncos gave up a total of 5,376 yards. They were ranked 9th, only giving up 193 yards a game. The weak spot was the run defense, which landed them 30th in the league. On the other side of the ball, Cutler got Denver ranked 13th overall and the pound game was ranked 9th in the league. In order for Denver to be a contender, they need to be able to stop the run and build on their offense this season.

OFF-SEASON UPGRADES

TYPE	ROUND	FIRST NAME	LAST NAME	SCHOOL/TEAM	POSITION
Free Agent	N/A	Boss	Bailey	Lions	LB
Free Agent	N/A	Darrell	Jackson	49ers	WR
Trade	N/A	Dewayne	Robertson	Jets	DT
Draft	1	Ryan	Clady	Boise State	T
Draft	1	Eddie	Royal	Virginia Tech	WR

SCOUTING REPORT

	DESCRIPTION	MAXIMIZING POTENTIAL	TIPS FOR OPPONENTS
STRENGTHS	Brandon Marshall is your best receiving option on the team. Feed him the ball.	Move him around via packages and get the ball to him.	Double him and keep an eye on him. Make them use someone else.
STRENGTHS	Champ Bailey is still one of the best corners in the game.	Shift coverage to the other side and let Champ lock down the assignment.	Why throw to his side? Work the other areas unless Champ blows coverage.
WEAKNESSES	The Broncos' running back corps is weak this season, since Henry has been released.	Try to get a passing game going to help out the run.	Play passes until they prove they can run.
WEAKNESSES	The Broncos got killed last year against the run, and were ranked 30th in the league.	Drop more men in the box and force them to pass.	Pound their lights out until they stop the run, and then use play action.

FRANCHISE MODE STRATEGY

Travis Henry is gone, which leaves the Broncos a bit thin at running back. If Selvin Young follows the standard set by previous Bronco backs, you should be okay here. More offensive linemen should be your priority.

KEY FRANCHISE INFORMATION

Cap Room: $34.29M
Key Rivals:
- Chargers, Chiefs, Raiders

Philosophy:
- Offense: West Coast
- Defense: 4-3

Highest Paid Players:
- C. Bailey
- D. Bly

Team Weapons:
- C. Bailey – Speed
- D.J. Williams – Brick Wall Defender

Best Young Players:
- S. Young
- E. Dumervil

TEAM STRATEGY

74

Many feel this will be a breakout year for Jay Cutler. If Coach Mike Shanahan's plug-and-play running game works, it just might be.

TEAM STRATEGY

▼ ROSTER AND **PACKAGE TIPS**

KEY PLAYER SUBSTITUTIONS

Position: TE
Substitution: Tony Scheffler
When: Global
Advantage: If you plan on throwing the ball more than running it with the Broncos, appointing Tony Scheffler as team's starting tight end is the right move to make. He is much faster than Daniel Graham. This allows him to stretch the deep middle of the field.

Position: RG
Substitution: Casey Wiegmann
When: Global
Advantage: There is no reason to have Casey Wiegmann sitting on the bench when he can move to right guard and upgrade the position. Montrae Holland's overall rating is 79, whereas Wiegmann's is 84. We think you will agree that this a good move.

Position: LE
Substitution: Jarvis Moss
When: Global
Advantage: This is a move that has to be made if you plan on getting any type of pass rush from the Broncos' defensive line. Moss's speed rating is several points higher than default starter John Engelberger's.

84	86	80
OVERALL	OFFENSE	DEFENSE

TEAM STRATEGY

#66 Tom Nalen *Center (C)*

▼ OFFENSIVE **STAR PLAYER**

Tom Nalen is one of the best centers in the game. He has led plenty of backs to success with his run-blocking skills. Nalen is also one of the main reasons that zone blocking protected Bronco quarterbacks over the years. He will be going to Canton, Ohio.

Run Block Strength	83
Run Block Footwork	88
Pass Block Strength	82
Pass Block Footwork	90

Player Weapon: None

#15 Brandon Marshall *Wide Receiver (WR)*

▼ OFFENSIVE **STAR PLAYER**

Now that Walker is gone, there is no doubt that Marshall will be the go-to guy this season. Marshall had an outstanding season with 1,325 yards, 7 touchdowns, and 102 receptions. His 6'4", 230 pound frame allows him to turn any catch into a big play.

Speed	92
Catch	89
Catch Traffic	90
Route Run	88

Player Weapons: Spec Catch Receiver, Possession Receiver

#6 Jay Cutler *Quarterback (QB)*

▼ OFFENSIVE **STAR PLAYER**

2007 was Cutler's first full season as the starting quarterback for the Denver Broncos. He put in a quality performance by passing for 3,497 yards and 20 TDs. He has good mobility and an absolute cannon for an arm. Use him with play action boot-legs to get out of the pocket.

Speed	74
Awareness	70
Throwing Power	95
Throwing Accuracy	86

Player Weapon: None

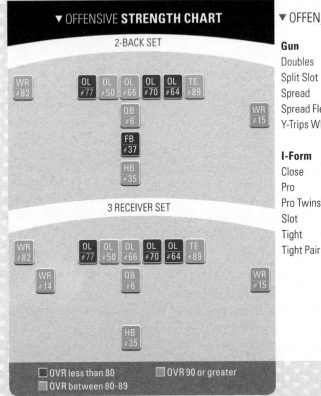

▼ OFFENSIVE **STRENGTH CHART**

2-BACK SET

WR #82 — OL #77 — OL #50 — OL #66 — OL #70 — OL #64 — TE #89 — WR #15
QB #6
FB #37
HB #35

3 RECEIVER SET

WR #82 — OL #77 — OL #50 — OL #66 — OL #70 — OL #64 — TE #89 — WR #15
WR #14 — QB #6
HB #35

☐ OVR less than 80 ☐ OVR 90 or greater
☐ OVR between 80-89

▼ OFFENSIVE **FORMATIONS**

Gun	Singleback
Doubles	Ace
Split Slot	Ace Pair Twins
Spread	Ace Twins
Spread Flex Wk	Base Flex
Y-Trips Wk	Doubles
	Empty Trey
I-Form	Y-Trips
Close	
Pro	**Strong**
Pro Twins	Pro Twins
Slot	
Tight	**Weak**
Tight Pair	Pro
	Pro Twins
	Tight Pair

▼ RECOMMENDED OFFENSIVE **AUDIBLE PACKAGES**

Singleback	Singleback	I-Form	Gun	Gun
Strong Stretch	Slants	Inside Zone	46 Z Cross	Dig Switch

▼ OFFENSIVE **PLAYCOUNTS**

Quick Pass:	19	Screen Pass:	13	Pitch:	9
Standard Pass:	90	Hail Mary:		Counter:	7
Shotgun Pass:	46	Inside Handoff:	32	Draw:	11
Play Action Pass:	65	Outside Handoff:	21	FB Run:	8

OFFENSE **KEY OFFENSIVE PLAYS**

Slants

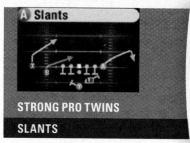

STRONG PRO TWINS

SLANTS

Slants have always been one of the most used and most effective routes in football. Use the Twin Slants as a quick striking play against the defense.

Success using this play will be based on the defender closest to the inside receiver.

The defender drops back to protect the deeper slant, leaving the shallow slant as a perfect option.

Cutler wastes no time and fires the pass to the receiver for an easy 10-yard gain.

FB Dive

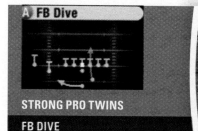

STRONG PRO TWINS

FB DIVE

Smash mouth football requires no elaborate explanation—just line up and run somebody over. The Denver Broncos have the horses to fit this scheme.

To have success running the FB Dive, it requires more of a pre-snap read than most running plays.

See the hole and waste no time getting in and out of it.

A good pre-snap read and a little manual control will keep this play yielding 5 to 6 yards a carry.

Curl Flat

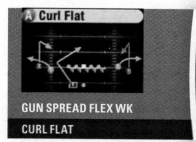

GUN SPREAD FLEX WK

CURL FLAT

One of the most unique plays in the Broncos' playbook is the Spread Flex WK Curl Flat. This play has built in slide protection and creates a nice advantage.

At the start of the play, the O-line runs back and to the right, creating space for the HB angle route.

The reads are simple and quick to make. The cornerback is playing off, so Cutler throws to the hook route.

Marshall makes the catch inside of the cornerback and turns up the field to gain more yards.

 DENVER BRONCOS DEFENSE

TEAM STRATEGY

#47 John Lynch *Safety (SS)*

▼ DEFENSIVE **STAR PLAYER**

When you think of hard-hitting safeties, John Lynch comes to mind. Even though he's losing a step, he still has big play ability. Lynch is a punishing run-stopper that can prevent big plays, in addition to being a great pass rusher.

Speed	85
Man Cover	50
Zone Cover	65
Hit Power	94

Player Weapon: Big Hitter

#24 Champ Bailey *Cornerback (CB)*

▼ DEFENSIVE **STAR PLAYER**

Champ Bailey is one of the top 3 corners in the game due to his speed, size, and great instincts. Bailey plays against some of the best wideouts in the game, and can shut down a side by himself. To this day, opponents fear throwing to his side of the field.

Speed	97
Man Cover	95
Zone Cover	95
Press	93

Player Weapons: Smart Corner, Shutdown Corner, Press Coverage Corner, Speed

#55 D.J. Williams *Linebacker (ROLB)*

▼ DEFENSIVE **STAR PLAYER**

Williams led the Broncos in tackles, logging 141 last season (with one sack). His speed and agility allows him to play from sideline to sideline. He controls the middle and plays the pass/run extremely well.

Speed	86
Tackling	92
Pursuit	90
Play Recog.	82

Player Weapon: Big Hitter

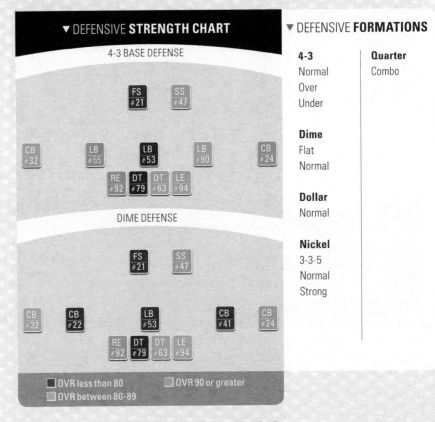

▼ DEFENSIVE **STRENGTH CHART**

4-3 BASE DEFENSE

DIME DEFENSE

■ OVR less than 80   □ OVR 90 or greater
□ OVR between 80-89

▼ DEFENSIVE **FORMATIONS**

4-3	Quarter
Normal	Combo
Over	
Under	

Dime
Flat
Normal

Dollar
Normal

Nickel
3-3-5
Normal
Strong

▼ RECOMMENDED DEFENSIVE **AUDIBLE PACKAGES**

4-3	4-3	Nickel	Dime	Quarter
2 Man Press	Fire Man	Cover 3	Cover 2	Man Up 3 Deep

▼ DEFENSIVE **PLAYCOUNTS**

Man Coverage:	45	Cover 2 Zone:	14	Man Blitz:	55
Man Zone:	34	Cover 3 Zone:	26	Zone Blitz:	64
Combo Coverage:	7	Deep Zone:	18	Combo Blitz:	13

DEFENSE **KEY DEFENSIVE PLAYS**

Ⓐ Cover 3 Press

4-3 OVER

COVER 3 PRESS

When a defense has players in the secondary like John Lynch and Champ Bailey, no matter what play is called, success is expected.

This defense is a 3 deep shell with the linebackers dropping into short curl zones.

The quarterback can't go to the short route, so he looks for the one-on-one match-up outside.

That proves to be a poor choice by the quarterback, as Bailey almost intercepts the pass.

Ⓐ Strong Man

NICKEL STRONG

STRONG MAN

There are some opponents that will play just like the team they use, always going deep. The Strong Man has a way of slowing this vertical attack.

The play is designed just like the NB blitz. At the snap, the cornerback will charge inside to pressure the quarterback.

The blitz doesn't get there but it makes the quarterback speed his reads up.

For some reason, the quarterback keeps throwing at Bailey, and again, he almost gets an interception.

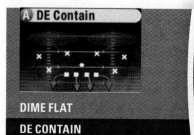

Ⓐ DE Contain

DIME FLAT

DE CONTAIN

When facing Snug formations, the Dime Flat DE Contain is a great defense to use. The corners play very aggressively, even though they are lined up further back.

This defense protects against the quick routes on the seam that most teams use when running the Snug.

Since the offense can't attack the interior, they try to hit the flats for a quick gain.

The cornerbacks play very aggressively, and the corner breaks on the ball and forces the receiver out of bounds.

TEAM STRATEGY

CLEVELAND BROWNS

▶ **Division** AFC North	▶ **Stadium** Cleveland Browns Stadium	▶ **Type** Open	▶ **Capacity** 73,200	▶ **Surface** Grass

▼ 2007 STANDINGS

Wins	Loses	Ties	PF	PA	Home	Road	vs. AFC	vs. NFC	vs. Div
10	6	0	402	382	7-1	3-5	7-5	3-1	3-3

▼ TEAM OVERVIEW

The Browns recently had an outstanding season in which they made a serious run for the playoffs. They have an excellent, well-balanced offense, but their defense is considerably weaker. The defense gave up 359 yards a game (30th). They gave up 230 in the air (24th) and 129 on the ground (27th). However, offensively, they racked up 232 in the air (12th) and 118 on the ground (8th). They can also score via special teams. In order for the Browns to repeat and expand on their success, they need to improve on the defensive side of the ball. Once they are able to achieve consistency on defense, their strong offense can really make an impact. Cleveland is the team to watch this season.

▼ OFF-SEASON UPGRADES

TYPE	ROUND	FIRST NAME	LAST NAME	SCHOOL/TEAM	POSITION
Free Agent	N/A	Rex	Hadnot	Dolphins	G
Trade	N/A	Shaun	Rogers	Lions	DT
Free Agent	N/A	Donté	Stallworth	Patriots	WR
Trade	N/A	Corey	Williams	Packers	DT
Draft	4	Beau	Bell	UNLV	LB

▼ SCOUTING REPORT

	DESCRIPTION	MAXIMIZING POTENTIAL	TIPS FOR OPPONENTS
STRENGTHS	Edwards and Winslow are becoming one of the best receiving combos in the league.	Use packages to move them around. It is hard to double team both receivers.	Double team them and shift coverage to the other side to give them different looks.
	Kamerion Wimbley is a sacking machine. Let him set the tone for the defense.	Use him in multiple blitz packages to help your secondary.	Set your pass protection accordingly and also use slide protection to his side.
WEAKNESSES	The only weakness for the Browns on the offensive side is the offensive line.	Use quick passing with a running game to help the line.	Apply pressure and run overloads to force a mismatch on the offensive line.
	The Browns' defense was listed 30th in the NFL, with 359 yards allowed per game.	Use zone blitzing schemes to help against the run/pass.	Use a balanced attack of run and pass to keep them unsure.

TEAM STRATEGY

FRANCHISE MODE STRATEGY

A shifty change of pace back would be a nice addition to the offensive attack. Defensively, look for another defensive tackle to provide depth behind Shaun Rogers. A speedy rushing end would be another good pick-up.

KEY FRANCHISE INFORMATION

Cap Room: $15.53M
Key Rivals:
- Bengals, Ravens, Steelers

Philosophy:
- Offense: Vertical Passing
- Defense: 3-4

Highest Paid Players:
- E. Steinbach
- S. Rohers

Team Weapons:
- K. Winslow – Possession Receiver
- J. Thomas – Pass Blocker

Best Young Players:
- J. Thomas
- K. Wimbley

88	**89**	**84**
OVERALL	OFFENSE	DEFENSE

▼ ROSTER AND **PACKAGE TIPS**

KEY PLAYER SUBSTITUTIONS

Position: QB
Substitution: Brady Quinn
When: Global
Advantage: This substitution is going to raise some eyebrows, but hear us out. Derek Anderson had a very good season last year, but Brady Quinn has the ability to be a franchise QB. If you play in a league, trade Anderson for a good cornerback.

Position: Slot
Substitution: Kellen Winslow
When: 4 and 5 receiver formations
Advantage: Kellen Winslow is one of the premier tight ends in the game. Moving him out in the slot in four and five wide formations ensures that he is always on the field. He is too effective as a pass receiver to be sitting on the bench at any time.

Position: CB
Substitution: A.J. Davis
When: Global
Advantage: A free safety is penciled in as the number 3 cornerback on the Browns' depth chart. While his overall rating might be better than any of the cornerbacks below him, he just isn't fast enough to keep up with most slot receivers in the game.

After blossoming in 2007 with 1,289 receiving yards and 16 TDs, Braylon Edwards and the Browns will remain a rising force in 2008.

TEAM STRATEGY

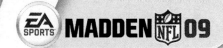

CLEVELAND BROWNS

TEAM STRATEGY

#17 Braylon Edwards *Wide Receiver (WR)*

▼ OFFENSIVE **STAR PLAYER**

He had his best season last year when he pulled down 80 receptions, 1,289 yards, and 16 touchdowns. He is showing why he was drafted in the first round by the Browns a few years ago. Edwards is indeed a top 10 wideout.

Speed	93
Catch	89
Catch Traffic	88
Route Run	93

Player Weapons: Quick Receiver, Spec Catch Receiver

#80 Kellen Winslow *Tight End (TE)*

▼ OFFENSIVE **STAR PLAYER**

Winslow was finally able to play a full season. When he did, he went off for 1,106 yards, pulled down 82 receptions, and scored 5 times. He is extremely hard to defend and is primed to have another great season if he stays healthy, with the addition of Stallworth.

Speed	85
Catch	87
Run Block	58
Pass Block	53

Player Weapons: Quick Receiver, Possession Receiver, Spec Catch Receiver

#31 Jamal Lewis *Halfback (HB)*

▼ OFFENSIVE **STAR PLAYER**

Many felt that Jamal Lewis was done. He proved everyone wrong with a great season. Lewis rushed for 1,304 yards with 298 carries and 9 touchdowns. He ran for 216 against the Bengals and scored 4 touchdowns against the Seahawks. He also averaged 4.4 yards a carry. Expect no less this season.

Speed	92
Agility	86
Trucking	97
Elusiveness	70

Player Weapons: Power Back, Stiff Arm Ball Carrier

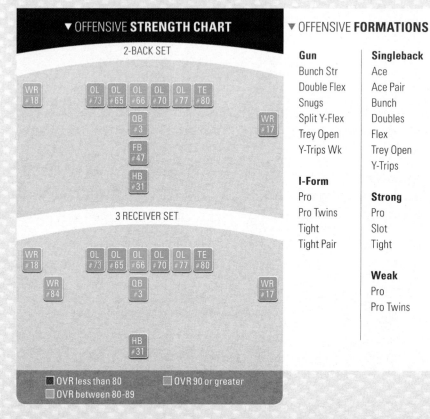

▼ OFFENSIVE **STRENGTH CHART**

2-BACK SET

WR #18 | OL #73 | OL #65 | OL #66 | OL #70 | OL #77 | TE #80 | WR #17
QB #3
FB #47
HB #31

3 RECEIVER SET

WR #18 | OL #73 | OL #65 | OL #66 | OL #70 | OL #77 | TE #80
WR #84 | QB #3 | WR #17
HB #31

☐ OVR less than 80   ☐ OVR 90 or greater
☐ OVR between 80-89

▼ OFFENSIVE **FORMATIONS**

Gun	Singleback
Bunch Str	Ace
Double Flex	Ace Pair
Snugs	Bunch
Split Y-Flex	Doubles
Trey Open	Flex
Y-Trips Wk	Trey Open
	Y-Trips

I-Form	
Pro	**Strong**
Pro Twins	Pro
Tight	Slot
Tight Pair	Tight

	Weak
	Pro
	Pro Twins

▼ RECOMMENDED OFFENSIVE **AUDIBLE PACKAGES**

Singleback	I-Form	Weak	Singleback	Gun
HB Sprint	Power O	Skinny Post	TE Post	Deep Curl

▼ OFFENSIVE **PLAYCOUNTS**

Quick Pass:	23	Screen Pass:	13	Pitch:	7
Standard Pass:	89	Hail Mary:		Counter:	10
Shotgun Pass:	51	Inside Handoff:	33	Draw:	12
Play Action Pass:	60	Outside Handoff:	12	FB Run:	8

OFFENSE **KEY OFFENSIVE PLAYS**

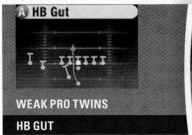

A HB Gut

WEAK PRO TWINS

HB GUT

Jamal Lewis keeps the tradition of what a Browns' back is. Use him to punish the defense and continuously bowl over oncoming defenders.

As the quarterback turns to give Lewis the ball, the defense seems to be in good position.

The fullback handles the linebacker that was sitting in the hole, and Lewis is now rumbling through.

Lewis is the type of back that punishes a defense on every run. Even in a crowd, he falls forward.

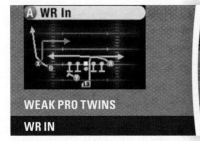

A WR In

WEAK PRO TWINS

WR IN

Because Jamal Lewis demands the attention of a defense, the pass routes of the WR In will be able to get open quite easily.

Not only does the defense have to deal with Lewis in the run game, but also in the passing game.

Every route seems to be open: Lewis in the flat, Winslow on the crossing, and Stallworth down the field.

The defense doesn't pay enough attention to Edwards, and pays for it with an elevated catch for a first down.

A Corner Strike

GUN BUNCH STRONG

CORNER STRIKE

This is a must-have play when running the Browns' offense. This play has a corner route and inside release corner, as well as a 2 level crossing route.

When facing man coverage, the tight receiver route will be open immediately after the ball is snapped.

If the defense doesn't present a good pass rush, look for the back running the out route to the left.

The back makes the catch in the flat and turns up field to pick up the first down on the play.

TEAM STRATEGY

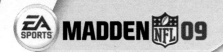

#92 Shaun Rogers *Defensive Tackle (DT)*

▼ DEFENSIVE **STAR PLAYER**

When you run the 3-4, you need a nose tackle that can play the run and generate pressure in the middle. Shawn does that and more. He even got an interception return for a touchdown last season, along with 8 sacks, making him the foundation the Browns need to win the battle in the trenches.

Speed	55
Strength	97
Power Moves	98
Finesse Moves	84

Player Weapon: Power Move D-Lineman

#99 Corey Williams *Defensive End (LE)*

▼ DEFENSIVE **STAR PLAYER**

The Giants showed that you need pressure to win Super Bowls. The Browns picked up Williams for this purpose. Last season, he had 35 tackles, 7 sacks, 3 forced fumbles, and 1 interception. He did all of this at defensive tackle. He will fit in well in the 3-4.

Speed	70
Strength	86
Power Moves	88
Finesse Moves	92

Player Weapon: Finesse Move D-Lineman

#95 Kamerion Wimbley *Linebacker (ROLB)*

▼ DEFENSIVE **STAR PLAYER**

This young player is a sack machine. He has generated 16 sacks in two seasons for the Browns. He has 51 tackles and 4 forced fumbles along with 5 sacks last season. Wimbley is known for using his speed and strength to aid his pass rushing ability, pass coverage, and run support.

Speed	85
Tackling	87
Pursuit	92
Play Recog.	78

Player Weapon: Brick Wall Defender

▼ DEFENSIVE **STRENGTH CHART**

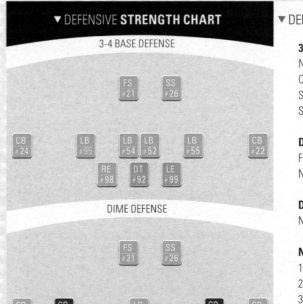

3-4 BASE DEFENSE

DIME DEFENSE

☐ OVR less than 80 ☐ OVR 90 or greater
☐ OVR between 80-89

▼ DEFENSIVE **FORMATIONS**

3-4	Quarter
Normal	Combo
Over	
Solid	
Stack	

Dime
Flat
Normal

Dollar
Normal

Nickel
1-5-5
2-4-5
3-3-5

▼ RECOMMENDED DEFENSIVE **AUDIBLE PACKAGES**

3-4	3-4	Nickel	Dime	Quarter
2 Man Under	MLB Storm Blitz	Cover 3	Cover 2	Man Up 3 Deep

▼ DEFENSIVE **PLAYCOUNTS**

Man Coverage:	42	Cover 2 Zone:	22	Man Blitz:	58
Man Zone:	38	Cover 3 Zone:	26	Zone Blitz:	58
Combo Coverage:	7	Deep Zone:	13	Combo Blitz:	7

DEFENSE **KEY DEFENSIVE PLAYS**

TEAM STRATEGY

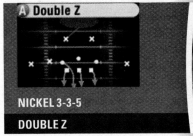

A Double Z
NICKEL 3-3-5
DOUBLE Z

The Double Z is a useful defense because even though it only rushes 4 defenders, the inside stunt by the linebacker helps bring pressure on the quarterback.

When the play starts, right away the d-end gets a clean release into the offensive back field.

The quarterback sees pressure from both sides and tries to avoid the rush.

Getting to the quarterback is half the battle. Taking him down for the sack is the key to success.

A Sam Snake
NICKEL 1-5-5
SAM SNAKE

Defending the run is a necessity. The 1-5-5 may not seem like the best choice, but it does a great job even against the jumbo run formations.

The keys to this play are the five linebackers. The linebackers can read the play without getting caught on blocks.

As the back approaches the line of scrimmage, the cornerback is setting a boundary to contain the run.

The back is brought down to the ground and does not gain any yards on the play.

A Double QB Spy
NICKEL 2-4-5
DBL QB SPY

Many times, the defense will face teams with quarterbacks that can roll out and hurt them with their feet and arm. The DBL QB will help contain that threat.

As the QB drops back to read the defense, he can see that we have solid coverage around the field.

There is still no clear passing lane, so the quarterback will have to force the pass into coverage.

Forced passes can be crucial, game-changing opportunities. The cornerback almost makes the interception.

TAMPA BAY BUCCANEERS

▶ **Division** NFC South   ▶ **Stadium** Raymond James Stadium   ▶ **Type** Open   ▶ **Capacity** 65,000   ▶ **Surface** Grass

▼ 2007 STANDINGS

Wins	Loses	Ties	PF	PA	Home	Road	vs. AFC	vs. NFC	vs. Div
9	7	0	334	270	6-2	3-5	1-3	8-4	5-1

▼ TEAM OVERVIEW

Tampa Bay has one of the best defenses in the league. They went about their business and got into the playoffs under the veteran leader Garcia. Defensively, the Bucs only gave up 16 points a game, 170 yards passing (2nd), 107 yards on the ground (17th), and a total of 278 yards a game (17th). On the other side of the ball, they scored 20 points a game (18th), 209 yards passing (16th), 117 yards on the ground (11th), and a grand total of 326 a game (18th). Tampa Bay relied on the defense to keep them in the game and used a balanced attack offensively to win games. The thing that helped them was Garcia managing the game in Gruden's West Coast system. Additionally, it was helpful to keep players healthy.

▼ OFF-SEASON UPGRADES

TYPE	ROUND	FIRST NAME	LAST NAME	SCHOOL/TEAM	POSITION
Free Agent	N/A	Marques	Douglas	49ers	DE
Free Agent	N/A	Warrick	Dunn	Falcons	RB
Free Agent	N/A	Jeff	Faine	Saints	C
Trade	N/A	Brian	Griese	Bears	QB
Draft	1	Aqib	Talib	Kansas State	CB

▼ SCOUTING REPORT

	DESCRIPTION	MAXIMIZING POTENTIAL	TIPS FOR OPPONENTS
STRENGTHS	Joey Galloway is your best option to go deep.	Use motion and packages to free him up and create mismatches.	You have to double him and pay attention to his alignment in every set.
	Ronde Barber year after year still produces and plays on a Pro Bowl level.	Match him up with the other team's best wideout.	Don't try him unless he has no safety help against your fastest wideout.
WEAKNESSES	Williams had a poor season last year and needs to step it up this season.	Use the passing game to help set up the run.	Use pass defense formations that have 4 man fronts. This can contain both run/pass.
	The only weakness is against the run. They were listed 17th.	Commit more men in the box and use 4-3/46 types of fronts.	Follow the golden rule--do it until they stop you. Pound their lights and use PA.

TEAM STRATEGY

FRANCHISE MODE STRATEGY

A second deep threat at wide receiver would open room for the Bucs' stable of running backs to operate. The Bucs are getting older on defense, so picking up some new young studs would pave the way for future success.

KEY FRANCHISE INFORMATION

Cap Room: $18.43M

Key Rivals:
- Falcons, Panthers, Saints

Philosophy:
- Offense: West Coast
- Defense: 4-3, Tampa 2

Highest Paid Players:
- D. Brooks
- G. Adams

Team Weapons:
- D. Brooks – Smart Linebacker
- R. Barber – Press Coverage Corner

Best Young Players:
- D. Joseph
- T. Jackson

91	86	95
OVERALL	OFFENSE	DEFENSE

▼ ROSTER AND **PACKAGE TIPS**

KEY PLAYER SUBSTITUTIONS

Position: HB
Substitution: Warrick Dunn
When: Global
Advantage: Warrick Dunn makes his way back to a Buccaneers uniform. Despite his age and compact body, he has proven on more than one occasion that he can carry the workload as the featured running back.

Position: HB2
Substitution: Carnell Williams
When: Global
Advantage: We could have easily bumped Carnell Williams up to the number one running back spot on the Buccaneers' depth chart, but with Dunn around, he makes for a solid number 2. In short yardage situations you can always package him in as the starter.

Position: LE
Substitution: Greg White
When: Global
Advantage: From a football video game standpoint, Greg White should be the team's starter at left end. He is just too good of a pass rusher not to be in the Tampa Bay lineup. His speed rating is considerably higher than Marques Douglas.

The oft-overlooked Jeff Garcia ran an efficient offense for the Bucs, whose stout defense should keep them in contention in 2008.

TEAM STRATEGY

TEAM STRATEGY

#84 Joey Galloway *Wide Receiver (WR)*

▼ OFFENSIVE **STAR PLAYER**

Many overlooked Galloway last season, and he made them pay. He pulled in 57 receptions, 1,014 yards, and 6 touchdowns. He was the go-to guy last season and will be this season as well. He has great hands, good speed, and the ability to run great double move routes.

Speed	97
Catch	88
Catch Traffic	82
Route Run	85

Player Weapon: Speed

#7 Jeff Garcia *Quarterback (QB)*

▼ OFFENSIVE **STAR PLAYER**

Everywhere this guy goes, he seems to play well in the West Coast system. His numbers won't knock you out of your chair (13 touchdowns, 2,440 passing yards, and 4 interceptions), but his 94.6 passing rating isn't bad. He manages games well and can get the job done every Sunday.

Speed	74
Awareness	88
Throwing Power	87
Throwing Accuracy	88

Player Weapon: None

#24 Carnell Williams *Halfback (HB)*

▼ OFFENSIVE **STAR PLAYER**

Williams had a terrible season last year. We all know that Gruden demands a consistent power run game. Williams was injured and only turned out 208 rushing yards, 54 carries, and 3 touchdowns. He is an excellent back for this system, and just needs to stay healthy.

Speed	92
Agility	93
Trucking	84
Elusiveness	88

Player Weapon: None

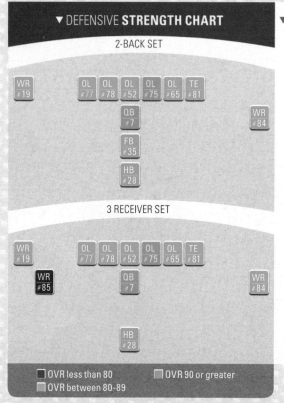

▼ DEFENSIVE **STRENGTH CHART**

2-BACK SET

3 RECEIVER SET

■ OVR less than 80 ■ OVR 90 or greater
■ OVR between 80-89

▼ OFFENSIVE **FORMATIONS**

Gun	Singleback
Doubles On	Ace
Snugs	Ace Pair Twins
Snugs Flip	Bunch
Split Slot	Doubles
Spread	Empty Bunch
Y-Trips Wk	Snugs
	Wing Trio
I-Form	
Pro	**Split**
Pro Twins	Slot
Tight	
	Strong
	Pro
	Tight Pair
	Weak
	Pro
	Pro Twins

▼ RECOMMENDED OFFENSIVE **AUDIBLE PACKAGES**

Singleback	Singleback	Split	Gun	Gun
HB Blast	TE Post	Drive RB Wheel	Y Shallow Cross	Slot Outs

▼ OFFENSIVE **PLAYCOUNTS**

Quick Pass:	13	Screen Pass:	9	Pitch:	6
Standard Pass:	98	Hail Mary:	1	Counter:	1
Shotgun Pass:	55	Inside Handoff:	27	Draw:	16
Play Action Pass:	52	Outside Handoff:	7		

OFFENSE **KEY OFFENSIVE PLAYS**

TEAM STRATEGY

HB DIVE

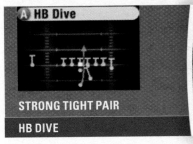

STRONG TIGHT PAIR

HB DIVE

1

2

3

There is a term used when referring to teams that have the ability to live off the run. It's called grown man football. Use the Dive to set this style.

Trust the play design and take the ball into the hole. Dives are open even when they look closed.

Graham gets behind his blockers and shows that he is no stranger to getting the tough yards.

He drags a few of the defenders for a ride as he picks up 5 yards through the heart of the defense.

SLOT CROSS

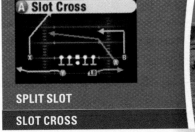

SPLIT SLOT

SLOT CROSS

1

2

3

There are some routes that are extremely effective and the slot cross is one of them. This route has been used by many on their way to success.

As the defense drops into coverage, read the middle of the field to see if the cross will be open.

The linebacker drops and takes away the cross, but it opens up the In route by the flanker.

A great read of the coverage. The throw turns into an easy catch and first down for the offense.

S OPTION ANGLE

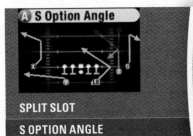

SPLIT SLOT

S OPTION ANGLE

1

2

3

Having two great routes in one play makes it hard for any defense to contain. The angle route and option route make this play explosive.

Once the play starts, the running back pulls the linebacker from the middle of the field with his outside release.

With the linebacker so wide, the back cuts back inside as the quarterback releases the ball.

The back gets the ball in his hands and picks up a first down for the offense.

TEAM STRATEGY

#55 Derrick Brooks *Linebacker (ROLB)*

▼ DEFENSIVE **STAR PLAYER**

He has been one of the two faces of the Tampa Bay defense from the Super Bowl. Brooks may be getting older, but still got 109 tackles last season with 2 forced fumbles. He lost a step, but always seems to be around the ball. His ticket is punched for Canton.

Speed	80
Tackling	90
Pursuit	90
Play Recog.	90

Player Weapon: Smart Linebacker

#20 Ronde Barber *Cornerback (CB)*

▼ DEFENSIVE **STAR PLAYER**

Barber is the other face that has been with the team for some time. One of the best cover 2 corners out there, Barber was the reason the Bucs' passing defense was ranked so high. He logged in 58 tackles, 1 sack, 1 forced fumble, and 2 interceptions. He's a sure Hall of Fame player.

Speed	88
Man Cover	78
Zone Cover	96
Press	97

Player Weapons: Smart Corner, Press Coverage Corner

#59 Cato June *Linebacker (LOLB)*

▼ DEFENSIVE **STAR PLAYER**

June was brought in to help with this top-rated defense last season. June had 69 tackles, one interception, and 1 forced fumble. He needs to work on those numbers to help improve the linebacking core. June is a player that moves and covers well.

Speed	84
Tackling	88
Pursuit	93
Play Recog.	85

Player Weapon: None

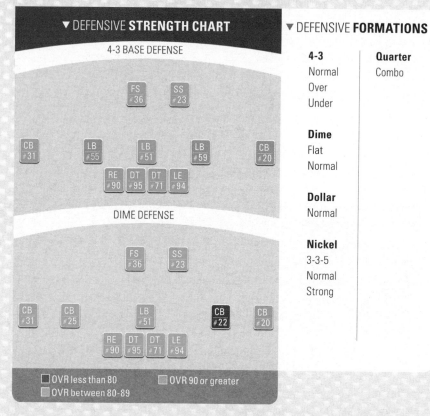

▼ DEFENSIVE **STRENGTH CHART**

▼ DEFENSIVE **FORMATIONS**

4-3	Quarter
Normal	Combo
Over	
Under	

Dime Flat / Normal

Dollar Normal

Nickel 3-3-5 / Normal / Strong

▼ RECOMMENDED DEFENSIVE **AUDIBLE PACKAGES**

4-3	4-3	Nickel	Dime	Quarter
2 Man Press	Thunder Smoke	Cover 3 Press	Cover 2	Cover 4

▼ DEFENSIVE **PLAYCOUNTS**

Man Coverage:	45	Cover 2 Zone:	14	Man Blitz:	55
Man Zone:	34	Cover 3 Zone:	26	Zone Blitz:	64
Combo Coverage:	7	Deep Zone:	18	Combo Blitz:	13

DEFENSE **KEY DEFENSIVE PLAYS**

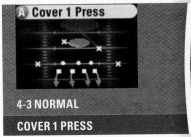

A Cover 1 Press

4-3 NORMAL

COVER 1 PRESS

The Cover 1 Press is a great run defense because the free safety plays a shallow zone, similar to Robber coverage. With him roaming underneath he can help stop the run.

As the quarterback turns to give the hand off, the defense has two defenders set to blow through the gap.

When the back gets the ball, the defensive end and linebacker are already behind the line and in his face.

The running back gets brought down just as he gets to the line of scrimmage. Yards are tough to come by.

A Zone Blitz

QUARTER

COMBO ZONE BLITZ

Some formations match up perfectly, and the Quarter Combo is great versus the Weak I Tight Pair. This Zone Blitz brings pressure up the middle and off the edges.

With two blitzing cornerbacks coming off the left edge, the offense will not be able to block both of them.

Instead of staying poised, the quarterback makes a rushed throw down the middle of the field.

Bad decision, but a great opportunity for the defense as the safety steps in front for an interception.

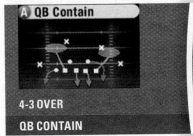

A QB Contain

4-3 OVER

QB CONTAIN

When facing a big and strong quarterback that likes to roll out to stretch the defense, the defense must be able to handle that. The 4-3 Over QB Contain does just that.

The benefit of contain coverage is that it forces mobile quarterbacks to stay in the pocket to make plays.

Some habits are hard to break and the quarterback just can't help but roll out of the pocket.

Once he started to roll out, the contain defender came up and made the sack.

ARIZONA CARDINALS

▶ **Division** NFC West ▶ **Stadium** University of Phoenix Stadium ▶ **Type** Open ▶ **Capacity** 63,400 ▶ **Surface** Grass

▼ 2007 STANDINGS

Wins	Loses	Ties	PF	PA	Home	Road	vs. AFC	vs. NFC	vs. Div
8	8	0	404	399	6-2	2-6	3-1	5-7	3-3

▼ TEAM OVERVIEW

The Arizona Cardinals have one of the best offenses out there. They scored 25 points a game (which ranks them 7th). They also picked up 254 yards in the air (5th), and 90 yards on the ground (29th) for 344 total yards per game. The problem lies on the defensive side. They gave up 24 points game (27th), 232 yards in the air (26th), and 97 yards on the ground (9th). The Cardinals used the run game to support the pass, but in the end, it was passing that helped them win. Fortunately, Arizona has two of the best wideouts in the league (Fitzgerald and Boldin) and a young gunslinger in Leinart. In addition, don't forget about Edge grinding out yards. They need to focus on improving their defense since scoring isn't a problem for them.

▼ OFF-SEASON UPGRADES

TYPE	ROUND	FIRST NAME	LAST NAME	SCHOOL/TEAM	POSITION
Free Agent	N/A	Clark	Haggans	Steelers	LB
Free Agent	N/A	Travis	LaBoy	Titans	DE
Free Agent	N/A	Bryan	Robinson	Bengals	DE
Draft	1	Dominique	Rodgers-Cromartie	Tennessee State	CB
Draft	2	Calais	Campbell	Miami	DE

▼ SCOUTING REPORT

	DESCRIPTION	MAXIMIZING POTENTIAL	TIPS FOR OPPONENTS
STRENGTHS	Boldin and Fitzgerald are one of the best wideout tandems in the league.	Move them around and look for favorable match-ups at all times.	Double team them and use some pressure to cut down time in the pocket.
STRENGTHS	Adrian Wilson is the best corner on the team. Roam with him.	Use zone blitzing coverages and roam the field with him.	Don't try his side and find him every down. He can be used in blitzes.
WEAKNESSES	The offensive line is the only weak spot for the Cards on offense.	Use the West Coast offensive scheme and a heavy rushing attack.	They say pressure bursts pipes. You need to use stunts to exploit weaknesses.
WEAKNESSES	The Cardinals' secondary is very poor. They were listed 26th in the league.	Play the pass because the rushing defense is ranked 9th.	Your best bet is a passing attack, because the Cardinals play the run well.

TEAM STRATEGY

FRANCHISE MODE STRATEGY

The Cardinals need some help in the middle of the offensive line if you are going to establish a running attack with Edge. Make picking up a pass rushing defensive end and a speedy corner your priority for the season.

KEY FRANCHISE INFORMATION

Cap Room: $740K

Key Rivals:
- 49ers, Rams, Seahawks

Philosophy:
- Offense: Run with Play Action
- Defense: 3-4 Hybrid

Highest Paid Players:
- L. Brown
- L. Fitzgerald

Team Weapons:
- L. Fitzgerald – Quick Receiver
- A. Boldin – Possession Receiver

Best Young Players:
- L. Brown
- G. Watson

78	82	74
OVERALL	OFFENSE	DEFENSE

▼ ROSTER AND **PACKAGE TIPS**

KEY PLAYER SUBSTITUTIONS

Position: RE

Substitution: Calais Campbell

When: 4-3 front

Advantage: This move depends on whether you plan to play a 4-3 front instead of a 3-4 front. If you plan on running a 4-3 front, move Calais Campbell to the right end. He will give you a legit pass rusher from his spot.

Position: DT

Substitution: Darnell Dockett

When: 4-3 front

Advantage: With Campbell moved to right end, Darnell Dockett can be moved inside at his natural position. By moving him inside, you get a defensive tackle who can defend the run and push the pocket up the middle when the offense passes the ball.

Position: CB

Substitution: Dominique Rodgers-Cromartie

When: Global

Advantage: Dominique Rodgers-Cromartie is a much faster cornerback than Eric Green, so making this move is a must if you plan on running any type of aggressive defensive scheme. Plus, it doesn't hurt that he is a few inches taller than Green.

Larry Fitzgerald and the Cardinals offense should continue to be a machine of offensive productivity, and if the changes they made on defense pay off, the Cardinals may fly high in 2008.

TEAM STRATEGY

93

 **ARIZONA CARDINALS** — OFFENSE

TEAM STRATEGY

#11 Larry Fitzgerald *Wide Receiver (WR)*
▼ OFFENSIVE **STAR PLAYER**

This man is a beast. He has good size, decent speed, great hands, and the ability to run outstanding routes. Fitzgerald didn't play a whole season, and still pulled in 100 receptions, 1,409 yards, and 10 touchdowns. He is the go-to guy for the Cards, and just needs to stay healthy.

Speed	93
Catch	95
Catch Traffic	95
Route Run	96

Player Weapon: Quick Receiver, Possession Receiver, Spec Catch Receiver, Hands

#81 Anquan Boldin *Wide Receiver (WR)*
▼ OFFENSIVE **STAR PLAYER**

Boldin is one of the better big body wideouts in the league. He's the type of player that can take a slant and make it an 80-yard touchdown. There is big play potential every time he touches the ball. He logged in 71 receptions, 853 yards, and 9 touchdowns last season.

Speed	91
Catch	93
Catch Traffic	99
Route Run	92

Player Weapon: Quick Receiver, Possession Receiver, Spec Catch Receiver, Hands

#32 Edgerrin James *Halfback (HB)*
▼ OFFENSIVE **STAR PLAYER**

Edge isn't the player he was when he was in Indy, but he is still a great runner. Last season, the Cardinals wanted to be a running team. Edge put in solid work with 324 carries, 1,222 yards a game, and 7 touchdowns. This is a major improvement from last season.

Speed	88
Agility	90
Trucking	92
Elusiveness	89

Player Weapons: Power Back, Stiff Arm Ball Carrier

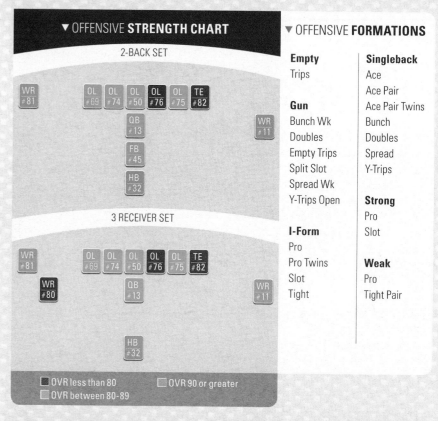

▼ OFFENSIVE **STRENGTH CHART**

▼ OFFENSIVE **FORMATIONS**

Empty
Trips

Gun
Bunch Wk
Doubles
Empty Trips
Split Slot
Spread Wk
Y-Trips Open

I-Form
Pro
Pro Twins
Slot
Tight

Singleback
Ace
Ace Pair
Ace Pair Twins
Bunch
Doubles
Spread
Y-Trips

Strong
Pro
Slot

Weak
Pro
Tight Pair

▼ RECOMMENDED OFFENSIVE **AUDIBLE PACKAGES**

Singleback	Singleback	I-Form	Gun	Gun
HB Counter	Quick Slants	Iso	X Follow	Pivot Z In

▼ OFFENSIVE **PLAYCOUNTS**

Quick Pass	21	Screen Pass	12	Pitch	7
Standard Pass	93	Hail Mary		Counter	9
Shotgun Pass	60	Inside Handoff	32	Draw	12
Play Action Pass	55	Outside Handoff	13	FB Run	8

OFFENSE **KEY OFFENSIVE PLAYS**

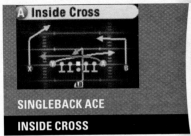

A Inside Cross

SINGLEBACK ACE

INSIDE CROSS

Crossing routes are great to use when facing both man and zone. The Inside Cross has been a play that always gets a wide open route for one of the tight ends.

1

The read is the same, whether facing man or zone. Read the linebackers to see where the route will open up.

2

The #1 tight end comes free as his route meshes with the route of the other tight end.

3

After making the catch the tight end is able to turn upfield and beat the defense for a first down.

A HB Sprint

SINGLEBACK ACE

HB SPRINT

Continue to dominate in the Singleback Ace set by taking advantage of Edgerrin James' skills as a running back. The HB Sprint showcases his talents.

1

Edge has to be happy when he sees all the great blocking in front of him.

2

Now that he has the ball, he sets up his blocks and starts to head outside to the corner.

3

Once Edgerrin hits the corner the defense is in trouble. He has already picked up a first down.

A Curl Combo

SINGLEBACK ACE PAIR

CURL COMBO

A good offense will be able to beat man, zone and blitz on any given play. The routes in the Curl Combo make this possible every time.

1

The defense looks to have the advantage here with the tight defense, but give it a second.

2

The flanker gets open on the outside because the flat route forced the corner to leave him alone.

3

Matt Leinart puts the ball in the perfect spot for Larry Fitzgerald to make the catch. He then turns up field for more yards.

TEAM STRATEGY

TEAM STRATEGY

#24 Adrian Wilson *Safety (SS)*

▼ DEFENSIVE **STAR PLAYER**

Adrian Wilson is one of the better safeties in the league. He is also the playmaker for the team. This Pro Bowler logged in 44 tackles with 2 interceptions last season. At 6'3" and 220 pounds, he covers a lot of area and can drop the hammer on opposing receivers.

Speed	89
Man Cover	65
Zone Cover	85
Hit Power	84

Player Weapon: None

#58 Karlos Dansby *Linebacker (ROLB)*

▼ DEFENSIVE **STAR PLAYER**

He had a great season last year playing outside. Dansby had 97 tackles, 4 forced fumbles, 3 interceptions, and 3.5 sacks last year. Clearly, he is the best linebacker on the team and they need him to repeat or improve on last season's numbers.

Speed	85
Tackling	86
Pursuit	93
Play Recog.	78

Player Weapon: Big Hitter, Brick Wall Defender, Smart Linebacker

#90 Darnell Dockett *Defensive Tackle (DT)*

▼ DEFENSIVE **STAR PLAYER**

Dockett was the leader on the line, leading the team with 9 sacks. He also had 58 tackles and forced 2 fumbles. He controlled the line of scrimmage and created plays when he got penetration. However, he needs additional help up front to make a bigger impact.

Speed	75
Strength	90
Power Moves	94
Finesse Moves	89

Player Weapon: Power Move D-Lineman

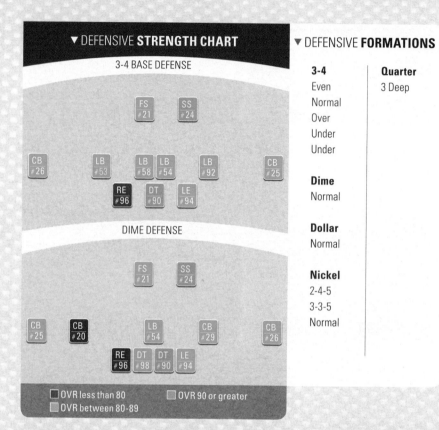

▼ DEFENSIVE **STRENGTH CHART**

3-4 BASE DEFENSE

FS #21 SS #24

CB #26 LB #53 LB #58 LB #54 LB #92 CB #25

RE #96 DT #90 LE #94

DIME DEFENSE

FS #21 SS #24

CB #25 CB #20 LB #54 CB #29 CB #26

RE #96 DT #98 DT #90 LE #94

☐ OVR less than 80   ☐ OVR 90 or greater
☐ OVR between 80-89

▼ DEFENSIVE **FORMATIONS**

3-4	Quarter
Even	3 Deep
Normal	
Over	
Under	
Under	
Dime	
Normal	
Dollar	
Normal	
Nickel	
2-4-5	
3-3-5	
Normal	

▼ RECOMMENDED DEFENSIVE **AUDIBLE PACKAGES**

3-4	3-4	Nickel	Dime	Quarter
2 Man Under	OLB Dogs Fire	Cover 3	Cover 2	Man Up 3 Deep

▼ DEFENSIVE **PLAYCOUNTS**

Man Coverage:	48	Cover 2 Zone:	21	Man Blitz:	55
Man Zone:	44	Cover 3 Zone:	33	Zone Blitz:	61
Combo Coverage:	9	Deep Zone:	16	Combo Blitz:	10

DEFENSE **KEY DEFENSIVE PLAYS**

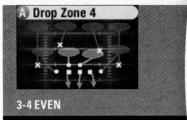

A Drop Zone 4

3-4 EVEN

DROP ZONE 4

1

2

3

Cover 4 is a great coverage to use when trying to keep the offense in front of the defenders and make them slow down their offensive attack.

The safety and linebackers are dropping back into coverage while still keeping an eye on the quarterback and receivers.

Alex Smith sees an opening in the defense and is going to try to fit the ball in to his receiver.

The benefit of the Cover 4 is that no receivers can get outside of the coverage.

A CB Fox Blitz

NICKEL 2-4-5

CB FOX BLITZ

1

2

3

In *Madden* there is a tendency by players to run toss plays to the weak side of the field. Using the Nickel 2-4-5 Fox Blitz the defense will be able to defend against this threat.

As soon as the quarterback calls for the snap the cornerback charges into the offensive backfield.

The back sees how deep into the backfield the corner is and has to try to adjust right away.

Rod Hood takes the perfect blitz angle and it pays off as he takes the back down for a loss.

A Fox Fire Zone

DIME NORMAL

FOX FIRE ZONE

1

2

3

The Fox Fire Zone is a defense designed to pressure the offense with a line stunt but remain strong in coverage in case the offense gets a pass off.

Karlos Dansby and Ralph Brown pressure the offensive tackle by rushing directly at him and forcing him into a decision.

Dansby is more of a threat so the tackle lets Brown run free. The defense doesn't care as long as one gets free.

Brown shows the offense that leaving him with a free run at the quarterback is a mistake. He drops Leinart in the backfield.

TEAM STRATEGY

SAN DIEGO CHARGERS

▶ **Division** AFC West   ▶ **Stadium** Qualcomm Stadium   ▶ **Type** Open   ▶ **Capacity** 71,500   ▶ **Surface** Grass

▼ 2007 STANDINGS

Wins	Loses	Ties	PF	PA	Home	Road	vs. AFC	vs. NFC	vs. Div
11	5	0	412	284	7-1	4-4	9-3	2-2	5-1

▼ TEAM OVERVIEW

The Bolts had a rough season early and turned it around late. Norv Turner got the ship rolling in the right direction, and a new star was born with Cromartie. The Bolts have a great core of players, and if everyone stays healthy, they can make another run this season. The offense is fine on the ground with 127 yards (7th), but passing was down with 187 yards a game (26th). The defense wasn't as good as last year, but they were solid. They only gave up 17 points a game (5th), 213 yards passing (14th), and 107 yards on the ground (16th). Hopefully, Turner can use his coaching skills to help Rivers gain more yards in the air. Plus, they need to improve on the defensive side of the ball.

▼ OFF-SEASON UPGRADES

TYPE	ROUND	FIRST NAME	LAST NAME	SCHOOL/TEAM	POSITION
Free Agent	N/A	L.J.	Shelton	Dolphins	T
Free Agent	N/A	Derek	Smith	49ers	LB
Draft	1	Antoine	Cason	Arizona	CB
Draft	3	Jacob	Hester	LSU	RB
Draft	5	Marcus	Thomas	UTEP	RB

▼ SCOUTING REPORT

	DESCRIPTION	MAXIMIZING POTENTIAL	TIPS FOR OPPONENTS
STRENGTHS	Tomlinson is a one man wrecking crew that led his team to the playoffs.	Like Keyshawn Johnson, give him the ball as much as possible.	He is hard to defend. You need to double him and sit on him.
	Merriman is the best at what he does. He wreaks havoc every single play.	Use him for blitzing and coverage. Keep the team off-balance.	Make sure you account for him on every play. He sheds blocks well.
WEAKNESSES	Jackson had all of the potential, but has never had the season expected in 2007.	Use compressed/grouping sets so he can get easier match-ups.	Use the top DB on him and double other weapons with safety help over top.
	The Chargers' safeties are the only weakness of this top-rated defense.	You need to create heavy pressure and be mindful of the offense's tendencies.	Use formations that have compressed or grouping sets. This can force isolation with safeties.

TEAM STRATEGY

FRANCHISE MODE STRATEGY
The Chargers are a pretty solid team from top to bottom. You have all the tools, so go for depth. A good possession receiver for the number 3 spot and nickelback should be your main focus.

KEY FRANCHISE INFORMATION

Cap Room: $18.07M
Key Rivals:
- Broncos, Chiefs, Raiders

Philosophy:
- Offense: Run with Play Action
- Defense: 3-4

Highest Paid Players:
- L. Tomlinson
- P. Rivers

Team Weapons:
- L. Tomlinson – Elusive Back
- A. Gates – Quick Receiver

Best Young Players:
- B. Davis
- E. Weddle

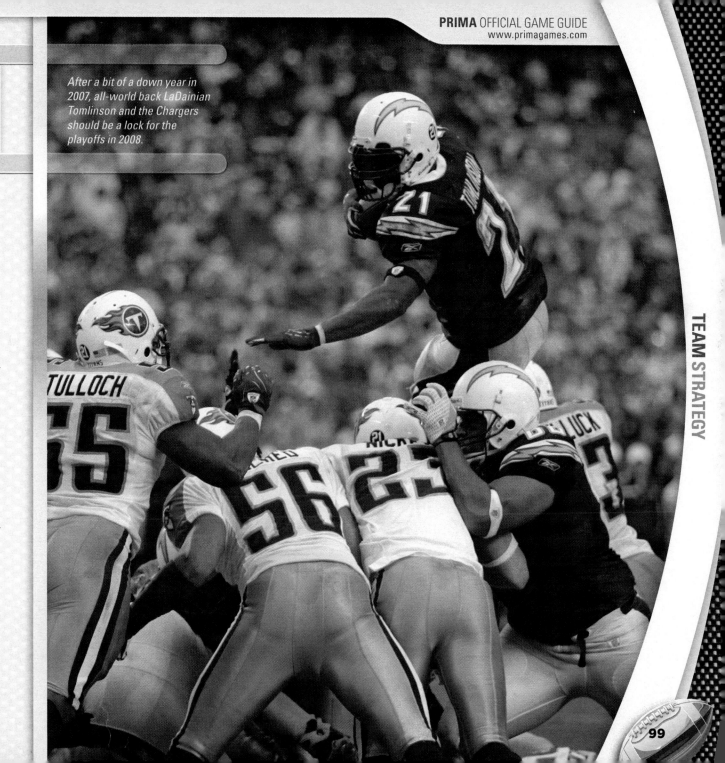

After a bit of a down year in 2007, all-world back LaDainian Tomlinson and the Chargers should be a lock for the playoffs in 2008.

TEAM STRATEGY

95	93	93
OVERALL	OFFENSE	DEFENSE

▼ ROSTER AND **PACKAGE TIPS**

KEY PLAYER SUBSTITUTIONS

Position: FB

Substitution: LaDainian Tomlinson

When: FB Dive/Decoy

Advantage: In real football, this move would probably not be made, but in *Madden,* players do this all the time. Having LaDainian Tomlinson lined up in the fullback spot when running the FB Dive means positive yardage.

Position: Slot

Substitution: Antonio Gates

When: Passing Situations

Advantage: Antonio Gates can be lined up just about anywhere on the field and cause some type of match-up problem. That's why putting him in the slot can really make the defense think about how to defend him.

Position: SE/FL

Substitution: Antonio Gates

When: Passing Situations

Advantage: We already suggested moving Gates into the slot, but let's take it one step further and move him outside at SE or FL. No cornerback in the game is going to be able to defend him. He is just too big and has good speed, even as an outside receiver.

TEAM STRATEGY

#21 LaDainian Tomlinson *Halfback (HB)*

▼ OFFENSIVE **STAR PLAYER**

Tomlinson is the best running back in the NFL. He has speed, power, excellent vision, and is hard to lay a hand on. He is also a weapon coming out of the backfield. He racked up 315 carries, 1,474 yards rushing, and 15 touchdowns. He also had over 400 yards receiving.

Speed	96
Agility	99
Trucking	92
Elusiveness	99

Player Weapons: Power Back, Elusive Back, Stiff Arm Ball Carrier, Speed

#85 Antonio Gates *Tight End (TE)*

▼ OFFENSIVE **STAR PLAYER**

This Pro Bowl player is one of the best tight ends out there to date. He has become the primary target for both Brees and Rivers. He had 984 yards receiving, 9 touchdowns, and 75 receptions. Gates is steady, so expect the same production this season.

Speed	88
Catch	90
Run Block	58
Pass Block	52

Player Weapons: Quick Receiver, Possession Receiver, Spec Catch Receiver

#89 Chris Chambers *Wide Receiver (WR)*

▼ OFFENSIVE **STAR PLAYER**

Chambers was brought in through a trade last season in order to help the receivers. The Chargers hoped that with the running game and Gates, this would allow Chambers to get good looks at the ball. Chambers lost a step, but is still a great option at wideout with the weapons they have.

Speed	94
Catch	88
Catch Traffic	87
Route Run	87

Player Weapon: Spec Catch Receiver

▼ OFFENSIVE **STRENGTH CHART**

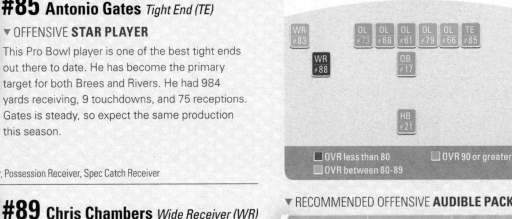

2-BACK SET

WR #83 | OL #73 | OL #68 | OL #61 | OL #79 | OL #66 | TE #85 | WR #89
QB #17
FB #34
HB #21

3 RECEIVER SET

WR #83 | OL #73 | OL #68 | OL #61 | OL #79 | OL #66 | TE #85 | WR #89
WR #88 | QB #17
HB #21

☐ OVR less than 80 ☐ OVR 90 or greater
☐ OVR between 80-89

▼ OFFENSIVE **FORMATIONS**

Gun	Wing Trio
Doubles	
Split Slot	**Split**
Split Y-Flex	Normal
Spread Y-Slot	
Y-Trips Open	**Strong**
	Pro
I-Form	Pro Twins
Pro	Tight Pair
Tight	Y-Flex
Tight Pair	
	Weak
Singleback	Pro
Ace	Pro Twins
Ace Pair	Tight Pair
Bunch	
Doubles	
F Wing	

▼ RECOMMENDED OFFENSIVE **AUDIBLE PACKAGES**

Singleback	Singleback	I-Form	Strong	Gun
HB Sprint	Slants	Iso	494 F Flat	Curl Flats

▼ OFFENSIVE **PLAYCOUNTS**

Quick Pass:	23	Screen Pass:	7	Pitch:	6
Standard Pass:	82	Hail Mary:		Counter:	9
Shotgun Pass:	45	Inside Handoff:	30	Draw:	9
Play Action Pass:	67	Outside Handoff:	18	FB Run:	11

OFFENSE **KEY OFFENSIVE PLAYS**

A Counter Wk

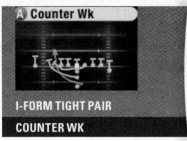

I-FORM TIGHT PAIR

COUNTER WK

LaDainian Tomlinson's skill as a running back is unparalleled. Use his speed and agility to really beat the defense with a counter play.

As soon as he has the ball, the defense looks to have him in their grasp.

This is why he is so valuable. LT makes a quick cut and totally leaves the defender grasping at air.

He is still cutting through the defense and picking up yards as he heads up the field.

A PA FL Clown

SINGLEBACK F WING

PA FL CLOWN

After establishing a running game with LaDainian, the play action pass is the next progression for the offense. This play even gets him into the pass routes.

Most play action passes don't send the back out into a pattern, but the FL Clown gets LT into the passing game.

At this point, the quarterback has Antonio Gates and LT open. Both are great options.

Rivers throws the ball to LT running the out route. He is able to turn up the field for a huge gain.

A TE Drag

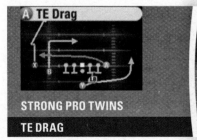

STRONG PRO TWINS

TE DRAG

High powered teams normally have no problem getting the ball down the field, and then struggle in the red zone. The TE Drag will help solve that problem.

Rivers reads the defense to see if he will be able to get the ball to Gates.

The defense is overplaying Gates so Rivers sees that they have left LT wide open in the flat.

It was a mistake to leave LT wide open. Now the defense has to figure out how to keep him from diving into the end zone again.

 SAN DIEGO CHARGERS — DEFENSE

#56 Shawne Merriman *Linebacker (ROLB)*

▼ DEFENSIVE **STAR PLAYER**

This man is an animal on the field. Merriman (a.k.a. "Lights Out") wreaks havoc on the field and sacrifices his body on every play. He had 12 sacks last season and 2 forced fumbles. He also had 68 tackles. This Pro Bowler is the heart of the defense.

Speed	87
Tackling	93
Pursuit	95
Play Recog.	78

Player Weapons: Big Hitter, Brick Wall Defender

#76 Jamal Williams *Defensive Tackle (DT)*

▼ DEFENSIVE **STAR PLAYER**

Williams is a tough defensive tackle that is one of the best run stoppers in the league. He anchors this line in the 3-4 scheme that they run in San Diego. He didn't have the season he did the year before last, but he's a player that is needed in the middle.

Speed	54
Strength	98
Power Moves	98
Finesse Moves	67

Player Weapon: Power Move D-Lineman

#93 Luis Castillo *Defensive Tackle (LE)*

▼ DEFENSIVE **STAR PLAYER**

Castillo is the type of power defensive end that you need in a 3-4 scheme. His job is to stop the run and allow the linebackers to get pressure on the quarterback. There is no other defensive end in a 3-4 scheme that plays the run as well as him.

Speed	70
Strength	95
Power Moves	96
Finesse Moves	75

Player Weapon: Power Move D-Lineman

TEAM STRATEGY

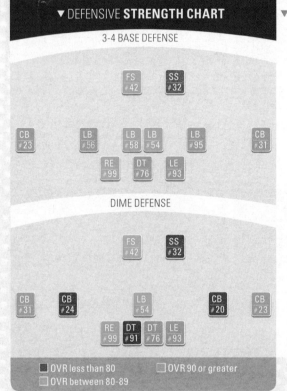

▼ DEFENSIVE **STRENGTH CHART**

3-4 BASE DEFENSE

DIME DEFENSE

■ OVR less than 80 □ OVR 90 or greater □ OVR between 80-89

▼ DEFENSIVE **FORMATIONS**

3-4	Quarter
Normal	Combo
Solid	
Stack	
Under	
Dime	
Flat	
Normal	
Dollar	
Normal	
Nickel	
2-4-5	
3-3-5	
Strong	

▼ RECOMMENDED DEFENSIVE **AUDIBLE PACKAGES**

3-4	43-43	Nickel	Dime	Quarter
2 Man Under	OLB Dogs Fire	Cover 3	Cover 2	Man Up 3 Deep

▼ DEFENSIVE **PLAYCOUNTS**

Man Coverage:	47	Cover 2 Zone:	22	Man Blitz:	56
Man Zone:	37	Cover 3 Zone:	26	Zone Blitz:	56
Combo Coverage:	7	Deep Zone:	13	Combo Blitz:	7

DEFENSE **KEY DEFENSIVE PLAYS**

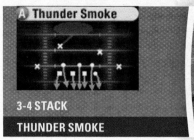

A Thunder Smoke

3-4 STACK

THUNDER SMOKE

Defense is supposed to be aggressive. The Chargers play defense with the mindset of getting behind the line of scrimmage and being disruptive.

As Fargas is about to get the ball, the defense is in position to shut him down from every angle.

The defensive end sets containment and shows Fargas that there will be no running outside.

The end starts to collapse onto the running back. Make the back turn inside and then clamp down.

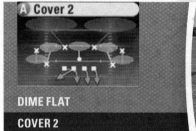

A Cover 2

DIME FLAT

COVER 2

Cover 2 defenses are being used more and more with teams that have great overall speed. The Chargers' defense fits this play call perfectly.

The key to the defense is to keep everything in front them, so that they can break on any pass.

With no wide open receivers, the quarterback will try to fit the ball between the two d-backs.

The cornerback undercuts the receiver and tries for the interception. No pick, but he breaks up the pass.

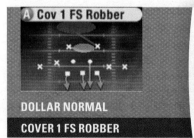

A Cov 1 FS Robber

DOLLAR NORMAL

COVER 1 FS ROBBER

This year, Cover 1 is going to be associated with many great play calls. The FS Robber is a solid defense that allows the safety to help out around the line.

Merriman is considered one of the best because of his natural ability to snuff out a play.

When he sees that the O-line is setting screen blocks, he follows the back to chase down the screen.

He meets the back as soon as he gets the ball and hits and strips him. No completion today.

TEAM STRATEGY

KANSAS CITY CHIEFS

▶ **Division** AFC West ▶ **Stadium** Arrowhead Stadium ▶ **Type** Open ▶ **Capacity** 79,400 ▶ **Surface** Grass

▼ 2007 STANDINGS

Wins	Loses	Ties	PF	PA	Home	Road	vs. AFC	vs. NFC	vs. Div
4	12	0	226	335	2-6	2-6	3-9	1-3	2-4

▼ TEAM OVERVIEW

The Chiefs are going through a rebuilding stage. They had a bad season last year, but are expected to improve this season, as they were given one of the best grades for drafting this season. They have two Pro Bowl players on the offensive side and are trying to improve on the defensive side of the ball. On the offensive side of the ball, the Chiefs are ranked 31st in points, only scoring 14 a game. They are also listed 31st in passing yards (198), and 32nd in the rushing department with 78 yards a game. On the other side, they are listed 13th in total yards (319), 5th is passing yards (188), and 28th against the run (130). They need to stop the run more effectively and return to the power run game.

▼ OFF-SEASON UPGRADES

TYPE	ROUND	FIRST NAME	LAST NAME	SCHOOL/TEAM	POSITION
Free Agent	N/A	Devard	Darling	Ravens	WR
Free Agent	N/A	Demorio	Williams	Falcons	LB
Draft	1	Glenn	Dorsey	LSU	DT
Draft	1	Brandon	Albert	Virginia	G
Draft	2	Brandon	Flowers	Virginia Tech	CB

▼ SCOUTING REPORT

	DESCRIPTION	MAXIMIZING POTENTIAL	TIPS FOR OPPONENTS
STRENGTHS	Tony Gonzales has changed the way we see tight ends. He is your best option.	Use packages to move him around and get him the ball.	You have to double him and force the player to go somewhere else.
	Derrick Johnson had 94 tackles, 4 sacks, 3 forced fumbles, and 2 interceptions... enough said.	You need to use him to generate pressure and to defend.	Give him something to do by flooding his area with routes.
WEAKNESSES	The quarterback situation is terrible since Trent Green left. This is hurting LJ.	You need to run the ball to help with the passing attack.	Focus on the run game and force them to throw. Always double Tony Gonzales.
	The defense plays the run very poorly. They're listed 28th in the NFL.	They have a talented defense overall. Use bigger fronts for the run.	Run the ball down their throat to force them to sit on the pound.

FRANCHISE MODE STRATEGY

Croyle and Huard have not yet established themselves as being franchise QBs. Consider drafting a QB if one becomes available. You will also need to get more help at receiver. On defense, the linebackers are getting old.

KEY FRANCHISE INFORMATION

Cap Room: $44.72M

Key Rivals:
- Broncos, Chargers, Raiders

Philosophy:
- Offense: Pro Style
- Defense: 4-3

Highest Paid Players:
- L. Johnson
- G. Dorsey

Team Weapons:
- T. Gonzalez – Quick Receiver
- L. Johnson – Power Back

Best Young Players:
- D. Bowe
- B. Pollard

71	68	72
OVERALL	OFFENSE	DEFENSE

The Chiefs and Larry Johnson should have more time and space to run their playbook in 2008 after shoring up their offensive and defensive lines via the draft with potential future stars.

▼ ROSTER AND **PACKAGE TIPS**

KEY PLAYER SUBSTITUTIONS

Position: WR
Substitution: Will Franklin
When: Global
Advantage: This move brings more speed at the wide receiver position by moving Will Franklin up to the number three or four receiver position without losing too much catching ability.

Position: RE
Substitution: Napoleon Harris
When: Global
Advantage: The Chiefs lost Jared Allen to the Vikings, so they don't have much of a pass rush along the defensive line. Napoleon Harris is the number 2 middle linebacker. Rather than having him ride the pine, move him to RE, and Tamba Hali to LE.

Position: DT
Substitution: Alfonso Boone
When: Global
Advantage: Alfonso Boone has a high strength rating, so he can easily be moved inside next to rookie Glenn Dorsey. This gives the Chiefs two effective run stoppers and pass rushers at both defensive tackle positions.

TEAM STRATEGY

KANSAS CITY CHIEFS — OFFENSE

#88 Tony Gonzalez *Tight End (TE)*

▼ OFFENSIVE STAR PLAYER

He is as steady as they come. The best tight end in the league and a Hall of Fame first time ballot when he hangs up the cleats, Gonzalez changed the game from this position. In a losing season he pulled in 99 receptions, 1,172 yards, and 5 touchdowns.

Speed	86
Catch	94
Run Block	55
Pass Block	50

Player Weapons: Quick Receiver, Possession Receiver, Spec Catch Receiver

#27 Larry Johnson *Halfback (HB)*

▼ OFFENSIVE STAR PLAYER

He had a bad season last year, but is still one of the best backs to date. His punishing running style beats defenders down. In the 4th quarter, he runs harder and stronger. The main problem is the line and lack of passing attack, in addition to running against loaded fronts.

Speed	92
Agility	90
Trucking	97
Elusiveness	85

Player Weapon: Power Back

#54 Brian Waters *Guard (LG)*

▼ OFFENSIVE STAR PLAYER

He is one of last few players left on a once great offensive line. Waters had led many backs to 1,000-yard seasons and pass protected very well. Currently, he is the best lineman on the line and the anchor. No one seals off the middle better than Waters.

Run Block Strength	95
Run Block Footwork	87
Pass Block Strength	92
Pass Block Footwork	82

Player Weapon: Crushing Run Blocker

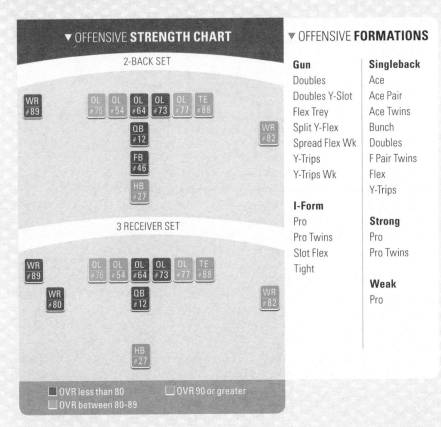

▼ OFFENSIVE STRENGTH CHART

2-BACK SET

WR #89 — OL #76 — OL #54 — OL #64 — OL #73 — OL #77 — TE #88 — WR #82
QB #12
FB #46
HB #27

3 RECEIVER SET

WR #89 — OL #76 — OL #54 — OL #64 — OL #73 — OL #77 — TE #88 — WR #82
WR #80 — QB #12 — WR #82
HB #27

☐ OVR less than 80   ☐ OVR 90 or greater   ☐ OVR between 80-89

▼ OFFENSIVE FORMATIONS

Gun	Singleback
Doubles	Ace
Doubles Y-Slot	Ace Pair
Flex Trey	Ace Twins
Split Y-Flex	Bunch
Spread Flex Wk	Doubles
Y-Trips	F Pair Twins
Y-Trips Wk	Flex
	Y-Trips
I-Form	
Pro	**Strong**
Pro Twins	Pro
Slot Flex	Pro Twins
Tight	
	Weak
	Pro

▼ RECOMMENDED OFFENSIVE AUDIBLE PACKAGES

Singleback	Singleback	I-Form	Gun	Gun
HB Dive	Flanker Dig	Power O	Smash	Drag Under

▼ OFFENSIVE PLAYCOUNTS

Quick Pass:	20	Screen Pass:	9	Pitch:	8
Standard Pass:	91	Hail Mary:		Counter:	11
Shotgun Pass:	63	Inside Handoff:	28	Draw:	10
Play Action Pass:	58	Outside Handoff:	12	FB Run:	8

TEAM STRATEGY

OFFENSE **KEY OFFENSIVE PLAYS**

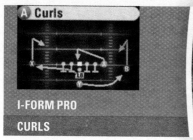

Ⓐ Curls
I-FORM PRO
CURLS

It is easy to run an offense with Gonzalez and Johnson. The I-Form Pro Curls is a play that lets the Chiefs put their featured players in great position for success.

1 Early on in the play, Croyle spots Tony G linking up in the middle of the field.

2 Because of the linebackers on both sides of Gonzalez, LJ in the flat is the best pass option.

3 Johnson makes the catch in the flat, and carries two defenders for a ride as he gains a first down.

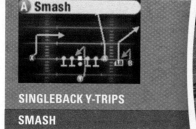

Ⓐ Smash
SINGLEBACK Y-TRIPS
SMASH

The Smash is very useful. The streak, corner, and hook route to the right side are sure to cause a receiver to spring wide open.

1 Tony Gonzalez holds the safety on the seam and prevents him from playing the slot's corner route.

2 Even after the quarterback misses the window to hit the corner route, the crossing route is an option as well as the hook.

3 The ball is thrown to the flanker who ran the hook, and he takes off up the field for a nice gain.

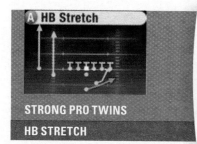

Ⓐ HB Stretch
STRONG PRO TWINS
HB STRETCH

Larry Johnson is a work horse. No matter how his numbers looked last year, he still can control a game with his aggressive running style.

1 Before even getting the ball in his hands, Johnson can see that his line has cleared some huge holes for him.

2 He picks up a crucial block from his fullback on a defender trying to force contain.

3 Now that Larry is in the clear, he presents a major problem for the defense. Move out the way.

 KANSAS CITY CHIEFS

DEFENSE

#59 Donnie Edwards *Linebacker (ROLB)*

▼ DEFENSIVE **STAR PLAYER**

Edwards is still one of the better OLBs. He logged in 104 tackles, 2 sacks, 1 forced fumble, and 1 interception. His numbers are consistent, and he is the leader of the defense. He has averaged over 100 tackles every single season that he has been in the league.

Speed	80
Tackling	88
Pursuit	90
Play Recog.	90

Player Weapon: Smart Linebacker

#23 Patrick Surtain *Cornerback (CB)*

▼ DEFENSIVE **STAR PLAYER**

Surtain was known as a shutdown corner for years. Now Surtain is getting slower, but still does a decent job of containing the deep pass. This 11-year vet made 58 tackles last season with 2 interceptions. Even though he's getting older, Surtain is as solid as they come.

Speed	90
Man Cover	90
Zone Cover	90
Press	84

Player Weapon: None

#56 Derrick Johnson *Linebacker (LOLB)*

▼ DEFENSIVE **STAR PLAYER**

Johnson put in some major work last season. He had 94 tackles, 4 sacks, 3 forced fumbles, and 2 interceptions. He is an athletic OLB that plays well from side to side, stuffs the run, and creates turnovers. Johnson is a playmaker that should be featured in every play.

Speed	87
Tackling	90
Pursuit	95
Play Recog.	85

Player Weapon: None

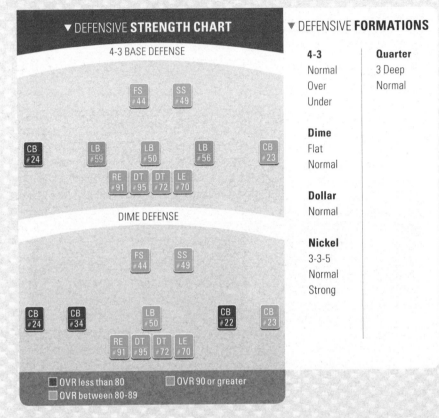

▼ DEFENSIVE **STRENGTH CHART**

4-3 BASE DEFENSE

DIME DEFENSE

☐ OVR less than 80   ☐ OVR 90 or greater
☐ OVR between 80-89

▼ DEFENSIVE **FORMATIONS**

4-3	Quarter
Normal	3 Deep
Over	Normal
Under	

Dime
Flat
Normal

Dollar
Normal

Nickel
3-3-5
Normal
Strong

▼ RECOMMENDED DEFENSIVE **AUDIBLE PACKAGES**

4-3	4-3	Nickel	Dime	Quarter
2 Man Under	Edge Sting	Cover 3	Cover 2	3 Deep Man

▼ DEFENSIVE **PLAYCOUNTS**

Man Coverage:	47	Cover 2 Zone:	14	Man Blitz:	54
Man Zone:	41	Cover 3 Zone:	28	Zone Blitz:	66
Combo Coverage:	8	Deep Zone:	19	Combo Blitz:	15

DEFENSE **KEY DEFENSIVE PLAYS**

A Mike Fire

4-3 UNDER

MIKE FIRE

1

2

3

Some of the best base defenses will have one linebacker blitzing. The Mike Fire brings the Middle linebacker to add pressure in the pass rush.

The quarterback is trying to fool the defense with play action; the linebacker has read it and continues to drop into coverage.

The offense hoped to hit the back in the flat, but the linebacker has taken that option away.

Instead, the quarterback now has to try his luck deep and the safeties almost intercept the pass on this risky throw.

A Spy 3 Blitz

4-3 NORMAL

SPY 3 BLITZ

1

2

3

Zone blitzing is an easy way to confuse an offense and create easy turnovers. The Spy 3 Blitz gives the defense a chance to do both of these things.

Cutler drops back pretty far, and in doing so, he gives the defensive end a straighter rush angle.

The ball needs to be thrown before Cutler takes a sack, so he tries to attack the sideline.

The safety has other thoughts as he steps in front of the pass and intercepts the ball, ending the drive.

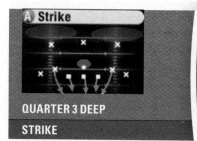

A Strike

QUARTER 3 DEEP

STRIKE

1

2

3

Bringing pressure with cornerbacks is much more of a threat to the offense than regular blitzes. The strike sends both inside corners and gets great pressure.

At the snap, both corners charge inside to blitz the quarterback. With all this speed, someone will reach the quarterback.

The problem for the offense is that with 3 outside rushers and only two blockers, someone will get free.

The corner breaks through and reaches the quarterback. He takes him down for a sack and loss of 10 yards.

TEAM STRATEGY

INDIANAPOLIS COLTS

▶ **Division** AFC South ▶ **Stadium** Lucas Oil Stadium ▶ **Type** Dome ▶ **Capacity** 63,000 ▶ **Surface** Field Turf

▼ 2007 STANDINGS

Wins	Loses	Ties	PF	PA	Home	Road	vs. AFC	vs. NFC	vs. Div
13	3	0	450	262	6-2	7-1	9-3	4-0	5-1

▼ TEAM OVERVIEW

The Colts made a nice run at the Super Bowl last season that was ended due to injuries to key players. They still have a great core and a winning formula. The key for them is that the defense improved and the offense remained steady behind the arm of Peyton Manning. The defense led the league in fewest number of points scored per game (16 points). They were also ranked 3rd in passing yards, and 15th against the run only giving up 106 yards a game. On the other side, Manning was 6th in passing yards with 252 yards a game, and 3rd in scoring with 28 points a game. The Colts did well in the rushing department with 166 yards a game. It's easy to guess what they will focus on once everyone has returned and is healthy.

▼ OFF-SEASON UPGRADES

TYPE	ROUND	FIRST NAME	LAST NAME	SCHOOL/TEAM	POSITION
Free Agent	N/A	Dominic	Rhodes	Raiders	RB
Draft	2	Mike	Pollack	Arizona State	G
Draft	3	Philip	Wheeler	Georgia Tech	LB
Draft	4	Jacob	Tamme	Kentucky	TE
Draft	5	Marcus	Howard	Georgia	LB

▼ SCOUTING REPORT

	DESCRIPTION	MAXIMIZING POTENTIAL	TIPS FOR OPPONENTS
STRENGTHS	Peyton Manning is clearly one of the best quarterbacks in the league.	The Colts have plenty of weapons. Share the wealth to prevent tendencies.	Mix up your coverages and where you send the heat.
STRENGTHS	Dwight Freeney is a pass-rushing animal, and every offensive lineman's nightmare.	Use stunts and send overload blitzes to free him up.	Stay away from him at all costs. Use slide protection and roll outs.
WEAKNESSES	Harrison isn't the wideout he once was after his injury from last season.	Put him in the slot so he can abuse weaker defenders.	Sit on him with an extra defender within your defensive scheme.
WEAKNESSES	The linebacking corps is fast, but aren't great at defending, so exploit them.	Use them in pass rushing situations and man coverage schemes.	Use play action passes and misdirection plays to get them out of position.

TEAM STRATEGY

FRANCHISE MODE STRATEGY

The Colts are pretty solid in all facets of the game. We would recommend looking for another runner to back up Addai. On defense, a shutdown corner would be a nice addition.

KEY FRANCHISE INFORMATION

Cap Room: $19.7M
Key Rivals:
- Jaguars, Patriots, Titans

Philosophy:
- Offense: Multiple
- Defense: 4-3, Cover 2

Highest Paid Players:
- P. Manning
- D. Freeney

Team Weapons:
- P. Manning – Smart QB
- B. Sanders – Big Hitter

Best Young Players:
- A. Bethea
- T. Ugoh

95	96	93
OVERALL	OFFENSE	DEFENSE

▼ ROSTER AND **PACKAGE TIPS**

KEY PLAYER SUBSTITUTIONS

Position: Slot
Substitution: Dallas Clark
When: Passing Situations
Advantage: Dallas Clark is a very effective receiver in the slot. His ability to make clutch catches can't be overlooked. With him in the slot, he can be motioned inside as a run blocker.

Position: WR4
Substitution: Dallas Clark
When: Global
Advantage: This sub follows along the same lines as the previous one. The only difference is that if we put him in the number four spot on the depth chart, he will line up in the slot on the right four wide sets; plus, we save our package option for another receiver.

Position: WR5
Substitution: Joseph Addai
When: Global
Advantage: When you look at the Colts' number five receiver, you will notice that Addai is just as good, if not better. If we sub him in, it means we don't have to package him and we still package in another receiver somewhere else in a 5WR formation.

Peyton Manning will be pointing the Colts toward another Super Bowl appearance in 2008.

TEAM STRATEGY

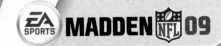
TEAM STRATEGY

#18 Peyton Manning *Quarterback (QB)*

▼ OFFENSIVE **STAR PLAYER**

Where should we start? Manning is one of the best quarterbacks in the league. No one put in the time and work that he has all year long. Peyton Manning is a master in his craft, and strives for perfection every time he is on the field.

Speed	59
Awareness	100
Throwing Power	96
Throwing Accuracy	99

Player Weapons: Smart Quarterback, Accurate Quarterback, Cannon Arm Quarterback

#88 Marvin Harrison *Wide Receiver (WR)*

▼ OFFENSIVE **STAR PLAYER**

Harrison has been called one of the best route runners in the NFL. He and Manning are one of the best passing combos in the league. Last season, he was plagued with an injury. This season, expect him to get back to hooking up with Manning.

Speed	92
Catch	97
Catch Traffic	91
Route Run	99

Player Weapons: Quick Receiver, Possession Receiver, Hands

#87 Reggie Wayne *Wide Receiver (WR)*

▼ OFFENSIVE **STAR PLAYER**

Wayne has become a great wideout in the NFL. He stepped up big last season and has been consistent for the past 3 seasons (with over 1,000 yards). Wayne pulled down 104 receptions, 1,510 yards in receptions, and 10 touchdowns. With Marvin back, expect the same production.

Speed	91
Catch	97
Catch Traffic	94
Route Run	97

Player Weapons: Quick Receiver, Possession Receiver, Hands

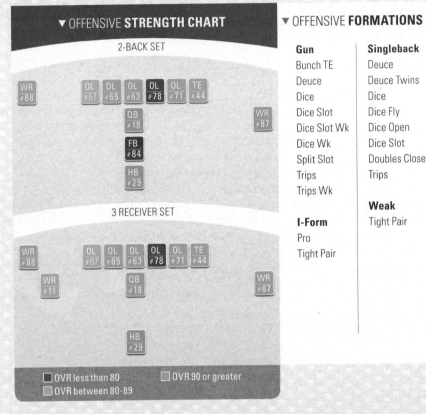

▼ OFFENSIVE **STRENGTH CHART**

2-BACK SET

WR #88 | OL #67 | OL #65 | OL #63 | OL #78 | OL #71 | TE #44 | WR #87
QB #18
FB #84
HB #29

3 RECEIVER SET

WR #88 | OL #67 | OL #65 | OL #63 | OL #78 | OL #71 | TE #44 | WR #87
WR #11 | QB #18
HB #29

☐ OVR less than 80   ☐ OVR 90 or greater
☐ OVR between 80-89

▼ OFFENSIVE **FORMATIONS**

Gun	**Singleback**
Bunch TE	Deuce
Deuce	Deuce Twins
Dice	Dice
Dice Slot	Dice Fly
Dice Slot Wk	Dice Open
Dice Wk	Dice Slot
Split Slot	Doubles Close
Trips	Trips
Trips Wk	
	Weak
I-Form	Tight Pair
Pro	
Tight Pair	

▼ RECOMMENDED OFFENSIVE **AUDIBLE PACKAGES**

Singleback	Singleback	Singleback	Gun	Gun
Stretch	Slants	Blunt Drive	Y Shallow Cross	WR Deep Hook

▼ OFFENSIVE **PLAYCOUNTS**

Quick Pass:	11	Screen Pass:	17	Pitch:	4
Standard Pass:	63	Hail Mary:	1	Counter:	8
Shotgun Pass:	78	Inside Handoff:	23	Draw:	17
Play Action Pass:	63	Outside Handoff:	26		

OFFENSE **KEY OFFENSIVE PLAYS**

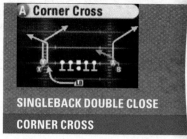

A Corner Cross

SINGLEBACK DOUBLE CLOSE

CORNER CROSS

Sometimes on offense it is possible to beat the defense just by the alignment of the receivers. The Double Close gives the Colts' receiver a great advantage versus any defense.

Marvin Harrison looks to run inside to take advantage of the vacant middle of the defense.

Once he sells the inside route, Harrison turns outside on the corner portion of the route.

After separating from the defender, Harrison has picked up a first down on the completion.

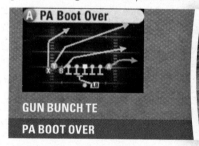

A PA Boot Over

GUN BUNCH TE

PA BOOT OVER

Peyton Manning has made a name for himself over the years as being the best play action quarterback in all of football. Use this play to take advantage of that ability.

Manning fakes the hand-off, and in doing so, freezes the defense. This spells trouble for the defense.

After getting the defense to freeze for a second, Manning has open crossing routes by both inside receivers.

Gonzalez makes the catch after turning up the field, and beats the defense for a first down.

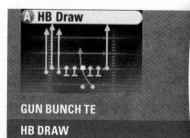

A HB Draw

GUN BUNCH TE

HB DRAW

Manning is so much of a threat with play action that the Colts can easily beat the defense with a good HB Draw.

When the play starts, the defense has to decide if this is a play action or a true run.

Addai sees the hole and gets in it quickly. This is exactly how the draw should work.

He is picking up tough yards as he churns his way through the middle of the defense.

TEAM STRATEGY

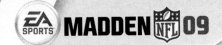

TEAM STRATEGY

#21 Bob Sanders *Safety (SS)*

▼ DEFENSIVE STAR PLAYER

Bob Sanders is now listed as one of the best safeties in the game. He is the leader of the defense when he is on the field. Sanders is a playmaker that forces turnovers, with 96 tackles, 3.5 sacks, and 2 interceptions.

Speed	93
Man Cover	80
Zone Cover	95
Hit Power	98

Player Weapons: Big Hitter, Smart Safety

#93 Dwight Freeney *Defensive End (RE)*

▼ DEFENSIVE STAR PLAYER

Dwight Freeney is a powerhouse. No one has the speed, power, and pass rushing agility in the league like Freeney. His motor runs nonstop and he gives tackles fits every single down. He was injured last season and the Colts missed his presence on the field. Be ready for his highly-anticipated return this season.

Speed	88
Strength	78
Power Moves	87
Finesse Moves	96

Player Weapon: Finesse Move D-Lineman

#98 Robert Mathis *Defensive End (LE)*

▼ DEFENSIVE STAR PLAYER

Mathis and Freeney serve as bookends on the line. We have seen that it's equally (or more) important to generate pressure with the line than with linebacker overloads. The Giants showed this, as did the Colts the year before. Mathis had gotten 7 sacks, 32 tackles, and 4 forced fumbles last season.

Speed	88
Strength	76
Power Moves	79
Finesse Moves	96

Player Weapon: Finesse Move D-Lineman

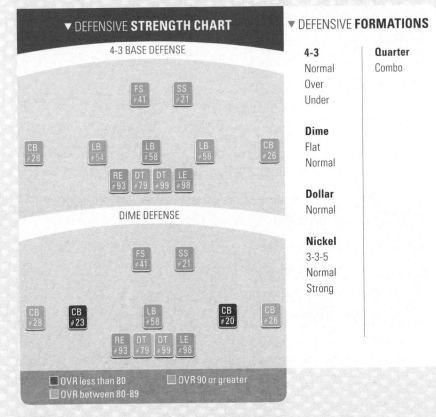

▼ DEFENSIVE **STRENGTH CHART**

4-3 BASE DEFENSE

DIME DEFENSE

☐ OVR less than 80   ☐ OVR 90 or greater
☐ OVR between 80-89

▼ DEFENSIVE **FORMATIONS**

4-3	**Quarter**
Normal	Combo
Over	
Under	

Dime
Flat
Normal

Dollar
Normal

Nickel
3-3-5
Normal
Strong

▼ RECOMMENDED DEFENSIVE **AUDIBLE PACKAGES**

4-3	4-3	Nickel	Dime	Quarter
2 Man Under	Free Fire	Cover 3	Cover 2	Man Up 3 Deep

▼ DEFENSIVE **PLAYCOUNTS**

Man Coverage:	45	Cover 2 Zone:	14	Man Blitz:	55
Man Zone:	44	Cover 3 Zone:	26	Zone Blitz:	64
Combo Coverage:	7	Deep Zone:	18	Combo Blitz:	13

DEFENSE KEY DEFENSIVE PLAYS

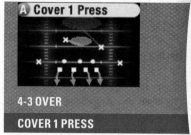

Ⓐ Cover 1 Press

4-3 OVER

COVER 1 PRESS

Run defense is extremely important. If a team can't stop the run, then play action passing will kill the defense. Look to the Cover 1 Press to handle the run.

When the offense starts the play, the linebackers are reading run and scraping down the line.

Taylor is trying to get to the edge but he sees that we have a sea of blue jerseys in pursuit.

As soon as the back crosses the line, the pursuing cornerback jumps on him and wraps him up for a short gain.

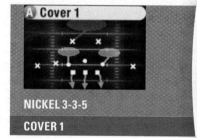

Ⓐ Cover 1

NICKEL 3-3-5

COVER 1

The Nickel 3-3-5 has one of the best Cover 1 defenses in all of *Madden*. This defense will make shallow routes hard to complete.

Both outside linebackers drop back into curl zones at the snap. Use this to take away routes on the seams.

The quarterback doesn't have any wide open routes, so he will try for the out route by the tight end.

When the ball reaches the tight end, so does the defense. They crush the receiver and prevent any extra gain on the play.

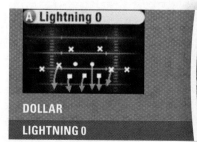

Ⓐ Lightning 0

DOLLAR

LIGHTNING 0

The Colts have one of the fastest defenses in the NFL. Take advantage of this wealth of speed and use the Lightning 0 to swarm the offense.

While the quarterback is taking his drop steps, the defense already has two defenders charging in clean.

The quarterback has to get rid of the ball quickly, but the defense still has coverage for hot reads.

The ball gets to the back but the linebacker is right on top of him, preventing a first down.

TEAM STRATEGY

115

DALLAS COWBOYS

▶ **Division** NFC East	▶ **Stadium** Texas Stadium	▶ **Type** Partial Dome	▶ **Capacity** 65,595	▶ **Surface** Texas Turf

▼ 2007 STANDINGS

Wins	Loses	Ties	PF	PA	Home	Road	vs. AFC	vs. NFC	vs. Div
13	3	0	455	325	6-2	7-1	3-1	10-2	4-2

▼ TEAM OVERVIEW

The Cowboys had a great season last year. They were one of the teams listed to go to the Super Bowl. The Dallas Cowboys were ranked 3rd in the league with 365.7 total yards offensively. They threw for 256 (3rd) and ran for 109 yards a game (17th). They scored a total of 28 points a game, which placed them 2nd in the league. On the defensive side of the ball, they were listed at 18th, giving up 20 points a game. Then they gave up a total of 307 yards per game which was 9th overall in the league. When you look at the yards, you see they gave up 213 in the air (13th) and only 94 yards on the ground (6th). Expect the same in 2009.

▼ OFF-SEASON UPGRADES

TYPE	ROUND	FIRST NAME	LAST NAME	SCHOOL/TEAM	POSITION
Trade	N/A	Adam	Jones	Titans	CB
Free Agent	N/A	Zach	Thomas	Dolphins	LB
Draft	1	Felix	Jones	Arkansas	RB
Draft	1	Mike	Jenkins	South Florida	CB
Draft	2	Martellus	Bennett	Texas A&M	TE

▼ SCOUTING REPORT

	DESCRIPTION	MAXIMIZING POTENTIAL	TIPS FOR OPPONENTS
STRENGTHS	Tony Romo is one of the more mobile QBs in the game and is able make things happen with his feet as well as his arm.	Use his mobility to take off and run when nothing opens down the field.	Be sure to have at least one defender in QB Spy if Romo takes off to run.
STRENGTHS	Marion Barber is one of the better power runners in the game and knows how to score inside the red zone.	Anytime you are near the goal line, use Barber to pound the ball in for an easy six points.	Put as many defenders in the box near the goal line to keep Barber out of the end zone.
WEAKNESSES	The Cowboys have only one legit home run hitter at receiver who can put fear in the defense: Terrell Owens.	Send Terrell Owens on deep passing routes to clear out room underneath for other Cowboy receivers.	Double up Terrell Owens and force Tony Romo to find other receivers.
WEAKNESSES	Roy Williams is the best in run support, but not strong against the pass because he doesn't have great coverage skills.	Have Williams play up in the box to defend the run. In passing situations, consider subbing him out.	If Williams is on the field, look to attack him with vertical pass route combos.

TEAM STRATEGY

FRANCHISE MODE STRATEGY

The Cowboys are stacked on both sides of the ball. Your main priority should be to create depth for the long term. Zach Thomas still has plenty of gas in the tank, but you will need a replacement eventually.

KEY FRANCHISE INFORMATION

Cap Room: $4.02M
Key Rivals:
- Eagles, Giants, Redskins, Texans

Philosophy:
- Offense: Multiple
- Defense: 3-4

Highest Paid Players:
- T. Romo
- T. Newman

Team Weapons:
- T. Owens – Possession Receiver
- D. Ware – Finess Move D-Lineman

Best Young Players:
- N. Folk
- M. Jenkins

96	96	93
OVERALL	OFFENSE	DEFENSE

▼ ROSTER AND **PACKAGE TIPS**

KEY PLAYER SUBSTITUTIONS

Position: HB

Substitution: Felix Jones

When: Passing Situations

Advantage: As far as catch ratings go, Marion Barber and Felix Jones are separated by only a few points. We like to have Jones in passing situations as our running back because of his speed.

Position: WR

Substitution: Terry Glenn

When: Global

Advantage: In *Madden,* Glenn is still a good receiver and should be the Cowboys' number 2 receiver. Patrick Crayton is a good receiver, but for now, he would be better served as the Cowboys' number 3 receiver for one more season.

Position: CB

Substitution: Mike Jenkins

When: Global

Advantage: This move depends on whether Pacman Jones is on the Cowboys' opening day roster or not. If he is, then he should be the number two cornerback. If he is not, then Mike Jenkins should be number 2, while Anthony Henry moves to nickelback.

Terrell Owens and the Cowboys will fly high in 2008 if the star-studded team with many strong personalities can jell together as a unit.

TEAM STRATEGY

TEAM STRATEGY

#81 Terrell Owens *Wide Receiver (WR)*

▼ OFFENSIVE **STAR PLAYER**

T.O. is one of the most consistent wideouts in the league, hands down. This man had 81 receptions, 1,355 yards, and 15 touchdowns. No one can guard him one-on-one; he also runs outstanding routes and reads coverages extremely well. Love him or hate him, he is a beast.

Speed	96
Catch	89
Catch Traffic	97
Route Run	96

Player Weapon: Quick Receiver, Possession Receiver, Speed

#82 Jason Witten *Tight End (TE)*

▼ OFFENSIVE **STAR PLAYER**

Witten is a top ten TE every year. He blocks well, runs routes, and has excellent hands. Witten is in the Pro Bowl almost every season, and led the team in receptions last season with 96. He also had 1,145 yards and 7 touchdowns. He last missed a start in 2003.

Speed	84
Catch	85
Run Block	59
Pass Block	52

Player Weapons: Quick Receiver, Possession Receiver

#9 Tony Romo *Quarterback (QB)*

▼ OFFENSIVE **STAR PLAYER**

Romo is reminiscent of a young Brett Favre. When he plays, he looks as comfortable as if he were in his backyard playing pitch and catch. He has an arm, and his mobility allows him to buy time to make plays. He threw for 4,211 yards with 36 touchdowns.

Speed	78
Awareness	80
Throwing Power	90
Throwing Accuracy	96

Player Weapon: Accurate Quarterback

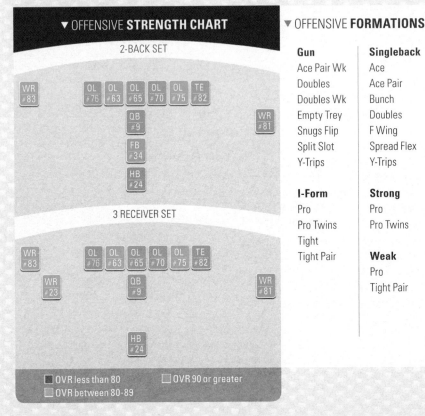

▼ OFFENSIVE **FORMATIONS**

Gun	Singleback
Ace Pair Wk	Ace
Doubles	Ace Pair
Doubles Wk	Bunch
Empty Trey	Doubles
Snugs Flip	F Wing
Split Slot	Spread Flex
Y-Trips	Y-Trips

I-Form	Strong
Pro	Pro
Pro Twins	Pro Twins
Tight	
Tight Pair	**Weak**
	Pro
	Tight Pair

▼ RECOMMENDED OFFENSIVE **AUDIBLE PACKAGES**

I-Form	Singleback	Singleback	Singleback	Gun
Iso Weak	Quick Slants	HB Dive	TE Post	WR In

▼ OFFENSIVE **PLAYCOUNTS**

Quick Pass:	22	Screen Pass:	12	Pitch:	9
Standard Pass:	80	Hail Mary:	1	Counter:	9
Shotgun Pass:	63	Inside Handoff:	33	Draw:	11
Play Action Pass:	62	Outside Handoff:	17		

OFFENSE KEY OFFENSIVE PLAYS

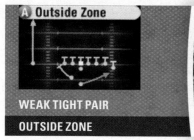

WEAK TIGHT PAIR

OUTSIDE ZONE

Marion Barber has proven that the run needs to be a part of the game plan when using the Cowboys. He is versatile, and is able to run inside and outside.

A running back is only as good as his blocking, and right away the O-line shows Barber the way to success.

Barber shows that setting up blocks is also a key to being considered a solid running back.

He fakes outside and then cuts inside to pick up key yards and a first down on the play.

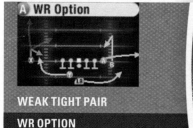

WEAK TIGHT PAIR

WR OPTION

Having success in the running game will make it that much easier to attack the defense in the passing game. Use the WR Option and T.O. to do this.

T.O. comes to the line, looks over the defense and sees that once he passes the corner it's over.

Romo laughs at 1-on-1 coverage against T.O. and delivers the ball as soon as he beats the press coverage.

T.O.'s speed, size and awareness are too much for the defense when he runs an option route.

GUN SPLIT SLOT

CROSS WEAK FLOOD

Cover 2 is going to be a thorn in many offenses' sides in *Madden NFL 09*. The Cross Weak Flood will help keep the chains moving and keep the offense from stalling on key drives.

As soon as the play starts, Romo reads the safeties and identifies them as being in Cover 2 Zone.

He has Crayton open over the middle and T.O showing open down field, but there is pressure from the defense.

The ball is dumped off to Crayton running over the middle and he cuts it up for a nice gain.

TEAM STRATEGY

TEAM STRATEGY

#94 Demarcus Ware *Linebacker (ROLB)*

▼ DEFENSIVE **STAR PLAYER**

Originally one of Parcell's picks, Ware is an animal. He gives tackles fits on the pass rush, and also plays the run well. Last season he had 84 tackles, 14 sacks, and caused 4 forced fumbles. He is the perfect player for the 3-4 scheme.

Speed	87
Tackling	94
Pursuit	99
Play Recog.	84

Player Weapons: Big Hitter, Brick Wall Defender

#55 Zach Thomas *Linebacker (MLB)*

▼ DEFENSIVE **STAR PLAYER**

Thomas has been a steady player throughout his career. He isn't the player he was before, but he is perfect for the 3-4 scheme they run in Dallas. What he brings to the Cowboys is leadership. He plays the run well and is always in position to make plays.

Speed	76
Tackling	97
Pursuit	95
Play Recog.	97

Player Weapons: Brick Wall Defender, Smart Linebacker

#41 Terence Newman *Cornerback (CB)*

▼ DEFENSIVE **STAR PLAYER**

The pass was a weakness of the Cowboys. The one corner that played well was Newman. He is a shutdown corner that has great speed and can make plays. Now with Jones on the other side, Newman may be able to improve on his 4 interceptions in 2007.

Speed	97
Man Cover	96
Zone Cover	90
Press	80

Player Weapon: Shutdown Corner, Speed

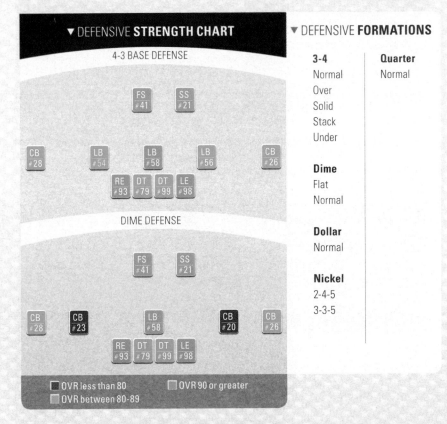

▼ DEFENSIVE **STRENGTH CHART**

4-3 BASE DEFENSE

FS #41 SS #21

CB #28 LB #54 LB #58 LB #56 CB #26

RE #93 DT #79 DT #99 LE #98

DIME DEFENSE

FS #41 SS #21

CB #28 CB #23 LB #58 CB #20 CB #26

RE #93 DT #79 DT #99 LE #98

☐ OVR less than 80 ☐ OVR 90 or greater
☐ OVR between 80-89

▼ DEFENSIVE **FORMATIONS**

3-4	Quarter
Normal	Normal
Over	
Solid	
Stack	
Under	

Dime
Flat
Normal

Dollar
Normal

Nickel
2-4-5
3-3-5

▼ RECOMMENDED DEFENSIVE **AUDIBLE PACKAGES**

3-4	3-4	Nickel	Dime	Quarter
2 Man Under	Sting Pinch	Cover 3	Cover 2 Buc	3 Deep Man

▼ DEFENSIVE **PLAYCOUNTS**

Man Coverage:	44	Cover 2 Zone:	23	Man Blitz:	55
Man Zone:	40	Cover 3 Zone:	26	Zone Blitz:	57
Combo Coverage:	6	Deep Zone:	14	Combo Blitz:	6

DEFENSE **KEY DEFENSIVE PLAYS**

TEAM STRATEGY

A MLB Blitz

3-4 UNDER

MLB BLITZ

It's no secret that the Cowboys have one of the best and most athletic line backing corps in the NFL. The MLB Blitz is a play that handles the run and pass well.

While Jason Campbell is turning to give the play action fake, Zach Thomas is blitzing the "A" gap.

Chris Canty and Bradi James are coming around the blind side of the quarterback to bring the pain.

Canty reaches Campbell and throws him to the turf for a sack, and loss of 9-yards on the play.

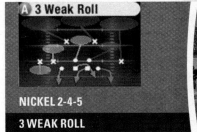

A 3 Weak Roll

NICKEL 2-4-5

3 WEAK ROLL

The 3 Weak Roll is a defense of choice because not only is it great versus the pass, but it can really throw a quarterback off with the different coverages to either side.

As the receivers start their routes, Zach Thomas is dropping back and reading the routes of both receivers.

The flanker is going to try and break inside while the slot heads out. Zach just sits and plays the quarterback's eyes.

Zach Thomas steps in front of the ball and picks off the pass. The 3 Weak Roll is a turnover creator.

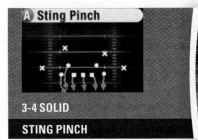

A Sting Pinch

3-4 SOLID

STING PINCH

One of the best ways to play the run is to make sure opponents don't get to the outside. The defense can always drop a safety in the box to handle the inside run.

Demarcus Ware shoots in off of the edge and immediately gets the fullback's attention.

He takes the fullback outside, before cutting underneath him to attack the running back.

Clinton Portis is a great running back, but when Demarcus Ware puts his hands on you, you're going down.

MIAMI DOLPHINS

▶ **Division** AFC East ▶ **Stadium** Dolphin Stadium ▶ **Type** Open ▶ **Capacity** 74,916 ▶ **Surface** Grass

▼ 2007 STANDINGS

Wins	Loses	Ties	PF	PA	Home	Road	vs. AFC	vs. NFC	vs. Div
1	15	0	267	437	1-7	0-8	1-11	0-4	0-6

▼ TEAM OVERVIEW

Miami has been going down since they lost Ricky Williams a few years ago. Many coaching changes and aging players have hurt the Dolphins. Now that they have Parcells in charge, things are looking up. He has always left teams in a better position than they were before he got there. He gets the most out of players and has an excellent eye for talent. The Dolphins were almost dead last in every single category on both sides of the ball. They did play the pass well by only giving up 188 yards in the air. The main problem was the weak offense. They only scored 16 points a game, which was 26th in the league. They averaged 189 yards in the air and 98 yards on the ground. In order to improve the defense, they need to be able to sustain drives to allow the defense to rest.

▼ OFF-SEASON UPGRADES

TYPE	ROUND	FIRST NAME	LAST NAME	SCHOOL/TEAM	POSITION
Trade	N/A	Jason	Ferguson	Cowboys	NT
Free Agent	N/A	Josh	McCown	Raiders	QB
Free Agent	N/A	Randy	Starks	Titans	DT
Draft	1	Jake	Long	Michigan	T
Draft	2	Phillip	Merling	Clemson	DE

▼ SCOUTING REPORT

	DESCRIPTION	MAXIMIZING POTENTIAL	TIPS FOR OPPONENTS
STRENGTHS	Ronnie Brown is a solid back that can be a handful when healthy.	Feed him the ball and use packages to move him around.	Play the run until they show you they can establish the pass.
	Jason Taylor is a Hall of Fame defensive end that generates good pressure outside.	He can play linebacker as well as defensive end.	Make sure you send extra help to take him out and use slide protection.
WEAKNESSES	The QB situation is awful. They were listed almost last in passing.	You need to run the ball to open up the pass.	Send pressure often to create turnovers. Make them show you they can pass.
	The best defensive players they have are Taylor and Porter; exploit this weakness.	Use Taylor and Porter in pass rushing packages.	Run a well-balanced attack to keep them on their toes. They don't have many playmakers.

TEAM STRATEGY

FRANCHISE MODE STRATEGY

The Dolphins have multiple young QBs, but a veteran back-up might be a good idea. Consider dealing Jason Taylor for numerous players and/or draft picks. You have a lot of work to do here.

KEY FRANCHISE INFORMATION

Cap Room: $15.92M

Key Rivals:
- Bills, Jets, Patriots

Philosophy:
- Offense: Run with Play Action
- Defense: 3-4

Highest Paid Players:
- J. Long
- J. Taylor

Team Weapons:
- J. Taylor – Finesse Move D-Lineman
- R. Brown – Power Back

Best Young Players:
- S. Satele
- J. Long

67	64	68
OVERALL	OFFENSE	DEFENSE

▼ ROSTER AND **PACKAGE TIPS**

KEY PLAYER SUBSTITUTIONS

Position: FB
Substitution: Ricky Williams
When: Situational
Advantage: We guarantee that if you play in an online league game, someone will move Ricky Williams to fullback at some point. He still has enough in the tank to be an effective ball carrier, especially when a fullback dive play is called.

Position: LE
Substitution: Phillip Merling
When: Global
Advantage: The sub is made to give the Dolphins another pass rusher at the defensive end position. Matt Roth is better off being moved inside where he can push the pocket. Having Merling at LE gives the Dolphins a rock solid one-two punch.

Position: CB
Substitution: Andre' Goodman
When: Global
Advantage: With a 93 speed rating, Andre' Goodman is more than capable of covering most of the slot receivers in the game. That's why we suggest moving him to the number 3 spot, so he can play nickelback and be on the field more.

Ronnie Brown and the Dolphins have nowhere to go but up, and under the guidance of the Big Tuna, the fish won't flounder as much in 2008.

TEAM STRATEGY

TEAM STRATEGY

#79 Jake Long *Tackle (LT)*

▼ OFFENSIVE **STAR PLAYER**

This is the number one pick this season for the Dolphins. When you rebuild, you want to make sure you have a solid line. Jake Long was listed as one of the best coming out this season. He has great size, good movement, seals off well, and punishes pass rushers.

Run Block Strength	95
Run Block Footwork	88
Pass Block Strength	92
Pass Block Footwork	77

Player Weapon: Crushing Run Blocker

#23 Ronnie Brown *Halfback (HB)*

▼ OFFENSIVE **STAR PLAYER**

Brown is a decent back that has all of the tools needed for success in the NFL. Parcells loves big backs that run hard. Brown was having a good season until he got injured. He had 602 yards, 119 carries, and 4 touchdowns in 7 starts.

Speed	91
Agility	91
Trucking	94
Elusiveness	84

Player Weapon: Power Back

#19 Ted Ginn *Wide Receiver (WR)*

▼ OFFENSIVE **STAR PLAYER**

Ted was the first round pick from last year that the team had great hopes for. He only had 420 yards receiving and 2 touchdowns. He is the best wideout they have and he has plenty of upside. His speed and agility makes him a threat to score at any time.

Speed	98
Catch	82
Catch Traffic	74
Route Run	83

Player Weapon: Speed

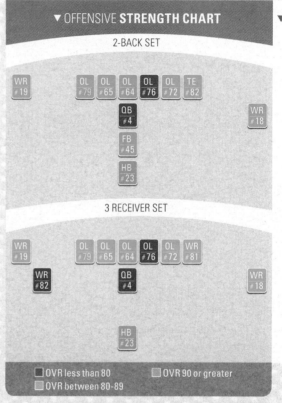

▼ OFFENSIVE **STRENGTH CHART**

2-BACK SET

WR #19 | OL #79 | OL #65 | OL #64 | OL #76 | OL #72 | TE #82 | WR #18
QB #4
FB #45
HB #23

3 RECEIVER SET

WR #19 | OL #79 | OL #65 | OL #64 | OL #76 | OL #72 | WR #81 | WR #18
WR #82 | QB #4
HB #23

☐ OVR less than 80   ☐ OVR 90 or greater
☐ OVR between 80-89

▼ OFFENSIVE **FORMATIONS**

Gun	Singleback
Wk	Ace
Doubles	Ace Pair
Doubles Wk	Bunch
Empty Trey	Doubles
Split Slot	F Wing
Y-Trips	Spread Flex
	Y-Trips
I-Form	
Pro	**Strong**
Pro Twins	Pro
Tight	Pro Twins
Tight Pair	
	Weak
	Pro
	Slot
	Tight Pair

▼ RECOMMENDED OFFENSIVE **AUDIBLE PACKAGES**

Singleback	I-Form	I-Form	Gun	Gun
HB Slam	Quick Slants	Power O	Strong Flood	Smash

▼ OFFENSIVE **PLAYCOUNTS**

Quick Pass:	23	Screen Pass:	12	Pitch:	9
Standard Pass:	85	Hail Mary:	1	Counter:	9
Shotgun Pass:	58	Inside Handoff:	34	Draw:	11
Play Action Pass:	63	Outside Handoff:	16		

OFFENSE **KEY OFFENSIVE PLAYS**

A Power O

SINGLEBACK F WING

POWER O

Ronnie Brown of the Dolphins is a good running back. Use the Power O and the auto motion in it, to help him shred the defense for big yards.

The backside guard will pull around the right side to add some blocking. Brown also has the FB as a blocker.

Brown has the ball with room to breathe. Now he has to set up his blocks to get the maximum gain.

Brown picks up the block from the fullback and then has all the running room he needs down the sideline.

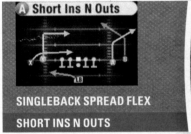

A Short Ins N Outs

SINGLEBACK SPREAD FLEX

SHORT INS N OUTS

Sometimes the best way to attack zone coverage is by trying to stretch it to the limit. The Spread Flex Ins N Outs gives the offense a way to attack zone coverage.

The safety and linebacker both drop to the middle of the field, letting the quarterback know to attack the seam.

The slot receiver has a lot of room to roam because of the way the safety and linebacker dropped into coverage.

The quarterback puts the ball perfectly on the spot and gives him a chance to pick up yards after the catch.

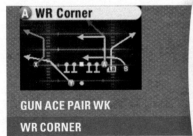

A WR Corner

GUN ACE PAIR WK

WR CORNER

Attack the defense with plays that will always give the offense an advantage. The WR Corner uses routes that attack the defense in multiple areas and are sure to get open.

At the snap both tight ends run up field to move the linebackers out of the way so that the flanker can run underneath.

With the void that the tight ends created by running off the linebackers, Ginn is wide open.

Ginn is already fast enough to beat defenders by himself, but by working off other routes he is more effective.

TEAM STRATEGY

TEAM STRATEGY

#99 Jason Taylor *Defensive End (RE)*

▼ DEFENSIVE **STAR PLAYER**

Taylor is the face of Miami, and one of the best pass rushers in the league. He had a great season (his 12th). He had 56 tackles, 11 sacks, 4 forced fumbles, and 1 interception, and hasn't missed a start since 1999.

Speed	85
Strength	77
Power Moves	75
Finesse Moves	96

Player Weapon: Finesse Move D-Lineman

#55 Joey Porter *Linebacker (ROLB)*

▼ DEFENSIVE **STAR PLAYER**

Joey was once one of the best OLBs in the game. Injuries and age have taken a toll on him, but he is still a great player. He had 65 tackles, 5 sacks, 1 forced fumble, and 2 interceptions. When he is healthy he can still bring it.

Speed	82
Tackling	91
Pursuit	92
Play Recog.	80

Player Weapons: Big Hitter, Brick Wall Defender

#91 Vonnie Holliday *Defensive Tackle (DT)*

▼ DEFENSIVE **STAR PLAYER**

Holliday was brought in to help with the pass rush. Holliday didn't have a great season last year, but he is still a useful pass rusher. He plays the run well, and can still get at the QB. He had only 2 sacks, 56 tackles, and one forced fumble.

Speed	63
Strength	86
Power Moves	86
Finesse Moves	74

Player Weapon: None

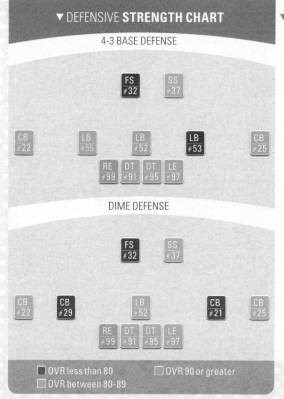

▼ RECOMMENDED DEFENSIVE **AUDIBLE PACKAGES**

4-3	4-3	Nickel	Dime	Quarter
2 Man Under	Fire Man	Cover 3	Cover 2	Man Up 3 Deep

▼ DEFENSIVE **PLAYCOUNTS**

Man Coverage:	45	Cover 2 Zone:	14	Man Blitz:	55
Man Zone:	34	Cover 3 Zone:	26	Zone Blitz:	64
Combo Coverage:	7	Deep Zone:	18	Combo Blitz:	13

DEFENSE **KEY DEFENSIVE PLAYS**

A Zone Blitz

4-3 UNDER

ZONE BLITZ

Zone Blitz schemes have been used to stop the run, such as the 4-3 Under Zone Blitz from the Dolphins defensive play.

Both the left outside linebacker and middle linebacker are sent in on a blitz.

The strong side defensive tackle will throw the offensive linemen's blocking off by dropping back in a zone.

If the offense tries to run towards their side, one of them will be in position to make the tackle.

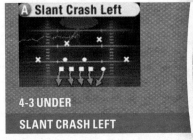

A Slant Crash Left

4-3 UNDER

SLANT CRASH LEFT

The 4-3 Under Slant Left is a good defense to call against play action because the defensive line is crashing towards the left side of the defensive line.

The right end is generally left unblocked and goes straight after the quarterback if he doesn't bite on the play fake.

The Jets quarterback tries to roll out after the fake and avoid being sacked.

The problem for the quarterback is the right end doesn't bite on the play fake.

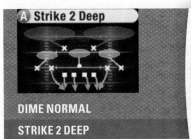

A Strike 2 Deep

DIME NORMAL

STRIKE 2 DEEP

The Dolphins have to be creative with their blitz schemes because the defense as a whole is not very strong. A creative zone defense to call is Dime Normal Strike 2 Deep.

This zone blitz sends the inside defensive backs in on blitzes from both sides of the field.

In most cases, the quarterback won't have much time to look deep down the field.

The quarterback is unable to get rid of the ball and the result is a date with the grass.

TEAM STRATEGY

PHILADELPHIA EAGLES

▶ **Division** NFC East   ▶ **Stadium** Lincoln Financial Field   ▶ **Type** Open   ▶ **Capacity** 67,594   ▶ **Surface** Grass

TEAM STRATEGY

FRANCHISE MODE STRATEGY

The offense is solid with no gaping holes. Focus your attention on acquiring an experienced MLB. The secondary is the strongest unit on the field, but sooner or later Dawkins is going to slow down. Be prepared.

KEY FRANCHISE INFORMATION

Cap Room: $22.79M

Key Rivals:
- Cowboys, Giants, Redskins

Philosophy:
- Offense: West Coast
- Defense: 4-3

Highest Paid Players:
- D. McNabb
- A. Samuel

Team Weapons:
- B. Westbrook – Elusive Back
- A. Samuel – Shutdown Corner

Best Young Players:
- O. Gaither
- C. Gocong

▼ 2007 STANDINGS

Wins	Loses	Ties	PF	PA	Home	Road	vs. AFC	vs. NFC	vs. Div
8	8	0	336	300	3-5	5-3	3-1	5-7	2-4

▼ TEAM OVERVIEW

The Eagles make a run for the Super Bowl every season. Unfortunately, they have struggled since their last Super Bowl appearance. The Eagles have troubles with retaining players and keeping them healthy (especially as they are getting older). This season, some changes have been made and they have worked the market. McNabb is coming back, and seems ready to show he still has what it takes to lead this team to the Super Bowl. The Eagles scored 21 points a game, threw for 234 yards (16th), and ran for 123 yards a game (8th). On the other side, they allowed only 18 points a game, 215 yards in the air (18th), and 95 yards on the ground. Now they have made moves to improve the pass defense with Samuel and getting Dawkins back.

▼ OFF-SEASON UPGRADES

TYPE	ROUND	FIRST NAME	LAST NAME	SCHOOL/TEAM	POSITION
Trade	N/A	Lorenzo	Booker	Dolphins	RB
Free Agent	N/A	Chris	Clemons	Raiders	DE
Free Agent	N/A	Asante	Samuel	Patriots	CB
Draft	2	Tevor	Laws	Notre Dame	DT
Draft	2	DeSean	Jackson	California	WR

▼ SCOUTING REPORT

	DESCRIPTION	MAXIMIZING POTENTIAL	TIPS FOR OPPONENTS
STRENGTHS	Westbrook is a premier back that is a big play waiting to happen.	Get the ball in his hands. He is the Eagles' offense.	Make sure you account for him and his alignment on every single play.
	Dawkins is the heart and soul of the Eagles' defense. His skills are unmatched.	Since the Eagles have good corners, you can move him around.	Don't throw in his area and look out for him on the rush.
WEAKNESSES	The Eagles have no go-to guy at the wideout position besides Westbrook.	Use Westbrook to set up easier pass coverage for wideouts.	Contain Westbrook and force them to make plays with other wideouts.
	The defensive line is weak against the run since they lost Trotter in 2006.	You need to use heavy fronts to slow down the run.	Pound the ball until they can slow it down. Then attack downfield passing.

91 OVERALL | 91 OFFENSE | 90 DEFENSE

▼ ROSTER AND **PACKAGE TIPS**

KEY PLAYER SUBSTITUTIONS

Position: HB
Substitution: Correll Buckhalter
When: Short Yardage
Advantage: As good as Brian Westbrook is, he is not a short yardage runner. Correll Buckhalter is a much bigger back, who has the power to move between the tackles and pick up the tough yardage inside.

Position: LE
Substitution: Chris Clemons
When: Global
Advantage: Juqua Parker has a higher overall than Chris Clemons, but it's only by a few points. We prefer to have Clemons in the line-up, primarily because he brings a little extra speed and is a better pass rusher.

Position: DT
Substitution: Trevor Laws
When: Long Passing Situations
Advantage: This move we make only in long pass situations. Trevor Laws is considerably faster than Brodrick Bunkley at the weak side tackle position. Laws's speed will allow him to get pressure up the middle quicker.

Brian Westbrook is one of the top three running backs in the league, and if the newly invigorated defense can hold up, the Eagles can soar again in 2008.

TEAM STRATEGY

TEAM STRATEGY

#36 Brian Westbrook *Halfback (HB)*

▼ OFFENSIVE **STAR PLAYER**

He is listed as a top 5 back. He is the prototype for the West Coast back needed to move the ball; Westbrook has hands, speed, and excellent running vision. He's hard to hit and changes direction at full speed. He had 278 carries, 1,333 yards rushing, and 7 touchdowns.

Speed	97
Agility	98
Trucking	78
Elusiveness	98

Player Weapons: Elusive Back, Speed

#73 Shawn Andrews *Guard (RG)*

▼ OFFENSIVE **STAR PLAYER**

Andrews is a steady guard that is an outstanding pass protector and opens holes for Westbrook. When he is in the game, he establishes the line from the first snap. He has been steady for some time now in the West Coast zone blocking scheme, and is the anchor of this line.

Run Block Strength	99
Run Block Footwork	79
Pass Block Strength	95
Pass Block Footwork	79

Player Weapon: Crushing Run Blocker, Pass Blocker

#5 Donovan McNabb *Quarterback (QB)*

▼ OFFENSIVE **STAR PLAYER**

McNabb is a great quarterback and was one of the best on the run. He isn't the runner he once was, but he is still hard to contain in the pocket. McNabb threw for 3,324 and had 14 touchdowns in 2007. This is a major accomplishment, considering all he had was Westbrook.

Speed	77
Awareness	83
Throw Power	95
Throwing Accuracy	85

Player Weapon: Cannon Arm Quarterback

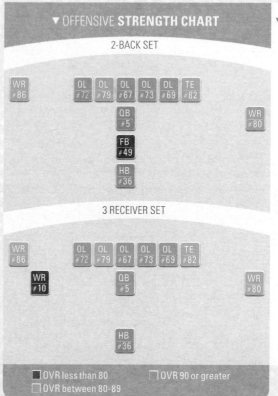

▼ OFFENSIVE **STRENGTH CHART**

2-BACK SET

WR #86 — OL #72 / OL #79 / OL #67 / OL #73 / OL #69 / TE #82 — WR #80
QB #5
FB #49
HB #36

3 RECEIVER SET

WR #86 — OL #72 / OL #79 / OL #67 / OL #73 / OL #69 / TE #82 — WR #80
WR #10 — QB #5 — WR #80
HB #36

- ■ OVR less than 80
- □ OVR 90 or greater
- □ OVR between 80–89

▼ OFFENSIVE **FORMATIONS**

Gun	Singleback
Bunch Wk	Ace Pair
Doubles	Ace Pair Twins
Snugs Flip	Bunch
Split	Double Flex
Split Y-Flex	Flex
Spread Y-Flex	Jumbo
Y-Trips Wk	Y-Trips

I-Form	Split
Pro	Slot
Pro Twins	
Slot Flex	**Strong**
Tight Pair	Pro
	Tight Pair

Weak
Pro

▼ RECOMMENDED OFFENSIVE **AUDIBLE PACKAGES**

Weak	I-Form	Singleback	Singleback	Gun
HB Gut	Quick Slants	Power O	Smash	Corner Strike

▼ OFFENSIVE **PLAYCOUNTS**

Quick Pass:	22	Screen Pass:	8	Pitch:	6
Standard Pass:	78	Hail Mary:	1	Counter:	10
Shotgun Pass:	55	Inside Handoff:	25	Draw:	13
Play Action Pass:	56	Outside Handoff:	17		

OFFENSE **KEY OFFENSIVE PLAYS**

A HB Cutback

SINGLEBACK DOUBLE FLEX

HB CUTBACK

1

2

3

This is a good run play to spread the defense out to open space up for Brian Westbrook. Use his speed to pick up yardage on the ground.

Right guard Shawn Andrews pulls to the right to become Westbrook's lead blocker.

We press down the Sprint button to shoot through the hole Andrews has opened up.

Once through the hole, we continue to hold the Sprint button to pick up more yards.

A Smash

SINGLEBACK DOUBLE FLEX

SMASH

1

1

2

3

The Smash pass concept has a receiver running a corner route, while another receiver runs a curl. This concept is very effective against Cover 2 zone.

Our first read is the flanker running the curl route. If no defenders cover him, that is where we throw the ball.

If he is covered, we then look for the slot receiver running the corner route.

We take control of the slot receiver and make the catch for a 17-yard pickup.

A X Follow

GUN SPREAD Y-FLEX

X FOLLOW

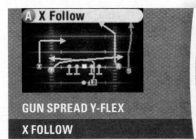
1

1

2

3

The Shotgun Spread Y-Flex X Follow has the flanker as the play's primary receiver. Another route we like is the out run by Westbrook.

Against man coverage, Westbrook is very hard to cover once he breaks to the sideline.

Notice the separation he gets on the defender covering him. This makes for an easy pitch and catch.

We make the grab and use Westbrook's speed to pick up extra yardage.

PHILADELPHIA EAGLES

TEAM STRATEGY

#22 Asante Samuel *Cornerback (CB)*

▼ DEFENSIVE STAR PLAYER

The Eagles knew that their passing defense was one of the weak spots last season. So they went out and spent the money for the best one on the market. Samuels is considered to be a speedy shutdown corner, and is a perfect fit.

Speed	93
Man Cover	94
Zone Cover	97
Press	90

Player Weapons: Smart Corner, Shutdown Corner

#26 Lito Sheppard *Cornerback (CB)*

▼ DEFENSIVE STAR PLAYER

Sheppard had been a steady corner over the years. Now with Samuel on the team, he doesn't have to line up with the best wideout every game. This move will allow Sheppard to make more plays on the ball and improve his numbers from last season.

Speed	94
Man Cover	94
Zone Cover	90
Press	82

Player Weapons: Smart Corner, Shutdown Corner

#20 Brian Dawkins *Safety (FS)*

▼ DEFENSIVE STAR PLAYER

The heart and soul of the defense, Dawkins is the leader on the field and one of the hardest hitters in the game. He has speed, great instincts, brings the wood, and is involved in every play and every down.

Speed	88
Man Cover	60
Zone Cover	85
Hit Power	94

Player Weapon: Big Hitter

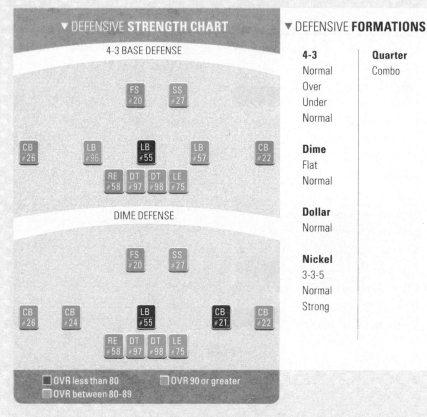

▼ DEFENSIVE STRENGTH CHART

4-3 BASE DEFENSE

FS #20 · SS #27

CB #26 · LB #96 · LB #55 · LB #57 · CB #22

RE #58 · DT #97 · DT #98 · LE #75

DIME DEFENSE

FS #20 · SS #27

CB #26 · CB #24 · LB #55 · CB #21 · CB #22

RE #58 · DT #97 · DT #98 · LE #75

☐ OVR less than 80   ☐ OVR 90 or greater
☐ OVR between 80-89

▼ DEFENSIVE FORMATIONS

4-3	Quarter
Normal	Combo
Over	
Under	
Normal	
Dime	
Flat	
Normal	
Dollar	
Normal	
Nickel	
3-3-5	
Normal	
Strong	

▼ RECOMMENDED DEFENSIVE AUDIBLE PACKAGES

4-3	4-3	Nickel	Dime	Quarter
2 Man Press	Fire Man	Cover 3	Cover 2	3 Deep Press

▼ DEFENSIVE PLAYCOUNTS

Man Coverage:	43	Cover 2 Zone:	15	Man Blitz:	56
Man Zone:	35	Cover 3 Zone:	24	Zone Blitz:	63
Combo Coverage:	8	Deep Zone:	19	Combo Blitz:	17

DEFENSE **KEY DEFENSIVE PLAYS**

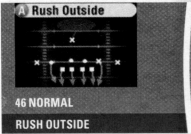

46 NORMAL

RUSH OUTSIDE

The Eagles have always been known for their aggressive defensive play calling. The 46 Normal Rush Outside is an example of a run defense they might run on a Sunday.

Strong safety Quintin Mikell is lined up near the line of scrimmage. He is sent in on an outside run blitz.

This puts him quickly into position to make a tackle on the ball carrier if he should try to run outside.

Mikell makes the tackle on Redskins running back Clinton Portis in the backfield.

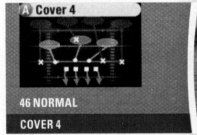

46 NORMAL

COVER 4

The 46 Normal Cover 4 gives the illusion that there may be some type of blitz called when really there is not.

With four defenders dropping back in deep zone coverage, there won't be much open deep.

The underneath coverage has three defenders dropping in zones to take away any short passes.

Once the ball is thrown up in the air, the Eagle defenders swarm quickly to the ball.

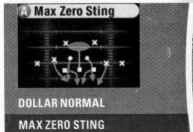

DOLLAR NORMAL

MAX ZERO STING

The Eagles love to dial up all kinds of elaborate blitz schemes to get pressure. The Max Zero Sting is a good example of one of those types of schemes.

The nose tackle drops back in a hook zone, while six defenders rush the quarterback.

At least one defender is going to shoot through a gap to get pressure on the quarterback.

With this type of heat, the quarterback won't be standing up very long.

TEAM STRATEGY

ATLANTA FALCONS

▶ **Division** NFC South ▶ **Stadium** Georgia Dome ▶ **Type** Dome ▶ **Capacity** 71,250 ▶ **Surface** Field Turf

▼ 2007 STANDINGS

Wins	Loses	Ties	PF	PA	Home	Road	vs. AFC	vs. NFC	vs. Div
4	12	0	259	414	3-5	1-7	1-3	3-9	1-5

▼ TEAM OVERVIEW

The Falcons have had a hard time getting the ship going in the right direction. They had a coach walk out on them during the season. Many changes needed to be made. On the offensive side of the ball, they were ranked 29th in points per game (16), gave up 301 yards a game (23rd), had 206 passing yards a game (18), and 96 rushing yards (26th). On the defensive side, they gave up 25 points a game (29th), 228 yards in the air (23rd), and 127 rushing yards a game (26th). The Falcons made a few changes and wanted to start off with a quarterback. Then they made some free agent moves as well.

▼ OFF-SEASON UPGRADES

TYPE	ROUND	FIRST NAME	LAST NAME	SCHOOL/TEAM	POSITION
Free Agent	N/A	Michael	Turner	Chargers	RB
Free Agent	N/A	Jason	Elam	Broncos	K
Draft	1	Matt	Ryan	Boston College	QB
Draft	1	Sam	Baker	USC	T
Draft	2	Curtis	Lofton	Oklahoma	LB

▼ SCOUTING REPORT

	DESCRIPTION	MAXIMIZING POTENTIAL	TIPS FOR OPPONENTS
STRENGTHS	Roddy White is your best option for the passing attack. Get him involved early.	Like all good weapons, move him around with different packages.	Double him and force them to pass to someone else.
	John Abraham is an animal on the line. He led the team in sacks.	To prevent double teams, use stunts to help increase sack potential.	Stay away from his side and look to see where he lines up.
WEAKNESSES	The quarterback situation is awful in Atlanta. Choose a rookie as starter this season.	You must use Turner and crew to generate a running game.	Double White and load the box. Apply pressure and mix up your coverages.
	The Falcons' defense was ranked 29th for the pass and 23rd against the run.	Use zone blitzing to get pressure and still have coverage downfield.	Using a balanced attack will keep them on their toes.

TEAM STRATEGY

FRANCHISE MODE STRATEGY

Matt Ryan is set to be the franchise QB, but he needs some new targets to throw to. Make finding a go-to deep threat receiver your number one priority. Try to choose a veteran cornerback until the youngsters find their stride.

KEY FRANCHISE INFORMATION

Cap Room: $33.72M
Key Rivals:
• Buccaneers, Panthers, Saints
Philosophy:
• Offense: Power Running
• Defense: 4-3
Highest Paid Players:
• M. Ryan
• K. Brooking
Team Weapons:
• J. Abraham – Finesse Move D-Lineman
• O. Muchelli – Crushing Run Blocker
Best Young Players:
• J. Anderson
• M. Ryan

67 OVERALL   68 OFFENSE   66 DEFENSE

▼ ROSTER AND **PACKAGE TIPS**

KEY PLAYER SUBSTITUTIONS

Position: QB
Substitution: Matt Ryan
When: Global
Advantage: Matt Ryan is the team's franchise quarterback, so he needs to be starting from day one. He has more speed and a stronger arm than Chris Redman. Ryan has some accuracy issues, but nothing that should keep him from starting.

Position: FS
Substitution: Jimmy Williams
When: Global
Advantage: Erik Coleman's overall rating is higher than Jimmy Williams's, but if you take a closer look at them both, it's clear who the starter should be. Williams is faster, better in man coverage, and stronger than Coleman.

Position: SS
Substitution: Daren Stone
When: Global
Advantage: Lawyer Milloy has made his mark in the league as one of the top safeties during that span. However, he has lost a step. At this point in his career, he would be better off playing in short yardage situations and letting Daren Stone start.

While No. 3 overall pick in the 2008 NFL draft Matt Ryan may be the new face of the Falcons franchise, he will have newly acquired veterans like RB Michael Turner and K Jason Elam to lean on.

TEAM STRATEGY

#1 Jason Elam *Kicker (K)*

▼ OFFENSIVE STAR PLAYER

Elam has been a solid kicker for years. This was a weak spot for the Falcons and they made a move to get one of the best kickers that was on the market. He is an accurate kicker that can kick outdoors, and be counted on to make 50 yarders.

Awareness	82
Kick Power	93
Kick Accuracy	92
Tackling	21

Player Weapon: None

#84 Roddy White *Wide Receiver (WR)*

▼ OFFENSIVE STAR PLAYER

Last season, White was the best wideout they had, pulling in 82 receptions, 1,202 yards, and 6 touchdowns. He is starting to come into his own. He uses his size to get inside position and has enough speed to get good yards after the catch.

Speed	93
Catch	84
Catch Traffic	86
Route Run	93

Player Weapon: Quick Receiver

#33 Michael Turner *Halfback (HB)*

▼ OFFENSIVE STAR PLAYER

Turner was another free agent pick-up; he has been the backup for LT for many seasons. When he came in he was a great runner. He has power, speed, and is a downhill runner. Additionally, he plays special teams.

Speed	92
Agility	86
Trucking	94
Elusiveness	78

Player Weapon: Power Back

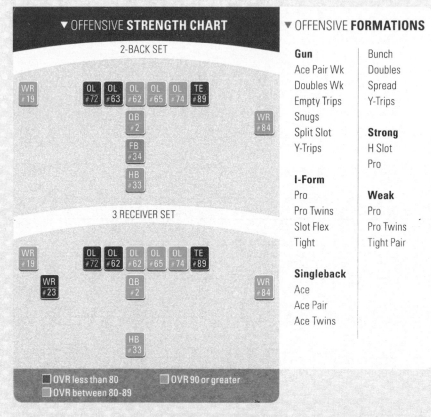

▼ OFFENSIVE STRENGTH CHART

2-BACK SET

WR #19 — OL #72 — OL #63 — OL #62 — OL #65 — OL #74 — TE #89 — WR #84 — QB #2 — FB #34 — HB #33

3 RECEIVER SET

WR #19 — OL #72 — OL #62 — OL #62 — OL #65 — OL #74 — TE #89 — WR #23 — QB #2 — WR #84 — HB #33

☐ OVR less than 80 ☐ OVR 90 or greater
☐ OVR between 80-89

▼ OFFENSIVE FORMATIONS

Gun
Ace Pair Wk
Doubles Wk
Empty Trips
Snugs
Split Slot
Y-Trips

I-Form
Pro
Pro Twins
Slot Flex
Tight

Singleback
Ace
Ace Pair
Ace Twins

Bunch
Doubles
Spread
Y-Trips

Strong
H Slot
Pro

Weak
Pro
Pro Twins
Tight Pair

▼ RECOMMENDED OFFENSIVE AUDIBLE PACKAGES

Singleback	I-Form	Strong	Singleback	Gun
Counter Wk	Curls	Power O	X Follow	Inside Switch

▼ OFFENSIVE PLAYCOUNTS

Quick Pass:	19	Screen Pass:	9	Pitch:	7
Standard Pass:	94	Hail Mary:		Counter:	11
Shotgun Pass:	52	Inside Handoff:	34	Draw:	12
Play Action Pass:	60	Outside Handoff:	12	FB Run:	9

OFFENSE **KEY OFFENSIVE PLAYS**

A HB Lead Toss

I-FORM TIGHT

HB LEAD TOSS

One of the better outside run plays in the game this year is the I-Form Tight HB Lead Toss. If the running back has some speed, there are yards to be gained.

1

With the fullback and left guard leading Michael Turner, there will be room to run.

2

Once to the outside, we continue to follow the left guard to the open field.

3

Turner has a few shake and bake moves. All it takes is one missed tackle and he is going in for six.

A FL Drive

I-FORM TIGHT

FL DRIVE

Regardless of whom the Falcons starting quarterback is, he will need short quick passing plays to move the ball through the air.

1

I-Form Tight FL Drive has Roddy White running a drag route from right to left.

2

If the defense is playing zone coverage, he will be open at some point for a quick bullet pass.

3

This pass play isn't going to net you a lot of yards, but it will help keep the chains moving.

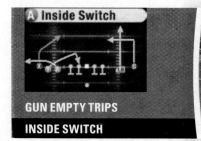

A Inside Switch

GUN EMPTY TRIPS

INSIDE SWITCH

The Gun Empty Trips Inside Switch is a good choice to get the ball quickly out of our quarterback's hands and to one of our receivers.

1

Our first read is the receiver running a flat route to the left. If he is open, we throw to him.

2

If not, we will look to throw to the receiver running the slant hook.

3

We throw a hard bullet pass to Roddy White as he hooks back towards our quarterback.

TEAM STRATEGY

 **ATLANTA FALCONS**

TEAM STRATEGY

#56 Keith Brooking *Linebacker (ROLB)*

▼ DEFENSIVE **STAR PLAYER**

Brooking has been with the Falcons for many years, and goes about his business to get things done. He is a hardnosed player that often finds himself around the ball, with 110 tackles last season and 2 sacks. He is the consistent leader on defense.

Speed	78
Tackling	90
Pursuit	90
Play Recog.	87

Player Weapon: None

#55 John Abraham *Defensive End (RE)*

▼ DEFENSIVE **STAR PLAYER**

He is an outstanding pass rusher when he is on the field; the main problem is him staying healthy. Last season, Abraham logged in 10 sacks and 4 forced fumbles. When he is on the field, he wreaks havoc every down. Just imagine what he could do in 16 games.

Speed	80
Strength	77
Power Moves	82
Finesse Moves	92

Player Weapon: Finesse Move D-Lineman

#59 Michael Boley *Linebacker (LOLB)*

▼ DEFENSIVE **STAR PLAYER**

Michael Boley was a fifth round draft pick for the Atlanta Falcons in 2005. In 2007 he notched 103 tackles and 3 QB sacks. He has plenty of speed and takes quality pursuit angles. He is decent in pass coverage with 4 picks the last two seasons.

Speed	85
Tackling	88
Pursuit	92
Play Recog.	80

Player Weapon: None

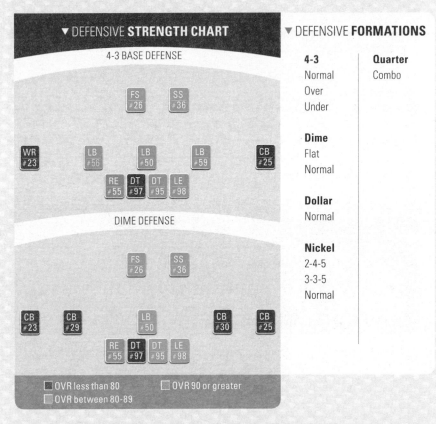

▼ DEFENSIVE **STRENGTH CHART**

4-3 BASE DEFENSE

FS #26 | SS #36

WR #23 | LB #56 | LB #50 | LB #59 | CB #25

RE #55 | DT #97 | DT #95 | LE #98

DIME DEFENSE

FS #26 | SS #36

CB #23 | CB #29 | LB #50 | CB #30 | CB #25

RE #55 | DT #97 | DT #95 | LE #98

☐ OVR less than 80 ☐ OVR 90 or greater
☐ OVR between 80-89

▼ DEFENSIVE **FORMATIONS**

4-3	**Quarter**
Normal	Combo
Over	
Under	
Dime	
Flat	
Normal	
Dollar	
Normal	
Nickel	
2-4-5	
3-3-5	
Normal	

▼ RECOMMENDED DEFENSIVE **AUDIBLE PACKAGES**

4-3	4-3	Nickel	Dime	Quarter
2 Man Under	Free Fire	Cover 3	Cover 2	Man Up 3 Deep

▼ DEFENSIVE **PLAYCOUNTS**

Man Coverage:	45	Cover 2 Zone:	16	Man Blitz:	59
Man Zone:	35	Cover 3 Zone:	27	Zone Blitz:	64
Combo Coverage:	7	Deep Zone:	19	Combo Blitz:	13

DEFENSE **KEY DEFENSIVE PLAYS**

GOAL LINE

JAM MIDDLE

A good inside run defense that defends the FB Dive is the Goal Line Jam Middle. This defense gets the linebacker in position to make the tackle.

With so many defenders on the line of scrimmage, it makes it tough for the line to account for each one.

This leaves the linebacker unblocked and allows him to be in the right spot to tackle the fullback.

The fullback is dropped for a loss in the backfield.

NICKEL 2-4-5

DOUBLE QB SPY

The Nickel 2-4-5 Double QB Spy is designed to prevent quarterbacks from taking off and running, but it also has other uses.

One of those other uses is to defend angle or circle routes from being run by running backs out of the backfield.

With the two inside linebackers playing QB Spy, they are in position to take away the running back's angle route.

The quarterback tries to throw to the running back, but the Falcons linebacker steps in front.

NICKEL 2-4-5

MLB BLITZ

A good blitz to bring heat on the quarterback is the Nickel 2-4-5 MLB Blitz. This defense sends both inside linebackers on an inside blitz.

The offensive line blocks to the inside to counter the pressure up the middle.

This leaves the right outside linebacker with a clean shot at putting quick pressure on the quarterback.

Keith Brooking comes in hard from the quarterback's blind side and is about to sack the quarterback.

TEAM STRATEGY

SAN FRANCISCO 49ERS

▶ **Division** NFC West ▶ **Stadium** Candlestick Park ▶ **Type** Open ▶ **Capacity** 70,207 ▶ **Surface** Grass

▼ 2007 STANDINGS

Wins	Loses	Ties	PF	PA	Home	Road	vs. AFC	vs. NFC	vs. Div
5	11	0	219	364	3-5	2-6	1-3	4-8	3-3

▼ TEAM OVERVIEW

The 49ers have a nice core of players, but are in the later part of rebuilding. They have made moves to improve the defense and have some great young players on the offensive side. The 49ers have hit the market to get key veteran players to help bring some leadership into the locker room. Last season, they ranked 32nd in total points (13.7), and racked up 237 total yards a game, 143 in passing, and 92 rushing yards (placing them 27th in the league). Defensively, they gave up 22.8 points per game (26th), 227 passing yards (22nd), and 118 on the ground (22nd). They really need to improve on the defensive side and hope that they get more consistency from the quarterback spot.

▼ OFF-SEASON UPGRADES

TYPE	ROUND	FIRST NAME	LAST NAME	SCHOOL/TEAM	POSITION
Free Agent	N/A	Isaac	Bruce	Rams	WR
Free Agent	N/A	DeShaun	Foster	Panthers	RB
Free Agent	N/A	Bryant	Johnson	Cardinals	WR
Draft	1	Kentwan	Balmer	North Carolina	DT
Draft	2	Chilo	Rachal	USC	G

▼ SCOUTING REPORT

	DESCRIPTION	MAXIMIZING POTENTIAL	TIPS FOR OPPONENTS
STRENGTHS	Frank Gore is your workhorse back, so make him the foundation of your scheme.	Feed him the ball as much as possible.	Show him extra attention at all times. You must contain him.
	Patrick Willis is a beast. He made 174 tackles, 4 sacks, and forced numerous turnovers.	Move him around through packages to generate pressure on the field.	Stay out of this man's way, and make sure you set your protection accordingly.
WEAKNESSES	The quarterback situation is awful for the 49ers. This hurts Frank Gore's running game.	Use big formations to get Davis involved in the passing attack.	Double Davis and play the run. Make them go elsewhere to move the ball.
	The 49ers' run defense is quite poor. They're ranked 22nd in the NFL.	You need to use 4-3/46 types of formations to slow down the run.	Pound this defense until they can stop you. Then exploit the pass through play action.

TEAM STRATEGY

FRANCHISE MODE STRATEGY

The 49ers have some good passing targets, but you might need to look for a QB if Alex Smith can't get the job done. Start looking for some younger secondary players and get help at defensive tackle.

KEY FRANCHISE INFORMATION

Cap Room: $21.69M

Key Rivals:
- Cardinals, Rams, Seahawks

Philosophy:
- Offense: Pass Heavy
- Defense: 3-4

Highest Paid Players:
- N. Clements
- A. Smith

Team Weapons:
- A. Lee – Big Foot Kicker
- P. Willis – Brick Wall Defender

Best Young Players:
- P. Willis
- V. Davis

72	66	77
OVERALL	OFFENSE	DEFENSE

▼ ROSTER AND **PACKAGE TIPS**

KEY PLAYER SUBSTITUTIONS

Position: WR
Substitution: Bryant Johnson
When: Global
Advantage: Bryant Johnson should be moved to the number 2 spot on the team's depth chart for the following reason. He is faster, runs better pass routes, can jump higher, and is a few inches taller than Arnaz Battle.

Position: Slot
Substitution: Vernon Davis
When: Passing Situations
Advantage: One of the faster tight ends in the game, Vernon Davis is a match up nightmare for linebackers, safeties, and in most cases, nickelbacks. By putting him in the slot, he can be even more effective in the red zone.

Position: LG
Substitution: Chilo Rachal
When: Global
Advantage: If you plan on running a lot of plays that require the left guard pulling, then this move makes sense. Chilo Rachal has considerably more speed than starter Adam Snyder. If you make this move, be aware that Rachal is not a better run or pass blocker than Snyder.

Frank Gore remains the primary engine in the 49ers offense in 2008, but if key youngsters like QB Alex Smith and TE Vernon Davis step up this year, the Niners can be competitive.

TEAM STRATEGY

TEAM STRATEGY

#21 Frank Gore *Halfback (HB)*
▼ OFFENSIVE **STAR PLAYER**

Gore is one of the top ten running backs in the league. He's the playmaker for this club, and a tough runner that breaks plenty of tackles and catches the ball well out of the backfield. All he needs is a passing attack to open lanes for him.

Speed	92
Agility	93
Trucking	92
Elusiveness	88

Player Weapon: Power Back

#80 Isaac Bruce *Wide Receiver (WR)*
▼ OFFENSIVE **STAR PLAYER**

Issac Bruce has been a great wideout over his career. The 49ers needed help at wideout, and brought him in with Jackson and Davis to help with the passing attack. In this stage of his career he will be more of a possession wideout, but he remains a great route runner.

Speed	87
Catch	92
Catch Traffic	82
Route Run	90

Player Weapon: Hands

#85 Vernon Davis *Tight End (TE)*
▼ OFFENSIVE **STAR PLAYER**

Davis has all of the tools to be a top shelf tight end. He has hands, speed, strength, and is a handful in the seam. The main problem with him is that he has no one connecting with him. He is due for some help and this could be the season.

Speed	92
Catch	84
Run Block	53
Pass Block	49

Player Weapon: None

▼ OFFENSIVE **STRENGTH CHART**

2-BACK SET / 3 RECEIVER SET

□ OVR less than 80　■ OVR 90 or greater　□ OVR between 80-89

▼ OFFENSIVE **FORMATIONS**

I-Form
Pro
Tight
Tight Pair

Rifle
Doubles
Doubles Y-Slot
Snugs Flip
Spread Flex Wk
Y-Trips

Singleback
Ace
Ace Pair
Bunch
Doubles
F Wing

Snugs Flip
Spread Flex
Trey Open
Y-Trips

Split
Slot

Strong
Pro
Pro Twins
Tight Pair

Weak
Pro
Tight Pair

▼ RECOMMENDED OFFENSIVE **AUDIBLE PACKAGES**

I-Form	Singleback	Strong	Singleback	Rifle
HB Power O	Slants	HB Dive	Short Ins N Outs	Corner Strike

▼ OFFENSIVE **PLAYCOUNTS**

Quick Pass:	25	Screen Pass:	11	Pitch:	7
Standard Pass:	86	Hail Mary:	1	Counter:	12
Shotgun Pass:	40	Inside Handoff:	29	Draw:	10
Play Action Pass:	63	Outside Handoff:	16		

OFFENSE **KEY OFFENSIVE PLAYS**

www.primagames.com

mage_ref id="13" />

RIFLE SNUGS FLIP

PA X CLOWN

mage_ref id="2" />

The PA X Clown has some tricky routes in it that can beat a variety of coverages. The double move route is especially nice.

While the quarterback is faking the handoff you should already be looking at the coverage to see what comes open.

We have time to wait for the deep cross to open up. Wait until the receiver finds a window in the zone.

We fire a strike and our receiver goes up to grab the pass.

mage_ref id="5" />

SINGLEBACK F WING

F WEAK LEAD

mage_ref id="3" />

The F Weak Lead uses auto motion by the fullback to bring him inside as a lead blocker. You can run a strong inside attack with this play.

As the line engages, we already can see that a hole will open up outside.

We have to hit the Sprint button to escape the defender shooting into the backfield.

Once we make our escape, we are off to the races down the sidelines.

mage_ref id="4" />

SPLIT SLOT

SLOT Z OUT

mage_ref id="11" />

Split back sets scream West Coast Offense. This play has some really nice route combinations with a backside curl and a flood on the right.

We really like to hit the angle route over the middle against man coverage. This route is very tough for defenders to follow.

As you can see, your fullback has eluded his defender and is running wide open over the middle.

We hit him with a pass and let him lower his shoulder on the secondary.

TEAM STRATEGY

143

 SAN FRANCISCO 49ERS · DEFENSE

#52 Patrick Willis *Linebacker (MLB)*

▼ DEFENSIVE **STAR PLAYER**

Patrick Willis had an outstanding season last year, in which he made 174 tackles, 4 sacks, and 2 forced fumbles. He is a young animal that has a nose for the ball and is a decent pass rusher. Willis also covers well from sideline to sideline, and is the playmaker on the defensive side.

Speed	91
Tackling	96
Pursuit	98
Play Recog.	85

Player Weapon: Big Hitter, Brick Wall Defender

#22 Nate Clements *Cornerback (CB)*

▼ DEFENSIVE **STAR PLAYER**

Clemens was brought in to fill the 49ers' need for a shutdown corner. Nate is a tough corner that plays all top wideouts. If you caught the ball against him, you earned it. He had 92 tackles, 3 forced fumbles, 1 sack, and 4 interceptions.

Speed	92
Man Cover	92
Zone Cover	85
Press	92

Player Weapon: Shutdown Corner, Press Coverage Corner

#94 Justin Smith *Defensive End (RE)*

▼ DEFENSIVE **STAR PLAYER**

Smith is the best pass rusher they have on the line. He had 2 sacks last season, but he made 78 tackles. He's a steady pass rusher that contains the run well and gives you a steady rush. He overpowers tackles to get pressure on quarterbacks and uses stunts.

Speed	75
Strength	82
Power Moves	88
Finesse Moves	79

Player Weapon: None

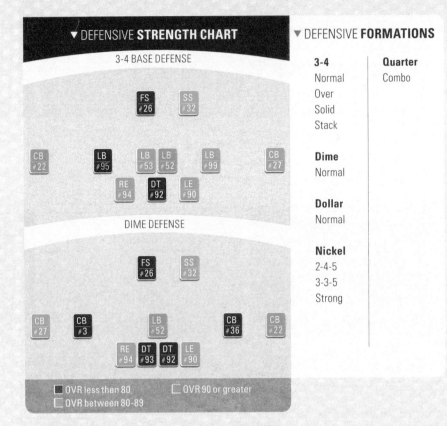

▼ DEFENSIVE **STRENGTH CHART**

3-4 BASE DEFENSE

DIME DEFENSE

- ■ OVR less than 80
- □ OVR between 80-89
- □ OVR 90 or greater

▼ DEFENSIVE **FORMATIONS**

3-4	Quarter
Normal	Combo
Over	
Solid	
Stack	

Dime
Normal

Dollar
Normal

Nickel
2-4-5
3-3-5
Strong

▼ RECOMMENDED DEFENSIVE **AUDIBLE PACKAGES**

3-4	3-4	Nickel	Dime	Quarter
2 Man Under	Storm Brave 1	Cover 3	Cover 2	Man Up 3 Deep

▼ DEFENSIVE **PLAYCOUNTS**

Man Coverage:	44	Cover 2 Zone:	20	Man Blitz:	54
Man Zone:	35	Cover 3 Zone:	16	Zone Blitz:	55
Combo Coverage:	6	Deep Zone:	11	Combo Blitz:	7

DEFENSE **KEY DEFENSIVE PLAYS**

A OLB Fire Man

3-4 STACK

OLB FIRE MAN

The Stack set from the 3-4 formation is one of the better run stoppers in the game. The stacked linebackers are protected from blockers and can get in to make plays.

Already you can see our defensive end scrape off the line. The left tackle had to pick up our blitzing linebacker.

The running back gets the ball, but our defender has already gotten into the backfield.

We make an easy tackle and get a loss on the play courtesy of the OLB Fire Man.

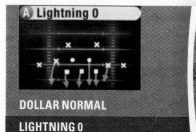

A Lightning 0

DOLLAR NORMAL

LIGHTNING 0

The Dollar Normal Lightning 0 is a high risk/high reward style of defense. You are bringing three additional blitzers with no safety help deep.

As we come to the line of scrimmage we see that the offense is in an empty set. This is tailor-made for our attacking defense.

The QB has just set his feet and already the heat is coming right into his face. He can't step up to throw.

Leinart tries to roll out, but is hammered by our defense. He lays the ball on the ground for a turnover.

A Cover 2 Sink

NICKEL 2-4-5

COVER 2 SINK

The purpose of this defense is to lock up the short areas of the field. The linebackers and cornerbacks blanket the field with two safeties helping out up top.

After the snap, you can see that the field is clogged up with defenders. There is nowhere for Leinart to go.

The quarterback sees a possible opening and tries to thread the pass in to his receiver.

Zone coverage is beefed up in *Madden NFL 09*. The Niners linebacker steps in and picks off the pass.

TEAM STRATEGY

ny NEW YORK GIANTS

▶ **Division** NFC East ▶ **Stadium** Giants Stadium ▶ **Type** Open ▶ **Capacity** 80,242 ▶ **Surface** Field Turf

TEAM STRATEGY

FRANCHISE MODE STRATEGY

Try to acquire a speedy back to complement Brandon Jacobs. The defensive line is as good as they come, so focus on getting help at outside linebacker. A quick cover corner would be a good acquisition as well.

KEY FRANCHISE INFORMATION

Cap Room: $22.75M
Key Rivals:
• Cowboys, Eagles, Redskins
Philosophy:
• Offense: Pro Style
• Defense: 4-3
Highest Paid Players:
• E. Manning
• K. McKenzie
Team Weapons
• O. Umenyiora – Finesse Move D-Lineman
• P. Burress – Spectacular Catch Receiver
Best Young Players:
B. Cofield
S. Smith

2007 STANDINGS

Wins	Loses	Ties	PF	PA	Home	Road	vs. AFC	vs. NFC	vs. Div
10	6	0	373	351	3-5	7-1	3-1	7-5	3-3

TEAM OVERVIEW

The New York Giants' last season was a great one. They went from not making it to the playoffs to one of the best runs in football history. They broke the record for road wins and had one of the best pass rushing defenses seen to date. They showed what team ball and a mean pass rush could do. The Giants are the favorites coming out this season, primed to repeat last year's success. They were balanced on the offensive side of the ball with 197 yards passing, 134 yards on the ground (4th), and 23 points a game (14th). The defense gave up 23 (17th) points a game, 207 yards in the air (11th), and played the run well only giving up 97 yards a game (8th).

OFF-SEASON UPGRADES

TYPE	ROUND	FIRST NAME	LAST NAME	SCHOOL/TEAM	POSITION
Free Agent	N/A	David	Carr	Panthers	QB
Free Agent	N/A	Sammy	Knight	Jaguars	S
Draft	1	Kenny	Phillips	Miami	S
Draft	2	Terrell	Thomas	USC	CB
Draft	3	Mario	Manningham	Michigan	WR

SCOUTING REPORT

	DESCRIPTION	MAXIMIZING POTENTIAL	TIPS FOR OPPONENTS
STRENGTHS	Eli Manning has come out of his shell, and this paid off last season.	Use the running game to set up the pass. He has weapons.	Mix up your coverages. Then take away Burress and Shockey.
STRENGTHS	Osi is relentless on the pass rush and can force you into bad passes.	Use stunts and multiple blitz packages to free up Osi.	When you pass, use slide protection to slow him down and run at him.
WEAKNESSES	Jacobs is a great power back, but his lack of speed kills the offense.	Use packages to get a faster back on the field.	Drop a lineman on him and use the defender to double someone else.
WEAKNESSES	The Giants' secondary is suspect at times, but the line protected them last season.	You need to use a strong pass rush to protect the weak secondary.	Use offensive overloads to expose weaknesses in the secondary and openings from blitz schemes.

94	94	92
OVERALL	OFFENSE	DEFENSE

▼ ROSTER AND **PACKAGE TIPS**

KEY PLAYER SUBSTITUTIONS

Position: HB

Substitution: Ahmad Bradshaw

When: Passing Situations

Advantage: Although Derrick Ward has a slightly better catch rating than Ahmad Bradshaw, he is not as fast. Having Bradshaw line up in passing situations gives you a more elusive back, who has the speed to go the distance when he touches the ball.

Position: FS

Substitution: Sam Madison

When: Global

Advantage: We suggest moving Sam Madison to free safety. By making this move, you lose speed, but upgrade the position by 11 overall points. Plus this move allows you to put Kevin Dockery into a starting role at cornerback. He is faster than Madison.

Position: SS

Substitution: Kenny Phillips

When: Global

Advantage: With Madison entrenched at free safety, we move Kenny Phillips to strong safety. This upgrades the strong safety position by adding more speed, range, and pass coverage.

Super Bowl XLII MVP Eli Manning, who came of age during the Giants' surprising playoff run last season, will ensure that Big Blue remains a force to be reckoned with for years to come.

TEAM STRATEGY

TEAM STRATEGY

#17 Plaxico Burress *Wide Receiver (WR)*

▼OFFENSIVE **STAR PLAYER**

He came up big when the Giants needed him last season, and is now a major threat on the field. He pulled in 70 receptions, had 1,025 yards receiving, and scored 12 touchdowns. Burress did this all while he was injured for most of the season. He's now the go-to guy for Manning.

Speed	93
Catch	92
Catch In Traffic	90
Route Run	93

Player Weapon: Quick Receiver, Possession Receiver, Spec Catch Receiver, Hands

#80 Jeremy Shockey *Tight End (TE)*

▼OFFENSIVE **STAR PLAYER**

Shockey is one of the most intense players you will ever see. He is very competitive and is a big play waiting to happen. No one can cover him, and his speed, size, hands, and blocking ability are unmatched. He was injured last season and is primed for a comeback.

Speed	84
Catch	85
Run Block	58
Pass Block	55

Player Weapon: Quick Receiver, Possession Receiver

#10 Eli Manning *Quarterback (QB)*

▼OFFENSIVE **STAR PLAYER**

Many have beaten this guy down from the day he was drafted. He also walked in his brother's shadow. Manning showed everyone that he is a great quarterback than could lead his team to the Super Bowl and win it all. Eli has great arm strength and also has mobility.

Speed	61
Awareness	88
Throw Power	93
Throw Accur.	94

Player Weapon: Accurate Quarterback

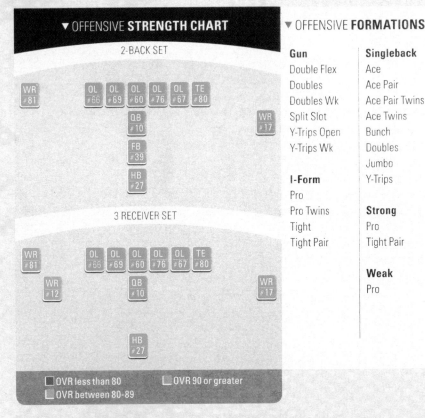

▼ OFFENSIVE **STRENGTH CHART**

2-BACK SET

- WR #81
- OL #66, OL #69, OL #60, OL #76, OL #67, TE #80
- QB #10
- WR #17
- FB #39
- HB #27

3 RECEIVER SET

- WR #81
- OL #66, OL #69, OL #60, OL #76, OL #67, TE #80
- WR #12
- QB #10
- WR #17
- HB #27

☐ OVR less than 80   ☐ OVR 90 or greater
☐ OVR between 80-89

▼ OFFENSIVE **FORMATIONS**

Gun	Singleback
Double Flex	Ace
Doubles	Ace Pair
Doubles Wk	Ace Pair Twins
Split Slot	Ace Twins
Y-Trips Open	Bunch
Y-Trips Wk	Doubles
	Jumbo
I-Form	Y-Trips
Pro	
Pro Twins	**Strong**
Tight	Pro
Tight Pair	Tight Pair
	Weak
	Pro

▼ RECOMMENDED OFFENSIVE **AUDIBLE PACKAGES**

Singleback	Singleback	I-Form	Gun	Gun
HB Sprint	Y Shallow Cross	Power 0	Drag Under	Corner Strike

▼ OFFENSIVE **PLAYCOUNTS**

Quick Pass:	19	Screen Pass:	9	Pitch:	8
Standard Pass:	79	Hail Mary:	1	Counter:	11
Shotgun Pass:	53	Inside Handoff:	29	Draw:	11
Play Action Pass:	63	Outside Handoff:	16		

OFFENSE **KEY OFFENSIVE PLAYS**

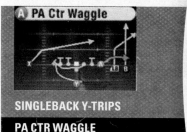

SINGLEBACK Y-TRIPS

PA CTR WAGGLE

After you have set up the run with Jacobs, play action is a great option for getting your receivers open down the field. Be sure to throw it quick.

Manning fakes the handoff to Jacobs and rolls out to his right.

Manning sets his feet and sees the tight end breaking open out in the flat. You can usually get him open.

Boss makes the grab and has a ton of open field in front of him. You can move the chains like crazy.

STRONG PRO

SPACING

Spacing plays try to get multiple receivers flooding the zones over the middle. The hook routes will look to find small open pockets and exploit them.

The defense has dropped into zone coverage. This usually is a problem when you want to throw short.

Jeremy Shockey finds a hole in the zone and tucks in to receive the pass from Manning.

He turns and looks for more yards down the field. If you can break a tackle you can get a big gain.

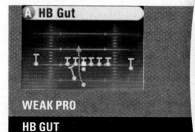

WEAK PRO

HB GUT

The HB Gut is a quick hitting power run play to the weak side of the line. Because of the fullback's alignment you will still have a lead blocker.

Jacobs gets the ball and has some daylight in front of him. Lay off the speed burst at first.

We break into the hole and tear down the field. Notice how our offensive line obliterated the defense.

Jacobs is a load to bring down for any defender. The Eagles are going to need two or three to make the tackle.

TEAM STRATEGY

#72 Osi Umenyiora *Defensive Tackle (RE)*

▼DEFENSIVE **STAR PLAYER**

Umenyiora has made a name for himself as one of the best pass rushers in the game. He got 53 tackles, 13 sacks, and 5 forced fumbles in 2007. He helped the Giants lead the league in sacks last season. He has speed, strength, and the best moves off the line.

Speed	85
Strength	78
Power Moves	92
Finesse Moves	96

Player Weapon: Finesse Move D-Lineman, Power Move D-Lineman

#91 Justin Tuck *Defensive End (DE)*

▼DEFENSIVE **STAR PLAYER**

Now that Michael Strahan has retired, Tuck steps into the left end position on a full-time basis. Fortunately, he has the skill set required to be a dominating force. He has the power moves to bowl over offensive lineman, and the speed to blow right by them as well.

Awareness	84
Speed	49
Throwing Power	86
Throwing Accuracy	91

Player Weapon: None

#58 Antonio Pierce *Linebacker (MLB)*

▼DEFENSIVE **STAR PLAYER**

Pierce was the missing ingredient that the Giants needed in the middle two seasons ago. Since he came, he has been a beast in the middle. He had 103 tackles, 1 sack, 1 forced fumble, and 1 interception last season. He does everything well and plays at a high level.

Speed	85
Tackling	94
Pursuit	95
Play Recog.	92

Player Weapon: Brick Wall Defender, Smart Linebacker

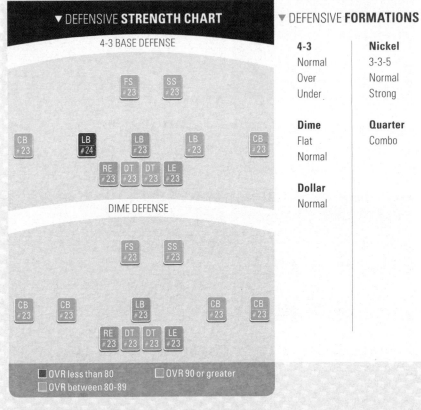

▼ DEFENSIVE **STRENGTH CHART**

4-3 BASE DEFENSE

| FS #23 | SS #23 |

| CB #23 | LB #24 | LB #23 | LB #23 | CB #23 |

| RE #23 | DT #23 | DT #23 | LE #23 |

DIME DEFENSE

| FS #23 | SS #23 |

| CB #23 | CB #23 | LB #23 | CB #23 | CB #23 |

| RE #23 | DT #23 | DT #23 | LE #23 |

■ OVR less than 80   □ OVR 90 or greater
□ OVR between 80-89

▼ DEFENSIVE **FORMATIONS**

4-3	Nickel
Normal	3-3-5
Over	Normal
Under	Strong
Dime	**Quarter**
Flat	Combo
Normal	
Dollar	
Normal	

▼ RECOMMENDED DEFENSE **AUDIBLE PACKAGES**

4-3	4-3	Nickel	Dime	Quarter
2 Man Under	Fire Man	Cover 3 Press	Cover 2	3 Deep Press

▼ DEFENSIVE **PLAYCOUNTS**

Man Coverage:	45	Cover 2 Zone:	14	Man Blitz:	55
Man Zone:	34	Cover 3 Zone:	26	Zone Blitz:	64
Combo Coverage:	7	Deep Zone:	18	Combo Blitz:	13

DEFENSE **KEY DEFENSIVE PLAYS**

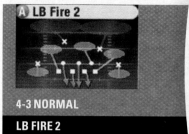

4-3 NORMAL
LB FIRE 2

Cover 2 defenses are solid choices within the red zone. The LB Fire 2 brings some heat up the middle and has nice zone coverage behind it.

As McNabb drops back, you can see that we have good coverage across the middle and in the flats.

The receiver turns for the ball, but our defender is approaching fast from behind him.

We smack the receiver the second that he catches the ball. It's a bad pass into zone coverage for only a 1-yard gain.

NICKEL NORMAL
OVER STORM BRAVE

There are times in the game when you just need to bring the heat after the quarterback. The Over Storm Brave fires two blitzers down the middle.

As soon as the ball is snapped, our linebacker breaks through the line and heads after McNabb.

McNabb is forced to make a quick throw or risk being sacked by our linebackers.

The pass was much too quick and bounces off the helmet of the tight end before he can break into his route.

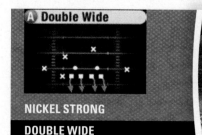

NICKEL STRONG
DOUBLE WIDE

The Double Wide play puts extra coverage on the two outside receivers. We like to call this on 3rd down and then manually cover the third receiver.

As the quarterback drops back to pass, he doesn't have too many uncovered options.

He fires off the pass on a quick curl hoping the receiver can break a tackle and get the first down.

We make the sure tackle short of the marker. We have a second defender in case the tackle is broken.

TEAM STRATEGY

JACKSONVILLE JAGUARS

▶ **Division** AFC South ▶ **Stadium** Jacksonville Municipal Stadium ▶ **Type** Open ▶ **Capacity** 82,000 ▶ **Surface** Grass

TEAM STRATEGY

FRANCHISE MODE STRATEGY

The Jaguars do not have any weaknesses anywhere on the field. You have the luxury of using your draft picks to grab the best available athlete and build depth at all positions. Keeping your young stars will be the biggest challenge.

KEY FRANCHISE INFORMATION

Cap Room: $1.25M
Key Rivals:
- Colts, Texans, Titans

Philosophy:
- Offense: Run with Play Action
- Defense: 4-3

Highest Paid Players:
- D. Garrard
- T. Williamson

Top Team Weapons:
- J. Henderson – Power Move D-Lineman
- R. Mathis – Shutdown Corner

Best Young Players:
- M. Jones-Drew
- M. Lewis

▼ 2007 STANDINGS

Wins	Loses	Ties	PF	PA	Home	Road	vs. AFC	vs. NFC	vs. Div
11	5	0	411	304	6-2	5-3	8-4	3-1	2-4

▼ TEAM OVERVIEW

Year after year, the Jaguars have played second fiddle to the Indianapolis Colts in the AFC South. One of the key reasons is they haven't been able to put much pressure on Peyton Manning. That's why the Jaguars drafted Derrick Harvey and Quentin Groves. Both should make an immediate impact and hopefully give the Jaguars some type of pass rush in this year's game.

The offense is in good hands at quarterback with the underrated David Garrard leading the team. At running back, the Jaguars have one of the best one-two punch combos in the league with Fred Taylor and Maurice Jones-Drew.

On defense, losing defensive tackle Marcus Stroud will certainly put a chink in the team's run defense armor. However, they still have defensive tackle John Henderson to control the middle.

▼ OFF-SEASON UPGRADES

TYPE	ROUND	FIRST NAME	LAST NAME	SCHOOL/TEAM	POSITION
Free Agent	N/A	Drayton	Florence	Chargers	CB
Free Agent	N/A	Jerry	Porter	Raiders	WR
Trade	N/A	Troy	Williamson	Vikings	WR
Draft	1	Derrick	Harvey	Florida	DE
Draft	2	Quentin	Groves	Auburn	DE

▼ SCOUTING REPORT

	DESCRIPTION	MAXIMIZING POTENTIAL	TIPS FOR OPPONENTS
STRENGTHS	The running combination of Fred Taylor and Maurice Jones-Drew is one of the best in the game.	Use Taylor to pound the ball inside, and Jones-Drew to run outside for an effective one-two punch.	Call inside run defenses to stop Taylor and call outside run defenses to stop Jones-Drew.
	Rashean Mathis is one of the best cornerbacks in the game and has the ability to lock down the receiver he is covering.	Leave Mathis on an island by himself and rotate the pass coverage to Brian Williams's side.	Don't attack Mathis often because he will pick a pass off from time to time; instead, attack Williams.
WEAKNESSES	The Jaguars' passing attack is not one of the stronger ones, due to the lack of a strong receiver to rely on.	Consider running the ball on first and second downs to keep from getting in third and long situations.	Stack the line of scrimmage with eight defenders to stop the run and force the Jaguars to pass.
	Rob Meier is now the Jaguars' number 2 defensive tackle. The question is: can he stop the run?	The best way to protect Meier is to call inside run blitzes to help prevent big gains.	Look to get the inside run game going by attacking Meier since he is not a strong run defender.

93	92	93
OVERALL	OFFENSE	DEFENSE

▼ ROSTER AND **PACKAGE TIPS**

KEY PLAYER SUBSTITUTIONS

Position: HB
Substitution: Maurice Jones-Drew
When: Outside Runs
Advantage: Package or sub Maurice Jones-Drew in anytime you plan on running the ball outside. This is not a knock on Fred Taylor, because he is more than capable. However, when you have a playmaker like Jones-Drew, he has to get his share of touches, too.

Position: WR
Substitution: Reggie Williams
When: Global
Advantage: For those of you who prefer taller receivers, moving Reggie Williams up the depth chart is a good move to make. At 6'4", he can do a lot of damage inside the red zone. Matt Jones is another tall receiver to consider moving up.

Position: LE
Substitution: Derrick Harvey
When: Global
Advantage: This sub improves the defensive line as a whole. Derrick Harvey is much faster than starter Paul Spicer, making him a bigger threat to put pressure on the quarterback. Spicer can now be moved to the number 2 spot at defensive tackle, where he instantly upgrades that position.

The dynamic Maurice Jones-Drew is complemented by ageless RB Fred Taylor and efficient QB David Garrard. If the Jaguars' moves on defense payoff, they will once again compete for the playoffs.

TEAM STRATEGY

TEAM STRATEGY

#28 Fred Taylor *Halfback (HB)*

▼OFFENSIVE **STAR PLAYER**

At age 32, Fred Taylor remains an elite back. Despite his age, he has not lost his step. Last season he rushed for 1,202 yards, which was his best since 2004. His nonstop motor allows him to run over defenders after the first initial contact. Look for him to post the same type of numbers this season.

Speed	93
Agility	94
Trucking	93
Elusiveness	93

Player Weapon: Power Back, Elusive Back

#32 Maurice Jones-Drew *Halfback (HB)*

▼OFFENSIVE **STAR PLAYER**

The other half of the Jaguars' two-headed rushing attack is the compact Maurice Jones-Drew. Despite his smallish frame, he is able to bust through would-be tacklers. Once out in the open field, he has extra speed that allows him to take the ball the distance.

Speed	95
Agility	95
Trucking	95
Elusiveness	93

Player Weapon: Power Back, Elusive Back

#9 David Garrard *Quarterback (QB)*

▼OFFENSIVE **STAR PLAYER**

When you look at David Garrard's passing numbers, nothing really stands out. However, he is in total control of the Jacksonville offense. Last season, he threw 18 touchdowns and 3 interceptions. His quarterback rating of 102.2 ranked him third in the league. His ability to make something happen when the play breaks down can't be overlooked.

Speed	77
Awareness	77
Throwing Power	93
Throwing Accur.	93

Player Weapon: Accurate Quarterback

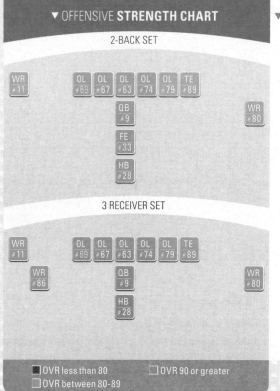

▼OFFENSIVE **STRENGTH CHART**

▼OFFENSIVE **FORMATIONS**

Gun
Doubles
Doubles Wing Wk
Split Slot
Spread Y-Flex
Trey Open
Y-Trips Wk

I-Form
Pro
Pro Twins
Tight Pair

Singleback
Ace
Ace Pair
Ace Pair Twins
Ace Twins
Bunch
Doubles
Flex
Y-Trips

Strong
Flex Twins
Pro
Tight

Weak
Pro
Pro Twins

▼ RECOMMENDED OFFENSIVE **AUDIBLE PACKAGES**

Singleback	Strong	Strong	Singleback	Gun
HB Dive	HB Option	Power O	Inside Cross	Corner Strike

▼ OFFENSIVE **PLAYCOUNTS**

Quick Pass:	25	Screen Pass:	7	Pitch:	5
Standard Pass:	81	Hail Mary:	2	Counter:	12
Shotgun Pass:	42	Inside Handoff:	29	Draw:	11
Play Action Pass:	68	Outside Handoff:	18		

OFFENSE **KEY OFFENSIVE PLAYS**

TEAM STRATEGY

A Iso Weak

I-FORM PRO

ISO WEAK

The I-Form Pro Iso Weak is a solid inside run play to pound between the tackles with Jacksonville Jaguar Fred Taylor.

1 We can either follow our fullback through the hole between the center and left guard, or bounce outside.

2 While in control of Taylor, we juke back inside and follow our FB through the open hole.

3 We burst through the hole and pick up a quick 7 yards before being tackled.

A PA Waggle

I-FORM PRO

PA WAGGLE

The I Form Pro PA Waggle complements the Iso Weak by giving the defense the same run action.

1 The play's primary receiver is Jerry Porter running a crossing route from left to right.

2 Another option to look for is the tight end running a delayed flat route to the right.

3 We take control of Marcedes Lewis and make the catch in the flat for a 6-yard gain.

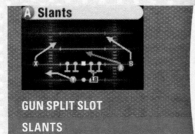

A Slants

GUN SPLIT SLOT

SLANTS

The Gun Split Slot Slants play has three receivers running slants, while the HB leaks out into the flat. This is a good pass play to beat the blitz.

1 The slot receiver is the play's primary receiver. Look to see if any defender drops over the middle.

2 Quarterback David Gerrard spots Dennis Northcutt wide open over the middle and throws him a bullet.

3 We take control of Northcutt and make the catch for an 8-yard pickup before being tackled.

JACKSONVILLE JAGUARS DEFENSE

TEAM STRATEGY

#27 Rashean Mathis *Cornerback (CB)*

▼DEFENSIVE **STAR PLAYER**

Teams tend not to throw towards Rashean Mathis. This is why his interception total took a nosedive in '07 as compared to '06 when he had 8 thefts. He still remains one of the best ball hawking corner-backs in the game. His ability to play man and zone coverage makes him very hard to throw against.

Speed	94
Man Cover	95
Zone Cover	92
Press	88

Player Weapon: Lock-Down Corner

#98 John Henderson *Defensive Tackle (DT)*

▼DEFENSIVE **STAR PLAYER**

Defensive tackle John Henderson is a big man who commands double team blocks to keep him from disrupting the opposing offense's pass and run game. When healthy and motivated, he is a destruc-tive force that can take over the game. Look for him to have a big season as the team's best inside interior lineman.

Speed	62
Strength	95
Power Moves	97
Finesse Moves	65

Player Weapon: Power Move D-Lineman

#54 Mike Peterson *Linebacker (MLB)*

▼DEFENSIVE **STAR PLAYER**

Over the last two seasons, Mike Peterson has been hit with a bad rash of injuries. These injuries have taken a toll on his ability to make plays. When healthy, he is able to make plays sideline to sideline, making him one of the leading middle linebackers in the game.

Speed	84
Tackling	93
Pursuit	97
Play Recog.	90

Player Weapon: Brick Wall Defender, Smart Linebacker

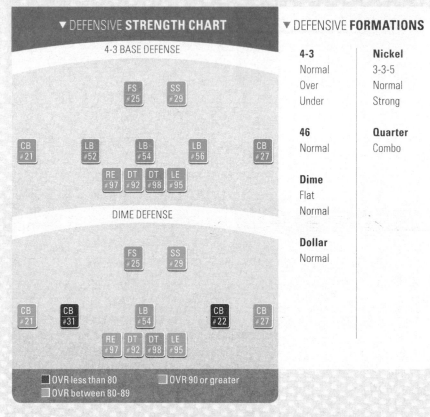

▼ DEFENSIVE **STRENGTH CHART**

4-3 BASE DEFENSE

FS #25 · SS #29

CB #21 · LB #52 · LB #54 · LB #56 · CB #27

RE #97 · DT #92 · DT #98 · LE #95

DIME DEFENSE

FS #25 · SS #29

CB #21 · CB #31 · LB #54 · CB #22 · CB #27

RE #97 · DT #92 · DT #98 · LE #95

☐ OVR less than 80 ☐ OVR 90 or greater
☐ OVR between 80-89

▼ DEFENSIVE **FORMATIONS**

4-3	Nickel
Normal	3-3-5
Over	Normal
Under	Strong
46	**Quarter**
Normal	Combo
Dime	
Flat	
Normal	
Dollar	
Normal	

▼ RECOMMENDED DEFENSIVE **AUDIBLE PACKAGES**

4-3	4-3	Nickel	Dime	Quarter
2 Man Under	Free Fire	Cover 2	Cover 3	3 Deep Press

▼ DEFENSIVE **PLAYCOUNTS**

Man Coverage:	42	Cover 2 Zone:	14	Man Blitz:	54
Man Zone:	34	Cover 3 Zone:	26	Zone Blitz:	63
Combo Coverage:	8	Deep Zone:	19	Combo Blitz:	17

DEFENSE **KEY DEFENSIVE PLAYS**

4-3 UNDER
CB DOGS ZONE

The 4-3 Under CB Dogs Zone has both cornerbacks blitzing from the outside to defend against the run game.

Against the stretch run play, outside linebacker Justin Durant is in good position to make the tackle.

Rashean Mathis comes in hard from his cornerback spot to force the RB back inside.

Colts' running back Joseph Addai is gang tackled by Durant and Mathis in the backfield for a loss.

NICKEL 3-3-5
COVER 3

The Nickel 3-3-5 Cover 3 is a solid zone defense to call that blankets the entire field, because it makes passing very difficult.

This defense is effective, because the nickelback and left outside linebacker cover the flats.

Outside linebacker Justin Durant sees the halfback leaking out in the backfield into the flat.

As soon as the halfback makes the catch, Durart makes the tackle for a minimal gain.

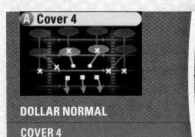

DOLLAR NORMAL
COVER 4

The Dollar Normal Cover 4 is a good defense to call to keep the Jaguars' defenders from giving up the big play deep.

The RCB, FS, SS, and LCB drop back in four deep coverage to defend the pass.

Colts' QB Peyton Manning tries to thread the needle to his receiver running the deep post.

SS Brian Williams steps in front of the Colts' receiver and knocks the ball down for an incomplete pass.

TEAM STRATEGY

NEW YORK JETS

| ▶ Division AFC East | ▶ Stadium Giants Stadium | ▶ Type Open | ▶ Capacity 80,242 | ▶ Surface Field Turf |

▼ 2007 STANDINGS

Wins	Loses	Ties	PF	PA	Home	Road	vs. AFC	vs. NFC	vs. Div
4	12	0	268	355	3-5	1-7	4-8	0-4	2-4

▼ TEAM OVERVIEW

The main two words this off-season were "spend money." The Jets spent a bunch of money on free agents to try to improve the team's 4-12 record in 2007. Players such as Alan Faneca, Damien Woody, and Calvin Pace are all expected to make huge impacts.

Thomas Jones is the team's work-horse on offense. With the new additions along the offensive line, he should see his rushing totals go up across the board. Wide receivers Laveranues Coles and Jerricho Cotchery are excellent targets to throw to.

The team looks like they will finally be able to implement the 3-4 defense with the chess pieces now in place. The Jets picked up former Panthers defensive tackle Kris Jenkins in a trade. He should force a lot of double teams and free up the inside linebackers to make plays.

▼ OFF-SEASON UPGRADES

TYPE	ROUND	FIRST NAME	LAST NAME	SCHOOL/TEAM	POSITION
Free Agent	N/A	Alan	Faneca	Steelers	G
Trade	N/A	Kris	Jenkins	Panthers	DT
Free Agent	N/A	Calvin	Pace	Cardinals	LB
Draft	1	Vernon	Gholston	Ohio State	DE
Draft	1	Dustin	Keller	Purdue	TE

▼ SCOUTING REPORT

	DESCRIPTION	MAXIMIZING POTENTIAL	TIPS FOR OPPONENTS
STRENGTHS	Kellen Clemons has a much stronger arm than Chad Pennington, making him much better at airing it out deep.	Send Laveranues Coles on a streak and then look to throw to him deep with Clemons's arm.	Although Clemons is strong, he has accuracy issues. Look to pick the pass off when the ball is aired out.
	Outside linebacker Vernon Gholston was drafted to put pressure on the quarterback with his speed from the outside.	Develop outside blitz schemes that allow Gholston to use his speed to put pressure on the quarterback.	Use slide protection or leave running backs in to pass block to the same side that Gholston lines up.
WEAKNESSES	Regardless of who is QB for the Jets, the passing game is going to be more difficult than most other teams.	Use Thomas Jones to pound the ball. He is a proven workhorse that can take pressure off the passing game.	Load the box with 8 and 9 defenders, and force the Jets' offense to have to throw the pass to beat you.
	David Barrett is a solid cornerback, but lacks top end speed to hang with elite receivers.	Make sure to leave a safety deep on the same side as Barrett; that way, there is a safety over the top to help.	Don't throw to the same side as Darrelle Revis. Instead, work the same side that Barrett lines up in.

FRANCHISE MODE STRATEGY

Pennington has been prone to injury, so finding a quality back-up is key. We recommend using the majority of your cap room and draft picks to work on your secondary. You may struggle with defending the pass until then.

KEY FRANCHISE INFORMATION

Cap Room: $2.33M

Key Rivals:
• Bills, Dolphins, Patriots

Philosophy:
• Offense: Multiple
• Defense: 3-4

Highest Paid Players:
• C. Pennington
• S. Ellis

Team Weapons:
• K. Rhodes – Smart Safety
• A. Faneca – Crushing Run Blocker

Best Young Players:
• D. Harris
• D. Revis

While the Jets made a splash in the offseason by signing some top-shelf talent, they will still need to rely on the steady play of WR Jerricho Cotchery and the rest of the team.

76	**76**	**75**
OVERALL	OFFENSE	DEFENSE

▼ ROSTER AND **PACKAGE TIPS**
KEY PLAYER SUBSTITUTIONS

Position: QB
Substitution: Kellen Clemens
When: Global
Advantage: This move really all depends on your style of play. If you like a pocket passer who has an accurate arm, then go with Chad Pennington. If you like to have some mobility and to throw deep, then go with Kellen Clemens.

Position: TE
Substitution: Dustin Keller
When: Global
Advantage: Having a fast tight end that can stretch the middle of the field is important in any passing game. Dustin Keller has a speed rating of 89, which is 11 points faster than Chris Baker, making him a bigger threat to make the catch deep.

Position: CB
Substitution: Justin Miller
When: Global
Advantage: This move isn't much of an improvement, but it does bring more speed to the nickelback position. Justin Miller's speed rating is 98, compared to Hank Poteat's speed rating of 88. If you send him on a blitz, he will get to the quarterback quicker.

TEAM STRATEGY

NEW YORK JETS

TEAM STRATEGY

#66 Alan Faneca *Guard (LG)*

▼OFFENSIVE STAR PLAYER

Alan Faneca is, by far, one of the best guards in the game. As a Steeler, he helped carve the way for running backs to find open running lanes. The Jets hope that he can do the same for them. He plays with a nasty mean streak and makes defenders pay for getting in his way.

Run Block Strength	95
Run Block Footwork	92
Pass Block Strength	90
Pass Block Footwork	86

Player Weapon: Crushing Run Blocker

#87 Laveranues Coles *Wide Receiver (WR)*

▼OFFENSIVE STAR PLAYER

The team's best playmaker on offense is Laveranues Coles. He is not a big receiver, but he does possess blazing elite receiver speed, which allows him to make big plays down the field. Despite his speed, the Jets don't throw long too often; instead, several of his catches are made underneath the coverage.

Speed	97
Catch	91
Catch In Traffic	95
Route Run	86

Player Weapon: Spec Catch Receiver, Possession Receiver, Hands, Speed

#49 Tony Richardson *Fullback (FB)*

▼OFFENSIVE STAR PLAYER

Over the years, fullback Tony Richardson has been known for his hard-nosed lead blocking. At age 36, he is not as effective of a runner, but he still opens plenty of holes to follow through. Look for the Jets to have him in the line up when they are near the goal line so he can do what he does best: open holes.

Speed	82
Run Block	63
Pass Block	50
Impact Block	82

Player Weapon: None

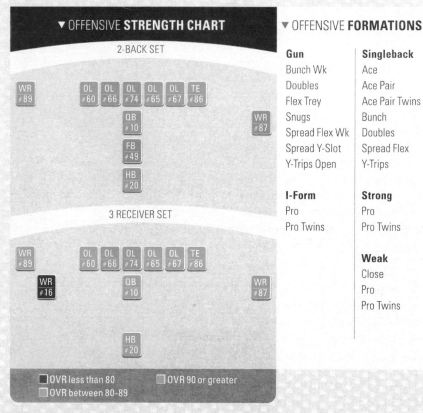

▼ OFFENSIVE STRENGTH CHART

2-BACK SET

WR #89 | OL #60 | OL #66 | OL #74 | OL #65 | OL #67 | TE #86 | WR #87
QB #10
FB #49
HB #20

3 RECEIVER SET

WR #89 | OL #60 | OL #66 | OL #74 | OL #65 | OL #67 | TE #86
WR #16 | QB #10 | WR #87
HB #20

☐ OVR less than 80   ☐ OVR 90 or greater
☐ OVR between 80-89

▼ OFFENSIVE FORMATIONS

Gun	Singleback
Bunch Wk	Ace
Doubles	Ace Pair
Flex Trey	Ace Pair Twins
Snugs	Bunch
Spread Flex Wk	Doubles
Spread Y-Slot	Spread Flex
Y-Trips Open	Y-Trips

I-Form	Strong
Pro	Pro
Pro Twins	Pro Twins

	Weak
	Close
	Pro
	Pro Twins

▼ RECOMMENDED OFFENSIVE AUDIBLE PACKAGES

Singleback	Singleback	Weak	Gun	Gun
HB Stretch	Slants	HB Gut	Corner Strike	Hitch Corners

▼ OFFENSIVE PLAYCOUNTS

Quick Pass:	21	Screen Pass:	7	Pitch:	5
Standard Pass:	68	Hail Mary:	1	Counter:	8
Shotgun Pass:	36	Inside Handoff:	25	Draw:	13
Play Action Pass:	58	Outside Handoff:	17		

OFFENSE KEY OFFENSIVE PLAYS

OFFENSE **KEY OFFENSIVE PLAYS**

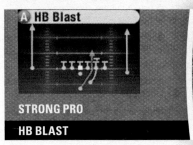

A HB Blast

STRONG PRO

HB BLAST

If you are looking to move the chains, you can't go wrong with giving Thomas Jones the ball on this play.

1 Follow the fullback through the hole between the center and left guard when the play is flipped.

2 If nothing opens up inside, look to bounce Jones outside where there may be running room.

3 We manage to pick up a tough 4 yards before being tackled.

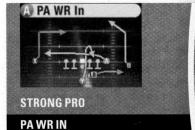

A PA WR In

STRONG PRO

PA WR IN

The Strong Pro PA WR In works off of the HB Blast. Look for Jerricho Cotchery running the dig from left to right.

1 The quarterback fakes the handoff to the halfback. Notice that a few defenders bite on the play fake.

2 As Cotchery breaks over the middle, we throw him a hard bullet pass.

3 We make the catch for about 8 yards and turn up the field for a few more.

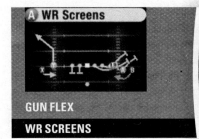

A WR Screens

GUN FLEX

WR SCREENS

Getting the ball to receiver Laveranues Coles is a must if you want to have success with the Jets' passing attack.

1 The Gun Flex WR Screens gets the ball to him by setting up a screen on the right side.

2 The key to this play is getting a few blocks by the big men out front.

3 If they are able to hold their blocks for long enough, there is big potential once to the outside.

TEAM STRATEGY

 **NEW YORK JETS**

TEAM STRATEGY

#25 Kerry Rhodes *Safety (SS)*

▼DEFENSIVE **STAR PLAYER**

One of the better overall safeties in the game is Kerry Rhodes. When he is able to freelance, he makes plays all over the field. This is evident by the 68 tackles, 2 sacks, and 5 interceptions he had last season. Look for a repeat performance as the Jets continue to build a strong secondary.

Speed	88
Man Cover	60
Zone Cover	90
Hit Power	80

Player Weapon: Smart Safety

#77 Kris Jenkins *Defensive Tackle (DT)*

▼DEFENSIVE **STAR PLAYER**

When he is able to keep his weight down, defensive tackle Kris Jenkins is a force to be reckoned with. With him taking on two defenders at once, he will free up the linebackers to make plays against the run and also free up defenders to shoot gaps to put pressure on the quarterback.

Speed	60
Strength	93
Power Moves	95
Finesse Moves	80

Player Weapon: Power Move D-Lineman

#92 Shaun Ellis *Defensive End (LE)*

▼DEFENSIVE **STAR PLAYER**

Clearly, the Jets' best pass rushing defensive linemen is Shaun Ellis. His sack totals don't necessarily reflect his ability to get to the quarterback, because he is often asked to keep containment and play to stop the run first. Because of this, he is not as aggressive as he could be in going after the quarterback.

Speed	69
Strength	87
Power Moves	90
Finesse Moves	75

Player Weapon: None

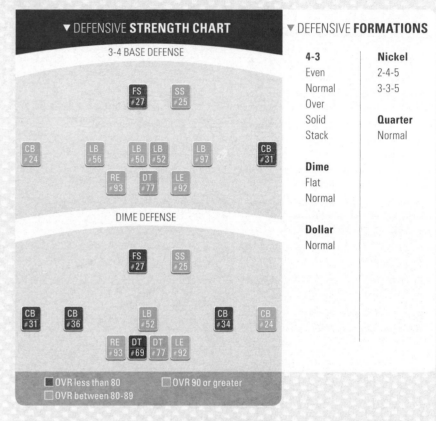

▼ DEFENSIVE **STRENGTH CHART**

3-4 BASE DEFENSE

FS #27 SS #25

CB #24 LB #56 LB #50 LB #52 LB #97 CB #31

RE #93 DT #77 LE #92

DIME DEFENSE

FS #27 SS #25

CB #31 CB #36 LB #52 CB #34 CB #24

RE #93 DT #69 DT #77 LE #92

☐ OVR less than 80
☐ OVR between 80-89
☐ OVR 90 or greater

▼ DEFENSIVE **FORMATIONS**

4-3	Nickel
Even	2-4-5
Normal	3-3-5
Over	
Solid	**Quarter**
Stack	Normal
Dime	
Flat	
Normal	
Dollar	
Normal	

▼ RECOMMENDED DEFENSIVE **AUDIBLE PACKAGES**

3-4	3-4	Nickel	Dime	Quarter
Cover 1 Press	OLB Dogs Fire	Cover 3	Cover 2	3 Deep Man

▼ DEFENSIVE **PLAYCOUNTS**

Man Coverage:	45	Cover 2 Zone:	22	Man Blitz:	59
Man Zone:	39	Cover 3 Zone:	26	Zone Blitz:	57
Combo Coverage:	6	Deep Zone:	14	Combo Blitz:	6

DEFENSE **KEY DEFENSIVE PLAYS**

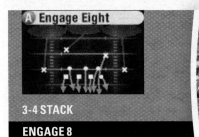

3-4 STACK
ENGAGE 8

The 3-4 Stack Engage 8 is a solid inside run defense to call to slow down the opposing offense's inside rushing attack.

Jets linebacker David Harris shoots through the gap and goes straight after the ball carrier.

Even Dolphins running back Ronnie Brown will have a hard time finding any daylight.

Harris gets penetration and is able to get to Brown before he ever gets to the line of scrimmage.

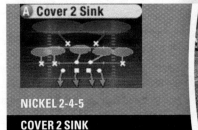

NICKEL 2-4-5
COVER 2 SINK

The Nickel 2-3-5 Cover 2 Sink does a good job of covering underneath portions of the field. The two safeties cover the deep halves.

One of the strengths of this defensive coverage is that it covers quick slants very well.

The left inside linebacker is perfectly positioned to pick the pass off or at least make the tackle.

David Harris steps in front of the receiver and picks the pass off.

DOLLAR NORMAL
STR EAGLE SLANT 3

Overloading one side of the offensive line with Jets' defenders is good a way to get quick pressure on the opposing quarterback.

The Dollar Normal Str Eagle Slant 3 has three pass rushers on the left side of the offensive line.

The defenders drop back, taking away any threat of the deep passing game.

Rookie linebacker Vernon Gholston gets to the quarterback before he can get the ball off.

TEAM STRATEGY

DETROIT LIONS

▶ **Division** NFC North ▶ **Stadium** Ford Field ▶ **Type** Dome ▶ **Capacity** 65,000 ▶ **Surface** Field Turf

2007 STANDINGS

Wins	Loses	Ties	PF	PA	Home	Road	vs. AFC	vs. NFC	vs. Div
7	9	0	346	444	5-3	2-6	3-1	4-8	3-3

TEAM OVERVIEW

Look for the Lions to be more of a hard-nosed team than ever. The team has taken on a new look since Rod Marinelli took control in 2006. Only 13 players remain of the team that Marinelli inherited.

With offensive coordinator Mike Martz now gone, look for the Lions' offensive playbook to be more balanced than it was in 2007. By running the ball more, this should free up passing lanes for standout receivers Roy Williams and Calvin Johnson.

The Lions traded away arguably their best defensive player in Shaun Rogers. It remains to be seen if anyone will be able to replace his ability to stop the inside run and put pressure on the quarterback up the gut. The secondary will be much improved to play the Tampa 2 scheme with new additions Brian Kelly and Leigh Bodden.

OFF-SEASON UPGRADES

TYPE	ROUND	FIRST NAME	LAST NAME	SCHOOL/TEAM	POSITION
Trade	N/A	Leigh	Bodden	Browns	CB
Free Agent	N/A	Brian	Kelly	Buccaneers	CB
Draft	1	Gosder	Cherilus	Boston College	T
Draft	2	Jordon	Dixon	Colorado	LB
Draft	3	Kevin	Smith	Central Florida	RB

SCOUTING REPORT

	DESCRIPTION	MAXIMIZING POTENTIAL	TIPS FOR OPPONENTS
STRENGTHS	Wide receivers Roy Williams and Calvin Johnson are two huge targets to look for when down inside the red zone.	Have Williams and Johnson run fades inside the red zone so they can jump up to make the catch.	Don't let Williams and Johnson beat you in the red zone. Call double coverage.
	Ernie Sims is excellent at tackling. His ability to chase down ball carriers cannot be overlooked.	Find ways to keep blockers off of Sims so that he can use his speed to bring ball carriers down.	Instead of running away from Sims, run towards him and force him to fight or shed blocks off.
WEAKNESSES	The Detroit Lions want to run the ball this season, but the big question is: who is going to carry the load?	We suggest going with rookie Kevin Smith because he can pick up the tough yardage inside.	Don't load up the box to stop the run. The Lions' passing game is much more effective than their run game.
	The Lions do not have an elite pass rusher at defensive end or defensive tackle to put pressure on the quarterback.	You will have to be creative to get pressure on the quarterback. Consider using zone blitz schemes.	Unless the Lions blitz, you will have all day in the pocket to pick the Lions' secondary apart.

TEAM STRATEGY

FRANCHISE MODE STRATEGY

Kitna is no spring chicken, so start looking for a future replacement. Look to get more help for the offensive line. Consider trading one of your receivers for a stud middle linebacker.

KEY FRANCHISE INFORMATION

Cap Room: $31.43M

Key Rivals:
- Bears, Packers, Vikings

Philosophy:
- Offense: Run with Play Action
- Defense: 4-3, Tampa 2

Highest Paid Players:
- C. Johnson
- C. Redding

Top Team Weapons:
- E. Sims – Big Hitter
- R. Williams – Spectacular Catch Receiver

Best Young Players:
- E. Sims
- C. Johnson

78	82	77
OVERALL	OFFENSE	DEFENSE

With a year under his belt, Calvin Johnson may be poised to put up numbers comparable to his eye-popping physical attributes as the Lions roar into 2008.

▼ ROSTER AND **PACKAGE TIPS**

KEY PLAYER SUBSTITUTIONS

Postion: FB
Substitution: Jerome Felton
When: Global
Advantage: This move is a must if you plan on playing with the Lions. We can't find any reason Jerome Felton shouldn't be the team's starting fullback. Felton is faster, a better blocker, and catches the ball better than default starter Jon Bradley.

Postion: TE
Substitution: Michael Gains
When: Global
Advantage: Here is another team that has a faster tight end at the number 2 spot. Michael Gaines has a higher overall rating than Dan Campbell. The only reason we may keep Campbell as our starter is because he is a better run blocker.

Postion: FS
Substitution: Gerald Alexander
When: Global
Advantage: Gerald Alexander has a little more range than starter Daniel Bullocks. However, if you make this move, keep in mind that Bullocks's awareness is higher and he has a slightly better catch rating.

TEAM STRATEGY

TEAM STRATEGY

#11 Roy Williams *Wide Receiver (WR)*

▼OFFENSIVE **STAR PLAYER**

Despite trade rumors circulating during the offseason, Roy Williams will remain a Lion. His ability to make spectacular catches around the goal line makes him an excellent target. With the Lions going to a more balanced attack, he may not put up big numbers, but 1,000 yards and 8 touchdown catches is not out of the question.

Speed	92
Catch	92
Catch In Traffic	86
Route Run	87

Player Weapon: Spec Catch Receiver, Hands

#81 Calvin Johnson *Wide Receiver (WR)*

▼OFFENSIVE **STAR PLAYER**

Calvin Johnson had high expectations last season as a rookie, but due to injuries and a complex passing system, he never really got on track. Johnson has the speed, height, and hands to be an elite receiver. It's just a matter of putting all those attributes together at the same time to make an impact on the field this season.

Awareness	84
Speed	49
Throwing Power	86
Throwing Accuracy	91

Player Weapon: Go-To-Guy/Stiff Arm, Possession Receiver, Quick Receiver, Spectacular Catch Receiver

#51 Dominic Raiola *Center (C)*

▼OFFENSIVE **STAR PLAYER**

If the Lions plan on getting the rushing game on track in 2008, it all starts by running the ball behind center Dominic Raiola. His athletic ability allows him to take good angles at opening holes in the run game. He is also a good pass blocker and keeps defensive tackles from getting much of a push up the middle.

Run Block Strength	84
Run Block Footwork	88
Pass Block Strength	86
Pass Block Footwork	85

Player Weapon: None

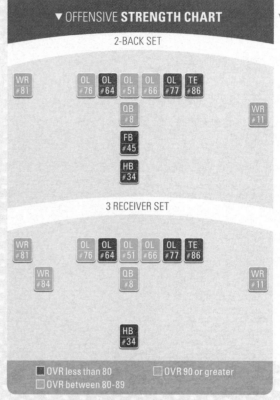

▼ OFFENSIVE **STRENGTH CHART**

2-BACK SET

WR #81 — OL #76, OL #64, OL #51, OL #66, OL #77, TE #86 — WR #11
QB #8
FB #45
HB #34

3 RECEIVER SET

WR #81 — OL #76, OL #64, OL #51, OL #66, OL #77, TE #86 — WR #11
WR #84 — QB #8
HB #34

■ OVR less than 80   □ OVR 90 or greater
□ OVR between 80-89

▼ OFFENSIVE **FORMATIONS**

Empty	Singleback
Trey Flex	Ace
	Doubles
I-Form	F Wing
Pro	Spread Flex
Pro Twins	Trey Open
Slot Flex	Wing Trio
Tight	Y-Trips
Rifle	**Split**
Doubles	Slot
Doubles Y-Slot	
Snugs Flip	**Strong**
Split Slot	Pro
Spread Flex Wk	Slot
Y-Trips	
	Weak
	H Pro
	H Slot

▼ RECOMMENDED OFFENSIVE **AUDIBLE PACKAGES**

Singleback	Strong	I-Form	Rifle	Empty
HB Counter	494 F Flat	Power 0	Corner Strike	Curl Flats

▼ OFFENSIVE **PLAYCOUNTS**

Quick Pass:	16	Screen Pass:	12	Pitch:	7
Standard Pass:	98	Hail Mary:	1	Counter:	8
Shotgun Pass:	50	Inside Handoff:	31	Draw:	15
Play Action Pass:	53	Outside Handoff:	14		

OFFENSE **KEY OFFENSIVE PLAYS**

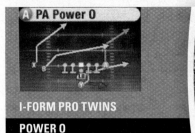

I-FORM PRO TWINS
POWER O

1

2

3

The Lions want to be more balanced this season. The I-Form Pro Twins Power O is a good play to start with.

Look to follow the fullback through the opening once the ball is handed off to the halfback.

If nothing opens up inside, look to bounce it to the left guard's side.

Once outside, press the sprint button and head towards the sideline.

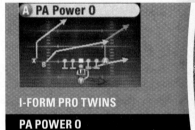

I-FORM PRO TWINS
PA POWER O

1

2

3

A good play action play that works in conjunction with the Power O is the PA Power O. The tight end is the play's primary receiver.

First, look for the tight end who is running the corner route. If he is not open, look for the fullback.

The tight end is covered running the corner route. The fullback is open in the flat.

If neither is open, look for the slot receiver running a crossing route left to right.

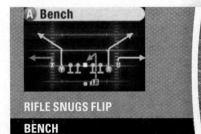

RIFLE SNUGS FLIP
BENCH

1

2

3

Calvin Johnson has plenty of speed to get open. We like to use the Rifle Snugs Flip Bench to get him open.

He runs up the field about 5 yards, and then makes a hard cut towards the sideline.

When he has gained some separation from his man, we throw him a bullet pass.

We make the catch about 7 yards past the line of scrimmage. We turn up the field and pick up a few more.

TEAM STRATEGY

 **DETROIT LIONS**

TEAM STRATEGY

#50 Ernie Sims *Linebacker (ROLB)*

▼DEFENSIVE **STAR PLAYER**

There is no question as to who is the star of the Lions' defensive unit. Last season, Ernie Sims racked up an amazing 134 tackles, which placed him 4th in the league. He is not often asked to blitz, but if called upon, he can get to the quarterback. He is a big time playmaker and needs to be on the field at all times.

Speed	90
Tackling	93
Pursuit	96
Play Recog.	72

Player Weapon: Big Hitter, Brick Wall Defender

#78 Cory Redding *Defensive Tackle (DT)*

▼DEFENSIVE **STAR PLAYER**

While he didn't put the same type of stats last season as he did the previous season, Redding still must be accounted for. He has the ability to push the pocket from his defensive tackle position. With Shawn Rogers now gone, it's imperative that Redding plays like his 2006 form and not his 2007 form.

Speed	70
Strength	88
Power Moves	88
Finesse Moves	78

#30 Leigh Bodden *Cornerback (CB)*

▼DEFENSIVE **STAR PLAYER**

Leigh Bodden had his best season as a cornerback by picking off 6 passes as a Cleveland Brown. He was traded to the Lions in the same deal that sent defensive tackle Shawn Rogers to the Browns. The Lions need Bodden to be a solid cornerback in the Tampa 2 to slow down the opposing offense's passing attack.

Speed	90
Man Cover	93
Zone Cover	87
Press	88

Player Weapon: Shutdown Corner

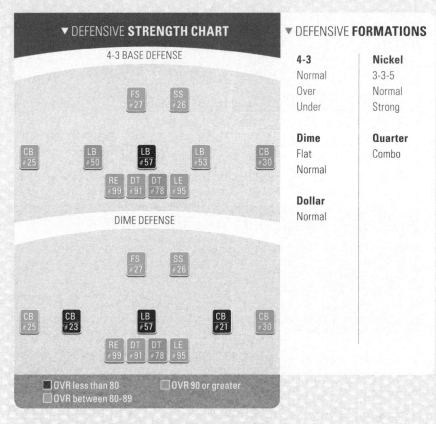

▼ **DEFENSIVE STRENGTH CHART**

4-3 BASE DEFENSE

FS #27 SS #26

CB #25 LB #50 LB #57 LB #53 CB #30

RE #99 DT #91 DT #78 LE #95

DIME DEFENSE

FS #27 SS #26

CB #25 CB #23 LB #57 CB #21 CB #30

RE #99 DT #91 DT #78 LE #95

- ■ OVR less than 80
- □ OVR between 80-89
- □ OVR 90 or greater

▼ DEFENSIVE **FORMATIONS**

4-3	Nickel
Normal	3-3-5
Over	Normal
Under	Strong
Dime	**Quarter**
Flat	Combo
Normal	
Dollar	
Normal	

▼ RECOMMENDED DEFENSIVE **AUDIBLE PACKAGES**

4-3	4-3	Nickel	Dime	Quarter
2 Man Press	LB Dogs	Cover 2	Cover 3	3 Deep Press

▼ DEFENSIVE **PLAYCOUNTS**

Man Coverage:	45	Cover 2 Zone:	14	Man Blitz:	55
Man Zone:	34	Cover 3 Zone:	26	Zone Blitz:	64
Combo Coverage:	7	Deep Zone:	18	Combo Blitz:	13

DEFENSE **KEY DEFENSIVE PLAYS**

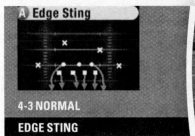

Ⓐ Edge Sting

4-3 NORMAL

EDGE STING

1

2

3

The Lions defense may have to incorporate a few more run blitz schemes to stop the outside rushing attack.

A good outside run defense is the 4-3 Over Edge Sting.

This run defense sends both outside linebackers on run blitz assignments.

If the running back tries to go outside, one of them will be in place to make the tackle.

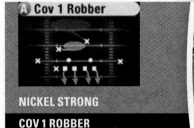

Ⓐ Cov 1 Robber

NICKEL STRONG

COV 1 ROBBER

1

2

3

The Nickel Strong Cov 1 Robber drops the strong safety over the deep middle, while the free safety plays robber underneath.

This pass coverage is helpful when an offense likes to have receivers run post routes.

Lions' strong safety Dwight Smith is in good position to pick the pass off or swat it down.

We take control of Smith and swat the pass away from the Packers' tight end.

Ⓐ Overload Blitz

DIME FLAT

OVERLOAD BLITZ

1

2

3

The Dime Flat Overload Blitz is designed to overload the left side of the offensive line with multiple pass rushers.

The left guard and left tackle are outnumbered. They can't block all three pass rushers.

Lions' right end Dewayne White is left unblocked, and has a clear path at the quarterback.

Packer Aaron Rodgers has no one open down the field and is about to be leveled.

TEAM STRATEGY

GREEN BAY PACKERS

▸ **Division** NFC North   ▸ **Stadium** Lambeau Field   ▸ **Type** Open   ▸ **Capacity** 72,928   ▸ **Surface** Grass

▼ 2007 STANDINGS

Wins	Loses	Ties	PF	PA	Home	Road	vs. AFC	vs. NFC	vs. Div
13	3	0	435	291	7-1	6-2	4-0	9-3	4-2

▼ TEAM OVERVIEW

The unexpected retirement of NFL Legend Brett Favre will certainly have an impact on the team's passing game, but not all is lost. Four year man Aaron Rogers is ready to be the trigger man. He should be able run the short quick passing game without too much of a letdown.

Packers running back Ryan Grant has enough speed and power to move the chains. His abilities will help prevent the opposing defense from sitting back and defending the pass. The Packers have an abundance of receivers to spread the ball around. Donald Driver and Greg Jennings are one of the better pass-catching tandems in the game.

The defense is led by defensive end sack master Aaron Kapman and tackling machine middle linebacker Nick Barnett. Both are disruptive players who will force opposing offenses to game plan around them.

▼ OFF-SEASON UPGRADES

TYPE	ROUND	FIRST NAME	LAST NAME	SCHOOL/TEAM	POSITION
Free Agent	N/A	Brandon	Chillar	Rams	LB
Draft	2	Jordy	Nelson	Kansas State	WR
Draft	2	Brian	Brohm	Louisville	QB
Draft	2	Patrick	Lee	Auburn	CB
Draft	3	Jermichael	Finley	Texas	TE

▼ SCOUTING REPORT

	DESCRIPTION	MAXIMIZING POTENTIAL	TIPS FOR OPPONENTS
STRENGTHS	Ryan Grant came on strong about midway though last season and never looked back. He will ease the transition for Aaron Rogers.	Give the ball to Grant plenty of times to open up passing lanes for Rogers.	Load the box with eight and nine fronts. Don't let Grant get the running game going.
STRENGTHS	Greg Jennings has a knack for getting in the end zone; leading the Packers to be one of the better red zone offenses in the league.	Anytime you are near the end zone, make sure Jennings is the primary target.	Force the Packers to throw to another receiver. Double-team him if he becomes a problem.
WEAKNESSES	Al Harris and Charles Woodson are two of the best press corners in the game, due to their physical style of play.	Anytime man coverage is called, be sure to put Harris and Woodson in press coverage.	Find plays that beat press coverage, because you will be seeing a lot of it when playing against the Packers.
WEAKNESSES	Anytime a young quarterback takes over an offense, expect the defense to call a lot of blitz packages to try and confuse him.	Run a lot of play action and quick developing pass plays to beat the blitz.	Dial up as many blitz packages as you can until Rogers shows he can beat them consistently.

FRANCHISE MODE STRATEGY

Time will tell if Aaron Rodgers can be the new franchise QB. While you wait, get a third cornerback to back up Harris and Woodson, who are both getting into their 30's. Other than that, draft for depth.

KEY FRANCHISE INFORMATION

Cap Room: $26.04M

Key Rivals:
- Bears, Lions, Vikings

Philosophy:
- Offense: West Coast
- Defense: 4-3

Highest Paid Players:
- C. Woodson
- K. Gbaja Biamila

Team Weapons:
- A. Kampman – Power Move D-Lineman
- C. Clifton – Pass Blocker

Best Young Players:
- A. Hawk
- G. Jennings

91
OVERALL

87
OFFENSE

92
DEFENSE

▼ ROSTER AND **PACKAGE TIPS**

KEY PLAYER SUBSTITUTIONS

Postion: RE

Substitution: Kabeer Gbaja-Biamila

When: Situational Pass Rusher

Advantage: Cullen Jenkins is a menace when it comes to stopping the run, but he is not the same pass rushing threat as KGB is. Another possible move is to move Jenkins inside at defensive tackle where he is a 91 overall and start KGB at RE.

Postion: 3RRB

Substitution: Ryan Grant

When: Global

Advantage: Ryan Grant has really good hands and there is no reason to sub him out in third down situations. While Brandon Jackson is good, Grant is better. You may also consider putting them in the backfield together.

Postion: FB

Substitution: John Kuhn

When: Passing Situations

Advantage: If you plan on throwing the ball more often than running it, consider starting John Kuhn at fullback. He brings more speed and has better hands than default starter Korey Hall.

It will be a brave new world for Ryan Grant and the Packers in 2008, but a stout defense and solid receiving corps should help smooth the transition for QB Aaron Rogers and the rest of the team.

TEAM STRATEGY

TEAM STRATEGY

#80 Donald Driver *Wide Receiver (WR)*

▼OFFENSIVE **STAR PLAYER**

Donald Driver didn't get in the end zone very much last season. As a matter of fact, he only managed to make two trips. However, he did lead the team in receptions and yards. Driver doesn't have top end speed, but he runs crisp routes that allow him to gain separation and get open just about anywhere on the field.

Speed	93
Catch	90
Catch In Traffic	90
Route Run	93

Player Weapon: Quick Receiver, Possession Receiver, Hands

#25 Ryan Grant *Halfback (HB)*

▼OFFENSIVE **STAR PLAYER**

Ryan Grant was an afterthought in New York and was traded to the Packers last offseason. With the Packers' running game struggling, Grant was inserted into the starting line-up. By the end of the season, he was one of the key reasons the Packers made it to all the way to the NFC Championship game.

Speed	93
Agility	88
Trucking	92
Elusiveness	77

Player Weapon: Power Back

#76 Chad Clifton *Tackle (LT)*

▼OFFENSIVE **STAR PLAYER**

One of the premier left tackles in the game today is Chad Clifton. His ability to keep top pass rushers off the quarterback makes him ideal for any team that likes to spread the offense. The Packers are one of those teams, and Clifton fits the mold perfectly.

Run Block Strength	93
Run Block Footwork	88
Pass Block Strength	95
Pass Block Footwork	92

Player Weapon: Pass Blocker

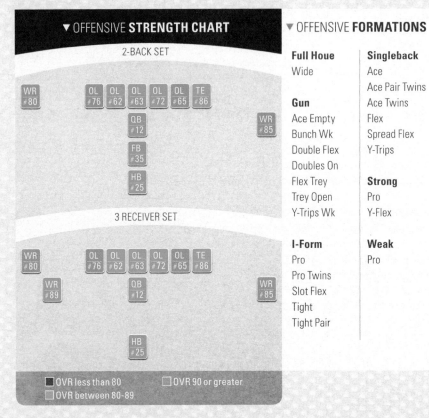

▼ OFFENSIVE **STRENGTH CHART**

2-BACK SET

WR #80 — OL #76, OL #62, OL #63, OL #72, OL #65, TE #86 — WR #85
QB #12
FB #35
HB #25

3 RECEIVER SET

WR #80 — OL #76, OL #62, OL #63, OL #72, OL #65, TE #86
WR #89 — QB #12 — WR #85
HB #25

■ OVR less than 80   □ OVR 90 or greater
□ OVR between 80-89

▼ OFFENSIVE **FORMATIONS**

Full Houe	Singleback
Wide	Ace
	Ace Pair Twins
Gun	Ace Twins
Ace Empty	Flex
Bunch Wk	Spread Flex
Double Flex	Y-Trips
Doubles On	
Flex Trey	**Strong**
Trey Open	Pro
Y-Trips Wk	Y-Flex
I-Form	**Weak**
Pro	Pro
Pro Twins	
Slot Flex	
Tight	
Tight Pair	

▼ RECOMMENDED OFFENSIVE **AUDIBLE PACKAGES**

Singleback	I-Form	Singleback	Gun	Gun
HB slam	Inside Cross	HB Slant	Deep Curl	Hitch Corners

▼ OFFENSIVE **PLAYCOUNTS**

Quick Pass:	14	Screen Pass:	7	Pitch:	4
Standard Pass:	76	Hail Mary:	2	Counter:	11
Shotgun Pass:	69	Inside Handoff:	27	Draw:	10
Play Action Pass:	61	Outside Handoff:	16		

OFFENSE **KEY OFFENSIVE PLAYS**

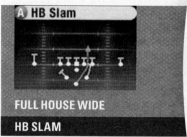

A HB Slam

FULL HOUSE WIDE

HB SLAM

The Full House Wide is regarded as one of the better running formations in the game. It just happens to be in the Packers playbook.

The HB Slam is one of the staple run plays you will find in this formation.

We cut back Packers' running back Ryan Grant and follow the tight end through the hole.

We pick up 5 yards before finally being brought down from behind.

A PA Middle

FULL HOUSE WIDE

PA MIDDLE

A good Full House Wide play action play to call once you establish the HB Slam with Grant is the PA Middle.

Aaron Rogers fakes the hand-off to Grant. Notice how a few of the defenders freeze.

Once the play fake is complete, we look for Greg Jennings on the Dig route.

We take control of Jennings just as the catch is made.

A Mesh

GUN BUNCH WK

MESH

The Mesh is a popular passing concept that is used by several NFL teams to keep the chains moving through the air.

The drag routes of two receivers cross each other in the middle of the field.

Against zone coverage, one of them is almost always open for a hard bullet pass.

If the catch is made on the run, there is usually some YAC to be gained.

TEAM STRATEGY

#74 Aaron Kampman *Defensive End (LE)*

▼DEFENSIVE **STAR PLAYER**

One of the least mentioned top defensive ends around the league is Aaron Kampman. He doesn't get the same recognition of some players in his position. Over the last two seasons, he has racked up a total of 27 sacks. There may not be a more consistent pass rusher than Kampman.

Speed	79
Strength	86
Power Moves	95
Finesse Moves	90

Player Weapon: Power Move D-Lineman

#31 Al Harris *Cornerback (CB)*

▼DEFENSIVE **STAR PLAYER**

Al Harris remains one of the top bump-n-run corners in the game. He uses his hands to get a hold of receivers at the line of scrimmage, thus slowing them down and preventing them from getting out in their pass routes. The only knock on him is some bigger receivers tend to give him problems.

Speed	88
Man Cover	95
Zone Cover	90
Press	98

Player Weapon: Smart Corner, Shutdown Corner, Press Coverage Corner

#50 A.J. Hawk *Linebacker (ROLB)*

▼DEFENSIVE **STAR PLAYER**

A.J. Hawk didn't have the same type of impact his second season as he did in the first season. Still, he is considered one of the hardest workers on the team. His speed allows him to make plays from sideline to sideline. He is an every down linebacker; when given space, he can make plays all over the field.

Speed	87
Tackling	92
Pursuit	94
Play Recog.	80

Player Weapon: Brick Wall Defender

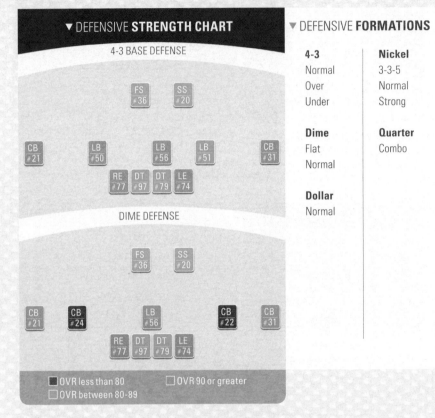

▼DEFENSIVE **STRENGTH CHART**

4-3 BASE DEFENSE

DIME DEFENSE

■ OVR less than 80 □ OVR 90 or greater
□ OVR between 80-89

▼DEFENSIVE **FORMATIONS**

4-3	Nickel
Normal	3-3-5
Over	Normal
Under	Strong

Dime	Quarter
Flat	Combo
Normal	

Dollar	
Normal	

▼ RECOMMENDED DEFENSIVE **AUDIBLE PACKAGES**

4-3	4-3	Nickel	Dime	Quarter
2 Man Press	Edge Sting	Cover 3	Cover 2	3 Deep Press

▼ DEFENSIVE **PLAYCOUNTS**

Man Coverage:	45	Cover 2 Zone:	14	Man Blitz:	55
Man Zone:	34	Cover 3 Zone:	26	Zone Blitz:	64
Combo Coverage:	7	Deep Zone:	18	Combo Blitz:	13

CB Blitz

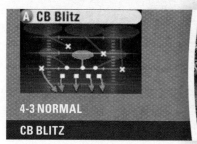

4-3 NORMAL

CB BLITZ

The 4-3 Normal CB Blitz has cornerback Charles Woodson blitzing from the left side of the offensive line.

If the offense calls an outside run play to his side, he will be in position to make the tackle.

The pass coverage is also solid with three defenders dropping back in deep coverage.

Woodson wraps the ball carrier up in the backfield before he has a chance to get to the line.

Zone Man X

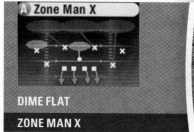

DIME FLAT

ZONE MAN X

If you are using the Packers, use the Dime Flat Zone Man X to throw off your opponent and hide your coverage.

This play puts cornerback Jarrett Bush in man coverage, while the rest of the defense plays zone.

If your opponent thinks man, he may attempt to throw a pass to the receiver covered by Bush.

If he does, he better watch for middle linebacker Nick Barnett dropping back in a hook zone.

2 Man Press

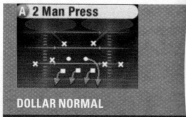

DOLLAR NORMAL

2 MAN PRESS

The Packers have two of the better pressing cornerbacks in the game. The Dollar Normal 2 Man Press showcases these talents.

Green Bay Packers' cornerback Al Harris jams his man at the line of scrimmage.

The safeties split out wide in 2 deep coverage to help prevent the deep ball.

Because the pass coverage is tight, there is a good chance of getting a coverage sack from a D-lineman.

TEAM STRATEGY

CAROLINA PANTHERS

▶ **Division** NFC South ▶ **Stadium** Bank Of America Stadium ▶ **Type** Open ▶ **Capacity** 73,504 ▶ **Surface** Grass

▼ 2007 STANDINGS

Wins	Loses	Ties	PF	PA	Home	Road	vs. AFC	vs. NFC	vs. Div
7	9	0	267	347	2-6	5-3	0-4	7-5	3-3

▼ TEAM OVERVIEW

The Panthers want to get back to pounding the ball and stopping the run on defense. They added some much needed punch along the offensive line by adding rookie offensive tackle Jeff Otah in the first round. On the defensive side of the ball, the defensive line has a lot of ques-tion marks and so stopping the run may be a huge task.

Steve Smith continues to be the Panthers' one consistent playmaker on offense, so getting him the ball is a must. The running game should be better with the improvement along the offensive line, plus the addition of rookie running back Jonathan Stewart.

The loss of defensive tackle Kris Jenkins to free agency and the retirement of defensive end Mike Rucker puts a sting on the Panthers' ability to stop the run.

▼ OFF-SEASON UPGRADES

TYPE	ROUND	FIRST NAME	LAST NAME	SCHOOL/TEAM	POSITION
Free Agent	N/A	D.J.	Hackett	Seahawks	WR
Free Agent	N/A	Muhsin	Muhammad	Bears	WR
Draft	1	Jonathan	Stewart	Oregon	RB
Draft	1	Jeff	Otah	Pittsburgh	T
Draft	3	Charles	Godfrey	Iowa	CB

▼ SCOUTING REPORT

	DESCRIPTION	MAXIMIZING POTENTIAL	TIPS FOR OPPONENTS
STRENGTHS	Steve Smith can outrun most cornerbacks in the game. With his speed, he gets deep and makes the big play down field.	Move Smith around and try to get him matched up with slower defend-ers. Look to go deep with him.	Keep an eye on Smith. Don't leave him matched up with a slower defender.
STRENGTHS	Julius Peppers remains a feared pass rusher. His athletic ability allows him to get around slower offensive tackles.	Find defenses where Peppers takes an outside rush assignment, this gives him a better pass rush angle.	If Peppers is getting too much pres-sure, slide protect the offensive line to his side to slow him down.
WEAKNESSES	Outside of Steve Smith, the Panthers don't really have another receiver to rely on for the big play deep down the field.	Use Smith as a decoy by sending him deep. This will help open passing lanes for the receivers underneath.	Double team Smith and force Jake Delhomme to throw underneath to receivers who are less talented.
WEAKNESSES	With defensive tackle Kris Jenkins now gone, the Panthers' inside run defense has gotten much easier to run on.	Consider putting an extra defender in the box to keep your opponent's rush-ing attack in check.	Pound the rock at the heart of the Panthers' defensive line to see if it can stop the run or not.

TEAM STRATEGY

FRANCHISE MODE STRATEGY

Finding a good pass-catching TE will give Steve Smith more room to work with. Julius Peppers needs more help on the line so he can avoid double teams. Try to get a veteran safety to lock down the secondary.

KEY FRANCHISE INFORMATION

Cap Room: $23.18M

Key Rivals:
- Buccaneers, Falcons, Saints

Philosophy:
- Offense: Power Running
- Defense: 4-3

Highest Paid Players:
- S. Smith
- J. Delhomme

Team Weapons:
- Steve Smith – Speed
- Julius Peppers – Finesse Move D-Lineman

Best Young Players:
- R. Marshall
- J. Steward

86 | 87 | 86
OVERALL | OFFENSE | DEFENSE

▼ ROSTER AND **PACKAGE TIPS**
KEY PLAYER SUBSTITUTIONS

Postion: HB
Substitution: Jonathan Stewart
When: Global
Advantage: Rookie running back Jonathan Stewart should be inserted into the starting lineup if you plan on playing with the Panthers. Default starter DeAngelo Williams has the same speed rating, but for the most part, the key HB ratings favor Stewart.

Postion: FS
Substitution: Charles Godfrey
When: Global
Advantage: Starting Charles Godfrey gives the Panthers some more range in the secondary. He is six points faster than starter Nate Salley. Six points may not seem like much, but when manually controlling him, you will notice a big difference.

Postion: FB
Substitution: DeAngelo Williams
When: Dual HB Looks
Advantage: Pairing DeAngelo Williams and Jonathan Stewart in the same backfield together gives the Panthers some flexibility, and will keep the defense guessing on who is getting the ball. Obviously, Williams isn't much of a lead blocker, so don't use him at fullback if you plan on pounding the ball inside.

While WR Steve Smith can catch just about any ball thrown his way, it will help to have a healthy Jake Delhomme to give the Panthers more space for their smashmouth style.

TEAM STRATEGY

TEAM STRATEGY

#89 Steve Smith *Wide Receiver (WR)*

▼OFFENSIVE **STAR PLAYER**

Despite the quarterback carousel in Carolina, Steve Smith still managed to catch 87 passes and went over 1,000 yards for the third season in a row. At 5'9", Smith is not going to beat cornerbacks with his strength. What he will do is use his speed to blow by defenders and make plays all over the field.

Speed	97
Catch	95
Catch In Traffic	95
Route Run	93

Player Weapon: Quick Receiver, Possession Receiver, Hands, Speed

#87 Muhsin Muhammad *Wide Receiver (WR)*

▼OFFENSIVE **STAR PLAYER**

Back for his second tour with the Panthers, Muhsin Muhammad gives the team a legit number two receiver. He runs solid pass routes, and his good hands allow him to make tough catches in traffic. Muhammad is a big target and will be called upon when the Panthers get in the red zone.

Speed	85
Catch	90
Catch In Traffic	84
Route Run	90

Player Weapon: Hands

#17 Jake Delhomme *Quarterback (QB)*

▼OFFENSIVE **STAR PLAYER**

Jake Delhomme was never able to shake the injury bug last season, which not only hurt his passing numbers, but also had a domino effect on the Panthers' overall offensive production. He is healthy again and looks to bounce back before the rash of injures derail his NFL career.

Speed	63
Awareness	82
Throwing Power	88
Throwing Accuracy	88

Player Weapon: None

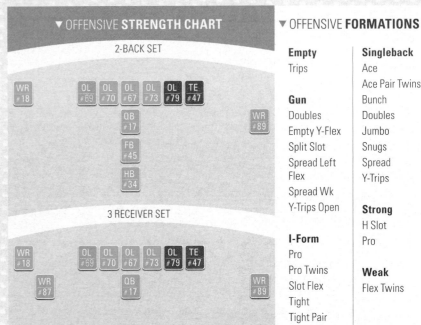

▼ **OFFENSIVE STRENGTH CHART**

2-BACK SET

WR #18 | OL #69 | OL #70 | OL #67 | OL #73 | OL #79 | TE #47 | WR #89
QB #17
FB #45
HB #34

3 RECEIVER SET

WR #18 | OL #69 | OL #70 | OL #67 | OL #73 | OL #79 | TE #47 | WR #89
WR #87 | QB #17
HB #34

☐ OVR less than 80   ☐ OVR 90 or greater
☐ OVR between 80-89

▼ **OFFENSIVE FORMATIONS**

Empty
Trips

Gun
Doubles
Empty Y-Flex
Split Slot
Spread Left Flex
Spread Wk
Y-Trips Open

I-Form
Pro
Pro Twins
Slot Flex
Tight
Tight Pair

Singleback
Ace
Ace Pair Twins
Bunch
Doubles
Jumbo
Snugs
Spread
Y-Trips

Strong
H Slot
Pro

Weak
Flex Twins

▼ RECOMMENDED OFFENSIVE **AUDIBLE PACKAGES**

Singleback	Strong	I-Form	Gun	Gun
HB Sprint	Y Shallow Cross	Stretch	Flat Combo	Double Cross

▼ OFFENSIVE **PLAYCOUNTS**

Quick Pass:	17	Screen Pass:	10	Pitch:	7
Standard Pass:	95	Hail Mary:	2	Counter:	9
Shotgun Pass:	52	Inside Handoff:	27	Draw:	12
Play Action Pass:	60	Outside Handoff:	17		

OFFENSE **KEY OFFENSIVE PLAYS**

(A) HB Dive

SINGLEBACK JUMBO

HB DIVE

The Panthers want to get back to pounding the ball inside. A good run play to start with is the Singleback Jumbo HB Dive.

1

With the extra tight ends in the line up, it gives the Singleback Jumbo HB Dive some extra punch.

2

We take control of DeAngelo Williams and look to run between the center and right guard.

3

Once through the hole, we cover the ball just as we are being tackled.

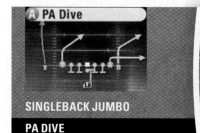

(A) PA Dive

SINGLEBACK JUMBO

PA DIVE

The Singleback Jumbo PA Dive is a good PA play to run after you have pounded the rock a few times with Williams.

1

The key to get this PA action play to work is getting the defense to bite on the play fake.

2

We like to air it out to speedster Steven Smith, who is running the fly route down the left sideline.

3

We take control of Smith and are able to get some separation from the defender as we make the catch.

(A) X-Clown

EMPTY TRIPS

X-CLOWN

A quick passing play to beat the blitz is the Empty Trips X-Clown. We like Ryne Robinson for our receiver.

1

Once the ball is snapped, we look for him first in the flat for a quick strike.

2

If he is not open in the flat, we look for D.J. Hackett on the deep post.

3

We make the catch in the flat, and take off down the field where we have open daylight.

TEAM STRATEGY

 **CAROLINA PANTHERS** DEFENSE

#90 Julius Peppers *Defensive End (RE)*

▼ DEFENSIVE **STAR PLAYER**

Last season was an enigma for one of the leading pass rushers of the last six seasons. Julius Peppers got to the quarterback just 2.5 times last season. The season before that, he registered 13 sacks. Peppers has way too much talent to have another down season; expect him to get back on top of his game in 2008.

Speed	87
Strength	80
Power Moves	84
Finesse Moves	97

Player Weapon: Big Hitter, Finesse Move D-Lineman

#52 Jon Beason *Linebacker (MLB)*

▼ DEFENSIVE **STAR PLAYER**

One of the most versatile middle linebackers in the league in only his second season, Jon Beason has established himself as a player that the opposing offense must account for. His speed and sure tackling ability allow him to make plays all over the field. He will again lead the team in tackles in 2008.

Speed	85
Tackling	94
Pursuit	97
Play Recog.	84

Player Weapon: Brick Wall Defender

#20 Chris Gamble *Cornerback (CB)*

▼ DEFENSIVE **STAR PLAYER**

Just like his last name, Chris Gamble likes to take chances when playing cornerback. When healthy, he will often gamble that his talents will allow him to make the big play. In most cases, the results are positive for the Panthers' defense. Last season, his interception total was down because he was fighting through injuries.

Speed	92
Man Cover	90
Zone Cover	90
Press	75

Player Weapon: None

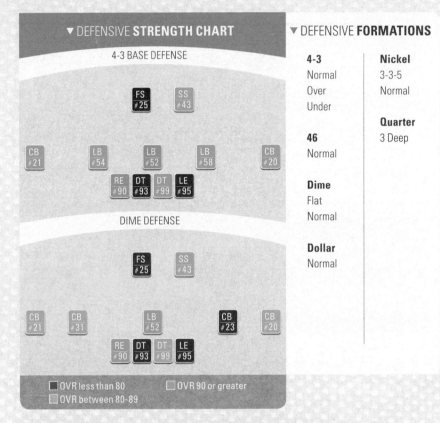

▼ DEFENSIVE **STRENGTH CHART**

4-3 BASE DEFENSE

FS #25 | SS #43
CB #21 | LB #54 | LB #52 | LB #58 | CB #20
RE #90 | DT #93 | DT #99 | LE #95

DIME DEFENSE

FS #25 | SS #43
CB #21 | CB #31 | LB #52 | CB #23 | CB #20
RE #90 | DT #93 | DT #99 | LE #95

☐ OVR less than 80   ☐ OVR 90 or greater
☐ OVR between 80-89

▼ DEFENSIVE **FORMATIONS**

4-3	**Nickel**
Normal	3-3-5
Over	Normal
Under	
	Quarter
46	3 Deep
Normal	
Dime	
Flat	
Normal	
Dollar	
Normal	

▼ RECOMMENDED DEFENSIVE **AUDIBLE PACKAGES**

4-3	4-3	Nickel	Dime	Quarter
2 Man Under	Free Fire	Cover 3	Cover 2	Quarters

▼ DEFENSIVE **PLAYCOUNTS**

Man Coverage:	40	Cover 2 Zone:	13	Man Blitz:	49
Man Zone:	38	Cover 3 Zone:	26	Zone Blitz:	63
Combo Coverage:	9	Deep Zone:	20	Combo Blitz:	19

DEFENSE **KEY DEFENSIVE PLAYS**

46 NORMAL
INSIDE BLITZ

The 46 Normal Inside Blitz is a natural inside run blitz scheme that many players implement into their defensive game plan.

Both the right outside and middle linebackers blitz the A and B gaps to shut down the inside run.

This makes it very hard for the running back to find any open lanes.

The running back gets to the line of scrimmage, but that's all he can muster against the Panthers stout run D.

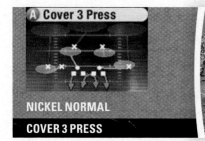

NICKEL NORMAL
COVER 3 PRESS

Not all defenses have to blitz to get pressure, especially when you have Julius Peppers on the D-line.

The Nickel Normal Cover 3 Press has the defenders jamming receivers at the line of scrimmage.

With three defenders dropping back, there won't be much open deep down the field.

With all the receivers covered, coverage sacks are common when calling this defense.

NICKEL 3-3-5
CB DOGS BLITZ

If your opponent likes to roll the quarterback out, a good play to prevent him from getting outside is the Nickel 3-3-5 CB Dogs Blitz.

This blitz sends both cornerbacks on a blitz from the left and right sides of the field.

The pass coverage is solid, but the flats are left open, provided that the quarterback can get ball there.

Panthers cornerback Chris Gamble sacks Buccaneers quarterback Jeff Garcia in the backfield.

TEAM STRATEGY

NEW ENGLAND PATRIOTS

▶ **Division** AFC East	▶ **Stadium** Gillette Stadium	▶ **Type** Open	▶ **Capacity** 68,756	▶ **Surface** Field Turf

▼ 2007 STANDINGS

Wins	Loses	Ties	PF	PA	Home	Road	vs. AFC	vs. NFC	vs. Div
16	0	0	589	274	8-0	8-0	12-0	4-0	6-0

TEAM STRATEGY

FRANCHISE MODE STRATEGY

Franchise QB? Check. Stable of receivers? Check. Dominant offensive line? Check. The linebacking corps is getting a bit long in the tooth so make plans to build for the future in the draft. Leave the offense alone.

KEY FRANCHISE INFORMATION

Cap Room: $5.97M
Key Rivals:
- Bills, Colts, Dolphins, Jets

Philosophy:
- Offense: Multiple
- Defense: Multiple

Highest Paid Players:
- T. Brady
- A. Thomas

Team Weapons:
- T. Brady – Smart QB
- R. Moss – Spectacular Catch Receiver

Best Young Players:
- S. Gostkowski
- L. Maroney

▼ TEAM OVERVIEW

Once again loaded to dominate the cyber gridiron, the Patriots have pretty much the same offensive power as in 2007. On defense, New England has reloaded the team with youth and athleticism. By signing linebacker Victor Hobson, and drafting linebacker Jerod Mayo, the Patriots are ready to dominate another season.

Any team that has Tom Brady at quarterback and Randy Moss at receiver is going to be explosive. Wes Welker and Jabar Gaffney give you two more solid receivers to throw to when Moss is double or triple-teamed.

The Patriots' defense needed to be young and fast at linebacker. With Hobson and Mayo in the mix, there should be no reason why creative blitz schemes can't be used to bring pressure on the opposing quarterback.

▼ OFF-SEASON UPGRADES

TYPE	ROUND	FIRST NAME	LAST NAME	SCHOOL/TEAM	POSITION
Free Agent	N/A	Fernando	Bryant	Lions	CB
Free Agent	N/A	Victor	Hobson	Jets	LB
Draft	1	Jerod	Mayo	Tennessee	LB
Draft	2	Terrence	Wheatley	Colorado	CB
Draft	3	Shawn	Crable	Michigan	LB

▼ SCOUTING REPORT

	DESCRIPTION	MAXIMIZING POTENTIAL	TIPS FOR OPPONENTS
STRENGTHS	Tom Brady established himself as the quarterback last year by breaking the most touchdowns passes in one season.	Brady's arm strength and accuracy rank among the best in the game, so airing out the ball won't be a problem.	The best to way to beat Brady is to get pressure in his face early and often.
STRENGTHS	Randy Moss is the game's best receiver because of his ability to stretch the defense deep.	Send Moss on deep routes to clear out passing lanes for the receivers underneath.	It's imperative to put a minimum of two defenders on Moss at all times or be prepared to be beaten deep.
WEAKNESSES	The Patriots don't really have a major weakness on offense, although their run game can be inconsistent at times.	Spread the defense by running four receiver sets, and then call a few dive plays to rack up the rushing yardage.	Your best bet is to let the Patriots run the ball rather than give up the deep pass.
WEAKNESSES	The Patriots' inside linebackers are not the fastest, so they could be liabilities in the pass game.	Because they are not very fast, it's best to have them drop back in zone coverage.	If man coverage is called, get a fast running back matched up with the Patriots' inside linebackers.

97	99	91
OVERALL	OFFENSE	DEFENSE

After throwing for 50 TDs (with 23 going to Randy Moss) and only 8 picks, setting a record for most points ever scored by a team, Tom Brady and the Patriots are equipped to go undefeated during the regular season—again.

▼ ROSTER AND **PACKAGE TIPS**

KEY PLAYER SUBSTITUTIONS

Postion: HB
Substitution: Kevin Faulk
When: Situational
Advantage: When you decide to go to the Gun and spread it out, we recommend putting Faulk in as your halfback. He has amazing hands for a running back and will be a lethal weapon coming out of the backfield.

Postion: MLB
Substitution: Jerod Mayo
When: Situational
Advantage: In situations where you are going up against a scrambling quarterback, Mayo is a good choice to bring in for spy coverage. He is significantly faster than Bruschi and would be a good player to blitz with.

Postion: FS
Substitution: Brandon Meriweather
When: Global
Advantage: We are splitting hairs here, but with a team like the Patriots, every spot is solid. Meriweather is a bit faster than Sanders, but his awareness is much lower. We only would make this sub if you plan on controlling the FS yourself.

TEAM STRATEGY

TEAM STRATEGY

#12 Tom Brady *Quarterback (QB)*

▼OFFENSIVE **STAR PLAYER**

When you look at all the qualities that make a great quarterback, look no further than Patriots quarterback Tom Brady. He is a strong-armed quarterback who is able to make the throw. He is always cool in the pocket and hardly makes mistakes. His ability to slide left or right in the pocket allows him to avoid being sacked.

Speed	64
Awareness	100
Throw Power	99
Throw Accur.	99

Player Weapon: Smart Quarterback, Accurate Quarterback, Cannon Arm Quarterback

#81 Randy Moss *Wide Receiver (WR)*

▼OFFENSIVE **STAR PLAYER**

All Randy Moss needed was a new team to show why he ranks among the best wide receivers to ever step on the field. Last season, he set a single season record by getting in the end zone 23 times. Some thought he lost his top end speed, but he proved them wrong by averaging 15.2 yards a catch.

Speed	98
Catch	97
Catch In Traffic	88
Route Run	94

Player Weapon: Quick Receiver, Spec Catch Receiver, Hands, Speed

#83 Wes Welker *Wide Receiver (WR)*

▼OFFENSIVE **STAR PLAYER**

Wes Welker is the perfect slot receiver. He runs textbook routes that allow him to get open underneath the coverage, and led the league with 112 catches. He is a very sure-handed receiver as he only dropped four catches the entire season. Look for another big season for the Patriots' number 2 primary receiver.

Speed	93
Catch	92
Catch In Traffic	95
Route Run	97

Player Weapon: Quick Receiver, Spec Catch Receiver, Hands

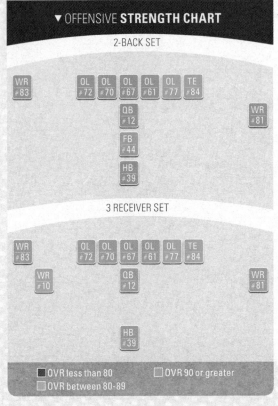

▼ OFFENSIVE **STRENGTH CHART**

2-BACK SET

WR #83 | OL #72 | OL #70 | OL #67 | OL #61 | OL #77 | TE #84 | WR #81
QB #12
FB #44
HB #39

3 RECEIVER SET

WR #83 | OL #72 | OL #70 | OL #67 | OL #61 | OL #77 | TE #84 | WR #81
WR #10 | QB #12
HB #39

■ OVR less than 80   □ OVR 90 or greater
□ OVR between 80-89

▼ OFFENSIVE **FORMATIONS**

Gun	I-Form
Bunch TE	Slot
Bunch Wk	Tight
Doubles	
Doubles Wk	**Singleback**
Empty Trips	Ace
Open	Ace Pair Twins
Snugs Flip	Doubles
Split Slot	Jumbo
Split Y-Flex	Snugs Flip
Spread	Trips Open
Spread Left On	Y-Trips
Spread Wk	
Spread Y-Flex	**Strong**
Trips Open	Slot
Y-Trips Open	

▼ RECOMMENDED OFFENSIVE **AUDIBLE PACKAGES**

Singleback	Singleback	Singleback	Gun	Gun
HB Stretch	TE Post	HB Cutback	Shallow Cross	Strong Flood

▼ OFFENSIVE **PLAYCOUNTS**

Quick Pass:	7	Screen Pass:	12	Pitch:	4
Standard Pass:	58	Hail Mary:	2	Counter:	6
Shotgun Pass:	117	Inside Handoff:	16	Draw:	19
Play Action Pass:	49	Outside Handoff:	21		

OFFENSE **KEY OFFENSIVE PLAYS**

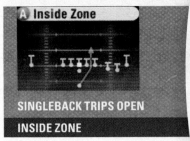

A Inside Zone

SINGLEBACK TRIPS OPEN

INSIDE ZONE

The Patriots like to spread the defense out when running the ball with their stud running back Laurence Maroney.

1 With the defenders spread out, it makes it very easy to find open running lanes.

2 Once through the hole, we press the speed burst button to get into open daylight.

3 We break a few tackles and pick up 9 yards before finally being brought down.

A PA FL Stretch

SINGLEBACK TRIPS OPEN

PA FL STRETCH

To keep the defense off-balance, we like to throw in the PA FL Stretch. This play works quite nicely once the Inside Zone run play is established.

1 The key is getting the defense to think run; if they do, there should be plenty of open receivers.

2 We launch a rocket deep to the best receiver in the game: Randy Moss.

3 We take control of him and get some separation as we make the catch deep down the field.

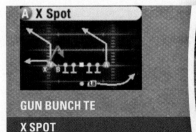

A X Spot

GUN BUNCH TE

X SPOT

Wes Welker has the knack for finding soft spots in the zone coverage. The Gun Bunch TE X Spot is a perfect example that showcases his talents.

1 Welker starts off by running a slant towards the middle.

2 He then hooks back towards the quarterback. It's at this point that the ball should be thrown.

3 Welker makes the catch for a 6-yard pick-up.

TEAM STRATEGY

TEAM STRATEGY

#96 Adalius Thomas *Linebacker (ROLB)*

▼DEFENSIVE **STAR PLAYER**

One of the team's most versatile linebackers, Adalius Thomas is rarely out of position to stop the run or defend the pass. As the season wore on, Thomas began to assert himself as the team's top linebacker. He registered 79 tackles and 6.5 sacks. With another season under the Patriots' system, his totals will only go up.

Speed	87
Tackling	90
Pursuit	90
Play Recog.	82

Player Weapon: None

#93 Richard Seymour *Defensive End (RE)*

▼DEFENSIVE **STAR PLAYER**

Very few defensive ends in a 3-4 base scheme can disrupt the passing game like Patriot Richard Seymour. He wasn't able to make an impact during the regular season due to injuries, but by the time playoffs came around, he was back in form by making life miserable for opposing quarterbacks.

Speed	71
Strength	92
Power Moves	96
Finesse Moves	82

Player Weapon: Power Move D-Lineman

#37 Rodney Harrison *Safety (SS)*

▼DEFENSIVE **STAR PLAYER**

Over the years, Rodney Harrison has been known as one of the hardest hitters in the league. Receivers always know where he is, because they don't want to be leveled to the ground. He is not as fast as he once was, but still has enough in the tank to make plays in the pass and run game.

Speed	84
Man Cover	45
Zone Cover	75
Hit Power	97

Player Weapon: Big Hitter, Smart Safety

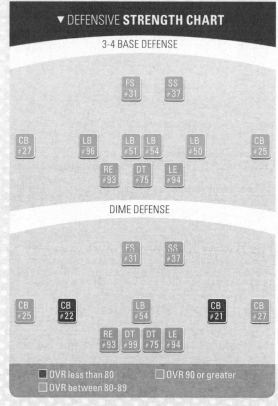

▼ DEFENSIVE **STRENGTH CHART**

3-4 BASE DEFENSE

FS #31 · SS #37
CB #27 · LB #96 · LB #51 · LB #54 · LB #50 · CB #25
RE #93 · DT #75 · LE #94

DIME DEFENSE

FS #31 · SS #37
CB #25 · CB #22 · LB #54 · CB #21 · CB #27
RE #93 · DT #99 · DT #75 · LE #94

■ OVR less than 80 ☐ OVR 90 or greater
☐ OVR between 80-89

▼ DEFENSIVE **FORMATIONS**

4-3	Nickel
Normal	1-5-5
Over	1-5-5 Prowl
Under	2-4-5
Stack	
Under	**Quarter**
	Combo
Dime	
Normal	
Dollar	
Normal	

▼ RECOMMENDED DEFENSIVE **AUDIBLE PACKAGES**

3-4	3-4	Nickel	Dime	Quarter
2 Man Under	OLB Dogs Fire	Cover 3	Cover 2	Cover 4

▼ DEFENSIVE **PLAYCOUNTS**

Man Coverage:	40	Cover 2 Zone:	23	Man Blitz:	61
Man Zone:	39	Cover 3 Zone:	25	Zone Blitz:	55
Combo Coverage:	5	Deep Zone:	12	Combo Blitz:	7

DEFENSE **KEY DEFENSIVE PLAYS**

A Weak Blitz

3-4 UNDER

WEAK BLITZ

The 3-4 Under Weak Blitz can be used either to pressure the quarterback or to stop the run.

1

Both Jerod Mayo and Adalius Thomas are sent on a blitz from the left side of the offensive line.

2

If the offense tries to run to their side, chances are the running back is going to be engulfed.

3

Mayo drags Jets running back Thomas Jones down from behind for a minimal gain.

A Cover 2

DOLLAR NORMAL

COVER 2

With a few new faces in the Patriots' secondary, playing Cover 2 zone defense is a good choice to defend short passes underneath.

1

Jets tight end Chris Baker runs a flat route to the right side of the field.

2

Cornerback Ellis Hobbs sees this and goes to cover Baker in the flat.

3

The pass is thrown and Hobbs jumps the route, looking to pick the pass off.

A Zone Blitz 2

NICKEL 1-5-5 PROWL

ZONE BLITZ 2

The Patriots like to mix up their blitz schemes by dropping and rushing different defenders in plays like the Zone Blitz 2.

1

The 1-5-5 Prowl has one defensive lineman and five linebackers in the box.

2

The zone blitzing sends the nickelback and four linebackers in on a blitz.

3

Quarterbacks often get confused by this and make poor decisions down the field.

TEAM STRATEGY

OAKLAND RAIDERS

▶ **Division** AFC West ▶ **Stadium** McAfee Coliseum ▶ **Type** Open ▶ **Capacity** 63,026 ▶ **Surface** Grass

TEAM STRATEGY

FRANCHISE MODE STRATEGY

The Raiders could use a couple of new passing targets and someone to guard Russell's blind side at left tackle. The Raiders have done well in the draft, but still have some spots to be filled on defense.

KEY FRANCHISE INFORMATION

Cap Room: $930K
Key Rivals:
- Broncos, Chargers, Chiefs

Philosophy:
- Offense: West Coast
- Defense: 4-3

Highest Paid Players:
- D. Hall
- J. Russell

Team Weapons:
- S. Lechler – Big Foot Kicker
- N. Asomugha – Shutdown Corner

Best Young Players:
- D. Hall
- D. McFadden

▼ 2007 STANDINGS

Wins	Loses	Ties	PF	PA	Home	Road	vs. AFC	vs. NFC	vs. Div
4	12	0	283	398	2-6	2-6	4-8	0-4	2-4

▼ TEAM OVERVIEW

The Raiders made some big acquisitions in the free agency market and drafted one of the most electrifying players in college football history. The question remains: can all the talent rejuvenate the once-proud franchise?

Offensively, the Raiders' rushing attack was one of the best in the game last season. The problem for any player using the Raiders is deciding who will carry the load. Do you stick with last year's starter and 1,000 yard rusher Justin Fargas or do you put in rookie hotshot Darren McFadden?

One thing is for sure about the Raiders' defense: It's going to be hard to pass on them. The team is deeper in the secondary with the addition of cornerback DeAngelo Hall. With Hall on one side and Nnamdi Asomugha on the other, the Raiders have two lockdown corners.

▼ OFF-SEASON UPGRADES

TYPE	ROUND	FIRST NAME	LAST NAME	SCHOOL/TEAM	POSITION
Trade	N/A	DeAngelo	Hall	Falcons	CB
Free Agent	N/A	Javon	Walker	Broncos	WR
Free Agent	N/A	Gibril	Wilson	Giants	S
Draft	1	Darren	McFadden	Arkansas	RB
Draft	4	Tyvon	Branch	Connecticut	CB

▼ SCOUTING REPORT

	DESCRIPTION	MAXIMIZING POTENTIAL	TIPS FOR OPPONENTS
STRENGTHS	The Raiders have one of the top running attacks in the game with an abundance of running backs, each with a different style.	Establish the inside and outside running game by switching out running backs based on the play.	Watch to see which RB lines up in the backfield. It will tell you whether it will be an inside or outside run.
	Derrick Burgess is by far the Raiders' best pass rusher along the defensive line. He consistently puts up solid sack numbers.	Manually control Burgess and use a variety of pass rushing moves to get to the quarterback.	Leave the tight end in to pass block. This will force him to take a wider angle at the quarterback.
WEAKNESSES	Quarterback JaMarcus Russell is young and still raw. He has a cannon for an arm, but he is very inaccurate.	Look to throw deep, but be prepared to take control of the receiver to make the catch if the pass is off target.	Take control of a safety centerfield. You can bet there will be at least one inaccurate pass thrown deep.
	Outside of Javon Walker, there is no proven receiver who can put fear in the defensive secondary.	Don't worry about going deep all too often; instead, work the short and mid range portions of the field.	Don't let Walker get deep without a safety over the top. It takes just one big play to change the game.

71	67	80
OVERALL	OFFENSE	DEFENSE

After a typical rookie season for an NFL QB, JaMarcus Russell is expected to continue his growth while the Raiders upgraded his backfield weapons by drafting rookie RB Darren McFadden.

▼ ROSTER AND **PACKAGE TIPS**

KEY PLAYER SUBSTITUTIONS

Postion: HB
Substitution: Darren McFadden
When: Global
Advantage: The Raiders spent a first round draft pick on McFadden, so you had better get him in the line-up. Fargas is fast, but McFadden is even faster. McFadden is much more elusive as well. He is a dangerous running back.

Postion: FB
Substitution: Oren O'Neal
When: Situational
Advantage: With two backs like McFadden and Fargus, you are going to want to run the ball and keep Russell out of long yardage situations. When you are looking to get your run game going, O'Neal can provide crushing lead blocks.

Postion: RE
Substitution: Greg Spires
When: Global
Advantage: Spires is a better player right now than Richardson. He is faster and has much more effective Finesse Moves. He is a bit older than Richardson, so he will need breaks from time to time to regain his stamina.

 # OAKLAND RAIDERS

OFFENSE

TEAM STRATEGY

#17 Javon Walker *Wide Receiver (WR)*

▼OFFENSIVE **STAR PLAYER**

Javon Walker looks to resurrect his career with the Silver and Black. His short stint in Denver was not as productive as he wanted. There is no question that he has big-time playmaking ability, as he has shown while in Green Bay. At 6'3" he makes for a big target, so it wouldn't be a surprise to see him lead the Raiders in receiving this season.

Speed	91
Catch	87
Catch In Traffic	87
Route Run	88

Player Weapon: Spec Catch Receiver

#20 Darren McFadden *Halfback (HB)*

▼OFFENSIVE **STAR PLAYER**

The Raiders never shy away from talented players even if they are already deep at one position. Darren McFadden joins an already crowded backfield. If he shows the same explosiveness he did in college, he won't have a problem becoming the Raiders' top running back.

Speed	97
Agility	96
Trucking	74
Elusiveness	92

Player Weapon: Elusive Back, Stiff Arm Ball Carrier, Speed

#2 JaMarcus Russell *Quarterback (QB)*

▼OFFENSIVE **STAR PLAYER**

With a full training camp under his belt, Jamarcus Russell is poised for a breakout season. He has a cannon for an arm and can make all the NFL throws. He is one of the biggest quarterbacks in the league, making him a very hard target to bring down. As long as he keeps his weight under control, he has a chance to be something special.

Speed	72
Awareness	59
Throw Power	98
Throw Accur.	87

Player Weapon: Cannon Arm Quarterback

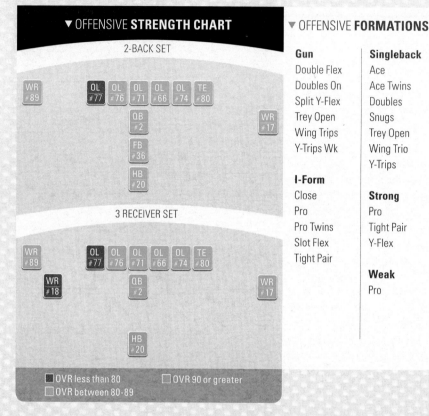

▼ OFFENSIVE **STRENGTH CHART**

▼ OFFENSIVE **FORMATIONS**

Gun
Double Flex
Doubles On
Split Y-Flex
Trey Open
Wing Trips
Y-Trips Wk

I-Form
Close
Pro
Pro Twins
Slot Flex
Tight Pair

Singleback
Ace
Ace Twins
Doubles
Snugs
Trey Open
Wing Trio
Y-Trips

Strong
Pro
Tight Pair
Y-Flex

Weak
Pro

▼ RECOMMENDED OFFENSIVE **AUDIBLE PACKAGES**

Singleback	Strong	I-Form	Gun	Gun
HB Counter	494 F Flat	Iso	HB Angle	Double Post

▼ OFFENSIVE **PLAYCOUNTS**

Quick Pass:	19	Screen Pass:	8	Counter:	9
Standard Pass:	85	Inside Handoff:	28	Draw:	11
Shotgun Pass:	54	Outside Handoff:	17	FB Run:	9
Play Action Pass:	60	Pitch:	6		

OFFENSE **KEY OFFENSIVE PLAYS**

A FB Fake HB Toss

I-FORM TIGHT PAIR

FB FAKE HB TOSS

One of the better run plays out of the Raiders' playbook to use with a speedy halfback is the I-Form Tight FB Fake HB Toss.

1 This play has the quarterback faking the ball off to the fullback.

2 Next, the quarterback will toss the ball to the halfback.

3 Once the halfback gets the ball, we take control of him and get outside quickly.

A PA TE Leak

I-FORM TIGHT PAIR

PA TE LEAK

The I Form Tight Pair PA TE Leak is often used around the goal line because defenses tend to pack in to stop the run.

1 The quarterback play fakes to the halfback. Often the defense will bite on the play fake.

2 First, we look to throw to the tight end running a corner route.

3 If he is covered, our next option is the fullback in the flat.

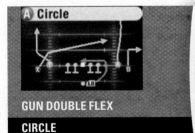

A Circle

GUN DOUBLE FLEX

CIRCLE

A low risk pass play out of the Raiders playbook to throw to the running back out of the backfield is the Gun Double Flex Circle.

1 The running back starts out by running towards the right sideline.

2 He breaks hard towards the middle of the field. He has gained separation from his man.

3 We make the catch about 10 yards down the field for a nice gain.

TEAM STRATEGY

 # OAKLAND RAIDERS

DEFENSE

TEAM STRATEGY

#21 Nnamdi Asomugha *Cornerback (CB)*

▼DEFENSIVE **STAR PLAYER**

One of the top cornerbacks in the game, Nnamdi Asomugha is able to lock down any receiver who lines up across from him. Last season, quarterbacks threw away from him because they feared he would pick the pass off. Not only a lockdown corner, he is also not afraid to stick his nose in to stop the run.

Speed	93
Man Cover	99
Zone Cover	90
Press	92

Player Weapon: Smart Corner, Shutdown Corner, Press Coverage Corner

#56 Derrick Burgess *Defensive End (LE)*

▼DEFENSIVE **STAR PLAYER**

Over the last three seasons, Derrick Burgess has been a menace to quarterbacks. He has racked up a total of 35 sacks during that time. He uses his speed to get around bigger offensive tackles. Once Burgess gets hold of the quarterback, it almost always results in a sack.

Speed	85
Strength	73
Power Moves	77
Finesse Moves	93

Player Weapon: Finesse Move D-Lineman

#52 Kirk Morrison *Linebacker (MLB)*

▼DEFENSIVE **STAR PLAYER**

One of the better middle linebackers at dropping back in pass coverage, Kirk Morrison has made a name for himself in the Silver and Black uniform. Last season, he picked the ball off 4 times and had 10 passes deflected. If the Raiders were a better team, Morrison would be in the Pro Bowl.

Speed	80
Tackling	95
Pursuit	96
Play Recog.	90

Player Weapon: Brick Wall Defender, Smart Linebacker

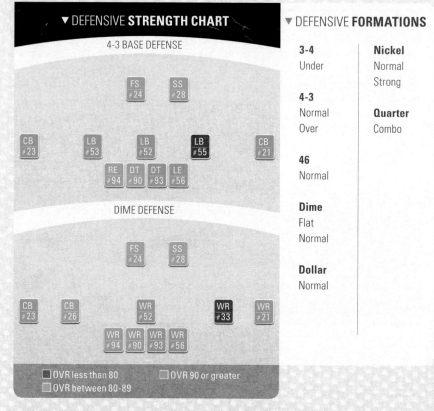

▼ DEFENSIVE **STRENGTH CHART**

4-3 BASE DEFENSE

DIME DEFENSE

☐ OVR less than 80   ☐ OVR 90 or greater
☐ OVR between 80-89

▼ DEFENSIVE **FORMATIONS**

3-4	**Nickel**
Under	Normal
	Strong
4-3	
Normal	**Quarter**
Over	Combo
46	
Normal	
Dime	
Flat	
Normal	
Dollar	
Normal	

▼ RECOMMENDED DEFENSIVE **AUDIBLE PACKAGES**

4-3	4-3	Nickel	Dime	Quarter
2 Man Under	Free Fire	Cover 3 Press	Cover 2	2 Man Under Spy

▼ DEFENSIVE **PLAYCOUNTS**

Man Coverage:	45	Cover 2 Zone:	16	Man Blitz:	52
Man Zone:	33	Cover 3 Zone:	23	Zone Blitz:	58
Combo Coverage:	8	Deep Zone:	16	Combo Blitz:	14

(A) Slant 1 OLB Fire

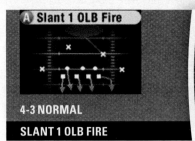

4-3 NORMAL

SLANT 1 OLB FIRE

Plays with defensive ends that are in DE Contain do a good job of defending different types of outside runs.

Left end Derrick Burgess is left unblocked as he goes outside to defend the run.

The running back has no chance, with Burgess set to make the tackle.

Burgess makes the tackle on the running back before he has a chance to pick up any yardage.

(A) Cover 2

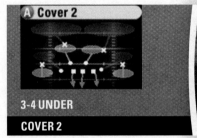

3-4 UNDER

COVER 2

The 3-4 Under is a solid defense to defend quick passes underneath, with most of the field blanketed by 8 defenders.

Both the Raiders' cornerbacks will jam the outside receivers at the line of scrimmage.

If the quarterback tries to throw a slant, the defenders underneath will be in position to make a play.

Left outside linebacker Robert Thomas jumps in front of the receiver to pick the pass off.

(A) CB Dogs Man

DIME NORMAL

CB DOGS MAN

The Dime Normal CB Dogs Man has two cornerbacks who blitz to put pressure on the quarterback from the outside.

With both cornerbacks blitzing, the free and strong safeties play man coverage on the outside receivers.

Raiders' cornerback Nnamdi Asomugha is left unblocked and has a clear path at the quarterback.

The quarterback doesn't see the blitz coming from the outside and is dropped to the ground for a sack.

TEAM STRATEGY

 ST. LOUIS RAMS

▸ **Division** NFC West ▸ **Stadium** Edward Jones Dome ▸ **Type** Dome ▸ **Capacity** 66,000 ▸ **Surface** Field Turf

▼ 2007 STANDINGS

Wins	Loses	Ties	PF	PA	Home	Road	vs. AFC	vs. NFC	vs. Div
3	13	0	263	438	1-7	2-6	0-4	3-9	1-5

▼ TEAM OVERVIEW

On paper, the Rams seemed to be one of the best teams last year, but a rash of injuries derailed the season in a hurry. This year, the Rams look healthy again and should be able rebound from last year's disappointment.

On offense, the Rams have good balance by being able to run and pass the ball. Marc Bulger and Torry Holt remain one of the top quarterback/receiver combos in the game. Running back Steven Jackson is an explosive runner who can take the rock to the house on any given play.

The Rams' defense suffered because their pass rush was lacking. That's why the Rams made defensive end Chris Long their first draft pick in the 2007 draft. With Long coming from one side, and Leonard Little from the other, they should be able to put the fear in opposing quarterbacks.

▼ OFF-SEASON UPGRADES

TYPE	ROUND	FIRST NAME	LAST NAME	SCHOOL/TEAM	POSITION
Free Agent	N/A	Jacob	Bell	Titans	G
Free Agent	N/A	Josh	Brown	Seahawks	K
Free Agent	N/A	Trent	Green	Dolphins	QB
Draft	1	Chris	Long	Virginia	DE
Draft	2	Donnie	Avery	Houston	WR

▼ SCOUTING REPORT

	DESCRIPTION	MAXIMIZING POTENTIAL	TIPS FOR OPPONENTS
STRENGTHS	Jackson is a big back that has become a top back in the league.	Feed this big man and allow him to wear down the defense.	Load the box and double Holt. You need help to take him down.
	Little is the best pass rusher they have. This guy is an animal.	Use stunts and overloads to get him free of double teams.	Stay away from him at all costs. His pass rush can cause turnovers.
WEAKNESSES	The offensive line has cost Bulger many injuries, and needs to do a better job of protecting him.	You need to use a short passing game with pound.	Create pressure and double Holt. You need to expose this weakness to create turnovers.
	The Rams' secondary isn't good at all. They don't have a shutdown corner.	Use zone blitzes and safety help deep.	Use the run to suck the secondary in and take a shot deep off PA.

TEAM STRATEGY

FRANCHISE MODE STRATEGY

Begin to look toward the future at receiver. Bruce and Bennett can still deliver, but are getting older. The Rams could use more depth at linebacker and cornerback. Use the draft to build these positions.

KEY FRANCHISE INFORMATION

Cap Room: $12.87M

Key Rivals:
• Cardinals, 49ers, Seahawks

Philosophy:
• Offense: Quick Passing
• Defense: 4-3

Highest Paid Players:
• M. Bulger
• C. Long

Top Team Weapons:
• Steven Jackson – Power Back
• T. Holt – Quick Receiver

Best Young Players:
• A. Carriker
• C. Long

77	80	70
OVERALL	OFFENSE	DEFENSE

▼ ROSTER AND **PACKAGE TIPS**

KEY PLAYER SUBSTITUTIONS

Postion: TE
Substitution: Anthony Becht
When: Situational
Advantage: McMichael is a great pass-catching TE, but there are times in the game when you need to put the ball in the hands of your best runner and burn up the block. You'll want Becht in the game, as he is a much stronger run blocker.

Postion: FB
Substitution: Richard Owens
When: Situational
Advantage: We've already mentioned that Becht is a good sub when you want to grind it out on the ground. Putting Owens in at fullback is another good option if you really want to pound the ball down the defense's throat.

Postion: WR
Substitution: Donnie Avery
When: Situational
Advantage: If you are going up against a team with slower corners, you might want to put Avery in as your number two receiver. He has much more speed than Drew Bennett and could put the hurt on your opponent deep.

Steven Jackson and the Rams were a better team than their record showed last year, and with the addition of Chris Long at DE they should be a contender if they can remain healthy.

TEAM STRATEGY

TEAM STRATEGY

#81 Torry Holt *Wide Receiver (WR)*

▼OFFENSIVE **STAR PLAYER**

Torry Holt has lost some speed due to knee injuries. However, he still runs some of the best pass patterns in the game. Last season, he had a team high of 93 receptions and made the Pro Bowl for a seventh time. With the old Rams' high octane offensive scheme back in place, his numbers should be equal or better than they were in 2007.

Speed	93
Catch	97
Catch In Traffic	81
Route Run	98

Player Weapon: Quick Receiver, Hands

#39 Steven Jackson *Halfback (HB)*

▼OFFENSIVE **STAR PLAYER**

Steven Jackson was not himself for most of last season due to injuries, but he still managed to go over 1,000 yards. For a big running back, Jackson has an extra gear that allows him to get into open space quickly. He is also an accomplished receiver out of the backfield, making him a double threat.

Speed	90
Agility	93
Trucking	98
Elusiveness	92

Player Weapon: Power Back, Elusive Back, Stiff Arm Ball Carrier

#10 Marc Bulger *Quarterback (QB)*

▼OFFENSIVE **STAR PLAYER**

One of the more accurate quarterbacks in the league over the last few seasons, Bulger never really got on track during the 2007 season. The offensive line was not able to give him enough time in the pocket to find open receivers. Because of that, he took a good amount of hits and his passes were thrown off target.

Speed	55
Awareness	86
Throw Power	90
Throw Accur.	94

Player Weapon: Accurate Quarterback

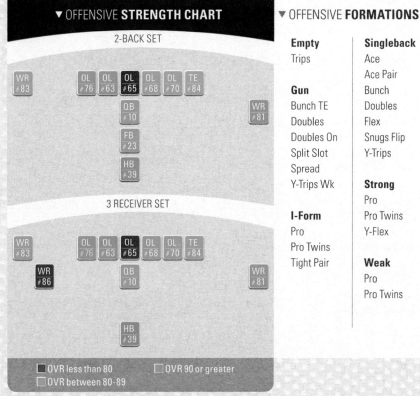

▼ OFFENSIVE **STRENGTH CHART**

2-BACK SET

WR #83 — OL #76 · OL #63 · OL #65 · OL #68 · OL #70 · TE #84 — WR #81

QB #10

FB #23

HB #39

3 RECEIVER SET

WR #83 — OL #76 · OL #63 · OL #65 · OL #68 · OL #70 · TE #84 — WR #81

WR #86 — QB #10 — WR #81

HB #39

- ■ OVR less than 80
- □ OVR between 80-89
- □ OVR 90 or greater

▼ OFFENSIVE **FORMATIONS**

Empty	Singleback
Trips	Ace
	Ace Pair
Gun	Bunch
Bunch TE	Doubles
Doubles	Flex
Doubles On	Snugs Flip
Split Slot	Y-Trips
Spread	
Y-Trips Wk	**Strong**
	Pro
I-Form	Pro Twins
Pro	Y-Flex
Pro Twins	
Tight Pair	**Weak**
	Pro
	Pro Twins

▼ RECOMMENDED OFFENSIVE **AUDIBLE PACKAGES**

Singleback	I-Form	Singleback	Singleback	Gun
HB Dive	Corner Strike	Power O	Slants	Corner Strike

▼ OFFENSIVE **PLAYCOUNTS**

Quick Pass:	24	Screen Pass:	10	Counter:	11
Standard Pass:	99	Inside Handoff:	30	Draw:	12
Shotgun Pass:	53	Outside Handoff:	15	FB Run:	8
Play Action Pass:	62	Pitch:	8		

OFFENSE **KEY OFFENSIVE PLAYS**

A HB Slam

SINGLEBACK DOUBLES
HB SLAM

Steven Jackson is one of the better running backs in the game. The Singleback Double HB Slam fits his style of running perfectly.

1 What we like about this play is that it's designed to run behind the Rams' strength on the offensive line.

2 Once to the line of scrimmage, we press the speed burst to get us into secondary.

3 We pick up a tough 10 yards before being tackled by two Seattle defenders.

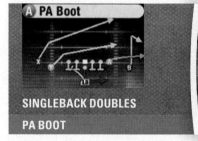

A PA Boot

SINGLEBACK DOUBLES
PA BOOT

The Singleback Doubles PA Boot gets the tight end running a delayed route open in the flat after we play fake to Jackson.

1 The tight end will act like he is going to pass block, while the quarterback is faking the handoff.

2 Once the play fake is over, the quarterback will bootleg to the right side of the field.

3 The tight end is open in the flat against man coverage as long as his defender bites on the play action.

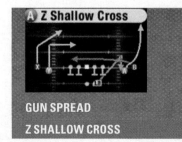

A Z Shallow Cross

GUN SPREAD
Z SHALLOW CROSS

Torry Holt remains one of the best route runners in the game. The Gun Spread Z Shallow Cross gets him open over the middle of the field.

1 There are a few options for Holt, depending on what type of pass coverage is called.

2 Is in most cases, he will be open at some point as he crosses the short middle of the field.

3 We take control of Holt just before the catch. If the ball is caught on the run, there is a good chance for some YAC.

TEAM STRATEGY

197

 ST. LOUIS RAMS

DEFENSE

TEAM STRATEGY

#91 Leonard Little *Defensive End (LE)*

▼DEFENSIVE **STAR PLAYER**

During his first 9 seasons in the league, Leonard Little has recorded 74 sacks. Last season (his tenth), he managed just 1. The main reason that he wasn't able to get pressure was injuries. With rookie Chris Long playing the opposite end, Little will receive fewer double teams. This should translate into more sacks for 2008.

Speed	84
Strength	75
Power Moves	72
Finesse Moves	88

Player Weapon: None

#51 Will Witherspoon *Linebacker (MLB)*

▼DEFENSIVE **STAR PLAYER**

Last season, Will Witherspoon was clearly the team's best defensive player. He led the team in tackles with 110 and in sacks with 7. At times, he was moved to outside linebacker to blitz the quarterback. With his cat-like speed, he is one of the best multipurpose middle linebackers in the game.

Speed	88
Tackling	93
Pursuit	98
Play Recog.	85

Player Weapon: Brick Wall Defender

#21 O.J. Atogwe *Safety (FS)*

▼DEFENSIVE **STAR PLAYER**

O.J. Atogwe came on strong in his second full season as the team's starting free safety. He had a team high of 8 interceptions. He has a wide range of speed, which allows him to cover the entire field and makes him the ideal center fielder for the Rams' aggressive defensive scheme. He is also solid in run support.

Speed	90
Man Cover	70
Zone Cover	85
Hit Power	74

Player Weapon: None

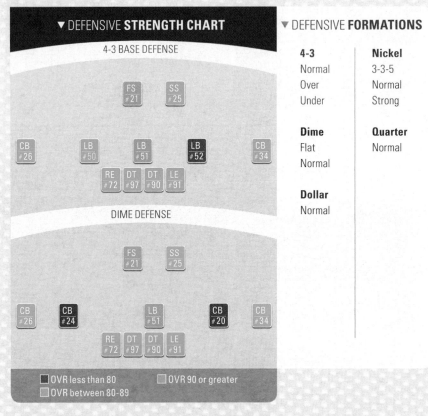

▼ DEFENSIVE **STRENGTH CHART**

4-3 BASE DEFENSE

FS #21 · SS #25
CB #26 · LB #50 · LB #51 · LB #52 · CB #34
RE #72 · DT #97 · DT #90 · LE #91

DIME DEFENSE

FS #21 · SS #25
CB #26 · CB #24 · LB #51 · CB #20 · CB #34
RE #72 · DT #97 · DT #90 · LE #91

☐ OVR less than 80 ☐ OVR 90 or greater
☐ OVR between 80-89

▼ DEFENSIVE **FORMATIONS**

4-3	**Nickel**
Normal	3-3-5
Over	Normal
Under	Strong

Dime	**Quarter**
Flat	Normal
Normal	

Dollar	
Normal	

▼ RECOMMENDED DEFENSIVE **AUDIBLE PACKAGES**

4-3	4-3	Nickel	Dime	Quarter
2 Man Under	Slant 1 OLB Fire	Cover 2	Cover 3 Press	1 Robber FS Lurk

▼ DEFENSIVE **PLAYCOUNTS**

Man Coverage:	45	Cover 2 Zone:	14	Man Blitz:	53
Man Zone:	35	Cover 3 Zone:	26	Zone Blitz:	63
Combo Coverage:	6	Deep Zone:	18	Combo Blitz:	12

DEFENSE **KEY DEFENSIVE PLAYS**

A Safety Blitz

4-3 NORMAL

SAFETY BLITZ

A good inside run defense to call on first down when playing with the Rams is the 4-3 Normal Safety Blitz.

1

It sends both safeties on a blitz through the gaps to blow up the inside running game.

2

The ball carrier will find it very tough to find an open hole with the safeties plugging the gaps.

3

The free safety gets to the ball carrier quickly and brings him down for a loss.

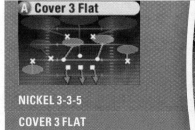

A Cover 3 Flat

NICKEL 3-3-5

COVER 3 FLAT

The Nickel Cover 3 Flat is a good defense to call to trick your opponent into throwing to the flat on the left side.

1

The running back runs a flat route. Notice right cornerback Tye Hill is sitting there, waiting for him.

2

The quarterback throws the pass in his direction.

3

Hill isn't able to pick the pass off, but he is in position to make the tackle as soon as the ball is caught.

A Ram Buck 1 Deep

QUARTER NORMAL

RAM BUCK

The Rams like to play an aggressive style of defense. The Quarter Normal Ram Buck 1 Deep brings some serious heat.

1

The linebacker and the second free safety on the field are sent in on a blitz.

2

At least one defender is usually unblocked and is able to get to the quarterback before he has time to throw.

3

Leonard Little wrestles Seattle's quarterback Matt Hasselbeck to the ground for a loss.

BALTIMORE RAVENS

▶ **Division** AFC North ▶ **Stadium** M&T Bank Stadium ▶ **Type** Open ▶ **Capacity** 71,008 ▶ **Surface** Momentum Turf

▼ 2007 STANDINGS

Wins	Loses	Ties	PF	PA	Home	Road	vs. AFC	vs. NFC	vs. Div
5	11	0	275	384	4-4	1-7	2-10	3-1	1-5

▼ TEAM OVERVIEW

The Ravens are going through a transition in 2008. Former head coach Brian Billick is gone and the team has a new franchise quarterback in Joe Flacco. What remains constant is the fact that the defense will be tough to run and pass on.

Until the quarterback situation is stable, running Willis McGahee will be the team's focal point on offense when it comes to moving the ball. Last season, he rushed for over 1,200 yards and got in the end zone 7 times. Wide receiver Derrick Mason will help make life easier for who-

ever starts at quarterback this season.

As long as Ray Lewis patrols the middle, being able to shut down the run shouldn't be much of a problem. The Ravens' secondary got a boost this offseason by signing former Raider Fabian Washington.

▼ OFF-SEASON UPGRADES

TYPE	ROUND	FIRST NAME	LAST NAME	SCHOOL/TEAM	POSITION
Free Agent	N/A	Brendon	Ayangadejo	Bears	LB
Free Agent	N/A	Frank	Walker	Packers	CB
Trade	N/A	Fabian	Washington	Raiders	CB
Draft	1	Joe	Flacco	Delaware	QB
Draft	2	Ray	Rice	Rutgers	RB

▼ SCOUTING REPORT

	DESCRIPTION	MAXIMIZING POTENTIAL	TIPS FOR OPPONENTS
STRENGTHS	Willis is the man you need in order for the Ravens to be successful.	Feed him and allow his production to open the passing attack.	Play the run and make them prove they can pass the ball.
	Ray Lewis is a future Hall of Fame player that is the total package.	Use him for 50% rush and 50% coverage. He does both quite well.	Be aware of him on every play. He can create turnovers to create momentum.
WEAKNESSES	Boller is the glaring weakness of this team. He hasn't panned out so far.	He needs a running game badly to set up the pass.	Load the box and send blitzers every down. Make sure you cover playmakers.
	Rolle isn't the shutdown corner he was when he was in Tennessee.	Keep safety help over the top of him. He gets beaten often.	Expose him early and often. Why try McAlister when you can beat up Rolle?

TEAM STRATEGY

FRANCHISE MODE STRATEGY

Finding a veteran QB would be a wise choice, as this team has the ability to win. Try to track down a playmaker at receiver to stretch the field. Pick up a young corner in the draft as the starters are getting older.

KEY FRANCHISE INFORMATION

Cap Room: $7.33M

Key Rivals:
- Bengals, Browns, Steelers

Philosophy:
- Offense: West Coast
- Defense: 3-4

Highest Paid Players:
- J. Ogden
- R. Lewis

Team Weapons:
- E. Reed – Smart Safety
- M. Stover – Accurate Kicker

Best Young Players:
- H. Ngata
- B. Grubbs

81	72	89
OVERALL	OFFENSE	DEFENSE

While Ray Lewis' physical skills may be eroding, his legendary leadership abilities ensure that the Ravens will remain tough on defense while a young offense finds its wings.

▼ ROSTER AND **PACKAGE TIPS**

KEY PLAYER SUBSTITUTIONS

Postion: LOLB

Substitution: Antwan Barnes

When: Global

Advantage: Antwan Barnes is an absolute speed burner for a linebacker. You'll want him in the game to blitz the quarterback. He is also a good choice to put in spy coverage on players like Vince Young and Tarvaris Jackson.

Postion: CB (Nickelback)

Substitution: Fabian Washington

When: Global

Advantage: If you need a player with the speed to hang with Randy Moss or Steve Smith, then Washington is your guy. Use him to double team these receivers or send him after the quarterback. He'll be in as fast as lightning.

Postion: SS

Substitution: Dawan Landry

When: Situational

Advantage: There isn't much to change up on the defensive side with the Ravens. This is a minor change, but every bit helps. If you are running SS blitz plays, put Landry in, as his speed will help him get in the backfield quicker.

TEAM STRATEGY

#85 Derrick Mason *Wide Receiver (WR)*

▼OFFENSIVE **STAR PLAYER**

Derrick Mason is not known for his speed, but he runs effective pass routes and is sure-handed. For the first time in his career, last season he went over the 100 reception mark, snagging 103 balls. If Mason plans to put up the same types of numbers in 2008, the Ravens need to settle on a quarterback quickly.

Speed	88
Catch	93
Catch In Traffic	84
Route Run	88

Player Weapon: Hands

#23 Willis McGahee *Halfback (HB)*

▼OFFENSIVE **STAR PLAYER**

The most reliable weapon that the Ravens had on offense last season was running back Willis McGahee. He managed to break the 1,200 yard mark, despite defenses loading up the box to stop the run. He also established himself as a solid receiver by catching 43 passes out the backfield.

Speed	92
Agility	93
Trucking	93
Elusiveness	79

Player Weapon: Power Back, Stiff Arm Ball Carrier

#86 Todd Heap *Tight End (TE)*

▼OFFENSIVE **STAR PLAYER**

Todd Heap's numbers were down in a big way last season due to his injuries and poor quarterback play. When healthy, he is able to draw double team coverage deep down the field. When this happens, the receivers on the outside often receive one-on-one coverage. If Heap is able to remain healthy, the Ravens' offensive production will receive a boost.

Speed	82
Catch	87
Run Block	58
Pass Block	52

Player Weapon: Quick Receiver, Possession Receiver

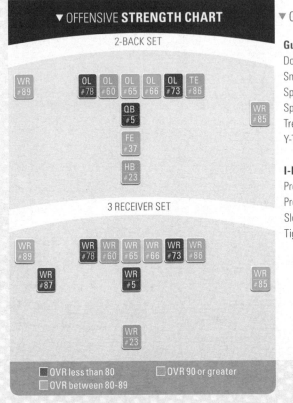

▼ OFFENSIVE **STRENGTH CHART**

2-BACK SET

WR #89 · OL #78 · OL #60 · OL #65 · OL #66 · OL #73 · TE #86 · WR #85 · QB #5 · FB #37 · HB #23

3 RECEIVER SET

WR #89 · WR #78 · WR #60 · WR #65 · WR #66 · WR #73 · WR #86 · WR #87 · WR #5 · WR #85 · WR #23

☐ OVR less than 80   ☐ OVR 90 or greater
☐ OVR between 80–89

▼ OFFENSIVE **FORMATIONS**

Gun	Singleback
Doubles	Ace
Snugs Flip	Ace Pair
Split Y-Flex	Ace Pair Twins
Spread Y-Flex	Bunch
Trey Open	Doubles
Y-Trips Wk	Wing Trio
	Y-Trips

I-Form	
Pro	Strong
Pro Twins	Pro
Slot	Tight Pair
Tight	Y-Flex

	Weak
	Pro
	Tight Pair

▼ RECOMMENDED OFFENSIVE **AUDIBLE PACKAGES**

I-Form	Singleback	Strong	Gun	Gun
Iso Weak	Quick Slants	Counter Weak	WR Deep Hook	Corner Strike

▼ OFFENSIVE **PLAYCOUNTS**

Quick Pass:	21	Screen Pass:	10	Counter:	9
Standard Pass:	86	Inside Handoff:	31	Draw:	12
Shotgun Pass:	50	Outside Handoff:	17	FB Run:	10
Play Action Pass:	65	Pitch:	6		

OFFENSE **KEY OFFENSIVE PLAYS**

A HB Blast

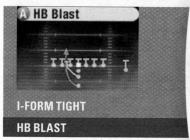

I-FORM TIGHT

HB BLAST

Ravens' Willis McGahee is the team's workhorse, so giving him the ball is a must. The I-Form Tight HB Blast is a solid play to move the chains.

Follow the fullback through the open hole he creates to avoid being tackled.

Sometimes you may need to take a stutter step and wait to see where the hole opens up.

We pick up a hard 6 yards before being tackled.

A PA Boot

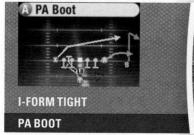

I-FORM TIGHT

PA BOOT

The I-Form Tight PA Boot works alongside the HB Blast. In addition, it gets tight end Todd Heap involved in the offense.

The quarterback play fakes the ball to McGahee to hold the defense.

We then take control of the quarterback, and roll him out to the right side, looking for Heap.

We spot Heap open in the flat and throw him a bullet pass for a 7-yard pick up.

A HB Screen

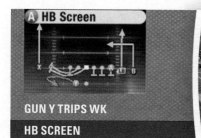

GUN Y TRIPS WK

HB SCREEN

With a young quarterback running the show in Baltimore, keeping things simple might be a wise decision in order to cut down on turnovers.

The Gun Y Trips WK HB Screen is a low risk pass play to keep the chains moving.

With the left guard and left tackle setting up the screen, there will be plenty of downfield blocking.

Roll the quarterback away from the side the screen is setting up to buy some extra time.

TEAM STRATEGY

#20 Ed Reed *Safety (FS)*

▼DEFENSIVE **STAR PLAYER**

One of two best safeties in the league, Ed Reed was all over the field last season. He managed to pick off a career high of 5 interceptions and deflected 13 passes. His incredible ball instincts put him in position to make plays in the run and pass game. At age 30, he is just now hitting his prime.

Speed	93
Man Cover	75
Zone Cover	90
Hit Power	85

Player Weapon: Smart Safety

#21 Chris McAlister *Cornerback (CB)*

▼DEFENSIVE **STAR PLAYER**

2 years ago, Chris McAlister was considered one of the top cornerbacks in the game. Since then, injuries and age have started to take their toll. He is still a physical cornerback with the talent to lock down receivers, but he just can't take as many chances as in years past or he will face getting beat deep.

Speed	93
Man Cover	92
Zone Cover	91
Press	93

Player Weapon: Smart Corner, Shutdown Corner, Press Coverage Corner

#52 Ray Lewis *Linebacker (MLB)*

▼DEFENSIVE **STAR PLAYER**

Just a few short years ago, Ray Lewis was not only the best middle linebacker in the game, but a player who could take a game over. At age 33, he has lost some of his speed, but he is still a force to be reckoned with when it comes to stopping inside runs because he can still tackle with the best of them.

Speed	82
Tackling	94
Pursuit	95
Play Recog.	95

Player Weapon: Big Hitter, Brick Wall Defender, Smart Linebacker

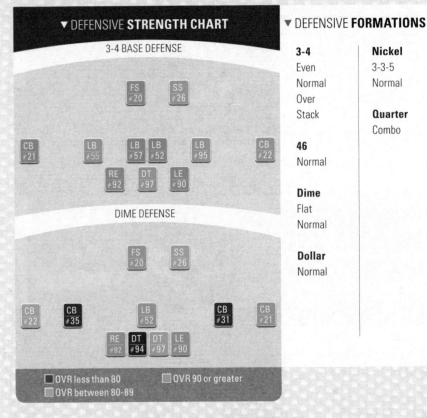

▼ DEFENSIVE **STRENGTH CHART**

3-4 BASE DEFENSE

FS #20 · SS #26
CB #21 · LB #55 · LB #57 · LB #52 · LB #95 · CB #22
RE #92 · DT #97 · LE #90

DIME DEFENSE

FS #20 · SS #26
CB #22 · CB #35 · LB #52 · CB #31 · CB #21
RE #92 · DT #94 · DT #97 · LE #90

☐ OVR less than 80   ☐ OVR 90 or greater
☐ OVR between 80-89

▼ DEFENSIVE **FORMATIONS**

3-4	Nickel
Even	3-3-5
Normal	Normal
Over	
Stack	**Quarter**
	Combo
46	
Normal	
Dime	
Flat	
Normal	
Dollar	
Normal	

▼ RECOMMENDED DEFENSIVE **AUDIBLE PACKAGES**

3-4	3-4	Nickel	Dime	Quarter
2 Man Under	OLB Dogs Fire	Cover 3	Cover 2	2 Man Press

▼ DEFENSIVE **PLAYCOUNTS**

Man Coverage:	45	Cover 3 Zone:	25	Combo Blitz:	11
Man Zone:	38	Deep Zone:	15		
Combo Coverage:	9	Man Blitz:	55		
Cover 2 Zone:	18	Zone Blitz:	58		

DEFENSE KEY DEFENSIVE PLAYS

A Mike Blitz

46 NORMAL

MIKE BLITZ

When looking to stop the run, there is no better defender over the years than Ravens' middle linebacker Ray Lewis.

The 46 Normal Mike Blitz puts him in perfect position to blow up any run that comes his way.

The ball carrier tries to run Lewis over, but that's not going to happen.

Lewis does what he does best: wrap up ball carriers.

A Cover 4 Buzz

3-4 STACK

COVER 4 BUZZ

The 3-4 Stack Cover 4 Buzz is a solid defense to run to defend the corner route, with both outside linebackers dropping back in buzz zones.

The quarterback looks down the field at the tight end, who is running a corner route.

With the left outside linebacker, left cornerback, and strong safety in coverage, the tight end won't be open.

The Ravens' strong safety steps in front of the tight end and picks the pass off.

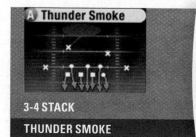

A Thunder Smoke

3-4 STACK

THUNDER SMOKE

A good defense to bring some serious heat from all directions when playing the Ravens is the 3-4 Stack Thunder Smoke.

With seven pass rushers, the offensive linemen won't be able pick them all up.

Outside linebacker Terrell Suggs shoots through the B Gap and goes straight after the quarterback.

The quarterback is unable to get the ball off and is dropped to the grass.

WASHINGTON REDSKINS

▶ **Division** NFC East ▶ **Stadium** FedEx Field ▶ **Type** Open ▶ **Capacity** 91,665 ▶ **Surface** Grass

▼ 2007 STANDINGS

Wins	Loses	Ties	PF	PA	Home	Road	vs. AFC	vs. NFC	vs. Div
9	7	0	334	310	5-3	4-4	2-2	7-5	3-3

▼ TEAM OVERVIEW

With Hall of Fame head coach Joe Gibbs retiring, the Redskins will take on a new look. Look for the Redskins to throw more often than when Gibbs was head coach. To prove our point, the Redskins' first three draft picks were two receivers and a tight end. The writing on the wall doesn't get any clearer than that.

With the additions of rookie receivers Devin Thomas and Malcolm Kelly, plus tight end Fred Davis, the Redskins are one of the deepest teams when it comes to the passing game. With starting receivers Santana Moss and Antwaan Randle El, along with All-Pro Tight End Chris Cooley, the Redskins should be able to move the ball through the air.

For the most part, the Redskins' defense that was rated among the top 10 in overall defense in 2007 remains intact.

▼ OFF-SEASON UPGRADES

TYPE	ROUND	FIRST NAME	LAST NAME	SCHOOL/TEAM	POSITION
Free Agent	N/A	Jerome	Mathis	Texans	WR
Draft	1	Devin	Thomas	Michigan State	WR
Draft	2	Fred	Davis	USC	TE
Draft	2	Malcolm	Kelly	Oklahoma	WR
Draft	3	Chad	Rinehart	Northern Iowa	G

▼ SCOUTING REPORT

	DESCRIPTION	MAXIMIZING POTENTIAL	TIPS FOR OPPONENTS
STRENGTHS	Portis is the heart and soul of the Skins, and is a well-rounded player.	You must feed him often to support Campbell's passing attack.	Play the run and force Campbell to beat you with his passing ability.
	Fletcher is one of the best MLBs in the game. He's the veteran leader.	Mix his roles up a bit, with 30% rush and 70% coverage.	Flood his area with routes. Give him something to do and read him.
WEAKNESSES	Campbell has all of the tools, but hasn't made a big impact yet.	He needs a West Coast offensive scheme with roll outs.	Send zone blitzes at him with spy. His accuracy isn't good on the run.
	Andre Carter is the only pass rushing defensive end they have right now.	The Skins need to use LBs to help generate heat.	Use a short passing game to exploit the aggressive blitz scheme. There will be holes.

TEAM STRATEGY

FRANCHISE MODE STRATEGY
The Redskins have some really nice players on offense. Focus your attention on the strong safety position and on getting some speed at cornerback. Your starters are solid, but lack in speed.

KEY FRANCHISE INFORMATION
Cap Room: $9.49M
Key Rivals:
• Cowboys, Eagles, Giants
Philosophy:
• Offense: West Coast
• Defense: 4-3
Highest Paid Players:
• C. Samuels
• C. Portis
Team Weapons:
• L. Fletcher-Baker – Brick Wall Defender
• C. Samuels – Crushing Run Blocker
Best Young Players:
• A. Montgomery
• M. Kelly

Clinton Portis, who rushed for 1,262 yards and 11 TDs in 2007, and the Redskins have a shot at making the playoffs again if the transition to a new offense goes smoothly and the defense stays solid.

88	85	90
OVERALL	OFFENSE	DEFENSE

▼ ROSTER AND **PACKAGE TIPS**

KEY PLAYER SUBSTITUTIONS

Postion: CB
Substitution: Fred Smoot
When: Global
Advantage: With teams like the Patriots out there, you need to have as much speed at cornerback as you possibly can. Smoot has better wheels than Springs. You'll need him to match up with the Randy Mosses of the world.

Postion: P
Substitution: Durant Brooks
When: Global
Advantage: Durant Brooks has a cannon for a leg and is just slightly less accurate than Derrick Frost. If you get in a game that comes down to field position, the extra distance on your punts could be important.

Postion: KR
Substitution: Devin Thomas
When: Global
Advantage: We like to have speed, speed, and more speed at the kick returner position. We recommend putting Devin Thomas in for Rock Cartwright. This will give you a lethal one-two combination with Antwaan Randle El.

TEAM STRATEGY

TEAM STRATEGY

#60 Chris Samuels *Tackle (LT)*

▼OFFENSIVE **STAR PLAYER**

Chris Samuels is one of the better offensive tackles in the game, and is often overlooked by bigger names at his position. He has played 66 straight games without missing a beat. The one weakness of his pass blocking skills is that he can be beaten by some pass rushers when they bull rush him to get by.

Run Block Strength	96
Run Block Footwork	88
Pass Block Strength	92
Pass Block Footwork	89

Player Weapon: Crushing Run Blocker, Pass Blocker

#26 Clinton Portis *Halfback (HB)*

▼OFFENSIVE **STAR PLAYER**

After a down year in 2006 due to injuries, Clinton Portis returned to form in a big way by rushing for over 1,200 yards and helping to lead the Redskins to the playoffs in 2007. Portis will have to learn a new offensive scheme, so the jury is out on his offensive production in 2008.

Speed	93
Agility	94
Trucking	88
Elusiveness	91

#89 Santana Moss *Wide Receiver (WR)*

▼OFFENSIVE **STAR PLAYER**

Of all the wide receivers on the Washington Redskins, Santana Moss is the most gifted. Last season, he caught 61 balls and racked up 808 receiving yards in just 14 games. Moss has playmaking abilities, but he is prone to injury and has a hard time beating press coverage.

Speed	97
Catch	86
Catch Traffic	81
Route Run	88

Player Weapon: Quick Receiver, Speed

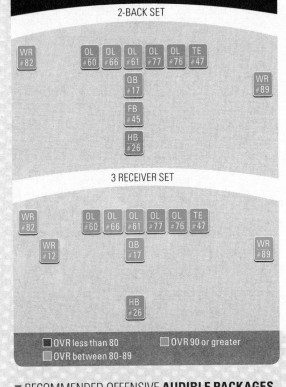

▼ OFFENSIVE **STRENGTH CHART**

2-BACK SET

WR #82 — OL #60 — OL #66 — OL #61 — OL #77 — OL #76 — TE #47 — WR #89
QB #17
FB #45
HB #26

3 RECEIVER SET

WR #82 — OL #60 — OL #66 — OL #61 — OL #77 — OL #76 — TE #47
WR #12 — QB #17 — WR #89
HB #26

☐ OVR less than 80 ☐ OVR 90 or greater
☐ OVR between 80-89

▼ OFFENSIVE **FORMATIONS**

Gun	Singleback
Doubles	Ace
Doubles Y-Slot	Ace Pair
Split Slot	Bunch
Spread Flex Wk	Doubles
Y-Trips	Flex
	Spread
I-Form	Y-Trips
Pro	
Pro Twins	**Split**
Slot Flex	Pro
Tight	
Tight Pair	**Strong**
	Pro
	Weak
	Pro
	Tight Pair

▼ RECOMMENDED OFFENSIVE **AUDIBLE PACKAGES**

I-Form	Singleback	I-Form	Singleback	Gun
Iso	Flanker Drive	Stretch	Slot Pivot	Y Corner

▼ OFFENSIVE **PLAYCOUNTS**

Quick Pass:	21	Screen Pass:	8	Pitch:	4
Standard Pass:	94	Hail Mary:	1	Counter:	14
Shotgun Pass:	45	Inside Handoff:	27	Draw:	9
Play Action Pass:	62	Outside Handoff:	18		

OFFENSE **KEY OFFENSIVE PLAYS**

A HB Gut

WEAK PRO

HB GUT

Running back Clinton Portis is the Redskins' primary running back who can get tough yards inside when called upon.

The Weak Pro HB Gut has Portis running to the left side of the offensive line.

The fullback makes a key block, which allows us to find open daylight.

We burst through the hole for a 4-yard pick-up.

A PA Deep Post

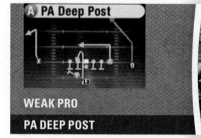

WEAK PRO

PA DEEP POST

Once we establish the HB Gut, we like to run some play action and go deep to Santana Moss on a fly route.

Jason Campbell fakes the handoff to Portis. The strong safety bites on the play fake.

This leaves Moss in one-on-one coverage with the left cornerback deep.

We take control of Moss and make the catch deep down the field for a big pick-up.

A Y Shallow Cross

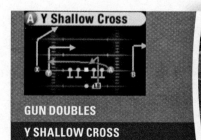

GUN DOUBLES

Y SHALLOW CROSS

We like to get tight end Chris Cooley involved in the Redskins' offense by running the Gun Doubles Y Shallow Cross.

This play has him running a shallow crossing route from right to left.

Against most coverages, his pass route is pretty much money; it's just a matter of waiting to get open.

Once the catch is made, Cooley is big enough to run a few defenders over while battling for yardage.

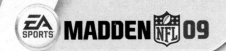

 # WASHINGTON REDSKINS

DEFENSE

#59 London Fletcher-Baker *Linebacker (MLB)*

▼DEFENSIVE **STAR PLAYER**

One of the most consistent middle linebackers over the last decade, London Fletcher continues to help improve his team's defense. In his first season with the Redskins, he led the team with 129 tackles. He even managed to pick off 3 passes, and took one of those in for a score.

Speed	82
Tackling	97
Pursuit	98
Play Recog.	93

Player Weapon: Brick Wall Defender, Smart Linebacker

#53 Marcus Washington *Linebacker (LOLB)*

▼DEFENSIVE **STAR PLAYER**

Marcus Washington never really got on track in 2007 due to injuries. When healthy, he is the team's best pass rushing linebacker. Despite missing a quarter of the season, he still managed to rack up 5 sacks. If he is able to remain healthy for the duration of this upcoming season, his sacks should increase.

Speed	82
Tackling	90
Pursuit	90
Play Recog.	85

#24 Shawn Springs *Cornerback (CB)*

▼DEFENSIVE **STAR PLAYER**

Shawn Springs is at his best when he is playing man coverage. At age 33, he has lost a few steps, but is still able to hang with most receivers around the league. He picked off four passes and made 62 tackles. For a cornerback to have that many tackles, it tells us that he is the complete package.

Speed	88
Man Cover	88
Zone Cover	92
Press	89

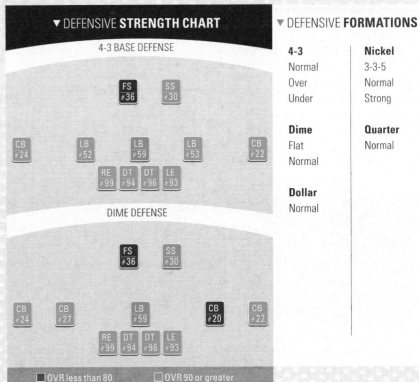

▼ DEFENSIVE **STRENGTH CHART**

4-3 BASE DEFENSE

FS #36 · SS #30

CB #24 · LB #52 · LB #59 · LB #53 · CB #22

RE #99 · DT #94 · DT #96 · LE #93

DIME DEFENSE

FS #36 · SS #30

CB #24 · CB #27 · LB #59 · CB #20 · CB #22

RE #99 · DT #94 · DT #96 · LE #93

☐ OVR less than 80   ☐ OVR 90 or greater
☐ OVR between 80-89

▼ DEFENSIVE **FORMATIONS**

4-3	Nickel
Normal	3-3-5
Over	Normal
Under	Strong

Dime	**Quarter**
Flat	Normal
Normal	

Dollar	
Normal	

▼ RECOMMENDED DEFENSIVE **AUDIBLE PACKAGES**

4-3	4-3	Nickel	Dime	Quarter
2 Man Under	Free Fire	Cover 3	Cover 2	3 Deep Man

▼ DEFENSIVE **PLAYCOUNTS**

Man Coverage:	45	Cover 2 Zone:	14	Man Blitz:	53
Man Zone:	35	Cover 3 Zone:	26	Zone Blitz:	63
Combo Coverage:	6	Deep Zone:	18	Combo Blitz:	12

DEFENSE **KEY DEFENSIVE PLAYS**

SS Blitz
4-3 OVER
SS BLITZ

When stopping the run, we like to call the 4-3 Over SS Blitz for extra run support. This often allows the SS to make the tackle.

We don't move him up near the line of scrimmage. Instead we want him to blitz from the default position on the field.

Reed Doughty sets his sights on the ball carrier as he gets near the line of scrimmage.

No offensive lineman picks up Doughty, and he is able to make the tackle on the ball carrier.

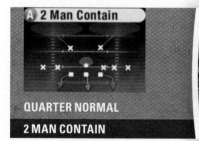

2 Man Contain
QUARTER NORMAL
2 MAN CONTAIN

The Quarter Normal 2 Man Contain is a good defense to prevent the quarterback from taking off out of the pocket.

If your opponent likes to run with his quarterback, this defense will make him think twice.

Both defensive ends are in QB Contain, while the linebacker plays QB Spy.

Even the more mobile quarterbacks will have a hard time trying to pick up yardage against this defense.

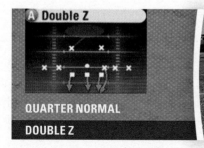

Double Z
QUARTER NORMAL
DOUBLE Z

The Quarter Normal Double puts the left cornerback and strong safety in man coverage on the outside receiver.

To add some pressure on the quarterback, the dimeback is sent in on a blitz from the left side.

With two defenders covering the flanker, it will be very hard for the quarterback to throw to him.

Cowboys quarterback Tony Romo is about to be sacked by Redskins cornerback Fred Smoot.

TEAM STRATEGY

NEW ORLEANS SAINTS

▶ **Division** NFC South ▶ **Stadium** Louisiana Superdome ▶ **Type** Dome ▶ **Capacity** 69,700 ▶ **Surface** Momentum Turf

▼ 2007 STANDINGS

Wins	Loses	Ties	PF	PA	Home	Road	vs. AFC	vs. NFC	vs. Div
7	9	0	379	388	3-5	4-4	1-3	6-6	3-3

▼ TEAM OVERVIEW

The Saints were explosive in 2007, despite key injuries to the top two running backs, which kept the running game from being much of a factor. Despite the rushing game never taking off, the passing game was among the best. What kept the Saints from reaching the playoffs was that the defense had a hard time stopping anyone.

Drew Brees ranks among the top quarterbacks in the league. He doesn't have the strongest arm, but he can make all the throws. Marques Colston has the speed and height to make defenses pay when he is left in one-on-one coverage.

The Saints signed a few new free agents to bolster the team's overall defense. Randall Gay, Dan Morgan, and Jonathan Vilma are all upgrades and will help improve a defense that gave up 348.1 yards per game last year.

▼ OFF-SEASON UPGRADES

TYPE	ROUND	FIRST NAME	LAST NAME	SCHOOL/TEAM	POSITION
Free Agent	N/A	Randall	Gay	Patriots	CB
Free Agent	N/A	Dan	Morgan	Panthers	LB
Trade	N/A	Jonathan	Vilma	Jets	LB
Draft	1	Sedrick	Ellis	USC	DT
Draft	2	Tracy	Porter	Indiana	CB

▼ SCOUTING REPORT

	DESCRIPTION	MAXIMIZING POTENTIAL	TIPS FOR OPPONENTS
STRENGTHS	Bush needs the ball in his hands at all times. His speed is unreal.	You need to move him around and get him the ball.	Shadow him, because he may line up anywhere, even at QB.
	McKenzie is the best corner they have. He needs to be on the best wideout.	Mix coverages with heat and allow his awareness to make plays.	He doesn't have great speed, so use double moves to get deep with your fast wideout.
WEAKNESSES	The Saints' offensive line isn't the best out there. They need to play better.	Use a West Coast-like scheme to help with pass protection.	Create pressure in different areas of the line every down. Use plenty of stunts.
	Their secondary isn't the best in the game, either. They only have Mike McKenzie.	You need to run zone blitzes with safety help deep to protect the deep pass.	Stretch the defense both vertically and horizontally. Attack deep early and often.

FRANCHISE MODE STRATEGY

You have some work to do to build up the middle of the offensive line. Until you do, the inside run game will suffer. As far as the defense goes, you will need to find some speed at corner through trades or the draft.

KEY FRANCHISE INFORMATION

Cap Room: $16.16M

Key Rivals:
- Buccaneers, Falcons, Panthers

Philosophy:
- Offense: West Coast
- Defense: 4-3

Highest Paid Players:
- D. Brees
- C. Grant

Team Weapons:
- D. Brees – Accurate QB
- J. Brown – Pass Blocker

Best Young Players:
- R. Bush
- S. Ellis

87	91	79
OVERALL	OFFENSE	DEFENSE

▼ ROSTER AND **PACKAGE TIPS**

KEY PLAYER SUBSTITUTIONS

Postion: HB

Substitution: Reggie Bush

When: Global

Advantage: Running the ball inside is tough in *Madden NFL 09*. We would rather have a player that can get to the corner lined up in the backfield. Bush is a more versatile player and can be lined up all over the field to attack the defense.

Postion: WR

Substitution: Devery Henderson

When: Global

Advantage: Sub Devery Henderson in as the third receiver. He has way too much speed to be left on the bench. Get him in the game and stretch the defense so that Patten and Colston can go to work underneath.

Postion: TE

Substitution: Mark Campbell

When: Situational

Advantage: If you are looking to ice the game by pounding the rock late in the fourth quarter, then Campbell is your guy. He is a stronger run blocker than Eric Johnson. In passing situations, you want Johnson's hands on the field.

If the Saints can play more consistent football in 2008, Marques Colston and his teammates have the firepower to return to the playoffs.

TEAM STRATEGY

213

NEW ORLEANS SAINTS

OFFENSE

#9 Drew Brees *Quarterback (QB)*

▼OFFENSIVE **STAR PLAYER**

Drew Brees started off the 2007 season by throwing 9 interceptions and just 1 touchdown in the first four games. In the last 12 games of the season, he caught fire by throwing 27 touchdowns and 12 interceptions. Brees does not have the strongest arm, but makes up for it with laser-like throws in the short and intermediate passing game.

Speed	64
Awareness	88
Throw Power	90
Throw Accur.	96

Player Weapon: Accurate Quarterback

#12 Marques Colston *Wide Receiver (WR)*

▼OFFENSIVE **STAR PLAYER**

One of the bigger receivers in the league, Marques Colston uses his body to shield smaller defenders. His ability to pick up chunks of yardage after the catch makes him a threat any time he touches the ball. When near the goal line, he is able to use his height and athleticism to out jump smaller defenders.

Speed	87
Catch	94
Catch Traffic	97
Route Run	91

Player Weapon: Quick Receiver, Possession Receiver, Hands

#25 Reggie Bush *Halfback (HB)*

▼OFFENSIVE **STAR PLAYER**

Reggie Bush may never be an every-down back because of his size. What he can do is make breathtaking moves that very few running backs can. His ability to take the ball the distance on any given play can't be ignored, whether it be in the backfield or lined up in the slot. Bush needs to be moved all around your scheme to showcase his many talents.

Speed	97
Agility	99
Trucking	66
Elusiveness	96

Player Weapon: Elusive Back, Speed

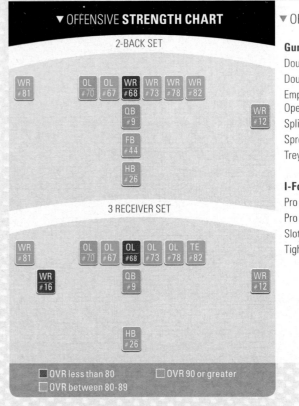

▼ OFFENSIVE **STRENGTH CHART**

2-BACK SET

WR #81 | OL #70 | OL #67 | WR #68 | WR #73 | WR #78 | WR #82 | WR #12

QB #9

FB #44

HB #26

3 RECEIVER SET

WR #81 | OL #70 | OL #67 | OL #68 | OL #73 | OL #78 | TE #82

WR #16 | QB #9 | WR #12

HB #26

☐ OVR less than 80   ☐ OVR 90 or greater
☐ OVR between 80-89

▼ OFFENSIVE **FORMATIONS**

Gun	Singleback
Double Flex	Ace
Doubles Wk	Ace Pair
Empty Trey	Ace Pair Twins
Open	Bunch
Split Slot	Flex
Spread	Snugs Flip
Trey Open	Spread
	Y-Trips
I-Form	
Pro	**Strong**
Pro Twins	Flex Twins
Slot	Pro
Tight Pair	
	Weak
	Flex Twins
	Pro
	Tight Pair

▼ RECOMMENDED OFFENSIVE **AUDIBLE PACKAGES**

Singleback	I-Form	Weak	Singleback	Gun
Counter Weak	Quick Slants	HB Gut	Curls	Smash

▼ OFFENSIVE **PLAYCOUNTS**

Quick Pass:	25	Screen Pass:	8	Pitch:	6
Standard Pass:	86	Hail Mary:	1	Counter:	12
Shotgun Pass:	50	Inside Handoff:	30	Draw:	11
Play Action Pass:	66	Outside Handoff:	18		

OFFENSE **KEY OFFENSIVE PLAYS**

TEAM STRATEGY

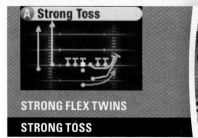

STRONG FLEX TWINS

STRONG TOSS

Toss plays are fairly effective in this year's game. A good toss play to call from the Saints' playbook is the Strong Flex Twins Strong Toss.

The right guard and fullback get out in front and set up the run blocking.

They wall off the defenders and allow us to get Deuce McAllister outside.

We find some open running room and pick up 8 yards before being tackled.

STRONG FLEX TWINS

WR STREAK

The Strong Flex Twins WR Streak sends speedster Marques Colston on a streak down the left sideline.

We look for him first, but if there is a safety playing over the top, we must look elsewhere.

Having a fast running back like Reggie Bush running a flat route makes things easy.

We use his speed after we make the catch to pick up positive yardage before being brought down.

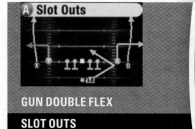

GUN DOUBLE FLEX

SLOT OUTS

Against man coverage, out routes run by slot receivers are a sure way to move the chains through the air with the Saints.

The Gun Double Flex Slot Outs has both receivers running slot routes to each side.

We throw to the slot receiver on the left once he breaks to the sideline.

We are able to get a few yards of separation and make the catch on the run.

NEW ORLEANS SAINTS

TEAM STRATEGY

#51 Jonathan Vilma *Linebacker (MLB)*

▼DEFENSIVE STAR PLAYER

The Saints needed a playmaker to play middle linebacker, so they signed one of the better ones in the game. Jonathan Vilma is an instant upgrade and will have a huge impact on the Saints' run defense, especially now that he is fully healed from last year's knee injury that shelved him for 9 games.

Speed	85
Tackling	91
Pursuit	95
Play Recog.	89

Player Weapon: Brick Wall Defender

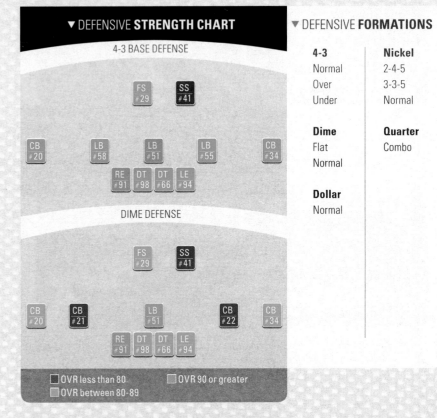

#91 Will Smith *Defensive End (RE)*

▼DEFENSIVE STAR PLAYER

Will Smith doesn't put up jaw-dropping numbers when it comes to sacks. What he does bring to the table is consistency. In his four seasons in the NFL, he has never had fewer than 7 sacks in a year. He has a none-stop motor and doesn't take plays off. He is also durable, having only missed two games during his short career.

Speed	82
Strength	80
Power Moves	85
Finesse Moves	93

Player Weapon: Finesse Move D-Lineman

#34 Mike McKenzie *Cornerback (CB)*

▼DEFENSIVE STAR PLAYER

Of all the Saints' cornerbacks, Mike McKenzie is the best. While he doesn't possess the same blazing speed, he is still a playmaker, as he returned two interceptions for touchdowns in 2007. In week 16 last season, he suffered a torn ACL, so there is some question if he will make it back in time for the start of the 2008 season.

Speed	90
Man Cover	94
Zone Cover	88
Press	80

Player Weapon: Shutdown Corner, Speed

▼ DEFENSIVE **FORMATIONS**

4-3	Nickel
Normal	2-4-5
Over	3-3-5
Under	Normal

Dime	**Quarter**
Flat	Combo
Normal	

Dollar	
Normal	

▼ RECOMMENDED DEFENSIVE **AUDIBLE PACKAGES**

4-3	4-3	Nickel	Dime	Quarter
2 Man Under	Free Fire	Cover 3	Cover 2	Man Up 3 Deep

▼ DEFENSIVE **PLAYCOUNTS**

Man Coverage:	45	Cover 2 Zone:	16	Man Blitz:	59
Man Zone:	34	Cover 3 Zone:	27	Zone Blitz:	64
Combo Coverage:	7	Deep Zone:	19	Combo Blitz:	13

DEFENSE **KEY DEFENSIVE PLAYS**

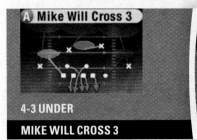

4-3 UNDER

MIKE WILL CROSS 3

A good inside run defense is the 4-3 Under Mike Will Cross. This defense has two linebackers stunting to confuse the run blocking.

Right outside linebacker Scott Fujita and middle linebacker Jonathan Vilma crisscross paths.

The fullback has to decide who to run block. He can't choose both of the linebackers.

The fullback chooses to block Fujita, leaving Vilma to make the tackle on the ball carrier.

NICKEL 2-4-5

COVER 2 QB SPY

The Nickel 2-4-5 Cover 2 QB spy drops the weak side defensive tackle in QB Spy. Both the corners play the flats.

The left cornerback sinks back a few yards, taking away the curl route.

As soon as he sees that running back in the flats, he closes in quickly.

The running back makes the catch, but is brought down quickly for a minimal gain.

NICKEL 2-4-5

INSIDE BLITZ 3

Getting pressure up the gut really throws the quarterback out of rhythm. One play that achieves this is the Inside Blitz.

If the inside linebackers get blocked, it will free up the nickelback to shoot through the B gap to get pressure.

The quarterback won't have much time in the pocket. If he doesn't get rid of it, he will be sacked.

The quarterback hangs on a bit too long and is brought down for a sack.

TEAM STRATEGY

 # SEATTLE SEAHAWKS

▶ **Division** NFC West ▶ **Stadium** Qwest Field ▶ **Type** Open ▶ **Capacity** 67,000 ▶ **Surface** Field Turf

▼ 2007 STANDINGS

Wins	Loses	Ties	PF	PA	Home	Road	vs. AFC	vs. NFC	vs. Div
10	6	0	393	291	7-1	3-5	2-2	8-4	5-1

TEAM STRATEGY

FRANCHISE MODE STRATEGY

The Seahawks' offense has some quality performers but is lacking in speed. Look for playmakers to stretch the defense. The defense is solid overall. Make good draft picks and find speed for the offense.

KEY FRANCHISE INFORMATION

Cap Room: $15.37M

Key Rivals:
• Cardinals, 49ers, Rams

Philosophy:
• Offense: West Coast
• Defense: 4-3

Highest Paid Players:
• J. Peterson
• W. Jones

Team Weapons:
• L. Tatupu – Brick Wall Defender
• P. Kerney – Power Move D-Lineman

Best Young Players:
• D. Tapp
• R. Sims

▼ TEAM OVERVIEW

One of the most consistent teams over the last decade has been the Seattle Seahawks. The main reason is that head coach Mike Holmgren has kept his players' focus year in and year out. This will be his last season, so his players would like nothing more than to send him out on top.

Offensively, the team is in good hands with Matt Hasselbeck. He put up solid passing numbers in 2007 despite the lack of a running game. None of the team's top four receivers are stars, but each one has a role in the passing game and does his job like a professional.

The Seahawks have stars on a defense that is often overlooked. Last season, as a unit, it ranked 7th. With pretty much the same line-up, the defense should only improve.

▼ OFF-SEASON UPGRADES

TYPE	ROUND	FIRST NAME	LAST NAME	SCHOOL/TEAM	POSITION
Free Agent	N/A	Julius	Jones	Cowboys	RB
Free Agent	N/A	Mike	Wahle	Panthers	G
Draft	1	Lawrence	Jackson	USC	DE
Draft	2	John	Carlson	Notre Dame	TE
Draft	4	Red	Bryant	Texas A&M	DT

▼ SCOUTING REPORT

	DESCRIPTION	MAXIMIZING POTENTIAL	TIPS FOR OPPONENTS
STRENGTHS	Matt Hasselbeck is regarded as one of the most accurate quarterbacks in the league with his trademark laser-like passes.	Run slants, drags, and other high percentage passes that utilize Hasselbeck's pinpoint accuracy.	Your best bet to beat Hassslebeck is to press him at the line to throw the timing off between his receivers.
	Patrick Kerney is one of the better defensive ends in the game. His motor and intensity rank him high.	Kerney is a one man wrecking crew. With rushing the quarterback, there is no need to blitz much.	Leave extra pass blockers on Kerney's side to prevent him from getting to your quarterback.
WEAKNESSES	Everyone knows that Seattle can pass the ball with the best of them. On the other hand, they can't run the ball.	If you plan on establishing a running game, try it from spread formations to open more running lanes.	Don't bother loading the box with safeties to stop the run; instead, leave them back to defend the pass.
	The Seahawks do not have an elite receiver to count on when a big play is needed or that the defense must scheme around.	Bobby Engram is not considered an elite receiver, but he knows how to catch the ball on crucial downs.	Focus on Engram and make sure he doesn't beat you in crucial third down situations.

87
OVERALL

88
OFFENSE

85
DEFENSE

The still underrated Matt Hasselbeck, who passed for 3,966 yards and 28 TDs in 2007, and the Seahawks remain one of the favorites to win the NFC West in 2008.

▼ ROSTER AND **PACKAGE TIPS**

KEY PLAYER SUBSTITUTIONS

Postion: TE

Substitution: John Carlson

When: Global

Advantage: John Carlson has more speed and better hands than Will Heller. When running with a West Coast Offense team like the Seahawks, you want to have a solid target at tight end. Carlson will give you more passing options.

Postion: CB (Nickelback)

Substitution: Josh Wilson

When: Global

Advantage: We recommend putting Josh Wilson in as your Nickelback (3rd corner). He is the fastest corner on the team and should be able to hang with just about any receiver you meet. He's great off the edge as a blitzer.

Postion: HB

Substitution: Maurice Morris

When: Situational

Advantage: When it comes to converting on passing downs, you want to have every possible advantage available to you. Morris has better hands than Julius Jones and should be put in the game when you plan on throwing the ball.

TEAM STRATEGY

TEAM STRATEGY

#8 Matt Hasselbeck *Quarterback (QB)*

▼OFFENSIVE **STAR PLAYER**

The Seattle Seahawks' running game was nonexistent last season, so the offense was based solely on Matt Hasselbeck's arm. He delivered in a big way by throwing for a franchise record of 3,966 yards. By throwing quick darts to receivers underneath, he was able to throw 28 touchdowns versus 12 interceptions.

Speed	66
Awareness	88
Throw Power	88
Throw Accur.	93

Player Weapon: Accurate Quarterback,

#83 Deion Branch *Wide Receiver (WR)*

▼OFFENSIVE **STAR PLAYER**

Deion Branch has yet to avoid the injury bug since coming to Seattle two years ago. When he is on the field, there is no question that he is a huge talent. He appeared in 11 games last season and managed to grab 49 balls. In the Seahawks' West Coast Offense, he has a chance to do bigger things if he stays healthy.

Speed	92
Catch	86
Catch Traffic	85
Route Run	92

Player Weapon: Quick Receiver

#71 Walter Jones *Tackle (LT)*

▼OFFENSIVE **STAR PLAYER**

Walter Jones remains the best offensive tackle in football, in spite of being 34 years old. His ability to pass block can't be underestimated. Even the best pass rushers have a hard time getting around him because he makes things look so easy. His run blocking is also top notch.

Run Block Strength	95
Run Block Footwork	90
Pass Block Strength	94
Pass Block Footwork	90

Player Weapon: Crushing Run Blocker, Pass Blocker

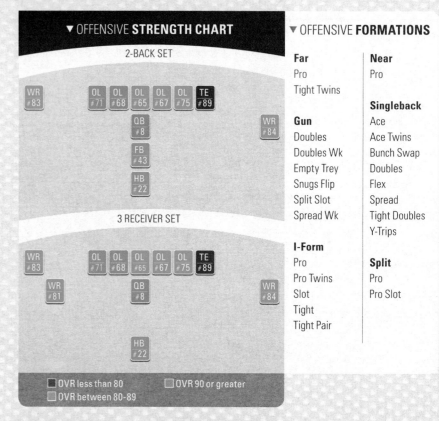

▼ OFFENSIVE **STRENGTH CHART**

2-BACK SET

WR #83 — OL #71 OL #68 OL #65 OL #67 OL #75 TE #89 — WR #84
QB #8
FB #43
HB #22

3 RECEIVER SET

WR #83 — OL #71 OL #68 OL #65 OL #67 OL #75 TE #89
WR #81 — QB #8 — WR #84
HB #22

☐ OVR less than 80 ☐ OVR 90 or greater
☐ OVR between 80-89

▼ OFFENSIVE **FORMATIONS**

Far	**Near**
Pro	Pro
Tight Twins	
	Singleback
Gun	Ace
Doubles	Ace Twins
Doubles Wk	Bunch Swap
Empty Trey	Doubles
Snugs Flip	Flex
Split Slot	Spread
Spread Wk	Tight Doubles
	Y-Trips
I-Form	
Pro	**Split**
Pro Twins	Pro
Slot	Pro Slot
Tight	
Tight Pair	

▼ RECOMMENDED OFFENSIVE **AUDIBLE PACKAGES**

I-Form	I-Form	Singleback	Singleback	Gun
Stretch	Slants	HB Draw	TE Post	Bench Switch

▼ OFFENSIVE **PLAYCOUNTS**

Quick Pass:	21	Screen Pass:	12	Pitch:	11
Standard Pass:	100	Hail Mary:	2	Counter:	13
Shotgun Pass:	53	Inside Handoff:	25	Draw:	13
Play Action Pass:	56	Outside Handoff:	16		

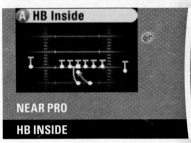

NEAR PRO
HB INSIDE

The Seahawks don't run the ball that much, but there are some good run plays to be found in their playbook, such as HB Inside.

This play has the halfback running inside between the left guard and center.

If nothing opens up inside, look to bounce outside for open daylight.

We manage to get past the line of scrimmage and pick up 5 yards.

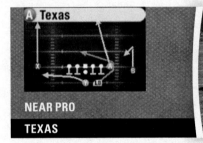

NEAR PRO
TEXAS

One of the staple plays in the West Coast Offense is the Texas. This play has the halfback running an angle route out of the backfield.

Against man coverage, it is very effective because the halfback will gain some separation from his man.

Once we see that he is open, we throw him a hard bullet pass over the middle.

We make the catch on the run and turn up the field for a nice gain.

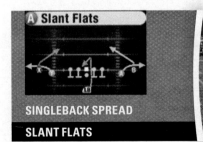

SINGLEBACK SPREAD
SLANT FLATS

What would any WCO be without a good amount of quick slant plays? One that we like to run is the Singleback Spread Slant Flats.

Quarterback Matt Hasselbeck is a highly accurate quarterback who doesn't make many mistakes.

While in control of him, we spot the split end running a quick slant on the left side of the field.

We throw him a bullet pass and he makes the catch on the run for an 8-yard pick-up.

TEAM STRATEGY

#59 Julian Peterson *Linebacker (ROLB)*
▼DEFENSIVE **STAR PLAYER**

Over the last two seasons, Julian Peterson has been a pain in the neck to opposing quarterbacks by racking up 19 sacks. His ability to put pressure on the quarterback helped make Seattle's pass defense one of the stronger ones in the league. Peterson is also one of the better cover linebackers in the game.

Speed	86
Tackling	90
Pursuit	98
Play Recog.	86

Player Weapon: Brick Wall Defender

#97 Patrick Kerney *Defensive End (LE)*
▼DEFENSIVE **STAR PLAYER**

Patrick Kerney made a huge splash in his first season as a Seattle Seahawk by registering 14 sacks. In three games alone, he had a total of 9 sacks. His non-stop motor and hard work ethic has allowed him to continue to be a strong player, regardless of him turning 32 in December.

Speed	78
Strength	84
Power Moves	93
Finesse Moves	86

Player Weapon: Power Move D-Lineman

#51 Lofa Tatupu *Linebacker (MLB)*
▼DEFENSIVE **STAR PLAYER**

Last season, Lofa Tatupu established himself as one of the top middle linebackers in the game by racking up a team-leading 109 tackles. He picked off another four passes for good measure. His leadership skills, athleticism, and intelligence make him the perfect middle linebacker in the NFL.

Speed	85
Tackling	96
Pursuit	98
Play Recog.	94

Player Weapon: Big Hitter, Brick Wall Defender, Smart Linebacker

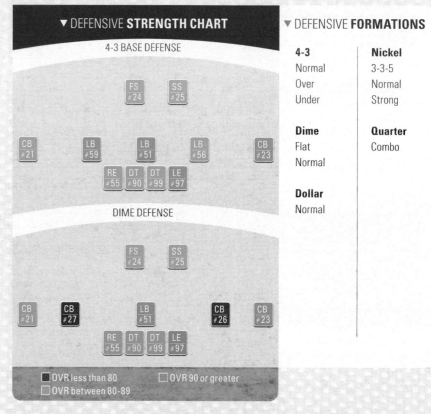

▼ DEFENSIVE **STRENGTH CHART**

4-3 BASE DEFENSE

FS #24 · SS #25
CB #21 · LB #59 · LB #51 · LB #56 · CB #23
RE #55 · DT #90 · DT #99 · LE #97

DIME DEFENSE

FS #24 · SS #25
CB #21 · CB #27 · LB #51 · CB #26 · CB #23
RE #55 · DT #90 · DT #99 · LE #97

■ OVR less than 80
□ OVR between 80-89
□ OVR 90 or greater

▼ DEFENSIVE **FORMATIONS**

4-3	Nickel
Normal	3-3-5
Over	Normal
Under	Strong

Dime	Quarter
Flat	Combo
Normal	

Dollar	
Normal	

▼ RECOMMENDED DEFENSIVE **AUDIBLE PACKAGES**

4-3	4-3	Nickel	Dime	Quarter
2 Man Under	Fire Man	Cover 3	Cover 2	3 Deep Press

▼ DEFENSIVE **PLAYCOUNTS**

Man Coverage:	45	Cover 2 Zone:	14	Man Blitz:	55
Man Zone:	34	Cover 3 Zone:	26	Zone Blitz:	64
Combo Coverage:	7	Deep Zone:	18	Combo Blitz:	13

DEFENSE **KEY DEFENSIVE PLAYS**

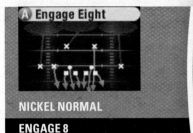

A Engage Eight

NICKEL NORMAL

ENGAGE 8

A good run defense to blow up inside run plays from the spread offense is the Nickel Normal Engage 8.

1 By sending eight defenders in on a run blitz, there won't be much room for the ball carrier to run.

2 Both the right outside linebacker and strong safety shoot through the B gaps.

3 The ball carrier has no chance to get back to the line of scrimmage.

A 9 Velcro

NICKEL NORMAL

9 VELCRO

One of the better pass coverages is the 9 Velcro. The Seattle Seahawks make this defense that much better with their high awareness.

1 By dropping nine defenders in pass coverage, there is not a lot of open space for the quarterback to find an open receiver.

2 The quarterback looks left to find an open receiver, but all of them are blanketed.

3 Despite only having a two man pass rush, the 9 Velcro can get a few coverage sacks.

A NB Blitz

NICKEL STRONG

NB BLITZ

When looking to bring some heat from the quarterback's blind side, try dialing up the Nickel Strong NB Blitz.

1 With both the right end and nickel-back blitzing, the left tackle is in a jam on who to block.

2 The right end is left unblocked and goes straight after the quarterback.

3 The quarterback can't get out of his way and is brought down hard to the turf.

TEAM STRATEGY

PITTSBURGH STEELERS

▶ **Division** AFC North   ▶ **Stadium** Heinz Field   ▶ **Type** Open   ▶ **Capacity** 65,050   ▶ **Surface** Grass

TEAM STRATEGY

FRANCHISE MODE **STRATEGY**

The Steelers are solid at the skill positions. Continue to build the offensive line with quality draft choices. Start looking for future replacements at MLB and ROLB. Your starters are great, but are over the 30-year mark.

KEY FRANCHISE INFORMATION

Cap Room: $5.56M
Key Rivals:
• Bengals, Browns, Ravens
Philosophy:
• Offense: Multiple
• Defense: 3-4
Highest Paid Players:
• B. Roethlisberger
• T. Polamalu
Team Weapons:
• T. Polamalu – Smart Safety
• C. Hampton – Power Move D-Lineman
Best Young Players:
• S. Holmes
• R. Mendenhall

▼ 2007 **STANDINGS**

Wins	Loses	Ties	PF	PA	Home	Road	vs. AFC	vs. NFC	vs. Div
10	6	0	393	269	7-1	3-5	7-5	3-1	5-1

▼ TEAM **OVERVIEW**

The Steelers need to get back to what they do best this season. Last season, they strayed from their strengths: pounding the ball on offense and playing aggressively on defense.

Ben Roethlisberger has become one of the top quarterbacks in the game.

He can make all the throws and is the team's leader. Willie Parker is one of the strongest running backs in the league. He doesn't have a lot of power, but he is shifty enough to make defenders miss.

Despite not being as aggressive last season, the Steelers' defense still ranked number 1 overall in total yards allowed. Strong safety Troy Polamalu had an off-year by his standards. He wasn't the same type of playmaker he has been in previous seasons. Expect him to bounce back in a big way and create turnovers.

▼ OFF-SEASON **UPGRADES**

TYPE	ROUND	FIRST NAME	LAST NAME	SCHOOL/TEAM	POSITION
Free Agent	N/A	Keyaron	Fox	Chiefs	LB
Free Agent	N/A	Justin	Hartwig	Panthers	C
Free Agent	N/A	Mewelde	Moore	Vikings	RB
Draft	1	Rashard	Mendenhall	Illinois	RB
Draft	2	Limas	Sweed	Texas	WR

▼ SCOUTING **REPORT**

	DESCRIPTION	MAXIMIZING POTENTIAL	TIPS FOR OPPONENTS
STRENGTHS	Ben Roethlisberger is a highly accurate QB. He is deadly if you simply let him stand in the pocket and find open receivers.	Use his accuracy to find different receivers in the passing game to keep the defense honest.	Be sure to play an aggressive, blitzing defense to keep pressure on Roethlisberger.
STRENGTHS	Willie Parker is one of the better speed runners in the game and is a threat to hit the home run every time he touches the ball.	Use sweeps and counters to take advantage of Parker's blazing speed.	Don't sleep on the Steelers' run game. Always be on guard; Parker can take it to the house.
WEAKNESSES	The offensive line is still a question mark for this team.	Make sure you roll out with Ben as much as possible so that defenses won't be able to key in on the QB.	Double up Hines Ward and force Big Ben to find another receiver.
WEAKNESSES	Troy Polamalu is as good as it gets in run support, as well as being strong against the pass because he has good coverage skills.	In passing situations, leave Polamalu on the field to strengthen your secondary.	If Polamalu is on the field, be careful of going deep to avoid throwing near Polamalu.

94	92	94
OVERALL	OFFENSE	DEFENSE

▼ ROSTER AND **PACKAGE TIPS**
KEY PLAYER SUBSTITUTIONS

Postion: HB
Substitution: Najah Davenport
When: Situational
Advantage: When you are in a passing situation, you want Davenport on the field. He has the best hands of all the running backs on the depth chart. He doesn't have Parker's speed, but he is more sure-handed.

Postion: MLB
Substitution: Lawrence Timmons
When: Situational
Advantage: Timmons is your fastest line-backer. If you are going up against a team that consistently runs with the quarter-back, then you will want to put him in the game. Use him to spy the QB and prevent him from taking off.

Postion: KR
Substitution: Nate Washington
When: Global
Advantage: Nate Washington has too much speed to only get on the field in four wide receiver situations. Put him in for Moore as a kick returner. He has all the tools to take the ball to the house anytime he gets his hands on it.

Look for Big Ben Roethlisberger, who threw for 32 TDs and only 11 interceptions, and a well-rounded Steelers team to compete for a Super Bowl XLIII berth if they can remain healthy.

TEAM STRATEGY

TEAM STRATEGY

#7 Ben Roethlisberger *Quarterback (QB)*
▼OFFENSIVE **STAR PLAYER**

After coming off of a down year in 2006, Ben Roethlisberger bounced back in a big way by throwing 32 touchdowns and only 11 interceptions. His QB Rating was his pro-career best of 104.1. As big as he is, Roethlisberger is able to make plays with his feet when nothing opens up downfield.

Speed	73
Awareness	87
Throw Power	95
Throw Accur.	91

Player Weapon: Cannon Arm Quarterback

#39 Willie Parker *Halfback (HB)*
▼OFFENSIVE **STAR PLAYER**

Since coming into the league in 2005, Willie Parker has been nothing short of spectacular. He has rushed for at least 1,200 yards in his first three seasons. Parker uses his straight line speed to get in and out of holes quickly. He won't break many tackles, but then again, it's hard to tackle what you can't catch.

Speed	97
Agility	94
Trucking	85
Elusiveness	90

Player Weapon: Speed

#86 Hines Ward *Wide Receiver (WR)*
▼OFFENSIVE **STAR PLAYER**

Hines Ward has made his mark in the NFL as a strong nosed receiver who is not afraid to make tough catches in traffic. He doesn't have the speed of some of the top receivers in the game, but he does have great hands and the drive to succeed. His run blocking is among the best, as far as receivers go.

Speed	87
Catch	93
Catch Traffic	97
Route Run	90

Player Weapon: Hands, Possession Receiver

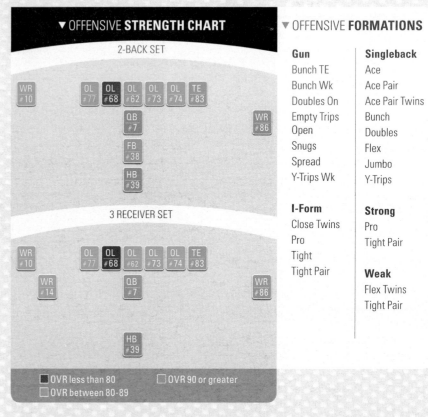

▼ OFFENSIVE **STRENGTH CHART**

2-BACK SET / 3 RECEIVER SET

☐ OVR less than 80 ☐ OVR between 80-89 ☐ OVR 90 or greater

▼ OFFENSIVE **FORMATIONS**

Gun	Singleback
Bunch TE	Ace
Bunch Wk	Ace Pair
Doubles On	Ace Pair Twins
Empty Trips	Bunch
Open	Doubles
Snugs	Flex
Spread	Jumbo
Y-Trips Wk	Y-Trips

I-Form	Strong
Close Twins	Pro
Pro	Tight Pair
Tight	
Tight Pair	**Weak**
	Flex Twins
	Tight Pair

▼ RECOMMENDED OFFENSIVE **AUDIBLE PACKAGES**

Singleback	Singleback	I-Form	Gun	Gun
Quick Pitch	TE Post	HB Counter Wk	Circle	Levels Switch

▼ OFFENSIVE **PLAYCOUNTS**

Quick Pass:	2	Screen Pass:	5	Pitch:	6
Standard Pass:	80	Hail Mary:	2	Counter:	15
Shotgun Pass:	57	Inside Handoff:	24	Draw:	10
Play Action Pass:	64	Outside Handoff:	16		

OFFENSE **KEY OFFENSIVE PLAYS**

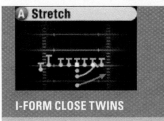

A Stretch

I-FORM CLOSE TWINS

STRETCH

Steelers halfback Willie Parker is one of the faster backs in the game. The I-Form Close Twins Stretch showcases his wheels.

Stretch plays take a little longer for the quarterback to hand off the ball.

As long as the blocking holds up, Parker can get outside where he can use his speed.

We pick up 9 yards before finally being brought down by the strong safety.

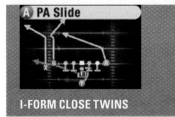

A PA Slide

I-FORM CLOSE TWINS

PA SLIDE

A good play action play to mix in with the I-Form Close Twins Stretch is the PA Slide. This play has several good options to throw to.

This play uses the same run action as the stretch play, except Big Ben play fakes to Willie Parker.

Once the play fake is done, we take control of Roethlisberger and roll him out to the left.

We throw to the fullback as he leaks out of the backfield and into the flat.

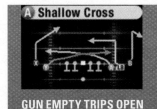

A Shallow Cross

GUN EMPTY TRIPS OPEN

SHALLOW CROSS

The Gun Empty Trips Open Shallow Cross is a high percentage pass play that has big play potential if the catch is made on the run.

Rookie receiver Limas Sweed brings some much needed speed to the Steelers' receiving unit.

With his speed coming across the middle of the field on a shallow cross, he is very hard to cover.

We make the catch and turn up the field for a 16-yard pickup.

TEAM STRATEGY

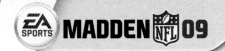

 # PITTSBURGH STEELERS

DEFENSE

TEAM STRATEGY

#43 Troy Polamalu *Safety (SS)*
▼DEFENSIVE **STAR PLAYER**

Injuries have taken their toll on Troy Polamalu over the last two seasons. Despite the injuries, he remains one of most feared safeties in the game. His ability to close in on ball carriers quickly and wrap them up is one of the key reasons that the Steelers' defense is one of the best in the game.

Speed	93
Man Cover	65
Zone Cover	85
Hit Power	90

Player Weapon: Big Hitter, Smart Safety

#98 Casey Hampton *Defensive Tackle (DT)*
▼DEFENSIVE **STAR PLAYER**

At 6'1" and 325 pounds, Steelers nose tackle Casey Hampton's job is not to make a lot of tackles or sacks. His primary job is to occupy as many blockers as he can on any given play, and let the Steelers' linebackers do the rest. Outside of the 2004 season, Hampton does not miss many games.

Speed	54
Strength	98
Power Moves	98
Finesse Moves	68

Player Weapon: Power Move D-Lineman

#51 James Farrior *Linebacker (MLB)*
▼DEFENSIVE **STAR PLAYER**

During his 11 year career in the NFL, James Farrior has racked up his share of tackles. Last season, he got more involved in the Steelers' complex blitz schemes by racking up 6½ sacks. Even though he is getting up there in age, he still drops back in pass coverage very well, making him a three down linebacker.

Speed	78
Tackling	93
Pursuit	96
Play Recog.	93

Player Weapon: None

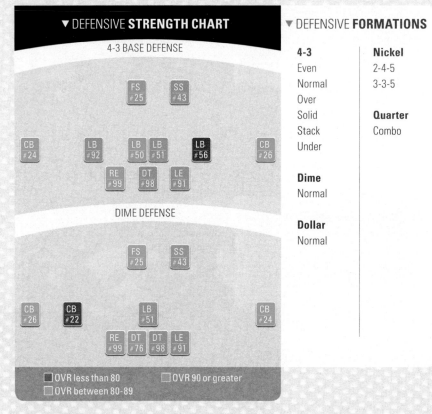

▼ **DEFENSIVE STRENGTH CHART**

4-3 BASE DEFENSE

DIME DEFENSE

☐ OVR less than 80   ☐ OVR 90 or greater
☐ OVR between 80-89

▼ DEFENSIVE **FORMATIONS**

4-3	Nickel
Even	2-4-5
Normal	3-3-5
Over	
Solid	**Quarter**
Stack	Combo
Under	
Dime	
Normal	
Dollar	
Normal	

▼ RECOMMENDED DEFENSIVE **AUDIBLE PACKAGES**

3-4	3-4	Nickel	Dime	Quarter
2 Man Under	OLB Dogs Fire	Cover 3	Cover 2	Man Up 3 Deep

▼ DEFENSIVE **PLAYCOUNTS**

Man Coverage:	47	Cover 2 Zone:	24	Man Blitz:	60
Man Zone:	39	Cover 3 Zone:	26	Zone Blitz:	60
Combo Coverage:	6	Deep Zone:	13	Combo Blitz:	7

DEFENSE **KEY DEFENSIVE PLAYS**

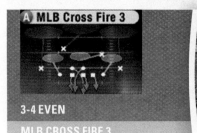

A MLB Cross Fire 3

3-4 EVEN

MLB CROSS FIRE 3

The Steelers are one of the more creative teams when it comes to run and pass blitzing schemes.

1

The 3-4 Even MLB Cross Fire 3 has both inside linebackers crossing each other.

2

This often confuses the offensive linemen about who to block.

3

Steelers' inside linebacker James Farrior brings the Bengals' ball carrier down for a loss.

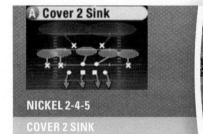

A Cover 2 Sink

NICKEL 2-4-5

COVER 2 SINK

We call the Nickel 2-4-5 Cover 2 Sink against players on offense who like to run a dink and dunk offense.

1

With five defenders dropping back in hook zones underneath, there is not much room to pass the ball.

2

The quarterback tries to thread the needle by throwing a bullet pass to the receiver over the middle.

3

It's a mistake, and one of the Steelers' defenders is able to step in front of the pass and pick it off.

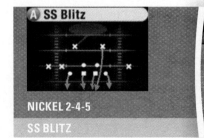

A SS Blitz

NICKEL 2-4-5

SS BLITZ

The Steelers are creative when it comes to drawing up blitz schemes to maximize their personnel.

1

One blitz we like to call that gets All Pro Strong Safety Troy Polamalu involved is the SS Blitz.

2

With his cat-like speed, he is able to blow by defenders quickly and go after the quarterback.

3

Most offenses tend to sputter because of his aggressive style of play.

TEAM STRATEGY

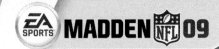
HOUSTON TEXANS

▶ **Division** AFC South   ▶ **Stadium** Reliant Stadium   ▶ **Type** Retractable Roof   ▶ **Capacity** 69,500   ▶ **Surface** Grass

▼ 2007 STANDINGS

Wins	Loses	Ties	PF	PA	Home	Road	vs. AFC	vs. NFC	vs. Div
8	8	0	379	384	6-2	2-6	5-7	3-1	1-5

▼ TEAM OVERVIEW

The Texans think this will be the year they make the playoffs for the first time. They didn't make any big splashes in free agency during the offseason. However, they did manage to add to the team's depth by signing Chris Brown, Chris Myers, and Jacques Reeves.

Matt Schuab leads the troops on the field. When given time to survey the field, he can carve up the opposing defense. Ahman Green and Brown should be a nice one-two punch, as long as they both can stay healthy.

With another year of seasoning, the hope is that the young defense will finally reach its potential and be able to keep opposing offenses out of the end zone. Mario Williams is starting to look like the number 1 overall draft pick the Texans used in 2006. Last season, he racked up a team high of 14 sacks.

▼ OFF-SEASON UPGRADES

TYPE	ROUND	FIRST NAME	LAST NAME	SCHOOL/TEAM	POSITION
Free Agent	N/A	Chris	Brown	Titans	RB
Trade	N/A	Chris	Myers	Broncos	C
Free Agent	N/A	Jacques	Reeves	Cowboys	CB
Draft	1	Duane	Brown	Virginia Tech	T
Draft	3	Antwaun	Molden	Eastern Kentucky	CB

▼ SCOUTING REPORT

	DESCRIPTION	MAXIMIZING POTENTIAL	TIPS FOR OPPONENTS
STRENGTHS	Matt Schaub is a much underrated QB. He has a nice arm and is a very accurate passer. He has decent speed as well.	Use his mobility to take off and run when nothing opens up down the field.	To be on the safe side, have at least one defender in QB Spy if Schaub decides to take off and run.
STRENGTHS	Andre Johnson is another underrated Texan. He has size and speed, and is a tremendous deep threat for Matt Schaub.	Send Johnson deep; there are not many corners that can keep up with a 6'3" receiver with good speed.	Don't cheat up, keep your safeties off the line because of Johnson's deep threat ability.
WEAKNESSES	Ahman Green is still the Texans featured back, but does he have what it takes to lead the Texans over the top?	Send Johnson on deep passing routes and hand off to Green to see if he can pick up at least 3 or 4 yards.	Double up Andre Johnson and force Schaub to find other ways to move the ball.
WEAKNESSES	Demeco Ryans is an outstanding MLB who can stuff the run as well as cover a top ranked TE.	In passing situations, let Ryans man up the offense's TE to take him out.	Keep Ryans honest by mixing up your play calling. This keeps him from predicting what's coming next.

TEAM STRATEGY

FRANCHISE MODE STRATEGY

Pick up a speed back via either trade or the draft. The offensive line needs some work and should be built up in the draft as well. Look for a veteran strong safety to help shore up the secondary.

KEY FRANCHISE INFORMATION

Cap Room: $22.41M
Key Rivals:
• Cowboys, Jaguars, Titans
Philosophy:
• Offense: Zone blocking run game
• Defense: 4-3
Highest Paid Players:
• A. Johnson
• M. Williams
Team Weapons:
• M. Williams – Power Move D-Lineman
• A. Johnson – Spectacular Catch Receiver
Best Young Players:
• M. Williams
• A. Okoye

78	79	79
OVERALL	OFFENSE	DEFENSE

▼ ROSTER AND **PACKAGE TIPS**

KEY PLAYER SUBSTITUTIONS

Position: WR

Substitution: Andre Davis

When: Global

Advantage: With Andre Davis at the number two receiver, you have two guys that can really stretch the field and put pressure on the defense. Move Kevin Walter to the slot and let him be your hands guy at that position.

Position: TE

Substitution: Mark Bruener

When: Situational

Advantage: Mark Bruener is a punishing run blocker from the tight end spot. In situations where you want to control the clock and pound the rock, you need him in the line-up. On passing downs, Owen Daniels is your guy.

Postion: LOLB

Substitution: Xavier Adibi

When: Situational

Advantage: When it is third down and you are pretty sure the offense is going to pass from a base set, sub in Adibi and let him get after the QB. He doesn't have the experience of the other linebackers, but he makes up for it in raw speed.

DE Mario Williams, who finally validated his No. 1 overall selection in the 2006 NFL Draft by recording 14 sacks and wreaking havoc in opponents' offensive backfield in 2007, and the Texans should continue to improve in 2008.

TEAM STRATEGY

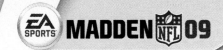

TEAM STRATEGY

#80 Andre Johnson *Wide Receiver (WR)*

▼OFFENSIVE **STAR PLAYER**

Despite missing nearly half of last season, Andre Johnson made 60 catches and got in the end zone 8 times. He has all the qualities of a superstar, and is on the verge of becoming one. At 6'3", he is very hard to defend for most defensive backs. His ability to out jump defenders makes him a great red zone target.

Speed	95
Catch	90
Catch Traffic	92
Route Run	94

Player Weapon: Quick Receiver, Possession Receiver, Hands

#81 Owen Daniels *Tight End (TE)*

▼OFFENSIVE **STAR PLAYER**

Owen Daniels is a good sized target with solid hands. In just his second season, he caught 63 balls and got in the end zone 3 times. He has decent speed that allows him to run seam routes down the middle of the field, and is also able to make the tough catches underneath.

Speed	85
Catch	85
Run Block	55
Pass Block	52

Player Weapon: None

#8 Matt Schaub *Quarterback (QB)*

▼OFFENSIVE **STAR PLAYER**

Matt Schaub is an accurate passer with good enough arm strength to make all the throws in the Texans' playbook. When he is able to stand in the pocket, he can deliver strikes to the Texans' receivers. However, there are some concerns about his durability. In his first season with the Texans, he missed 5 games due to injuries.

Speed	62
Awareness	78
Throw Power	88
Throw Accur.	92

Player Weapon: None

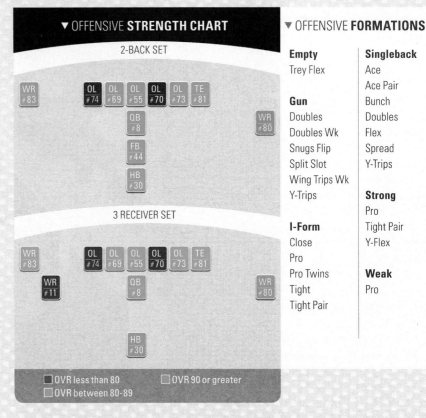

▼ OFFENSIVE **STRENGTH CHART**

2-BACK SET

WR #83 — OL #74 | OL #69 | OL #55 | OL #70 | OL #73 | TE #81 — WR #80 — QB #8 — FB #44 — HB #30

3 RECEIVER SET

WR #83 — OL #74 | OL #69 | OL #55 | OL #70 | OL #73 | TE #81 — WR #80 — WR #11 — QB #8 — HB #30

☐ OVR less than 80   ☐ OVR 90 or greater
☐ OVR between 80-89

▼ OFFENSIVE **FORMATIONS**

Empty	Singleback
Trey Flex	Ace
	Ace Pair
Gun	Bunch
Doubles	Doubles
Doubles Wk	Flex
Snugs Flip	Spread
Split Slot	Y-Trips
Wing Trips Wk	
Y-Trips	**Strong**
	Pro
I-Form	Tight Pair
Close	Y-Flex
Pro	
Pro Twins	**Weak**
Tight	Pro
Tight Pair	

▼ RECOMMENDED OFFENSIVE **AUDIBLE PACKAGES**

Singleback	Singleback	I-Form	Gun	Gun
Stretch	X Follow	Iso	Backs Cross	Curl Flats

▼ OFFENSIVE **PLAYCOUNTS**

Quick Pass:	22	Screen Pass:	7	Pitch:	8
Standard Pass:	98	Hail Mary:	1	Counter:	12
Shotgun Pass:	51	Inside Handoff:	30	Draw:	11
Play Action Pass:	65	Outside Handoff:	19		

OFFENSE **KEY OFFENSIVE PLAYS**

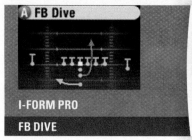

A FB Dive
I-FORM PRO
FB DIVE

The I-Form Pro FB Dive One is one of the better quick inside running plays. This play may not pick up a lot of yards, but it's generally good for 3 or 4.

Texans quarterback Matt Schaub quickly sticks the ball in the full-back's hands.

Once the fullback gets the ball, we take control of him and press the sprint button.

Once through the hole, we press down on the cover up button to ensure that we don't fumble the ball.

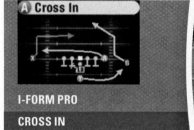

A Cross In
I-FORM PRO
CROSS IN

A good intermediate pass play from the Texans' playbook is the I-Form Pro Cross In. Kevin Walter is the play's primary receiver.

Walter will take an inside release and then run straight up the field.

He then will break across the middle about 8 yards down the field.

We take control of him and make the catch on the run for a 12-yard pick-up.

A Comebacks
GUN Y TRIPS
COMEBACKS

Comeback routes are very effective against man coverage, but the quarterback needs time in the pocket to wait for the receivers to run them.

One of the better receivers in the game is Andre Johnson. He happens to be the play's primary receiver.

Because of his route running ability, he is able to gain separation once he comes back on his route.

He is a sure-handed receiver who doesn't drop too many passes thrown his way.

TEAM STRATEGY

 **HOUSTON TEXANS**   DEFENSE

TEAM STRATEGY

#59 DeMeco Ryans *Linebacker (MLB)*

▼DEFENSIVE **STAR PLAYER**

In just two seasons in the NFL, Demeco Ryans has already established himself as one of the best middle linebackers in the league. Last season, he racked up a team high of 127 tackles, sacked the quarterback twice, and even picked off a pass for good measure. The future is bright for this rising defensive star.

Speed	84
Tackling	96
Pursuit	97
Play Recog.	87

Player Weapon: Brick Wall Defender

#90 Mario Williams *Defensive End (RE)*

▼DEFENSIVE **STAR PLAYER**

In his rookie season, Mario Williams was expected to have a huge impact in the NFL. However, things didn't go as planned, and some analysts were calling him a first round bust. In his second season, he turned things around and became the impact player the Texans thought he would by racking up 14 sacks.

Speed	86
Strength	85
Power Moves	95
Finesse Moves	95

Player Weapon: Finesse Move D-Lineman, Power Move D-Lineman

#56 Morlon Greenwood *Linebacker (ROLB)*

▼DEFENSIVE **STAR PLAYER**

Not the biggest playmaker on the Texans' defense, but one of the more consistent ones is weak outside linebacker Morlon Greenwood. He finished second in total tackles with 119. If there is one thing lacking from his game, it is that he doesn't get much pressure on the quarterback, as he only recorded one sack last season.

Speed	85
Tackling	89
Pursuit	91
Play Recog.	81

Player Weapon: Brick Wall Defender

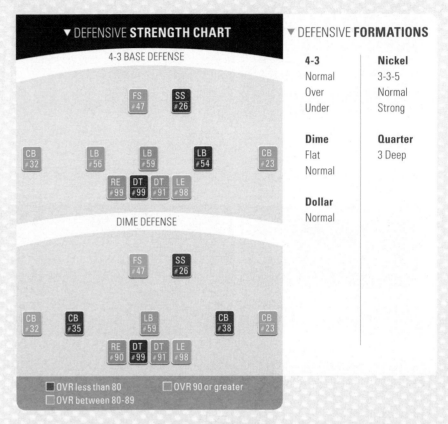

▼ DEFENSIVE **STRENGTH CHART**

4-3 BASE DEFENSE

FS #47   SS #26

CB #32   LB #56   LB #59   LB #54   CB #23

RE #99   DT #99   DT #91   LE #98

DIME DEFENSE

FS #47   SS #26

CB #32   CB #35   LB #59   CB #38   CB #23

RE #90   DT #99   DT #91   LE #98

☐ OVR less than 80   ☐ OVR 90 or greater
☐ OVR between 80-89

▼ DEFENSIVE **FORMATIONS**

4-3	**Nickel**
Normal	3-3-5
Over	Normal
Under	Strong

Dime	**Quarter**
Flat	3 Deep
Normal	

Dollar	
Normal	

▼ RECOMMENDED DEFENSIVE **AUDIBLE PACKAGES**

4-3	4-3	Nickel	Dime	Quarter
2 Man Press	Slant Crash Left	Cover 3	Cover 2	Man Up 3 Deep

▼ DEFENSIVE **PLAYCOUNTS**

Man Coverage:	43	Cover 2 Zone:	13	Man Blitz:	50
Man Zone:	38	Cover 3 Zone:	26	Zone Blitz:	64
Combo Coverage:	8	Deep Zone:	19	Combo Blitz:	15

DEFENSE **KEY DEFENSIVE PLAYS**

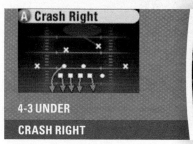

A Crash Right
4-3 UNDER
CRASH RIGHT

A good run defense to call if the offense likes to run plays to the left side of the offensive line is the 4-3 Under Crash Right.

Mario Williams isn't known as a great run stopper, but this defense puts him in good position to make a stop.

With Williams's speed, he gets into the backfield quickly and targets the ball carrier.

Once Williams gets his arms wrapped around him, it's very hard to break away from him.

A 4 Buzz Flats
4-3 OVER
4 BUZZ FLATS

The 4-3 Over 4 Buzz Flats is a solid defense to call to defend the pass all over the field with nine Texan defenders dropping in zones.

Both defensive ends drop into flat coverage, and the two outside linebackers drop in buzz zones.

The receiver looks open as he breaks to the sideline, but looks can be deceiving.

The left outside linebacker gets a speed burst at the last second and is able to swat the pass away.

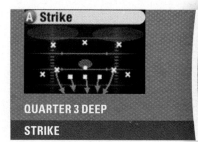

A Strike
QUARTER 3 DEEP
STRIKE

The Quarter 3 Deep Strike brings good pressure from the Texans dimebacks who are blitzing both sides of the offensive line.

The offensive tackles will block both the defensive ends, allowing the defensive backs to come in without being blocked.

Because of their speed, they can avoid slower offensive linemen without being blocked.

Even if the quarterback is mobile, he will find it hard to avoid being sacked.

TENNESSEE TITANS

▶ **Division** AFC South ▶ **Stadium** LP Field ▶ **Type** Open ▶ **Capacity** 68,798 ▶ **Surface** Grass

▼ 2007 STANDINGS

Wins	Loses	Ties	PF	PA	Home	Road	vs. AFC	vs. NFC	vs. Div
10	6	0	301	297	5-3	5-3	7-5	3-1	4-2

▼ TEAM OVERVIEW

The Titans surprisingly made the playoffs in 2007 and are looking for a repeat performance in 2008. The team didn't make many moves during the offseason. The biggest move was bringing back offensive coordinator Mike Heimerdinger. His multiple offensive schemes should make the offense more productive and ultimately score more points.

Former Falcons tight end Alge Crumpler gives quarterback Vince Young a dependable target who can stretch the middle of the field. The offensive line remains one of the team's biggest strengths, and should open plenty of holes for running backs Lendale White and rookie Chris Johnson.

Defensive end Kyle Vanden Bosch and defensive tackle Albert Haynesworth are able to generate a lot of pressure. Because they are able to get to the quarterback consistently, the Titans' secondary doesn't have to cover receivers for as long.

▼ OFF-SEASON UPGRADES

TYPE	ROUND	FIRST NAME	LAST NAME	SCHOOL/TEAM	POSITION
Free Agent	N/A	Alge	Crumpler	Falcons	TE
Free Agent	N/A	Jevon	Kearse	Eagles	DE
Free Agent	N/A	Jake	Scott	Colts	G
Draft	1	Chris	Johnson	East Carolina	RB
Draft	2	Jason	Jones	Eastern Michigan	DL

▼ SCOUTING REPORT

	DESCRIPTION	MAXIMIZING POTENTIAL	TIPS FOR OPPONENTS
STRENGTHS	Vince Young has to be one of the best young QBs in the game. He has a nice arm, the size, and major speed.	Use his mobility to run when nothing opens down the field. Then hit one of your receivers deep for a quick TD.	To be on the safe side, always have at least one defender in QB Spy if Young decides to take off.
STRENGTHS	LenDale White is a bruising running back. His QB is faster than he is, but he can pick up those tough yards.	Feed White the ball with HB Dives and HB Slams to open up the short passing game for Young.	Do not sleep on Lendale White. Always have one of your safeties down in the box.
WEAKNESSES	The Titans do have not a serious deep threat at the wideout position. The offensive playcalling will have to be creative.	Be prepared to run the football with Young or White. Get the TE in the game, and use the FB.	Be patient playing against the Titans. Do not underestimate their receiving corps.
WEAKNESSES	Keith Bulluck is still a solid MLB. He is just as tenacious as ever and a force to be reckoned with. He anchors the defense.	Have Bulluck play up in the box to defend the run. In passing situations, let him man up the offense's TE.	Keep Bulluck honest by mixing up your play calling. This will prevent him from predicting what is coming.

FRANCHISE MODE STRATEGY

Vince Young needs some targets at receiver. Make this priority number one. The secondary will struggle against teams with multiple fast receivers. You'll need to find a fast cover guy to match up with these threats.

KEY FRANCHISE INFORMATION

Cap Room: $20.41M

Key Rivals:
- Colts, Jaguars, Texans

Philosophy:
- Offense: Multiple
- Defense: 4-3

Highest Paid Players:
- V. Young
- M. Roos

Team Weapons:
- A. Haynesworth – Power Move D-Lineman
- K. Bulluck – Brick Wall Defender

Best Young Players:
- C. Finnegan
- M. Griffin

89
OVERALL

84
OFFENSE

91
DEFENSE

The multi-dimensional Vince Young and the no-nonsense Titans both must get back to what they're best at if the Titans are going to compete for a playoff berth in 2008.

TEAM STRATEGY

▼ ROSTER AND **PACKAGE TIPS**

KEY PLAYER SUBSTITUTIONS

Postion: HB

Substitution: Chris Johnson

When: Situational

Advantage: Chris Johnson has a ridiculous amount of speed at his disposal. Anytime you want to attack the perimeter of the defense, you have to put him in the game. Sweeps, tosses, and counters are right up his alley.

Postion: LE

Substitution: Jevon Kearse

When: Global

Advantage: We prefer to have defensive ends with the speed to get after the QB. Kearse has significantly more speed than Fisher and is our choice at LE. You can't forget the importance of speed, especially against fast QBs.

Postion: WR

Substitution: Brandon Jones

When: Global

Advantage: We prefer to have Brandon Jones as our number one receiver. He is slightly faster than Roydell Williams and has better hands. The three receivers on the Titans are basically interchangeable, but every little advantage helps.

TEAM STRATEGY

#68 Kevin Mawae *Center (C)*

▼OFFENSIVE **STAR PLAYER**

Despite being 37, Tennessee Titan Kevin Mawae still ranks among the better centers in the game. He is the team's leader along the offensive line. He is able to open up lanes by pulling to block and can still lock down in pass protection. Mawae is a true warrior who is nearing the end of a great career.

Run Block Strength	91
Run Block Footwork	92
Pass Block Strength	93
Pass Block Footwork	90

Player Weapon: None

#83 Alge Crumpler *Tight End (TE)*

▼OFFENSIVE **STAR PLAYER**

Alge Crumpler is a dependable tight end who can stretch the middle of the field, and will be a big target when the Titans are near the end zone. He has lost some speed, but still knows how to get open. Look for Crumpler to be the team's top pass catcher in 2008.

Speed	78
Catch	82
Run Block	60
Pass Block	50

Player Weapon: None

#10 Vince Young *Quarterback (QB)*

▼OFFENSIVE **STAR PLAYER**

Last season, Vince Young's quarterback percentage was much higher than in his rookie season. He completed over 63 percent of his passes. Young is at his best when he is able to get out of the pocket and make things happen with his arm or legs. He wasn't able to do this last season due to injuries.

Speed	90
Awareness	70
Throw Power	93
Throw Accur.	84

Player Weapon: Speed Quarterback

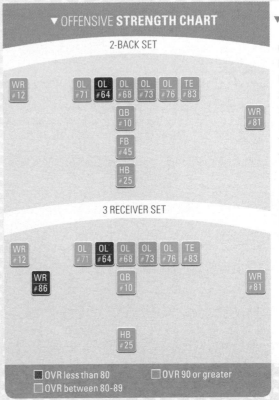

▼ OFFENSIVE **STRENGTH CHART**

2-BACK SET

WR #12 | OL #71 | OL #64 | OL #68 | OL #73 | OL #76 | TE #83 | WR #81
QB #10
FB #45
HB #25

3 RECEIVER SET

WR #12 | OL #71 | OL #64 | OL #68 | OL #73 | OL #76 | TE #83
WR #86 | QB #10 | WR #81
HB #25

☐ OVR less than 80   ☐ OVR 90 or greater
☐ OVR between 80-89

▼ OFFENSIVE **FORMATIONS**

Gun	**Singleback**
Doubles On	Ace
Doubles Wk	Ace Pair
Snugs	Ace Pair Twins
Split Slot	Ace Twins
Spread Wk	Bunch
Trey Open	Doubles
Wing Trips	Flex
	Spread
I-Form	Y-Trips
H Pro	
H Slot Flex	**Strong**
H Twins	H Pro
	H Twins
	Weak
	H Pro
	H Twin TE

▼ RECOMMENDED OFFENSIVE **AUDIBLE PACKAGES**

Singleback	Singleback	Strong	Gun	Gun
HB Stretch	TE Post	HB Dive	689 Hook	Corner Strike

▼ OFFENSIVE **PLAYCOUNTS**

Quick Pass:	21	Screen Pass:	15	Pitch:	14
Standard Pass:	81	Hail Mary:	3	Counter:	12
Shotgun Pass:	56	Inside Handoff:	24	Draw:	14
Play Action Pass:	67	Outside Handoff:	20		

OFFENSE KEY OFFENSIVE PLAYS

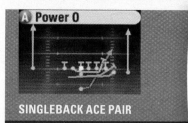

A Power O

SINGLEBACK ACE PAIR

POWER O

The Titans must be able to run the ball with LenDale White. A powerful running play that will get the tough yardage is the Power O.

The tight end on the left side is sent in auto motion to the right to add an extra run blocker.

With the extra tight end blocking, it helps spring White to the open field.

White isn't fast, but he is hard to bring down with just one defender.

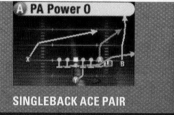

A PA Power O

SINGLEBACK ACE PAIR

PA POWER O

With the run game now established, it's time to mix in some play action by running the PA Power O.

The tight end on the left does the same auto motion as in the Power O run play.

The tight end is the play's primary receiver, but we like to look to Justin Gage on the crossing route.

We make the catch in stride and pick up another 5 yards down the field.

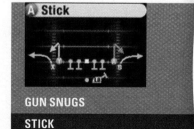

A Stick

GUN SNUGS

STICK

The Gun Snugs Stick is a good underneath pass play to call against zone coverage because of the short routes that the receivers run.

Vince Young can be somewhat erratic on deep throws. That is why we like to keep it simple by running the stick route.

Once the receivers turn towards Young, we throw a hard bullet pass.

This play won't pick up a lot of yardage, but it lowers the risk of passes being picked off.

TEAM STRATEGY

#53 Keith Bulluck *Linebacker (ROLB)*
▼DEFENSIVE **STAR PLAYER**

Bulluck did not register as many tackles last season as he has in previous seasons. A lot of that had to do with the overall improvement of the entire defense. He did manage to pick off five passes, although three of those came in one game. He is not much of a pass rusher, but he does excel in pass coverage.

Speed	86
Tackling	91
Pursuit	92
Play Recog.	86

Player Weapon: Big Hitter, Brick Wall Defender

#92 Albert Haynesworth *Defensive Tackle (DT)*
▼DEFENSIVE **STAR PLAYER**

If you ask most scouts who the best defensive tackle is in the game today, most would answer, "Titan Albert Haynesworth." No offensive interior linemen can handle him because he is just too big, too explosive, and too strong at the point of attack. These attributes allow him to be a disruptive force in both the run and pass game.

Speed	64
Strength	98
Power Moves	98
Finesse Moves	77

Player Weapon: Power Move D-Lineman

#24 Chris Hope *Safety (SS)*
▼DEFENSIVE **STAR PLAYER**

Chris Hope is one of the Titans' leaders on defense. Last season, he wasn't himself due to a season-ending injury to the neck that he sustained in November. When he is on the field, he is very good in run support and has enough speed to drop back in pass coverage. Look for him to rebound in 2008.

Speed	88
Man Cover	65
Zone Cover	85
Hit Power	85

Player Weapon: None

▼DEFENSIVE **STRENGTH CHART**

4-3 BASE DEFENSE / DIME DEFENSE

☐ OVR less than 80 ☐ OVR 90 or greater ☐ OVR between 80-89

▼DEFENSIVE **FORMATIONS**

4-3	Nickel
Normal	3-3-5
Over	Normal
Under	Strong
Dime	**Quarter**
Flat	Combo
Normal	
Dollar	
Normal	

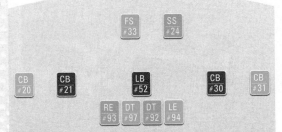

▼ RECOMMENDED DEFENSIVE **AUDIBLE PACKAGES**

4-3	4-3	Nickel	Dime	Quarter
2 Man Under	Fire Man	Cover 3	Cover 2	3 Deep Press

▼ DEFENSIVE **PLAYCOUNTS**

Man Coverage:	45	Cover 2 Zone:	14	Man Blitz:	55
Man Zone:	34	Cover 3 Zone:	26	Zone Blitz:	64
Combo Coverage:	7	Deep Zone:	18	Combo Blitz:	13

PRIMA OFFICIAL GAME GUIDE
www.primagames.com

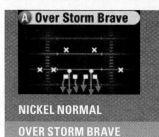

A Over Storm Brave

NICKEL NORMAL

OVER STORM BRAVE

A good Nickel Normal run defense to call to blow up run plays from spread formations is the Over Storm Brave.

This defense is designed to get two linebackers involved in blowing up the ball carrier in the backfield.

With both of them blitzing, one usually is not blocked by an offensive linemen.

The ball carrier is unable to find an open running lane and is tackled at the line of scrimmage.

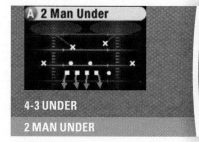

A 2 Man Under

4-3 UNDER

2 MAN UNDER

The 4-3 Under 2 Man Under is a good base defense to call on first down because it is solid against both the run and pass.

With five defenders playing man coverage underneath, it is effective at covering running backs and tight ends.

If the quarterback looks up top, both safeties drop back deep to make sure no receiver gets past them.

The left cornerback is able to get up in the air and knock the pass away for an incomplete pass.

A Zone Blitz

4-3 OVER

ZONE BLITZ

A good zone blitz that brings heat from right outside linebacker Keith Bulluck is the 4-3 Over Zone Blitz.

With Bulluck and Ryan Fowler blitzing, they create an overload on the left side of the offensive line.

The left tackle blocks the right end, allowing for Bullock to rush the quarterback untouched.

An offensive lineman tries to save his quarterback from taking a vicious hit, but he is too late.

TEAM STRATEGY

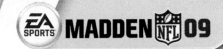

MINNESOTA VIKINGS

▶ **Division** NFC North ▶ **Stadium** Herbert H. Humphrey Metrodome ▶ **Type** Dome ▶ **Capacity** 64,121 ▶ **Surface** Astroplay

▼ 2007 STANDINGS

Wins	Loses	Ties	PF	PA	Home	Road	vs. AFC	vs. NFC	vs. Div
8	8	0	365	311	5-3	3-5	2-2	6-6	3-3

▼ TEAM OVERVIEW

A "win now" attitude was blowing in the cold Minneapolis air this past offseason. The Vikings opened their wallets and spent 29 million in guarantees to receiver Bernard Berrian and safety Madiue Williams. The big splash this offseason was trading for pass rush specialist Jared Allen. The Vikings gave up multiple draft picks to reel him in.

Adrian Peterson came on the scene as the rookie with a loud thunder. His electrifying runs from last season have energized the Vikings' fans. Many believe this may be the year that Minnesota gets back into the playoffs, due to the strong running game led by Peterson.

Defensively, the Vikings are better on paper than they were a year ago. With the addition of Allen, putting pressure on the quarterback won't be a problem. The run defense will be just as stout as it was in 2007.

▼ OFF-SEASON UPGRADES

TYPE	ROUND	FIRST NAME	LAST NAME	SCHOOL/TEAM	POSITION
Trade	N/A	Jared	Allen	Chiefs	DE
Free Agent	N/A	Bernard	Berrian	Bears	WR
Free Agent	N/A	Madieu	Williams	Bengals	S
Draft	2	Tyrell	Johnson	Arkansas State	S
Draft	5	John David	Booty	USC	QB

▼ SCOUTING REPORT

	DESCRIPTION	MAXIMIZING POTENTIAL	TIPS FOR OPPONENTS
STRENGTHS	Tavaris Jackson has the pleasure of being a QB for a team that has the game's best RB, Adrian Peterson.	Use Jackson's mobility to run when nothing opens down the field. Then hit one of your receivers deep for a quick TD.	To be on the safe side, always have at least one defender in QB Spy if Jackson decides to take off and run.
STRENGTHS	Adrian Peterson is fast and elusive. If a defense brings eight in the box, audible to a pass play and send Peterson out in the flats.	Feed Peterson the ball with HB Dives, HB Slams, and HB Sweeps to open up the short passing game for Jackson.	Play the run first because of the presence of Peterson.
WEAKNESSES	The QB position is still a big question mark. The Vikings have confidence in Jackson, but he has yet to realize his full potential.	Be prepared to run the football with Jackson or Peterson. Get the TE in the game, and use the FB.	Don't overplay the run because Jackson has a burner in his arsenal named Bernard Berrian.
WEAKNESSES	The Vikings' defense is tough as a unit. No one player stands out, but they are good against the run and have a tremendous pass rush.	Keep pressure on opposing offenses. Blitz unexpectedly and force the offense to make mistakes.	Keep the Vikings' defense honest by mixing up your plays. This prevents them from predicting what's coming.

TEAM STRATEGY

FRANCHISE MODE STRATEGY

Tarvaris Jackson is still growing as a player, so a veteran QB would be a nice pickup. The defense is strong all around. Begin searching for a replacement for 35-year old Pat Williams at DT.

KEY FRANCHISE INFORMATION

Cap Room: $4.69M

Key Rivals:
- Bears, Lions, Packers

Philosophy:
- Offense: West Coast
- Defense: 4-3, Tampa 2

Highest Paid Players:
- J. Allen
- S. Hutchinson

Team Weapons:
- P. Williams – Power Move D-Lineman
- S. Hutchinson – Crushing Run Blocker

Best Young Players:
- A. Peterson
- R. Edwards

By breaking the NFL single-game rushing record with 296 yards eight games into his career, and averaging 5.6 yards per carry in 2007, Adrian Peterson and a stout defense make the Vikings a Super Bowl threat if they get consistent play from their QBs.

90	85	96
OVERALL	OFFENSE	DEFENSE

▼ ROSTER AND **PACKAGE TIPS**

KEY PLAYER SUBSTITUTIONS

Position: Slot WR

Substitution: Aundrae Allison

When: Situational

Advantage: Allison has more speed than the starting slot receiver Bobby Wade. There are situations when you want to really stretch the defense, especially when you have established the run with Adrian Peterson. Allison fills this role well.

Position: TE

Substitution: Jim Kleinsasser

When: Situational

Advantage: Kleinsasser is a vastly superior run blocker to the starting tight end, Visanthe Shiancoe. You will want to put him in the game whenever you are looking to pound the rock with Adrian Peterson. He's a powerful blocker.

Position: CB

Substitution: Tyrell Johnson

When: Situational

Advantage: If you are looking to bring the heat out of the Dime formation, consider subbing in Tyrell Johnson as the 4th cornerback. He has blazing speed and can be used to blitz, or as a QB Spy. He can hang with the fastest QBs.

TEAM STRATEGY

TEAM STRATEGY

#76 Steve Hutchinson *Guard (LG)*

▼OFFENSIVE STAR PLAYER

One of the key reasons that the Vikings' rushing attack is so strong is based on the signing of left guard Steve Hutchinson a few years ago. His ability to open gaping holes that a freight train can run through can't be underestimated. He is one of the more athletic guards in the game and doesn't commit many penalties.

Run Block Strength	99
Run Block Footwork	93
Pass Block Strength	90
Pass Block Footwork	84

Player Weapon: Crushing Run Blocker

#28 Adrian Peterson *Halfback (HB)*

▼OFFENSIVE STAR PLAYER

Adrian Peterson burst on the NFL scene in a big way as a rookie by breaking the single-game rushing record against the San Diego Chargers. During the 14 games he played in, he rushed for 1,341 yards and got in the end zone 12 times. His one weakness is his ability to stay healthy.

Speed	96
Agility	98
Trucking	92
Elusiveness	99

Player Weapon: Power Back, Elusive Back, Stiff Arm Ball Carrier, Speed

#87 Bernard Berrian *Wide Receiver (WR)*

▼OFFENSIVE STAR PLAYER

The Vikings hope that Bernard Berrian can be the team's big play receiver that has been lacking since Moss left a few years back. If Berrian can stretch the field, it will open more running lanes for the Vikings' vaunted rushing attack. Last season with the Bears' porous passing attack, he still managed to catch 71 passes.

Speed	97
Catch	82
Catch Traffic	78
Route Run	82

Player Weapon: Speed

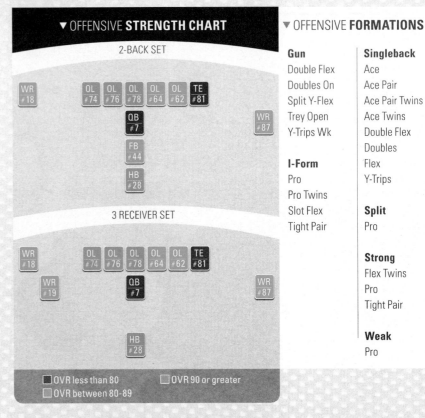

▼ OFFENSIVE STRENGTH CHART

2-BACK SET

WR #18 | OL #74 · OL #76 · OL #78 · OL #64 · OL #62 · TE #81 | WR #87
QB #7
FB #44
HB #28

3 RECEIVER SET

WR #18 | OL #74 · OL #76 · OL #78 · OL #64 · OL #62 · TE #81
WR #19 | QB #7 | WR #87
HB #28

☐ OVR less than 80 ☐ OVR 90 or greater
☐ OVR between 80-89

▼ OFFENSIVE FORMATIONS

Gun	Singleback
Double Flex	Ace
Doubles On	Ace Pair
Split Y-Flex	Ace Pair Twins
Trey Open	Ace Twins
Y-Trips Wk	Double Flex
	Doubles
I-Form	Flex
Pro	Y-Trips
Pro Twins	
Slot Flex	**Split**
Tight Pair	Pro
	Strong
	Flex Twins
	Pro
	Tight Pair
	Weak
	Pro

▼ RECOMMENDED OFFENSIVE AUDIBLE PACKAGES

I-Form	Singleback	I-Form	Gun	Gun
HB Counter Wk	Slot Drive	Stretch	Corner Strike	Circle

▼ OFFENSIVE PLAYCOUNTS

Quick Pass:	23	Screen Pass:	15	Pitch:	5
Standard Pass:	89	Hail Mary:	2	Counter:	11
Shotgun Pass:	50	Inside Handoff:	27	Draw:	11
Play Action Pass:	67	Outside Handoff:	19		

OFFENSE **KEY OFFENSIVE PLAYS**

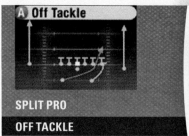

Ⓐ Off Tackle

SPLIT PRO

OFF TACKLE

The Vikings have to establish the run if they plan to score any points on offense. A good run play to begin with is the Split Pro Off Tackle.

This Off Tackle play has Adrian Peterson running off tackle to the right side of the offensive line.

We like to pop Peterson outside where he can use his power and speed to pick up yardage.

If nothing opens up, we can always cut back inside to pick up positive yardage.

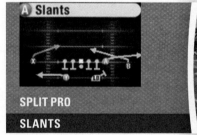

Ⓐ Slants

SPLIT PRO

SLANTS

Keeping it simple is best when making passes with Tarvaris Jackson. The Split Pro Slants is one of those simple pass plays.

If Peterson is open in the flat, he is a good option to throw to.

If not, we look to throw next to rookie Sidney Rice running the slant on the left side.

We make the catch for a 7-yard pick-up. If he breaks a tackle, he may go all the way with his speed.

Ⓐ Strong Flood

GUN TREY OPEN

STRONG FLOOD

Plays that flood the zone with multiple receivers running at different depths are a great way to attack this type of pass coverage.

When running this play, we like to start by first looking to the receiver in the flat.

If he is not open, we then look for the receiver running the 10-yard out.

We spot him open and throw him a hard bullet pass. We make the catch for an 11-yard pick-up.

TEAM STRATEGY

TEAM STRATEGY

#94 Pat Williams *Defensive Tackle (DT)*

▼DEFENSIVE **STAR PLAYER**

Defensive tackle Pat Williams presents a major road block for any team trying to establish an inside power running game. His ability to force two blockers to block him makes it very easy for the Viking linebackers to make tackles. Williams is not much of a pass rusher because he doesn't move well.

Speed	56
Strength	99
Power Moves	99
Finesse Moves	69

Player Weapon: Power Move D-Lineman

#69 Jared Allen *Defensive End (RE)*

▼DEFENSIVE **STAR PLAYER**

The Vikings signed defensive end Jared Allen this off-season to improve the team's lack of a consistent pass push. Last season with the Kansas City Chiefs, he led the league in sacks with 15 in just 14 games. Allen is as explosive as he is disruptive. Offensive tackles just don't have the athleticism to shut him down consistently.

Speed	84
Strength	76
Power Moves	88
Finesse Moves	96

Player Weapon: Finesse Move D-Lineman

#42 Darren Sharper *Safety (SS)*

▼DEFENSIVE **STAR PLAYER**

Voted to the NFC Pro last season, Darren Sharper continues to play at a high level at 32. He is one of the few safeties in the league that excels in run and pass defense. In 2007, he racked up 63 tackles and picked off four passes. A true leader on and off the field, Shaper remains one of the best in the league at his position.

Speed	88
Man Cover	80
Zone Cover	90
Hit Power	75

Player Weapon: Smart Safety

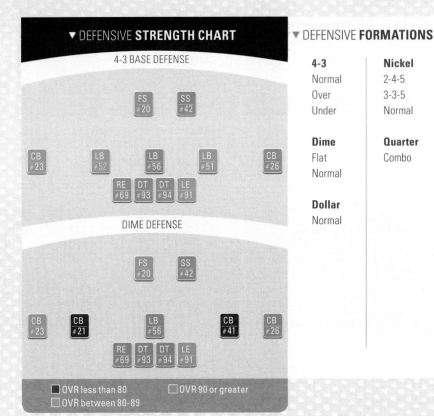

▼ DEFENSIVE **STRENGTH CHART**

4-3 BASE DEFENSE

FS #20   SS #42

CB #23   LB #52   LB #56   LB #51   CB #26

RE #69   DT #93   DT #94   LE #91

DIME DEFENSE

FS #20   SS #42

CB #23   CB #21   LB #56   CB #41   CB #26

RE #69   DT #93   DT #94   LE #91

■ OVR less than 80   □ OVR 90 or greater
□ OVR between 80-89

▼ DEFENSIVE **FORMATIONS**

4-3	Nickel
Normal	2-4-5
Over	3-3-5
Under	Normal
Dime	**Quarter**
Flat	Combo
Normal	
Dollar	
Normal	

▼ RECOMMENDED DEFENSIVE **AUDIBLE PACKAGES**

4-3	4-3	Nickel	Dime	Quarter
2 Man Under	Thunder Smoke	Cover 3	Cover 2	3 Deep Press

▼ DEFENSIVE **PLAYCOUNTS**

Man Coverage:	45	Cover 2 Zone:	16	Man Blitz:	55
Man Zone:	35	Cover 3 Zone:	27	Zone Blitz:	64
Combo Coverage:	7	Deep Zone:	19	Combo Blitz:	13

DEFENSE **KEY DEFENSIVE PLAYS**

TEAM STRATEGY

4-3 UNDER
SAM SHOOT FIRE 2

With the Vikings' defensive line, you don't have to run the blitz all that often. If you do call these types of plays, try the Sam Shoot Fire 2.

This defense sends Ben Leber in on a run blitz from the right side of the offensive line.

Even if he does not get to the running back, one of the defensive tackles will.

Big man Kevin Williams brings down the Packers' running back just as he gets to the line of scrimmage.

NICKEL 2-4-5
UNDER STRONG

Any defense that has a defender dropping back in buzz zones is a good defense to call to defend corner routes ran by the slot receiver.

The Nickel 2-4-5 Under Strong has the nickelback dropping back in a buzz zone.

The receiver breaks to the corner, but both the nickelback and right cornerback are in position.

The receiver tries to go up for the pass, but he is unable to make the catch with two defenders blanketing him.

DIME NORMAL
FOX FIRE ZONE

The Dime Normal Fox Fire Zone overloads the right side of the offensive line with multiple defenders while dropping 6 defenders in pass coverage.

Linebacker E.J. Henderson and defensive back Charles Gordon are sent in on a blitz.

The right tackle can block only one of them, so he must choose quickly.

In most cases, he will block Gordon first, but at other times he will block Henderson.

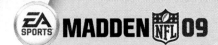

FRANCHISE MODE

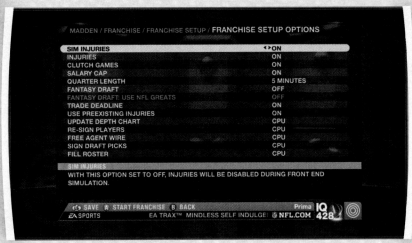

MADDEN / FRANCHISE / FRANCHISE SETUP / **FRANCHISE SETUP OPTIONS**

SIM INJURIES	◄►ON
INJURIES	ON
CLUTCH GAMES	ON
SALARY CAP	ON
QUARTER LENGTH	5 MINUTES
FANTASY DRAFT	OFF
FANTASY DRAFT: USE NFL GREATS	OFF
TRADE DEADLINE	ON
USE PREEXISTING INJURIES	ON
UPDATE DEPTH CHART	CPU
RE-SIGN PLAYERS	CPU
FREE AGENT WIRE	CPU
SIGN DRAFT PICKS	CPU
FILL ROSTER	CPU

SIM INJURIES
WITH THIS OPTION SET TO OFF, INJURIES WILL BE DISABLED DURING FRONT END SIMULATION.

◄ SAVE Ⓐ START FRANCHISE Ⓑ BACK
EA SPORTS   EA TRAX™ MINDLESS SELF INDULGE ▶ NFL.COM

▲ *Franchise Mode settings*

If you've ever surfed the Internet looking at the NFL transactions or have a copy of every Pre-Draft magazine, then Franchise Mode is for you. Even if you aren't this intense, but are curious about being behind the wheel of an NFL team for more than just a couple of games, then you owe Franchise Mode a look.

Franchise Mode puts you in charge of all the big decisions. You manage the roster, call the plays, execute the plays, scout the draft, make the picks, and then sign the players. If things aren't going well on the field or with your personnel, then you have nobody to blame but the man in the mirror.

Fortunately, we are here to help take you through the ins and outs of owning a team in *Madden NFL 09*. We'll show you how to build a team from scratch using a Fantasy Draft, or take a current team and build it into a dynasty.

STARTING YOUR FRANCHISE

Franchise Mode begins with a pretty simple decision. You have to decide which team you want to take control of. One choice would be to grab a top line team and try to build a multi-championship dynasty. Another option is to grab a weaker team and try to help them out of the cellar.

The final option is to totally start from scratch with a Fantasy Draft. We'll discuss that more in a bit. First,

let's take a look at the options you have for setting up your franchise.

The key elements you should consider are whether you want to have a salary cap, the length of quarters for your games, the fantasy draft, and whether you wish to have injuries turned on. Your other choices involve how much power you want to give the CPU to update the depth chart, sign players, bid on free agents, and take care of other roster needs.

FANTASY DRAFT

SUPER BOWL RESULTS

NEW ORLEANS SAINTS 36   NEW ENGLAND PATRIOTS 41

▲ *Will you take home the title?*

With the Fantasy Draft turned on, all of the current NFL players are placed in one big draft pool. This is one of the most fun ways to play Franchise Mode. You'll draft 49 rounds of NFL players and work to assemble your very own dream team. Now you have the chance to build a team to fit your personal style of play. Would you like to run a college-style shotgun spread attack? If pounding the ball is your favorite style of play, load up on linemen and a stud running back. You can also create another Steel Curtain defense and try to prove the old adage "Defense Wins Championships" to be true.

When you decide to play a Fantasy Draft, know that you will be in for some serious work. If you want to do it right, you'll be involved with at least the first 10 rounds of the draft. After that, you can let the CPU sim the rest of the picks if you are tired of managing it. Part of being prepared is knowing the roster requirements you will need to fill by the end of the day. The draft is 49 rounds long and works in a snake fashion. The first pick of the first round in the draft will pick last in the second round, and so on.

ROSTER REQUIREMENTS

#	OFFENSE
3	Quarterbacks (QB)
3	Halfbacks (HB)
1	Fullback (FB)
4	Wide Receivers (WR)
2	Tight Ends (TE)
4	Offensive Tackles (LT, RT)
4	Offensive Guards (LG, RG)
2	Centers (C)

#	DEFENSE
4	Defensive Ends (LE, RE)
3	Defensive Tackles (DT)
4	Outside Linebackers (LOLB, ROLB)
2	Middle Linebackers (MLB)
4	Cornerbacks (CB)
2	Free Safeties (FS)
2	Strong Safeties (SS)

#	SPECIAL TEAMS
1	Kicker (K)
1	Punter (P)

PHILOSOPHY

▲ *Brady makes an ideal Franchise QB*

Everybody has different opinions about which positions are the most important. It can be a bit intimidating as you approach your very first fantasy draft. To help you out in this task, we have created a draft priority list to help you grab an entire team in just 25 picks. Take a couple of practice runs at the Fantasy Draft before you commit to playing a full season. The good news is, unlike in real life, you can get a do-over on your draft. These are just guidelines and not hard and fast rules. If you have an amazing player that is a game changer available, then grab him up even if it doesn't follow the list. Keep an eye on what positions are getting run off the board; you may have to adjust your strategy a bit.

ROUND	POSITION	NOTES
1	Quarterback	You can't win without scoring. The QB is the leader of the offense. Look for a quarterback with an accurate arm and enough throwing power to get the ball there in time. If you like to run, find a QB that also has decent speed.
2	Defensive End	Defensive linemen get off their block quicker in *Madden NFL 09*. This position can be a game changer.
3	Offensive Tackle	An elite left tackle will enable you to send more backs out into pass patterns.
4	Cornerback	You'll need serious speed to match up with the top receivers in the game.
5	Halfback	If you can find a back with power, speed, and elusiveness, you can control the game and grind out the yards.
6	Wide Receiver	Speeds, hands, and a high route running rating are your best bets at this position.
7	Defensive Tackle	A big body here can go a long way towards shutting down the run.
8	Defensive End	Get another speed rusher to go after the QB.
9	Offensive Tackle	Make sure you get a player that fits your style of offense. Good run and pass blockers can be hard to find.
10	Middle Linebacker	The QB of the defense. Get someone with great awareness and speed here.
11	Tight End	If you want to throw it around, look for a pass catcher. Otherwise, get a bruising run blocker.
12	Outside Linebacker	Outside linebackers need to be fast, especially at ROLB. Draft the fastest one and don't worry about his other attributes.
13	Center	Look for a center with high awareness and pass blocking ability. These two attributes will go a long way in protecting the QB up the middle.
14	Cornerback	Find another guy here that can hang with the league's best receivers.
15	Strong Safety	Go for a big hitter here to punish receivers coming over the middle.
16	Wide Receiver	This is your vertical route runner. Load up on speed and stretch the defense.
17	Defensive Tackle	Go for size for the second interior D-lineman. Stuff the run.
18	Outside Linebacker	Look for high speed, pursuit, and tackling ratings from this position.
19	Offensive Guard	The second guard will probably have to be average at best.
20	Free Safety	Speed, awareness, and good jumping ability are the key ratings to look for.
21	Fullback	For West Coast offenses, look for a good pass catcher. Otherwise, find a guy that can level linebackers.
22	Halfback	It's becoming true that you can't win with just one great back in the NFL. Find a quality back-up.
23	Offensive Guard	You've got the QB and now you've got two guys to protect him.
24	Kicker	Most decent kickers perform about the same. Any middle of the road guy will do here.
25	Punter	Grab a punter with a powerful leg to pin the other team deep.

FRANCHISE MODE

FRANCHISE MODE

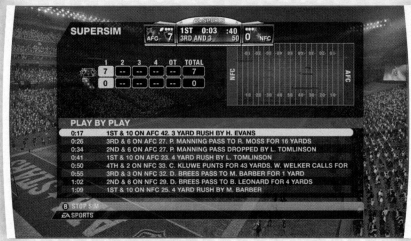

▲ Use SuperSim to speed through games

▲ Hiring a Scouting Agency will help with the NFL Draft

REGULAR SEASON

The regular season is self-explanatory. Play your games or sim them. For optimum results, try to play the games yourself. The Simming engine is great when you're short on time, but we like to be in full control of our team both on and off the field.

There are a couple of things to watch out for while going through the season. If you have turned the Trade Deadline on, you'll only have the first six weeks of the regular season to

▲ See how opponents stack up

make trades. After that, you'll just have to deal with what you have on your team. You will be able to sign Free Agents to replace players lost to injury or to shake up your roster a bit.

You can offer to make a specific trade with another team, or you can place a player on the trading block. When you place a player on the trading block, you can select a position with a ratings range, or a draft pick that you would accept in exchange for that player. Within seconds the CPU will let you know if you have any takers.

OFF-SEASON SCHEDULE

Each year, you will have a batch of things that need to be completed in the off-season before you can move

on. You will need to sign new coaches if there are holes in your staff. If you have a hot team, you will often lose your coordinators to head coaching jobs. One of the best signings you can make is to pick up a Scouting Agency. We'll discuss this more later, but you'll be able to follow twenty college players at a time instead of the default five.

You'll see players retire after you shore up your coaching staff. Don't be surprised to see some of your older stars hang up their cleats. For example, in our first season with the Patriots, both Tedy Bruschi and Rodney Harrison called it a career. If you don't prepare for older guys leaving, you could get stuck with a huge hole in your line-up.

Resigning current players can be a minefield of trouble for you and your

▲ Retirement can catch you off guard

franchise. Remember, you don't have unlimited funds. There is a salary cap in place unless you turned it off at the beginning of your Franchise set-up. If you are playing with a Fantasy Draft, you might lose a pile of players here. Be cautious when it comes to signing players. If you get in too far you'll have trouble filling out your roster and you won't be able to sign your draft picks. It is best to sign your older players to short-term deals so you won't be stuck with their big salaries when their skills decline. Go for young future studs with a couple of veterans in key positions.

▲ *You can't always keep your stars*

THE DRAFT

Most players that hop into Franchise Mode are mostly focused on the draft and free agency. Draft junkies live for this part of the game. *Madden NFL 09* has in-season scouting that allows you to follow potential college draft picks as your year progresses. You'll start out being able to scout five players at a time. If you hire a top-line scouting agency, you'll be able to follow up to twenty players. The longer you scout a player, the more information you can find out about him.

▲ *Scout as many players as you can*

You'll see the combined stats for everybody, but by scouting them, you can unearth even more data about

them. You won't see actual ratings until after you sign players, but you can get a good feel for how they are going to work out based on the scout's comments. You can scout a player for a couple of weeks and then move on to another. Once draft day arrives, you'll go on the clock. You can choose to view the available players that you have scouted at any time in the draft.

▲ *Don't miss your pick*

MONEY SAVING TIPS

It doesn't take much to run into a cash crunch if you have a lot of superstars on your team. It takes some discipline and planning to keep your roster manageable, but still have enough talent to win. You need to make the decision as to whether you want to mortgage the future for a shot at the title today, or build slowly for longevity.

▲ *Sponsors have requirements, too*

▲ *The Colts are excited to be playing in their new stadium*

Here are a couple of tips to help you maximize your cash flow and stay under the cap.

▶ Be smart about signing players. The longer the contract, the better it is for your cap. Raise the signing bonus and sign long-term deals, and eventually you'll have a cap-friendly roster. On the other hand, avoid long-term deals with older players. Their skill will deteriorate, but you'll be stuck with a big cap hit.

▶ If you have quality depth, trade away big contracts for future draft picks. You'll stay young, and more importantly, you'll remain within your budget.

▶ Be on the lookout for additional sources of revenue. Get good enough and you'll get a local media contract. You can also pick up sponsorship deals. Upgrade your stadium and you'll put more fans in the seats.

FRANCHISE MODE

▲ *Creating a player from scratch*

In NFL Superstar Mode, you take control of everything about your player. You will go to the NFL Combine, attend Training Camp, go to practice, play in games, talk to the press, and negotiate for new contracts. Your goal is to become an NFL Hall of Famer.

You have three different options when it comes to beginning your Superstar: Create-A-Superstar, Play As Rookie, or Import NCAA Legend.

CREATE-A-SUPERSTAR

Create-A-Superstar allows you to build up a player from scratch. You begin with Player Info, which allows you to name your player, choose a position, and pick your dominant hand.

Stage two is to determine your build. You can make yourself just about as big or small as you want. Have arms

▲ *Performing the QB Challenge drill*

like pythons, or go for a more sinewy look. We chose to be a prototypical Strong Safety in this example. We'll have plenty of size to drop the hammer on any receiver trying to come across the middle.

Next, you'll determine your player's

equipment and accessories. You control everything from wristbands to ankle tape. Get your guy looking just like you want. Fortunately, you can change your accessories at any time.

The final step is to go through a series of drills to get your basic statistics in place. You'll have the option of choosing the type of player you wish to be at the position you have chosen. For example, you can be a Balanced QB, Pocket QB, or a Scrambling QB. Different drills will be required depending on your choices.

PLAY AS ROOKIE

▲ *Play as a Rookie*

Option number two is to take control of a current NFL Rookie. Do you want to see how you would do as Darren McFadden with the Oakland Raiders? Well, here is your chance. Another option would be to take the helm as Matt Ryan, the new franchise quarterback of the Atlanta Falcons. On the defensive side of the ball, try Jerod Mayo (MLB). When the Patriots' Tedy Bruschi hangs up his cleats, you'll be the go-to guy on a stacked team. Take your pick of any of the NFL draft choices. We recommend avoiding

offensive linemen, as this is not the most fun position to play in the game.

IMPORT NCAA LEGEND

▲ *Campus Legend goes to camp*

Finally, option three is to import your Campus Legend from *NCAA Football 09* into the game. If you have the Prima Guide for *NCAA Football 09,* you'll remember our Heisman QB, Donovan Ingley. We'll use him for the rest of this section. If you choose to import an NCAA Legend, you won't run the same drills as you did with Create-A-Player. Your beginning ratings will be based on your NCAA career.

ROAD TO THE DRAFT

▲ *Our first agent signing*

Now that you have birthed your superstar, it's time to get ready for the

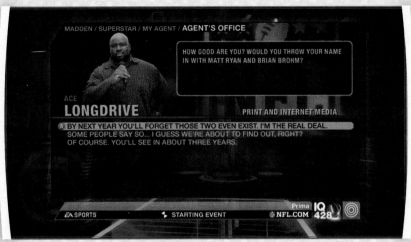

▲ *Interviews help establish your player's attitude*

▲ *Our new contract is fairly lucrative*

FRANCHISE MODE

draft. If you chose to play as a current rookie, you will skip this step. Step one is to hire an agent to represent you in contract negotiations. When you visit the Agent Directory, you can see who is interested in you, as well as view their ratings in several different categories. The higher you are rated coming out of college, the more choices you will have on this screen. If possible, try to get an agent that will give you access to the Performance Institute. This will allow you to train skills that are most important to your position and improve your ratings. In the beginning, you won't have a ton of choices. If you grow into a top player, you'll have the agents knocking down your door.

There are three parts to the pre-draft process. You'll take an IQ test that will help establish the mental capacity of your player. You have to answer ques-

tions within the time period. Do your best, but keep an eye on the clock. You will face comparison questions to test your vocabulary, and number sequencing drills to determine your logic skills.

▲ *Taking the IQ Test*

The interview part of the pre-draft process allows you to further establish the character of your player. You have a number of choices here based on how you want your player to be perceived. You can, of course, toe the line and be politically correct with your answers. It's fun, however, to be the brash prima

donna and run your mouth.

The final aspect of the pre-draft process involves individual workouts and the combine. You get to perform position specific drills as well as the all-important 40-yard dash and bench press. You will want to practice the drills in Mini Games mode so that you can perform when it counts.

You will typically go somewhere between the second and third rounds, depending on how well you performed. The Chargers in the third round of the draft pick up our NCAA Legend.

YOUR CAREER

Once you have been drafted, it's up to you to become a Hall of Fame player. The less you sim and the more you play yourself, the faster your player will improve. Training camp and the

Performance Institute will help you improve your ratings.

▲ *Superstars continue to improve*

After a couple of years, you will have the chance to become a Free Agent and chase the money. If you have a good situation, go for the glory and not the cash.

▲ Do you have what it takes to top the Leaderboard?

Each year, the most competitive players in the game connect to the Internet and prepare to do battle against players all around the world. People that only play against the CPU are often stunned when they first venture into the shark-infested waters of online play.

The CPU will mix up their plays and rarely run the same play more than a couple of times. Against a human opponent, you can find yourself abused by the same play over and over again until you adjust. Players will blitz every down and throw it deep on you all day. Others will move players around in creative ways and constantly create mismatches for themselves.

In this section of the guide, we'll take a look at the most common tactics you will see, and give you tips on how you can survive and dominate online play.

During the course of online play, you will typically run into one of these standard styles of offense.

GROUND POUNDER/ CLOCK BALLER

Clock Ballers have one main goal in mind. They want to control the clock, hold the ball, and grind away at you. You will often see this strategy pulled out at the end of the game, or in a tournament setting like the EA SPORTS Madden Challenge. The Madden Challenge has 2-minute quarter games

in the early rounds. This strategy can eat up the whole half without too much trouble. Playing against players like this can be like beating your head against the wall for hours at a time. They are content to grab 3-4 yards a play and ease their way down the field. Be aware: just because a player runs this scheme, it doesn't mean they can't throw it on you.

You are going to have to bring extra players up in the box when you go against the Ground Pounder. Watch your pursuit angles and make sure you hold them to minimum gains as often as possible. If you are able to get the ball carrier in a crowd of defenders, use the strip ball button to try to create a fumble. Put 8-9 players down in the box and use the Run Commit feature on first down. If you can get them in 3rd and long, you'll succeed against this type of player.

On offense, you will want to get out in front as quickly as possible. Force them to abandon their ground game and get out of their comfort zone. It might even be worth trying an onside kick after a score to pick up an extra possession. You can also give the Clock Baller a dose of his own medi-

cine and slow down the play when you have the ball. Just don't get out of your rhythm and mess up your own game.

When teams are looking to run the ball down your throat, they will often break out a play like the Full House Weak HB Sweep.

They will then put the weak side back in motion to the same side as the sweep. This will overload the defense with numerous blockers leading the way for the halfback.

▲ Jackson goes in motion

To counter the out and out running attack, you have to take some extreme measures. In this example, we are going to attack the run with the 46 Normal Strong Blitz. Use the defensive line audibles to crash the line out. Next, use the linebacker audibles to send all of the linebackers on the blitz. Finish things off with press coverage.

▲ Full House Weak HB Sweep

▲ 46 Normal Strong Blitz

You will want to take control of the free safety and check the pass first. If the offense is running, you will use him to be the contain defender. In this particular play, the linebackers shoot through the gap in the middle of the line. If the play call was a counter or inside run, it would be toast.

▲ *The LB shoots right up the middle*

Our cornerback is able to get off the line clean and has a great pursuit angle on the running back. We continue to control the free safety and get him in position to make the stop, should the corner not be able to make the tackle.

▲ *The HB is stuffed in the backfield*

Now it is second and long. The Ground Pounder has been shaken out of his comfort zone and has to look to throw the ball.

▲ *Engram is wide open on the slant route*

AERIAL ASSAULT

Although some players like to run, the vast majority of *Madden NFL 09* players will choose to move it through the air. Moving the ball through the air is still the tactic of choice for most players. There are numerous ways to approach the passing game, and you will see them all at one time or another. Some players like to go with a West Coast style of offense. They will dink and dunk the ball down the field, throwing lots of crossing routes and slants. Others favor the long ball. They will try to roll out and go deep on you. Shotgun passing attacks are another favorite, especially against opponents that blitz every play. Players will go into the Gun with 4 or 5 receivers and throw it all over the place.

The most dangerous of these, of course, is the balanced player that will show you a bit of everything. Think Peyton Manning and the Colts here. They will throw from Singleback Slot sets, Gun Spread sets, and then go into I-Form Tight and run play action routes to the tight ends. These players can be a real problem to deal with on offense.

West Coast offenses are very efficient and are sort of like the Ground Pounders of the passing game. Those that run the WCO will need to be able to make quick reads and correct decisions with the ball, as this is a timing offense. Use your defenders to fill the passing lanes. Play underneath zones, drop linemen into hook zones, and otherwise try to clog up the field. These players can be tough to sack, so you will want to mix up your blitzes. Throw in some bump-n-run coverage as well as mixed man/zone defenses.

A typical play you will run into is the Split Pro Slants from the Seahawks playbook. This is the West Coast offense at its best. Against man coverage, the slants will be open all day long. This is true even if bump-n-run coverage is applied.

We don't want to just come out in zone all the time. Instead, we want to bait the offense into making a mistake. We call 4-3 Normal 2 Man Under, and make two adjustments at the line of scrimmage. Both the MLB and RE are put in hook zones using Individual Defensive Hot Routes.

▲ *Put the RE and MLB in hook zones*

When the ball is snapped, the QB takes a quick look at the WR and reads man coverage. He fires the ball in without hesitation. Julius Peppers has dropped back and is in perfect position to pick off the pass.

You could put all the linebackers in hook zones using the linebacker

▲ *Peppers forces the turnover*

▲ *Jones will be wide open*

ONLINE STRATEGIES

audibles, but this would leave the halfback wide open in the flat. Instead, drop the RE in zone and let the ROLB play Jones in man coverage.

Most deep lobbers do not work on their skills as far as reading pass coverages. They will often have a favorite receiver and like to just throw the ball up and go get it with their user-catching skills. They are going to struggle this year as the strafe catch is gone, but they can still be dangerous. You need to work on your stick skills so that you can make plays yourself. When going up against teams like the Patriots and Panthers, you have to have safety help over the top. Randy Moss and Steve Smith will be open deep all day against single man coverage. Go into practice mode and put yourself on defense. Practice against the Hail Mary play and work on manual defense.

The most difficult type of player to defend is the one that throws short, medium, and deep balls. They don't have a favorite receiver and will throw to the first guy they see open. You are going to have to throw everything but the kitchen sink at them to stop their attack. Disguise your coverages using

Individual Defensive Hot Routes, blitz from different angles, and manually control defenders to guard their favorite spots on the field.

MOBILE QUARTERBACK ATTACK

With Michael Vick out of the picture, these players aren't as prevalent or dangerous as they use to be. However, there are still players like Tarvaris Jackson and of course Vince Young who can run this type of attack. Players that favor the Mobile QB will constantly put your containment to the test. They will get outside on you and force you to break off coverage to defend them. Against these types of players, you really don't want to flush them out of the pocket. Instead, you want to contain rush on the outside and leave players in QB Spy to hold onto the middle. Remember, having a player in QB Spy that is much slower than the quarterback won't help you. The QB will just wave as he runs right past the defender.

One of the best ways to defend this type of player is by using Man/Zone

▲ *Vince Young rolls out right*

▲ *Our corner blitz sacks him*

coverages. Coverages with man on one side and zone on the other will make it tough to figure out which way to roll out of the pocket. You can also send blitzers from the wide side of the field.

Force the QB to roll to the short side and run out of room. You can also send a steady diet of corner blitzes from the QB's throwing side. So if he is right-handed, blitz from the right and make him throw across his body. Many players that run this style of offense completely fall apart when you take away their bread and butter schemes.

▲ *Hustling back to the line*

NO HUDDLE OFFENSE

The No Huddle Offense is the Mr. Hyde to the Clock Baller's Dr. Jekyll. This player is just as frustrating to deal with as you can never get into a good groove. One type of No Huddle player will go at you right from the snap. He will have all of his audibles set just like he wants and will hit you again and again to go for the quick score. With Formation Audibles in the game, he has even more options to attack you.

The other type of No Huddle player will just do it in certain situations. If he has success on a play and knows you are in a bad defensive call, he'll keep running no huddle and punishing your bad play call. You'll often have to call a timeout just to catch your breath here.

Use your audibles and formations audibles to change your play and coverages up. As a last resort, go offside while the other team is coming to the line. This will let you pick a new play and force the offense to go to the play selection screen. Sometimes a timeout is worth more than 5 yards, especially when it is early in the drive.

In addition, use your Individual Playmaker Hot Routes and manual player movement to adjust to what your opponent is doing and force him to make a mistake.

▲ *A bunched compression set*

▲ *Gun Bunch TE*

ONLINE STRATEGIES

COMPRESSION OFFENSE

The Compression Offense has taken the tournament scene by storm over the last few years. If you have attended an EA SPORTS Madden Challenge event, then you are sure to have seen the compression in action. West Coast Offense teams have run this style of offense in the NFL for years, and it has been fully adapted for use in *Madden NFL 09* as well.

Compressed sets have bunches of players lined up in one area to create confusion for the coverage. These players are often lined up tight to the line of scrimmage to give them plenty of room to run outbreaking routes.

With the majority of the offense loaded up on one side of the field, the single backside post or slant can

come wide open. With all the players grouped in tight, it can make it really easy to read man versus zone coverage.

Good compression users can be very tough to defend. You have two main weapons at your disposal. First, you can send the blitz and run bump-n-run pressure. Many compression players will send all five receivers out in pass patterns. You can often get in with at least one defender. The next option is to mix up your coverages and hot route defensive linemen to drop into coverage as well. Clog up the passing lanes and try to make a mess of things so that reads are tough. Mix in some Man/Zone combo defenses to make things tougher for the quarterback.

▲ *Gun Bunch Wk*

Defensively, you will typically encounter three different types of players online.

BEND DON'T BREAK

▲ *Make red zone chances count*

Bend But Don't Break players do not want to give up the big plays. They will sit back and keep all of the offensive players in front of them. Their idea is to force a third and long situation, or catch the offense in a mistake. These players thrive in creating turnovers and playing great red zone defense. When going up against these types of players, you have to be patient. Take what the offense gives you and work your way down the field. Don't throw into double coverage and be ready to execute in the red zone. You have to score inside the twenty on a consistent basis if you

▲ *A typical All Coverage Scheme*

▲ *The Colts are lined up to bring the heat*

are to beat this player.

There is another version of this scheme that you will also run into online. This is the All Coverage scheme. Players will use Individual Defensive Hot Routes to drop all of their linemen back into zone coverage. They may rush one player, but will typically throw 10 or 11 into coverage. Use delay routes with deep clear out routes to bust up this style of defense.

AGGRESSIVE

Teams like the Philadelphia Eagles are known to always be on the attack on defense. You will see this online in the form of players that like to bring the heat on each and every play. They like to play on the knife's edge and aren't afraid to give up a big play every once in a while. They believe they can force you to make enough mistakes to

lose. Be ready for a ton of bump-n-run coverage coming your way.

There are several different types of aggressive players. One uses blitzes based on the framework of the game. They will use shifts and stunts to overload one side of the field and try to get more blitzers in than the offense can handle. Others will pay a more freewheeling style of defense by moving players all over the field, stacking defenders behind each other, and manually pass rushing from all different angles.

They seek to create what are referred to as Nano Blitz Packages. The pressure comes on the quarterback within just seconds of the snap.

Slide Protection has been added to the Next Gen versions of *Madden NFL 09* this season. It will be your main defense against blitz-happy players. Typically, blitzers have a couple of

favorite points of attack. Use Slide Protection to direct your offensive line to plug these gaps. You will also need to leave at least one back in to pass block. Using a Tight End as a blocker can be another effective strategy. This will often change up the whole blocking scheme and thwart the Nano attack. Use your slants, screens, quick outs, and dumps to your backs to counter the quick heat that nanos bring. If you can make an aggressive player pay for his behavior, you will force him to back off so you can run your offense.

BALANCED

Players who are not predictable are always the toughest to handle. Defenders who call a mix of man and zone coverages as well as timely blitzes can be rough to go up against. They typically understand what each defensive play is trying to accomplish and know how to take away the danger spots on the field. They will often pull an occasional nano out, but don't make them the focal point of their offense. If you want to be a top tier online player, then you should strive to be this sort of player. No matter what the offense throws at you, you will have an answer. Like a chameleon, you need to be able to change things up at will.

When you attack this player on offense, you will have to mix things up. Run from passing sets, throw from running sets, and do whatever you have to do to be unpredictable.

▲ *Play solid defense and get after those receivers*

DEPTH CHARTS

 ## CHICAGO BEARS

POS	OVR	FIRST NAME	LAST NAME
C	93	Olin	Kreutz
C	67	Anthony	Oakley
CB	91	Charles	Tillman
CB	91	Nathan	Vasher
CB	78	Danieal	Manning
CB	78	Trumaine	McBride
DT	96	Tommie	Harris
DT	79	Dusty	Dvoracek
DT	78	Anthony	Adams
FB	84	Jason	McKie
FS	87	Mike	Brown
FS	73	Josh	Gattis
HB	80	Matt	Forte
HB	80	Cedric	Benson
HB	78	Adrian	Peterson
K	93	Robbie	Gould
LE	89	Adewale	Ogunleye
LE	76	Israel	Idonije
LG	78	Terrence	Metcalf
LG	78	Josh	Beekman
LOLB	79	Hunter	Hillenmeyer
LOLB	70	Michael	Okwo
LT	79	Chris	Williams
LT	73	John	St. Clair
MLB	98	Brian	Urlacher
MLB	69	Rod	Wilson
P	82	Brad	Maynard
QB	79	Rex	Grossman
QB	76	Kyle	Orton
RE	85	Alex	Brown
RE	84	Mark	Anderson
RG	85	Roberto	Garza
RG	68	Tyler	Reed
ROLB	95	Lance	Briggs
ROLB	73	Jamar	Williams
RT	85	John	Tait
RT	70	Kirk	Barton
SS	83	Brandon	McGowan
SS	73	Craig	Steltz
TE	86	Desmond	Clark
TE	85	Greg	Olsen
WR	82	Marty	Booker
WR	81	Devin	Hester
WR	79	Earl	Bennett
WR	77	Mark	Bradley

 ## CINCINNATI BENGALS

POS	OVR	FIRST NAME	LAST NAME
C	79	Eric	Ghiaciuc
C	68	Dan	Santucci
CB	84	Deltha	O'Neal
CB	83	Johnathan	Joseph
CB	80	Leon	Hall
CB	67	David	Jones
DT	83	John	Thornton
DT	83	Domata	Peko
DT	76	Pat	Sims
FB	87	Jeremi	Johnson
FS	76	Marvin	White
FS	72	Ethan	Kilmer
HB	84	Rudi	Johnson
HB	82	Kenny	Watson
HB	80	Chris	Perry
K	90	Shayne	Graham
LE	84	Antwan	Odom
LE	73	Frostee	Rucker
LG	83	Stacy	Andrews
LG	82	Andrew	Whitworth
LOLB	78	Rashad	Jeanty
LOLB	74	Darryl	Blackstock
LT	88	Levi	Jones
LT	73	Anthony	Collins
MLB	78	Dhani	Jones
MLB	77	Ahmad	Brooks
P	82	Kyle	Larson
QB	96	Carson	Palmer
QB	75	Ryan	Fitzpatrick
RE	83	Robert	Geathers
RE	74	Jonathan	Fanene
RG	86	Bobbie	Williams
RG	62	Nate	Livings
ROLB	82	Keith	Rivers
ROLB	67	Brandon	Johnson
RT	92	Willie	Anderson
RT	75	Scott	Kooistra
SS	80	Nedu	Ndukwe
SS	79	Dexter	Jackson
TE	81	Reggie	Kelly
TE	81	Ben	Utecht
WR	97	Chad	Johnson
WR	95	T.J.	Houshmandzadeh
WR	77	Andre	Caldwell
WR	76	Jerome	Simpson

BUFFALO BILLS

POS	OVR	FIRST NAME	LAST NAME
C	83	Melvin	Fowler
C	75	Jason	Whittle
CB	93	Terrence	McGee
CB	82	Jabari	Greer
CB	82	Leodis	McKelvin
CB	77	Will	James
DT	94	Marcus	Stroud
DT	84	Kyle	Williams
DT	83	John	McCargo
FB	78	Darian	Barnes
FS	83	Ko	Simpson
FS	83	George	Wilson
HB	90	Marshawn	Lynch
HB	79	Fred	Jackson
HB	74	Dwayne	Wright
K	92	Rian	Lindell
LE	83	Chris	Kelsay
LE	79	Ryan	Denney
LG	91	Derrick	Dockery
LG	72	Christian	Gaddis
LOLB	90	Angelo	Crowell
LT	97	Jason	Peters
LT	71	Patrick	Estes
MLB	82	Paul	Posluszny
MLB	82	John	DiGiorgio
P	89	Brian	Moorman
QB	79	J.P.	Losman
QB	79	Trent	Edwards
RE	92	Aaron	Schobel
RE	75	Chris	Ellis
RG	83	Brad	Butler
RG	78	Duke	Preston
ROLB	87	Kawika	Mitchell
ROLB	79	Keith	Ellison
ROLB	72	Alvin	Bowen
RT	86	Langston	Walker
RT	69	Kirk	Chambers
SS	92	Donte	Whitner
SS	72	Bryan	Scott
TE	78	Robert	Royal
TE	72	Derek	Schouman
WR	91	Lee	Evans
WR	79	James	Hardy
WR	78	Roscoe	Parrish
WR	77	Josh	Reed

DENVER BRONCOS

POS	OVR	FIRST NAME	LAST NAME
C	89	Tom	Nalen
C	85	Casey	Wiegmann
CB	97	Champ	Bailey
CB	89	Dre'	Bly
CB	78	Domonique	Foxworth
CB	76	Karl	Paymah
DT	84	Dewayne	Robertson
DT	79	Marcus	Thomas
DT	78	Alvin	McKinley
FB	79	Cecil	Sapp
FB	78	Mike	Bell
FS	79	Hamza	Abdullah
FS	74	Marquand	Manuel
HB	84	Selvin	Young
HB	81	Michael	Pittman
K	70	Matt	Prater
LE	81	Jarvis	Moss
LE	81	John	Engelberger
LG	87	Ben	Hamilton
LG	76	Dylan	Gandy
LOLB	82	Boss	Bailey
LOLB	81	Nate	Webster
LT	79	Ryan	Clady
MLB	74	Niko	Koutouvides
MLB	70	Jordan	Beck
P	77	Sam	Paulescu
QB	86	Jay	Cutler
QB	79	Patrick	Ramsey
RE	90	Elvis	Dumervil
RE	82	Ebenezer	Ekuban
RG	79	Montrae	Holland
RG	76	Kory	Lichtensteiger
ROLB	95	D.J.	Williams
ROLB	75	Jamie	Winborn
RT	79	Erik	Pears
RT	79	Chris	Kuper
RT	78	Ryan	Harris
SS	92	John	Lynch
SS	83	Marlon	McCree
TE	86	Daniel	Graham
TE	84	Tony	Scheffler
WR	93	Brandon	Marshall
WR	86	Darrell	Jackson
WR	84	Brandon	Stokley
WR	77	Eddie	Royal

CLEVELAND BROWNS

POS	OVR	FIRST NAME	LAST NAME
C	89	Hank	Fraley
C	82	LeCharles	Bentley
CB	84	Eric	Wright
CB	82	Brandon	McDonald
CB	78	Daven	Holly
CB	68	A.J.	Davis
DT	94	Shaun	Rogers
DT	72	Louis	Leonard
DT	70	Ahtyba	Rubin
FB	92	Lawrence	Vickers
FS	84	Brodney	Pool
FS	84	Gary	Baxter
HB	90	Jamal	Lewis
HB	77	Jerome	Harrison
HB	77	Jason	Wright
K	91	Phil	Dawson
LE	90	Corey	Williams
LE	85	Shaun	Smith
LG	95	Eric	Steinbach
LG	79	Lennie	Friedman
LOLB	85	Willie	McGinest
LOLB	78	Antwan	Peek
LT	97	Joe	Thomas
MLB	85	D'Qwell	Jackson
MLB	84	Andra	Davis
P	81	Dave	Zastudil
QB	87	Derek	Anderson
QB	82	Brady	Quinn
RE	87	Robaire	Smith
RE	68	Melila	Purcell
RG	90	Rex	Hadnot
RG	77	Seth	McKinney
ROLB	88	Kamerion	Wimbley
ROLB	70	Shantee	Orr
RT	89	Kevin	Shaffer
RT	84	Ryan	Tucker
SS	87	Sean	Jones
SS	68	Steve	Cargile
TE	97	Kellen	Winslow
TE	79	Steve	Heiden
WR	95	Braylon	Edwards
WR	85	Donte	Stallworth
WR	83	Joe	Jurevicius
WR	81	Travis	Wilson
WR	73	Josh	Cribbs

TAMPA BAY BUCCANEERS

POS	OVR	FIRST NAME	LAST NAME
C	88	Jeff	Faine
C	76	Dan	Buenning
CB	92	Ronde	Barber
CB	82	Phillip	Buchanon
CB	80	Aqib	Talib
CB	72	Sammy	Davis
DT	87	Jovan	Haye
DT	84	Chris	Hovan
DT	79	Ryan	Sims
FB	87	B.J.	Askew
FS	87	Tanard	Jackson
FS	84	Eugene	Wilson
HB	85	Warrick	Dunn
HB	85	Carnell	Williams
HB	84	Earnest	Graham
K	89	Matt	Bryant
LE	86	Marques	Douglas
LE	82	Kevin	Carter
LG	85	Arron	Sears
LG	78	Anthony	Davis
LOLB	91	Cato	June
LOLB	74	Quincy	Black
LT	87	Luke	Petitgout
LT	76	Donald	Penn
MLB	89	Barrett	Ruud
MLB	71	Teddy	Lehman
P	84	Josh	Bidwell
QB	90	Jeff	Garcia
QB	77	Brian	Griese
RE	88	Gaines	Adams
RE	85	Greg	White
RG	93	Davin	Joseph
RG	78	Jeremy	Zuttah
ROLB	93	Derrick	Brooks
ROLB	68	Adam	Hayward
RT	87	Jeremy	Trueblood
RT	63	Chris	Denman
SS	88	Jermaine	Phillips
SS	74	Sabby	Piscitelli
TE	83	Alex	Smith
TE	79	Ben	Troupe
WR	88	Joey	Galloway
WR	80	Ike	Hilliard
WR	79	Maurice	Stovall
WR	78	Michael	Clayton

 ARIZONA CARDINALS

POS	OVR	FIRST NAME	LAST NAME
C	80	Al	Johnson
C	73	Lyle	Sendlein
CB	86	Roderick	Hood
CB	83	Eric	Green
CB	82	Dominique	R-Cromartie
CB	69	Ralph	Brown
DT	93	Darnell	Dockett
DT	80	Gabe	Watson
DT	79	Alan	Branch
FB	88	Terrelle	Smith
FS	89	Antrel	Rolle
FS	78	Aaron	Francisco
HB	92	Edgerrin	James
HB	76	Marcel	Shipp
HB	73	J.J.	Arrington
K	82	Neil	Rackers
LE	83	Antonio	Smith
LE	79	Calais	Campbell
LG	85	Reggie	Wells
LG	66	Scott	Peters
LOLB	82	Bertrand	Berry
LOLB	75	Travis	LaBoy
LT	86	Mike	Gandy
LT	65	Elliot	Vallejo
MLB	86	Gerald	Hayes
MLB	85	Karlos	Dansby
P	73	Dirk	Johnson
QB	85	Kurt	Warner
QB	85	Matt	Leinart
RE	76	Joe	Tafoya
RE	74	Kenny	Iwebema
RG	79	Deuce	Lutui
RG	74	Elton	Brown
ROLB	85	Clark	Haggans
ROLB	85	Chike	Okeafor
RT	85	Levi	Brown
RT	66	Brandon	Keith
SS	96	Adrian	Wilson
SS	70	Oliver	Celestin
TE	78	Leonard	Pope
TE	76	Troy	Bienemann
WR	97	Larry	Fitzgerald
WR	95	Anquan	Boldin
WR	77	Early	Doucet
WR	74	Jerheme	Urban

SAN DIEGO CHARGERS

POS	OVR	FIRST NAME	LAST NAME
C	94	Nick	Hardwick
C	77	Cory	Withrow
CB	93	Quentin	Jammer
CB	92	Antonio	Cromartie
CB	79	Antoine	Cason
CB	73	Cletis	Gordon
DT	97	Jamal	Williams
DT	80	Brandon	McKinney
DT	64	Keith	Jackson
FB	83	Jacob	Hester
FB	76	Andrew	Pinnock
FS	85	Clinton	Hart
FS	71	Paul	Oliver
HB	99	LaDainian	Tomlinson
HB	79	Darren	Sproles
K	94	Nate	Kaeding
LE	93	Luis	Castillo
LE	66	Ryon	Bingham
LG	94	Kris	Dielman
LG	73	Scott	Mruczkowski
LOLB	92	Shaun	Phillips
LOLB	75	Marques	Harris
LT	93	Marcus	McNeill
LT	62	Tony	Pape
MLB	86	Stephen	Cooper
MLB	80	Derek	Smith
P	86	Mike	Scifres
QB	90	Philip	Rivers
QB	82	Billy	Volek
RE	86	Igor	Olshansky
RE	83	Jacques	Cesaire
RG	88	Mike	Goff
RG	70	Erik	Robertson
ROLB	97	Shawne	Merriman
ROLB	72	Jyles	Tucker
RT	80	Jeromey	Clary
RT	75	L.J.	Shelton
SS	79	Eric	Weddle
SS	67	Brian	Bonner
TE	99	Antonio	Gates
TE	76	Brandon	Manumaleuna
WR	91	Chris	Chambers
WR	89	Vincent	Jackson
WR	79	Eric	Parker
WR	79	Buster	Davis

DEPTH CHARTS

DEPTH CHARTS

 KANSAS CITY CHIEFS

POS	OVR	FIRST NAME	LAST NAME
C	76	Rudy	Niswanger
C	73	Wade	Smith
CB	89	Patrick	Surtain
CB	79	Brandon	Flowers
CB	70	Tyron	Brackenridge
CB	69	Dimitri	Patterson
DT	84	Glenn	Dorsey
DT	83	Ron	Edwards
DT	78	Tank	Tyler
FB	78	Oliver	Hoyte
FS	85	Jarrad	Page
FS	71	Jon	McGraw
HB	94	Larry	Johnson
HB	79	Kolby	Smith
HB	75	Jamaal	Charles
K	76	Billy	Cundiff
LE	84	Alfonso	Boone
LE	75	Turk	McBride
LG	91	Brian	Waters
LG	71	Tre	Stallings
LOLB	93	Derrick	Johnson
LOLB	70	Pat	Thomas
LT	81	Branden	Albert
LT	75	Will	Svitek
MLB	84	Napoleon	Harris
MLB	65	Nate	Harris
P	94	Dustin	Colquitt
QB	78	Brodie	Croyle
QB	78	Damon	Huard
RE	86	Tamba	Hali
RE	68	Johnny	Dingle
RG	78	Adrian	Jones
RG	76	Herb	Taylor
ROLB	93	Donnie	Edwards
ROLB	84	Demorrio	Williams
RT	80	Damion	McIntosh
RT	71	Anthony	Alabi
SS	87	Bernard	Pollard
SS	70	DaJuan	Morgan
TE	98	Tony	Gonzalez
TE	76	Brad	Cottam
WR	90	Dwayne	Bowe
WR	77	Devard	Darling
WR	76	Jeff	Webb
WR	75	Will	Franklin

 INDIANAPOLIS COLTS

POS	OVR	FIRST NAME	LAST NAME
C	96	Jeff	Saturday
C	74	Steve	Justice
CB	87	Kelvin	Hayden
CB	87	Marlin	Jackson
CB	77	Tim	Jennings
CB	76	Dante	Hughes
DT	86	Ed	Johnson
DT	82	Raheem	Brock
DT	78	Darrell	Reid
FB	79	Jacob	Tamme
FS	93	Antoine	Bethea
FS	75	Melvin	Bullitt
HB	91	Joseph	Addai
HB	83	Dominic	Rhodes
HB	77	Kenton	Keith
K	93	Adam	Vinatieri
LE	95	Robert	Mathis
LE	79	Keyunta	Dawson
LG	90	Ryan	Lilja
LG	64	Jamey	Richard
LOLB	81	Tyjuan	Hagler
LOLB	68	Ramon	Guzman
LT	81	Tony	Ugoh
LT	68	Michael	Toudouze
MLB	91	Gary	Brackett
MLB	74	Phillip	Wheeler
P	87	Hunter	Smith
QB	99	Peyton	Manning
QB	73	Jim	Sorgi
RE	95	Dwight	Freeney
RE	81	Josh	Thomas
RG	78	Mike	Pollak
RG	77	Charlie	Johnson
ROLB	87	Freddie	Keiaho
ROLB	70	Clint	Session
RT	93	Ryan	Diem
RT	67	Corey	Hilliard
SS	99	Bob	Sanders
SS	76	Matt	Giordano
TE	93	Dallas	Clark
TE	75	Tom	Santi
WR	97	Reggie	Wayne
WR	94	Marvin	Harrison
WR	80	Anthony	Gonzalez
WR	75	Devin	Aromashodu

DALLAS COWBOYS

POS	OVR	FIRST NAME	LAST NAME
C	94	Andre	Gurode
C	70	Cory	Procter
CB	95	Terence	Newman
CB	88	Anthony	Henry
CB	82	Mike	Jenkins
CB	73	Orlando	Scandrick
DT	84	Jay	Ratliff
DT	80	Tank	Johnson
DT	68	Remi	Ayodele
FB	83	Deon	Anderson
FS	90	Ken	Hamlin
FS	67	Courtney	Brown
HB	93	Marion	Barber
HB	80	Felix	Jones
HB	77	Tashard	Choice
K	89	Nick	Folk
LE	82	Marcus	Spears
LE	71	Jason	Hatcher
LG	89	Kyle	Kosier
LG	77	Pat	McQuistan
LOLB	89	Greg	Ellis
LOLB	80	Anthony	Spencer
LT	94	Flozell	Adams
LT	78	Doug	Free
MLB	94	Zach	Thomas
MLB	87	Bradie	James
P	95	Mat	McBriar
QB	94	Tony	Romo
QB	78	Brad	Johnson
RE	84	Chris	Canty
RE	67	Stephen	Bowen
RG	97	Leonard	Davis
RG	68	Joe	Berger
ROLB	98	DeMarcus	Ware
ROLB	80	Bobby	Carpenter
RT	88	Marc	Colombo
RT	77	James	Marten
SS	88	Roy	Williams
SS	76	Pat	Watkins
TE	97	Jason	Witten
TE	80	Martellus	Bennett
WR	98	Terrell	Owens
WR	86	Terry	Glenn
WR	82	Patrick	Crayton
WR	73	Sam	Hurd

MIAMI DOLPHINS

POS	OVR	FIRST NAME	LAST NAME
C	88	Samson	Satele
C	64	Mike	Byrne
CB	86	Will	Allen
CB	80	Michael	Lehan
CB	73	Travis	Daniels
CB	72	Andre'	Goodman
DT	84	Jason	Ferguson
DT	84	Vonnie	Holliday
DT	79	Randy	Starks
FB	89	Reagan	Mauia
FS	77	Jason	Allen
FS	77	Renaldo	Hill
HB	92	Ronnie	Brown
HB	83	Ricky	Williams
HB	76	Jalen	Parmele
K	88	Jay	Feely
LE	81	Phillip	Merling
LE	80	Matt	Roth
LG	89	Justin	Smiley
LG	71	Donald	Thomas
LOLB	78	Reggie	Torbor
LOLB	76	Charlie	Anderson
LT	85	Jake	Long
LT	65	Ike	Ndukwe
MLB	85	Channing	Crowder
MLB	81	Akin	Ayodele
P	76	Brandon	Fields
QB	79	Josh	McCown
QB	78	John	Beck
RE	98	Jason	Taylor
RE	67	Lionel	Dotson
RG	77	Steve	McKinney
RG	76	Shawn	Murphy
ROLB	88	Joey	Porter
ROLB	68	Edmond	Miles
RT	87	Vernon	Carey
RT	65	Julius	Wilson
SS	83	Yeremiah	Bell
SS	77	Keith	Davis
TE	82	Anthony	Fasano
TE	79	David	Martin
WR	84	Ernest	Wilford
WR	82	Ted	Ginn
WR	72	Derek	Hagan
WR	69	Greg	Camarillo

PHILADELPHIA EAGLES

POS	OVR	FIRST NAME	LAST NAME
C	92	Jamaal	Jackson
C	68	Nick	Cole
CB	96	Asante	Samuel
CB	93	Lito	Sheppard
CB	91	Sheldon	Brown
CB	78	Joselio	Hanson
DT	84	Mike	Patterson
DT	84	Brodrick	Bunkley
DT	79	Trevor	Laws
FB	66	Dan	Klecko
FS	92	Brian	Dawkins
FS	73	Quintin	Demps
HB	97	Brian	Westbrook
HB	82	Correll	Buckhalter
HB	75	Tony	Hunt
K	82	David	Akers
LE	87	Juqua	Parker
LE	85	Chris	Clemons
LG	88	Todd	Herremans
LG	75	Scott	Young
LOLB	81	Chris	Gocong
LOLB	73	Rocky	Boiman
LT	95	William	Thomas
LT	76	Winston	Justice
MLB	79	Stewart	Bradley
MLB	68	Pago	Togafau
P	74	Saverio	Rocca
QB	92	Donovan	McNabb
QB	78	Kevin	Kolb
RE	93	Trent	Cole
RE	75	Bryan	Smith
RG	96	Shawn	Andrews
RG	80	Max	Jean-Gilles
ROLB	87	Omar	Gaither
ROLB	64	Akeem	Jordan
RT	90	Jon	Runyan
RT	60	King	Dunlap
SS	83	Quintin	Mikell
SS	78	Sean	Considine
TE	85	L.J.	Smith
TE	80	Kris	Wilson
WR	87	Kevin	Curtis
WR	86	Reggie	Brown
WR	78	DeSean	Jackson
WR	76	Jason	Avant

 ATLANTA FALCONS

POS	OVR	FIRST NAME	LAST NAME
C	82	Todd	McClure
C	75	Alex	Stepanovich
CB	79	Von	Hutchins
CB	78	Chris	Houston
CB	77	Chevis	Jackson
CB	76	David	Irons
DT	82	Jonathan	Babineaux
DT	78	Trey	Lewis
DT	77	Kindal	Moorehead
FB	90	Ovie	Mughelli
FS	80	Erik	Coleman
FS	77	Jimmy	Williams
HB	88	Michael	Turner
HB	82	Jerious	Norwood
HB	75	Jason	Snelling
K	90	Jason	Elam
LE	83	Jamaal	Anderson
LE	70	Derrick	Jones
LG	77	Justin	Blalock
LG	75	Quinn	Ojinnaka
LOLB	87	Michael	Boley
LOLB	76	Stephen	Nicholas
LT	78	Sam	Baker
LT	69	Renardo	Foster
MLB	81	Curtis	Lofton
MLB	65	Tony	Taylor
P	77	Michael	Koenen
P	74	Saverio	Rocca
QB	83	Matt	Ryan
QB	82	Chris	Redman
RE	92	John	Abraham
RE	76	Chauncey	Davis
RG	85	Kynan	Forney
RG	72	D'Anthony	Batiste
ROLB	89	Keith	Brooking
ROLB	74	Robert	James
RT	84	Todd	Weiner
RT	75	Tyson	Clabo
SS	82	Lawyer	Milloy
SS	74	Daren	Stone
TE	68	Ben	Hartsock
TE	66	Martrez	Milner
WR	89	Roddy	White
WR	80	Laurent	Robinson
WR	79	Harry	Douglas
WR	79	Michael	Jenkins

 SAN FRANCISCO 49ERS

POS	OVR	FIRST NAME	LAST NAME
C	85	Eric	Heitmann
C	73	Cody	Wallace
CB	92	Nate	Clements
CB	88	Walt	Harris
CB	79	Shawntae	Spencer
CB	77	Reggie	Smith
DT	79	Aubrayo	Franklin
DT	77	Ronald	Fields
DT	75	Joe	Cohen
FB	85	Moran	Norris
FS	79	Mark	Roman
FS	75	Dashon	Goldson
HB	93	Frank	Gore
HB	82	DeShaun	Foster
HB	77	Michael	Robinson
K	90	Joe	Nedney
LE	83	Isaac	Sopoaga
LE	76	Kentwan	Balmer
LG	82	Adam	Snyder
LG	78	Chilo	Rachal
LOLB	85	Manny	Lawson
LOLB	72	Jay	Moore
LT	86	Joe	Staley
LT	71	Qasim	Mitchell
MLB	96	Patrick	Willis
MLB	80	Jeff	Ulbrich
P	96	Andy	Lee
QB	79	Alex	Smith
QB	79	Shaun	Hill
RE	89	Justin	Smith
RE	75	Ray	McDonald
RG	84	David	Baas
RG	75	Tony	Wragge
ROLB	79	Tully	Banta-Cain
ROLB	74	Parys	Haralson
RT	88	Jonas	Jennings
RT	61	Damane	Duckett
SS	87	Michael	Lewis
SS	73	Keith	Lewis
TE	87	Vernon	Davis
TE	73	Delanie	Walker
WR	85	Isaac	Bruce
WR	82	Bryant	Johnson
WR	82	Arnaz	Battle
WR	77	Jason	Hill

 NEW YORK GIANTS

POS	OVR	FIRST NAME	LAST NAME
C	92	Shaun	O'Hara
C	75	Grey	Ruegamer
CB	88	Sam	Madison
CB	86	Aaron	Ross
CB	83	Kevin	Dockery
CB	80	Corey	Webster
DT	87	Fred	Robbins
DT	85	Barry	Cofield
DT	75	Jay	Alford
DT	68	Rodney	Leisle
FB	88	Madison	Hedgecock
FS	82	James	Butler
FS	80	Kenny	Phillips
HB	87	Brandon	Jacobs
HB	82	Ahmad	Bradshaw
HB	81	Derrick	Ward
K	85	Lawrence	Tynes
LE	94	Justin	Tuck
LG	91	Rich	Seubert
LOLB	81	Mathias	Kiwanuka
LOLB	72	Zak	DeOssie
LT	93	David	Diehl
LT	75	Guy	Whimper
MLB	95	Antonio	Pierce
MLB	73	Jonathan	Goff
P	81	Jeff	Feagles
QB	93	Eli	Manning
QB	76	David	Carr
RE	97	Osi	Umenyiora
RE	74	Dave	Tollefson
RG	95	Chris	Snee
RG	78	Kevin	Boothe
ROLB	78	Danny	Clark
ROLB	77	Gerris	Wilkinson
RT	93	Kareem	McKenzie
RT	69	Adam	Koets
SS	83	Sammy	Knight
SS	77	Michael	Johnson
TE	95	Jeremy	Shockey
TE	80	Kevin	Boss
WR	96	Plaxico	Burress
WR	86	Amani	Toomer
WR	83	Steve	Smith
WR	78	Mario	Manningham
WR	72	Sinorice	Moss

DEPTH CHARTS

DEPTH CHARTS

 JACKSONVILLE JAGUARS

POS	OVR	FIRST NAME	LAST NAME
C	93	Brad	Meester
C	68	Dennis	Norman
CB	95	Rashean	Mathis
CB	85	Drayton	Florence
CB	75	Scott	Starks
CB	73	Trae	Williams
DT	95	John	Henderson
DT	86	Rob	Meier
DT	77	Derek	Landri
FB	91	Greg	Jones
FS	92	Reggie	Nelson
FS	70	Jamaal	Fudge
HB	94	Fred	Taylor
HB	91	Maurice	Jones-Drew
HB	74	Chauncey	Washington
K	86	Josh	Scobee
LE	87	Paul	Spicer
LE	81	Derrick	Harvey
LG	94	Vince	Manuwai
LG	72	Uche	Nwaneri
LOLB	83	Justin	Durant
LOLB	78	Clint	Ingram
LT	90	Khalif	Barnes
LT	72	Richard	Collier
MLB	93	Mike	Peterson
MLB	69	Tony	Gilbert
P	77	Adam	Podlesh
QB	92	David	Garrard
QB	77	Cleo	Lemon
RE	86	Reggie	Hayward
RE	79	Quentin	Groves
RG	91	Maurice	Williams
RG	74	Tutan	Reyes
ROLB	92	Daryl	Smith
ROLB	73	Brian	Iwuh
RT	87	Tony	Pashos
RT	66	Andrew	Carnahan
SS	87	Brian	Williams
SS	79	Gerald	Sensabaugh
TE	84	Marcedes	Lewis
TE	80	George	Wrighster
WR	86	Jerry	Porter
WR	83	Reggie	Williams
WR	81	Dennis	Northcutt
WR	78	Troy	Williamson

 NEW YORK JETS

POS	OVR	FIRST NAME	LAST NAME
C	93	Nick	Mangold
C	71	Will	Montgomery
CB	88	Darrelle	Revis
CB	79	Hank	Poteat
CB	77	Dwight	Lowery
CB	75	David	Barrett
DT	92	Kris	Jenkins
DT	74	C.J.	Mosley
DT	70	Sione	Pouha
FB	90	Tony	Richardson
FS	78	Abram	Elam
FS	71	Artrell	Hawkins
HB	88	Thomas	Jones
HB	82	Leon	Washington
HB	80	Jesse	Chatman
K	86	Mike	Nugent
LE	86	Shaun	Ellis
LE	67	Mike	Devito
LG	95	Alan	Faneca
LG	73	Jacob	Bender
LOLB	87	Calvin	Pace
LOLB	79	Bryan	Thomas
LT	84	D'Brickashaw	Ferguson
LT	68	Clint	Oldenburg
MLB	90	David	Harris
MLB	85	Eric	Barton
P	79	Ben	Graham
QB	81	Chad	Pennington
QB	77	Kellen	Clemens
RE	87	Kenyon	Coleman
RE	72	Kareem	Brown
RG	87	Brandon	Moore
RG	69	Robert	Turner
ROLB	82	Vernon	Gholston
ROLB	68	Matt	Chatham
RT	88	Damien	Woody
RT	68	Wayne	Hunter
SS	96	Kerry	Rhodes
SS	77	Eric	Smith
TE	80	Chris	Baker
TE	80	Dustin	Keller
WR	91	Laveranues	Coles
WR	89	Jerricho	Cotchery
WR	76	Brad	Smith
WR	73	Wallace	Wright

 DETROIT LIONS

POS	OVR	FIRST NAME	LAST NAME
C	87	Dominic	Raiola
C	71	Corey	Hulsey
CB	90	Leigh	Bodden
CB	82	Brian	Kelly
CB	78	Keith	Smith
CB	76	Travis	Fisher
DT	91	Cory	Redding
DT	83	Chuck	Darby
DT	76	Shaun	Cody
FB	78	Jerome	Felton
FB	68	Jon	Bradley
FS	82	Daniel	Bullocks
FS	80	Gerald	Alexander
HB	79	Kevin	Smith
HB	78	Tatum	Bell
K	91	Jason	Hanson
LE	82	Jared	DeVries
LE	76	Ikaika	Alama-Francis
LG	79	Edwin	Mulitalo
LG	75	Manny	Ramirez
LOLB	84	Paris	Lenon
LOLB	74	Alex	Lewis
LT	84	Jeff	Backus
LT	77	Jonathan	Scott
MLB	78	Jordon	Dizon
MLB	69	Buster	Davis
P	81	Nick	Harris
QB	84	Jon	Kitna
QB	77	Drew	Stanton
RE	86	Dewayne	White
RE	79	Corey	Smith
RG	80	Stephen	Peterman
RG	71	Jon	Dunn
ROLB	94	Ernie	Sims
ROLB	68	Anthony	Cannon
RT	79	Gosder	Cherilus
RT	74	George	Foster
SS	86	Dwight	Smith
SS	73	Kalvin	Pearson
TE	79	Michael	Gaines
TE	78	Dan	Campbell
WR	92	Roy	Williams
WR	91	Calvin	Johnson
WR	87	Shaun	McDonald
WR	84	Mike	Furrey

 GREEN BAY PACKERS

POS	OVR	FIRST NAME	LAST NAME
C	86	Scott	Wells
C	72	Allen	Barbre
CB	93	Al	Harris
CB	92	Charles	Woodson
CB	76	Jarrett	Bush
CB	76	Pat	Lee
DT	86	Ryan	Pickett
DT	82	Johnny	Jolly
DT	77	Justin	Harrell
FB	86	Korey	Hall
FB	85	John	Kuhn
FS	86	Nick	Collins
FS	77	Aaron	Rouse
HB	87	Ryan	Grant
HB	81	Brandon	Jackson
K	88	Mason	Crosby
LE	97	Aaron	Kampman
LE	76	Mike	Montgomery
LG	82	Junius	Coston
LG	77	Daryn	Colledge
LOLB	82	Brady	Poppinga
LOLB	80	Brandon	Chillar
LT	95	Chad	Clifton
LT	68	Breno	Giacomini
MLB	94	Nick	Barnett
MLB	75	Abdul	Hodge
P	80	Jon	Ryan
QB	83	Aaron	Rodgers
QB	80	Brian	Brohm
RE	92	Cullen	Jenkins
RE	88	Kabeer	Gbaja Biamila
RG	87	Jason	Spitz
RG	76	Josh	Sitton
ROLB	94	A.J.	Hawk
ROLB	71	Tracy	White
RT	94	Mark	Tauscher
RT	68	Tony	Moll
SS	87	Atari	Bigby
SS	67	Charlie	Peprah
TE	83	Donald	Lee
TE	77	Jermichael	Finley
WR	93	Greg	Jennings
WR	92	Donald	Driver
WR	84	James	Jones
WR	78	Jordy	Nelson

CAROLINA PANTHERS

POS	OVR	FIRST NAME	LAST NAME
C	82	Ryan	Kalil
C	75	Geoff	Hangartner
CB	88	Chris	Gamble
CB	88	Ken	Lucas
CB	83	Richard	Marshall
CB	70	Dante	Wesley
DT	83	Ma'ake	Kemoeatu
DT	78	Darwin	Walker
DT	77	Damione	Lewis
FB	87	Brad	Hoover
FS	77	Nate	Salley
FS	77	Charles	Godfrey
HB	85	DeAngelo	Williams
HB	83	Jonathan	Stewart
HB	76	LaBrandon	Toefield
K	92	John	Kasay
LE	78	Charles	Johnson
LE	77	Tyler	Brayton
LG	88	Travelle	Wharton
LG	79	Evan	Mathis
LOLB	87	Thomas	Davis
LOLB	73	James	Anderson
LT	90	Jordan	Gross
LT	73	Frank	Omiyale
MLB	93	Jon	Beason
MLB	76	Dan	Connor
P	82	Jason	Baker
QB	85	Jake	Delhomme
QB	79	Matt	Moore
RE	96	Julius	Peppers
RE	76	Stanley	McClover
RG	82	Jeremy	Bridges
RG	77	Keydrick	Vincent
ROLB	84	Landon	Johnson
ROLB	80	Na'il	Diggs
RT	78	Jeff	Otah
RT	67	Rueben	Riley
SS	85	Chris	Harris
SS	68	C.J.	Wilson
TE	78	Jeff	King
TE	75	Gary	Barnidge
WR	98	Steve	Smith
WR	86	D.J.	Hackett
WR	84	Muhsin	Muhammad
WR	76	Dwayne	Jarrett

 ## NEW ENGLAND PATRIOTS

POS	OVR	FIRST NAME	LAST NAME
C	95	Dan	Koppen
C	66	Dan	Connolly
CB	87	Ellis	Hobbs
CB	83	Fernando	Bryant
CB	79	Jason	Webster
CB	77	Terrence	Wheatley
DT	94	Vince	Wilfork
DT	81	Mike	Wright
DT	70	Le Kevin	Smith
FB	84	Heath	Evans
FB	78	Kyle	Eckel
FS	86	Brandon	Meriweather
FS	86	James	Sanders
HB	90	Laurence	Maroney
HB	81	Kevin	Faulk
K	92	Stephen	Gostkowski
LE	90	Ty	Warren
LE	67	Santonio	Thomas
LG	96	Logan	Mankins
LG	80	Russ	Hochstein
LOLB	88	Mike	Vrabel
LOLB	71	Pierre	Woods
LT	95	Matt	Light
LT	69	Wesley	Britt
MLB	86	Tedy	Bruschi
MLB	82	Jerod	Mayo
P	74	Chris	Hanson
QB	99	Tom	Brady
QB	76	Matt	Cassel
RE	96	Richard	Seymour
RE	87	Jarvis	Green
RG	94	Stephen	Neal
RG	73	Billy	Yates
ROLB	95	Adalius	Thomas
ROLB	74	Shawn	Crable
RT	86	Nick	Kaczur
RT	77	Ryan	O'Callaghan
SS	94	Rodney	Harrison
SS	78	Tank	Williams
TE	87	Benjamin	Watson
TE	79	Marcus	Pollard
WR	99	Randy	Moss
WR	94	Wes	Welker
WR	82	Jabar	Gaffney
WR	78	Chad	Jackson

 ## OAKLAND RAIDERS

POS	OVR	FIRST NAME	LAST NAME
C	86	John	Wade
C	83	Jake	Grove
CB	96	Nnamdi	Asomugha
CB	93	DeAngelo	Hall
CB	80	Stanford	Routt
CB	72	Tyvon	Branch
DT	91	Tommy	Kelly
DT	83	Terdell	Sands
DT	79	Gerard	Warren
FB	84	Justin	Griffith
FB	80	Oren	O'Neal
FS	87	Michael	Huff
FS	71	Hiram	Eugene
HB	85	Darren	McFadden
HB	85	Justin	Fargas
K	81	Sebastian	Janikowski
LE	92	Derrick	Burgess
LE	76	Kalimba	Edwards
LG	85	Robert	Gallery
LG	66	Chris	Morris
LOLB	79	Robert	Thomas
LOLB	78	Sam	Williams
LT	78	Kwame	Harris
LT	70	Mario	Henderson
MLB	92	Kirk	Morrison
MLB	62	Ricky	Brown
P	97	Shane	Lechler
QB	83	JaMarcus	Russell
QB	76	Andrew	Walter
RE	81	Greg	Spires
RE	72	Jay	Richardson
RG	86	Cooper	Carlisle
RG	81	Paul	McQuistan
ROLB	82	Thomas	Howard
ROLB	67	Jon	Alston
RT	83	Cornell	Green
RT	66	Mark	Wilson
SS	87	Gibril	Wilson
SS	74	Jarrod	Cooper
TE	83	Zach	Miller
TE	77	John	Madsen
WR	87	Javon	Walker
WR	82	Ronald	Curry
WR	76	Drew	Carter
WR	72	Johnnie Lee	Higgins

ST. LOUIS RAMS

POS	OVR	FIRST NAME	LAST NAME
C	79	Brett	Romberg
C	77	Mark	Setterstrom
CB	87	Fakhir	Brown
CB	86	Tye	Hill
CB	77	Ronald	Bartell
CB	75	Jonathan	Wade
DT	89	Adam	Carriker
DT	84	La'Roi	Glover
DT	74	Cliff	Ryan
FB	83	Brian	Leonard
FB	72	Richard	Owens
FS	90	O.J.	Atogwe
FS	73	Jerome	Carter
HB	97	Steven	Jackson
HB	77	Antonio	Pittman
K	91	Josh	Brown
LE	87	Leonard	Little
LE	76	Victor	Adeyanju
LG	94	Jacob	Bell
LOLB	79	Chris	Draft
LOLB	72	Quinton	Culberson
LT	91	Orlando	Pace
LT	77	Adam	Goldberg
MLB	92	Will	Witherspoon
MLB	68	Tim	McGarigle
P	90	Donnie	Jones
QB	89	Marc	Bulger
QB	81	Trent	Green
RE	84	Chris	Long
RE	82	James	Hall
RG	81	Richie	Incognito
RG	75	Nick	Leckey
ROLB	85	Pisa	Tinoisamoa
ROLB	66	Vince	Hall
RT	85	Alex	Barron
RT	76	John	Greco
SS	82	Corey	Chavous
SS	75	Todd	Johnson
TE	84	Randy	McMichael
TE	77	Anthony	Becht
WR	94	Torry	Holt
WR	82	Drew	Bennett
WR	78	Reche	Caldwell
WR	76	Donnie	Avery
WR	75	Keenan	Burton

DEPTH CHARTS

BALTIMORE RAVENS

POS	OVR	FIRST NAME	LAST NAME
C	84	Chris	Chester
C	72	Adrien	Clarke
CB	94	Chris	McAlister
CB	84	Samari	Rolle
CB	77	Fabian	Washington
CB	76	Corey	Ivy
DT	88	Kelly	Gregg
DT	78	Justin	Bannan
DT	66	J'Vonne	Parker
FB	86	Le'Ron	McClain
FS	98	Ed	Reed
FS	72	Haruki	Nakamura
HB	91	Willis	McGahee
HB	80	Ray	Rice
HB	77	Cory	Ross
K	95	Matt	Stover
LE	90	Trevor	Pryce
LE	82	Dwan	Edwards
LG	93	Jason	Brown
LG	73	David	Hale
LOLB	84	Jarret	Johnson
LOLB	81	Antwan	Barnes
LT	79	Adam	Terry
LT	78	Jared	Gaither
MLB	94	Ray	Lewis
MLB	90	Bart	Scott
P	80	Sam	Koch
QB	79	Joe	Flacco
QB	78	Kyle	Boller
RE	91	Haloti	Ngata
RE	68	Amon	Gordon
RG	88	Ben	Grubbs
RG	72	Mike	Kracalik
ROLB	88	Terrell	Suggs
ROLB	77	Gary	Stills
RT	79	Marshal	Yanda
RT	71	Oniel	Cousins
SS	88	Dawan	Landry
SS	74	Tom	Zbikowski
TE	91	Todd	Heap
TE	76	Daniel	Wilcox
WR	87	Derrick	Mason
WR	85	Mark	Clayton
WR	78	Demetrius	Williams
WR	70	Marcus	Smith

WASHINGTON REDSKINS

POS	OVR	FIRST NAME	LAST NAME
C	84	Casey	Rabach
C	67	Justin	Geisinger
CB	89	Carlos	Rogers
CB	88	Shawn	Springs
CB	87	Fred	Smoot
CB	74	Justin	Tyron
DT	88	Cornelius	Griffin
DT	85	Anthony	Montgomery
DT	75	Kedric	Golston
FB	85	Mike	Sellers
FS	76	Stuart	Schweigert
FS	75	Reed	Doughty
HB	91	Clinton	Portis
HB	84	Ladell	Betts
HB	73	Rock	Cartwright
K	82	Shaun	Suisham
LE	84	Phillip	Daniels
LE	72	Demetric	Evans
LG	86	Pete	Kendall
LG	73	Chad	Rinehart
LOLB	89	Marcus	Washington
LOLB	70	Khary	Campbell
LT	96	Chris	Samuels
LT	76	Stephon	Heyer
MLB	96	London	Fletcher-Baker
MLB	74	H.B.	Blades
P	80	Durant	Brooks
QB	86	Jason	Campbell
QB	85	Todd	Collins
RE	88	Andre	Carter
RE	74	Erasmus	James
RG	92	Randy	Thomas
RG	83	Jason	Fabini
ROLB	88	Rocky	McIntosh
ROLB	65	Rian	Wallace
RT	90	Jon	Jansen
RT	78	Todd	Wade
SS	93	LaRon	Landry
SS	71	Vernon	Fox
TE	92	Chris	Cooley
TE	77	Fred	Davis
WR	87	Santana	Moss
WR	83	Antwaan	Randle El
WR	81	Malcolm	Kelly
WR	80	Devin	Thomas

NEW ORLEANS SAINTS

POS	OVR	FIRST NAME	LAST NAME
C	78	Matt	Lehr
C	75	Jonathan	Goodwin
CB	89	Mike	McKenzie
CB	82	Randall	Gay
CB	78	Jason	Craft
CB	76	Tracy	Porter
DT	85	Brian	Young
DT	84	Sedrick	Ellis
DT	80	Hollis	Thomas
FB	85	Mike	Karney
FS	81	Josh	Bullocks
FS	81	Kevin	Kaesviharn
HB	86	Deuce	McAllister
HB	86	Reggie	Bush
HB	79	Aaron	Stecker
K	85	Martin	Gramatica
LE	87	Charles	Grant
LE	66	Josh	Savage
LG	82	Jamar	Nesbit
LG	79	Andy	Alleman
LOLB	84	Scott	Fujita
LOLB	83	Mark	Simoneau
LT	94	Jammal	Brown
LT	72	Jermon	Bushrod
MLB	91	Jonathan	Vilma
MLB	64	Marvin	Mitchell
P	78	Steve	Weatherford
QB	94	Drew	Brees
QB	77	Mark	Brunell
RE	90	Will	Smith
RE	80	Bobby	McCray
RG	84	Jahri	Evans
RG	69	Tim	Duckworth
ROLB	80	Scott	Shanle
ROLB	64	Troy	Evans
RT	82	Jon	Stinchcomb
RT	72	Carl	Nicks
SS	79	Roman	Harper
SS	69	Chris	Reis
TE	80	Eric	Johnson
TE	77	Mark	Campbell
WR	94	Marques	Colston
WR	81	David	Patten
WR	79	Lance	Moore
WR	77	Robert	Meachem

SEATTLE SEAHAWKS

POS	OVR	FIRST NAME	LAST NAME
C	82	Chris	Spencer
C	77	Chris	Gray
CB	88	Kelly	Jennings
CB	79	Jordan	Babineaux
CB	77	Josh	Wilson
CB	94	Marcus	Trufant
DT	87	Rocky	Bernard
DT	83	Marcus	Tubbs
DT	80	Brandon	Mebane
FB	88	Leonard	Weaver
FB	76	Owen	Schmitt
FS	87	Deon	Grant
FS	68	C.J.	Wallace
HB	84	Julius	Jones
HB	80	Maurice	Morris
K	79	Olindo	Mare
LE	95	Patrick	Kerney
LE	77	Baraka	Atkins
LG	90	Mike	Wahle
LG	68	Steve	Vallos
LOLB	89	LeRoy	Hill
LOLB	69	Lance	Laury
LT	95	Walter	Jones
LT	73	Floyd	Womack
MLB	97	Lofa	Tatupu
MLB	75	D.D.	Lewis
P	75	Ryan	Plackemeier
QB	91	Matt	Hasselbeck
QB	82	Seneca	Wallace
RE	83	Darryl	Tapp
RE	78	Lawrence	Jackson
RG	80	Rob	Sims
RG	76	Mansfield	Wrotto
ROLB	95	Julian	Peterson
ROLB	69	Will	Herring
RT	86	Sean	Locklear
RT	72	Ray	Willis
SS	86	Brian	Russell
SS	80	Mike	Green
TE	79	John	Carlson
TE	66	Will	Heller
WR	87	Bobby	Engram
WR	87	Deion	Branch
WR	83	Nate	Burleson
WR	73	Ben	Obomanu

PITTSBURGH STEELERS

POS	OVR	FIRST NAME	LAST NAME
C	85	Justin	Hartwig
C	79	Sean	Mahan
CB	89	Ike	Taylor
CB	89	Deshea	Townsend
CB	84	Bryant	McFadden
CB	71	William	Gay
DT	96	Casey	Hampton
DT	82	Chris	Hoke
DT	69	Scott	Paxson
FB	83	Carey	Davis
FS	83	Ryan	Clark
FS	75	Anthony	Smith
HB	93	Willie	Parker
HB	81	Rashard	Mendenhall
HB	80	Najeh	Davenport
K	84	Jeff	Reed
LE	94	Aaron	Smith
LE	75	Travis	Kirschke
LG	76	Chris	Kemoeatu
LG	69	Darnell	Stapleton
LOLB	79	LaMarr	Woodley
LOLB	70	Arnold	Harrison
LT	88	Marvel	Smith
LT	77	Trai	Essex
MLB	92	James	Farrior
MLB	86	Larry	Foote
P	79	Daniel	Sepulveda
QB	95	Ben	Roethlisberger
QB	78	Charlie	Batch
RE	84	Brett	Keisel
RE	70	Nick	Eason
RG	87	Kendall	Simmons
RG	69	Matt	Lentz
ROLB	93	James	Harrison
ROLB	75	Bruce	Davis
RT	83	Willie	Colon
RT	81	Max	Starks
SS	98	Troy	Polamalu
SS	76	Tyrone	Carter
TE	92	Heath	Miller
TE	73	Matt	Spaeth
WR	90	Hines	Ward
WR	85	Santonio	Holmes
WR	80	Limas	Sweed
WR	77	Nate	Washington

 ## HOUSTON TEXANS

POS	OVR	FIRST NAME	LAST NAME
C	80	Chris	Myers
C	71	Chris	White
CB	87	Dunta	Robinson
CB	82	Fred	Bennett
CB	77	Jacques	Reeves
CB	74	DeMarcus	Faggins
DT	92	Amobi	Okoye
DT	76	Travis	Johnson
DT	75	Anthony	Maddox
FB	81	Vonta	Leach
FS	82	Will	Demps
FS	75	Nick	Ferguson
HB	82	Ahman	Green
HB	79	Chris	Brown
HB	76	Darius	Walker
K	88	Kris	Brown
LE	80	Anthony	Weaver
LE	71	Earl	Cochran
LG	83	Chester	Pitts
LG	73	Kasey	Studdard
LOLB	74	Zac	Diles
LOLB	74	Kevin	Bentley
LT	78	Ephraim	Salaam
LT	76	Duane	Brown
MLB	95	DeMeco	Ryans
MLB	69	Ben	Moffitt
P	77	Matt	Turk
QB	85	Matt	Schaub
QB	79	Sage	Rosenfels
RE	97	Mario	Williams
RE	78	N.D.	Kalu
RG	77	Fred	Weary
RG	77	Mike	Brisiel
ROLB	89	Morlon	Greenwood
ROLB	75	Chaun	Thompson
RT	82	Eric	Winston
RT	72	Rashad	Butler
SS	79	Glenn	Earl
SS	78	C.C.	Brown
TE	88	Owen	Daniels
TE	74	Mark	Bruener
WR	96	Andre	Johnson
WR	80	Kevin	Walter
WR	78	Andre	Davis
WR	76	Jacoby	Jones

 ## TENNESSEE TITANS

POS	OVR	FIRST NAME	LAST NAME
C	94	Kevin	Mawae
C	65	Jason	Murphy
CB	88	Cortland	Finnegan
CB	88	Nick	Harper
CB	75	Reynaldo	Hill
CB	71	Eric	King
DT	98	Albert	Haynesworth
DT	86	Tony	Brown
DT	73	Kevin	Vickerson
FB	84	Ahmard	Hall
FS	88	Michael	Griffin
FS	78	Vincent	Fuller
HB	84	LenDale	White
HB	78	Chris	Henry
HB	77	Chris	Johnson
K	91	Rob	Bironas
LE	81	Bryce	Fisher
LE	81	Jevon	Kearse
LG	77	Leroy	Harris
LG	77	Eugene	Amano
LOLB	89	David	Thornton
LOLB	67	Josh	Stamer
LT	88	Michael	Roos
LT	75	Daniel	Loper
MLB	79	Ryan	Fowler
MLB	79	Stephen	Tulloch
P	77	Craig	Hentrich
QB	88	Vince	Young
QB	79	Kerry	Collins
RE	93	Kyle	Vanden Bosch
RE	74	Jason	Jones
RG	92	Jake	Scott
RG	68	Enoka	Lucas
ROLB	97	Keith	Bulluck
ROLB	75	Stanford	Keglar
RT	88	David	Stewart
RT	66	Michael	Otto
SS	92	Chris	Hope
SS	77	Calvin	Lowry
TE	86	Alge	Crumpler
TE	81	Bo	Scaife
WR	80	Brandon	Jones
WR	80	Justin	Gage
WR	79	Roydell	Williams
WR	77	Justin	McCareins

 ## MINNESOTA VIKINGS

POS	OVR	FIRST NAME	LAST NAME
C	95	Matt	Birk
C	73	John	Sullivan
CB	91	Antoine	Winfield
CB	83	Cedric	Griffin
CB	79	Marcus	McCauley
CB	77	Charles	Gordon
DT	98	Pat	Williams
DT	97	Kevin	Williams
DT	76	Ellis	Wyms
FB	85	Thomas	Tapeh
FS	88	Madieu	Williams
FS	80	Tyrell	Johnson
HB	95	Adrian	Peterson
HB	88	Chester	Taylor
HB	76	Maurice	Hicks
K	90	Ryan	Longwell
LE	83	Ray	Edwards
LE	70	Jayme	Mitchell
LG	98	Steve	Hutchinson
LG	70	Brian	Daniels
LOLB	81	Ben	Leber
LOLB	69	Vinny	Ciurciu
LT	96	Bryant	McKinnie
LT	65	Chase	Johnson
MLB	92	E.J.	Henderson
MLB	69	Derrick	Pope
P	82	Chris	Kluwe
QB	79	Tarvaris	Jackson
QB	77	Gus	Frerotte
RE	97	Jared	Allen
RE	82	Brian	Robison
RG	88	Anthony	Herrera
RG	80	Artis	Hicks
ROLB	87	Chad	Greenway
ROLB	71	Rufus	Alexander
RT	87	Ryan	Cook
RT	73	Marcus	Johnson
SS	92	Darren	Sharper
SS	79	Michael	Boulware
TE	79	Visanthe	Shiancoe
TE	78	Jim	Kleinsasser
WR	85	Bernard	Berrian
WR	83	Sidney	Rice
WR	81	Bobby	Wade
WR	77	Robert	Ferguson

DEPTH CHARTS

The following offensive and defensive lists include every player who is rated approximately 75 or above in his position, and have been sorted by overall rating. However, the overall rating is just a starting point. Each list includes additional attributes related to the position. Consider these attributes when you search for the perfect player to complement your team.

Centers (C)

OVR	FIRST NAME	LAST NAME	RUN BLOCK STRENGTH	RUN BLOCK FOOTWORK	PASS BLOCK STRENGTH	PASS BLOCK FOOTWORK
96	Jeff	Saturday	90	94	96	97
95	Matt	Birk	92	96	90	94
95	Dan	Koppen	90	92	95	97
94	Andre	Gurode	95	86	94	70
94	Nick	Hardwick	95	88	89	88
94	Kevin	Mawae	91	92	93	90
93	Olin	Kreutz	90	90	92	92
93	Nick	Mangold	88	92	92	92
93	Brad	Meester	95	94	92	90
92	Jamaal	Jackson	94	78	84	86
92	Shaun	O'Hara	92	88	93	92
89	Hank	Fraley	94	78	91	75
89	Tom	Nalen	83	88	82	90
88	Jeff	Faine	84	85	87	92
88	Samson	Satele	90	80	88	85
87	Dominic	Raiola	84	88	86	85
86	John	Wade	87	75	88	76
86	Scott	Wells	82	79	82	89
85	Justin	Hartwig	90	86	88	84
85	Eric	Heitmann	88	77	85	73
85	Jeremy	Newberry	92	84	87	78
85	Casey	Wiegmann	82	89	82	90
84	Chris	Chester	84	89	80	87
84	Casey	Rabach	89	76	85	80
83	Melvin	Fowler	87	79	85	76
83	Jake	Grove	87	87	87	83
82	LeCharles	Bentley	88	70	87	65
82	Mike	Flynn	86	78	86	72
80	Mike	Flanagan	85	87	86	93
80	Al	Johnson	86	69	84	65
79	Brett	Romberg	85	85	85	85
78	Matt	Lehr	84	76	82	73
77	Chris	Gray	82	68	84	68
77	Mark	Setterstrom	80	88	78	86
77	Cory	Withrow	86	78	82	74
76	Dan	Buenning	88	74	85	69
76	Rudy	Niswanger	85	75	80	72
75	Jonathan	Goodwin	83	68	83	68
75	Geoff	Hangartner	84	78	82	78
75	Grey	Ruegamer	85	55	80	64

Fullbacks (FB)

OVR	FIRST NAME	LAST NAME	SPEED	RUN BLOCK	PASS BLOCK	IMPACT BLOCK
92	Lawrence	Vickers	78	72	50	90
91	Greg	Jones	86	62	50	85
90	Ovie	Mughelli	66	74	48	90
90	Tony	Richardson	82	63	50	82
89	Reagan	Mauia	82	72	45	86
88	Madison	Hedgecock	70	74	57	90
88	Terrelle	Smith	66	78	60	92
88	Leonard	Weaver	86	62	50	66
87	B.J.	Askew	82	67	55	75
87	Brad	Hoover	78	64	54	70
87	Jeremi	Johnson	72	70	52	85
87	Lorenzo	Neal	65	82	54	98
86	Korey	Hall	80	68	48	87
86	Le'Ron	McClain	77	70	50	82
85	Mike	Karney	77	65	51	82
85	John	Kuhn	78	63	52	78
85	Moran	Norris	74	74	48	85
85	Mike	Sellers	72	70	64	80
85	Thomas	Tapeh	82	60	50	75
84	Heath	Evans	85	58	52	70
84	Justin	Griffith	80	60	52	72
84	Ahmard	Hall	77	65	54	90
84	Jason	McKie	74	68	55	88
83	Deon	Anderson	78	66	47	79
83	Carey	Davis	85	58	44	65
83	Brian	Leonard	86	54	48	60
81	Dan	Kreider	63	74	50	96
81	Vonta	Leach	70	66	52	82
80	Oren	O'Neal	76	73	40	82
79	Cecil	Sapp	86	54	47	66
79	Jacob	Tamme	87	52	54	65
78	Darian	Barnes	66	68	52	90
78	Mike	Bell	87	55	48	55
78	Jameel	Cook	74	63	55	76
78	Kyle	Eckel	78	60	52	65
78	Jerome	Felton	76	60	40	72
78	Oliver	Hoyte	74	68	52	80
76	Peyton	Hillis	87	54	48	64
76	Andrew	Pinnock	75	63	45	75
76	Owen	Schmitt	78	62	44	78

OFFENSIVE PLAYER LIST

Halfbacks (HB)

OVR	FIRST NAME	LAST NAME	SPEED	AGILITY	TRUCKING	ELUSIVENESS
99	LaDainian	Tomlinson	96	99	92	99
97	Steven	Jackson	90	93	98	92
97	Brian	Westbrook	97	98	78	98
95	Adrian	Peterson	96	98	92	99
94	Larry	Johnson	92	90	97	85
94	Fred	Taylor	93	94	93	93
93	Marion	Barber	92	94	99	85
93	Frank	Gore	92	93	92	88
93	Willie	Parker	97	94	85	90
92	Ronnie	Brown	91	91	94	84
92	Edgerrin	James	88	90	92	89
91	Joseph	Addai	93	93	84	94
91	Maurice	Jones-Drew	95	95	95	93
91	Willis	McGahee	92	93	93	79
91	Clinton	Portis	93	94	88	91
90	Jamal	Lewis	92	86	97	70
90	Marshawn	Lynch	93	93	95	86
90	Laurence	Maroney	93	90	94	82
88	Thomas	Jones	90	90	90	82
88	Chester	Taylor	90	94	86	87
88	Michael	Turner	92	86	94	78
87	Ryan	Grant	93	88	92	77
87	Brandon	Jacobs	90	87	98	80
86	Reggie	Bush	97	99	66	96
86	Deuce	McAllister	89	86	93	72
85	Warrick	Dunn	92	94	65	88
85	Carnell	Williams	92	93	84	88
85	DeAngelo	Williams	93	94	80	95
84	Shaun	Alexander	84	78	94	70
83	Dominic	Rhodes	89	91	88	80
83	Jonathan	Stewart	93	93	90	82
83	Ricky	Williams	90	88	84	80
82	Ahmad	Bradshaw	93	95	83	86
82	Correll	Buckhalter	91	88	88	74
81	Rashard	Mendenhall	92	92	91	80
81	Sammy	Morris	87	84	88	78
81	Michael	Pittman	89	86	85	80
81	Derrick	Ward	89	90	84	85
80	Cedric	Benson	87	84	87	80
79	Chris	Brown	88	86	80	78
79	Michael	Bush	89	86	87	77
78	Pierre	Thomas	91	92	77	86
77	Tashard	Choice	90	88	82	80
76	LaBrandon	Toefield	87	85	84	74
75	Gary	Russell	87	90	86	76

Left Guard (LG)

OVR	FIRST NAME	LAST NAME	RUN BLOCK STRENGTH	RUN BLOCK FOOTWORK	PASS BLOCK STRENGTH	PASS BLOCK FOOTWORK
98	Steve	Hutchinson	99	93	90	84
96	Logan	Mankins	90	96	96	97
95	Alan	Faneca	95	92	90	86
95	Eric	Steinbach	93	96	95	95
94	Jacob	Bell	90	93	89	84
94	Kris	Dielman	94	88	90	86
94	Vince	Manuwai	96	88	92	82
93	Jason	Brown	95	88	90	80
91	Derrick	Dockery	96	85	88	75
91	Rich	Seubert	93	88	91	82
91	Brian	Waters	95	87	92	82
90	Ryan	Lilja	85	93	89	92
90	Mike	Wahle	87	88	87	93
89	Kyle	Kosier	89	84	89	80
89	Justin	Smiley	92	85	90	78
88	Todd	Herremans	88	86	89	82
88	Travelle	Wharton	88	88	89	90
87	Ben	Hamilton	80	88	84	86
86	Pete	Kendall	84	84	88	84
85	Robert	Gallery	90	85	89	75
85	Arron	Sears	90	82	91	80
85	Reggie	Wells	86	84	86	82
84	Ruben	Brown	90	65	92	55
83	Stacy	Andrews	92	70	88	72
83	Chester	Pitts	87	86	85	82
82	Junius	Coston	91	70	88	70
82	Jamar	Nesbit	84	78	87	78
82	Adam	Snyder	87	85	85	78
82	Andrew	Whitworth	93	80	91	78
80	Russ	Hochstein	84	75	87	78
79	Andy	Alleman	82	78	84	80
79	Lennie	Friedman	85	70	80	78
78	Josh	Beekman	88	82	86	80
78	Anthony	Davis	89	76	84	76
78	Terrence	Metcalf	87	70	85	68
78	Chilo	Rachal	92	76	89	70
77	Eugene	Amano	82	66	82	65
77	Leroy	Harris	87	77	88	72
77	Pat	McQuistan	86	78	88	74
76	Dylan	Gandy	82	73	84	80
76	Chris	Kemoeatu	91	71	85	67
76	Claude	Terrell	90	80	85	70
75	Quinn	Ojinnaka	80	66	84	70
75	Manny	Ramirez	92	65	85	58
75	Scott	Young	84	65	84	64

OFFENSIVE STRATEGY

ROSTER ATTRIBUTES

Left Tackle (LT)

OVR	FIRST NAME	LAST NAME	RUN BLOCK STRENGTH	RUN BLOCK FOOTWORK	PASS BLOCK STRENGTH	PASS BLOCK FOOTWORK
97	Jason	Peters	92	89	97	96
97	Joe	Thomas	96	97	97	97
96	Bryant	McKinnie	98	92	97	90
96	Chris	Samuels	96	88	95	89
95	Chad	Clifton	93	88	95	92
95	Walter	Jones	95	90	94	90
95	Matt	Light	91	94	97	98
95	William	Thomas	96	92	95	93
94	Flozell	Adams	98	88	98	83
94	Jammal	Brown	93	89	95	92
93	David	Diehl	92	88	93	86
93	Marcus	McNeill	97	92	95	89
91	Orlando	Pace	92	88	95	85
90	Khalif	Barnes	93	92	93	91
90	Jordan	Gross	88	91	91	92
88	Levi	Jones	90	88	92	87
88	Michael	Roos	93	88	92	92
88	Marvel	Smith	93	88	92	72
88	Tony	Ugoh	90	84	91	80
87	Luke	Petitgout	86	85	91	86
86	Mike	Gandy	89	78	89	72
86	Joe	Staley	85	94	90	93
85	Jake	Long	95	88	92	77
84	Jeff	Backus	88	78	91	75
84	D'Brickashaw	Ferguson	88	80	89	80
84	Wayne	Gandy	90	71	89	70
83	Barry	Sims	89	79	90	74
81	Branden	Albert	90	84	92	82
80	Roman	Oben	87	65	86	65
79	Ryan	Clady	86	83	91	82
78	Sam	Baker	88	84	91	86
78	Doug	Free	84	80	87	85
78	Jared	Gaither	88	75	92	85
78	Kwame	Harris	86	84	88	80
78	Ephraim	Salaam	85	80	87	85
77	Trai	Essex	84	76	88	76
77	Adam	Goldberg	85	64	86	60
77	Jonathan	Scott	80	85	87	85
76	Duane	Brown	89	79	93	83
76	Stephon	Heyer	88	70	90	60
76	Winston	Justice	87	80	85	65
76	Donald	Penn	85	67	86	66
75	Will	Svitek	85	85	86	85
75	Guy	Whimper	80	84	84	82
75	Daniel	Loper	80	75	85	74

Quarterback (QB)

OVR	FIRST NAME	LAST NAME	SPEED	AWARENESS	THROW POWER	THROW ACCURACY
99	Tom	Brady	64	100	99	99
99	Peyton	Manning	59	100	96	99
96	Carson	Palmer	54	93	97	95
95	Ben	Roethlisberger	73	87	95	91
94	Drew	Brees	65	88	90	96
94	Tony	Romo	78	80	90	96
93	Eli	Manning	61	88	93	94
92	David	Garrard	77	77	93	93
92	Donovan	McNabb	77	83	95	85
91	Matt	Hasselbeck	66	88	88	93
90	Jeff	Garcia	74	88	87	88
90	Philip	Rivers	64	87	87	95
89	Marc	Bulger	55	86	90	94
88	Vince	Young	90	70	93	84
87	Derek	Anderson	58	77	96	89
86	Jason	Campbell	69	77	93	85
86	Jay	Cutler	74	70	95	86
85	Todd	Collins	52	86	86	92
85	Jake	Delhomme	63	82	88	88
85	Matt	Leinart	60	78	87	92
85	Matt	Schaub	62	78	88	92
85	Kurt	Warner	46	88	88	92
84	Jon	Kitna	60	78	89	89
83	Aaron	Rodgers	66	72	90	88
83	JaMarcus	Russell	72	59	98	87
83	Matt	Ryan	63	72	93	87
82	Brady	Quinn	71	69	89	86
82	Chris	Redman	56	78	87	90
82	Billy	Volek	55	78	90	88
82	Seneca	Wallace	85	72	84	82
81	Trent	Green	48	83	86	90
81	Chad	Pennington	55	78	82	94
80	Brian	Brohm	64	65	91	88
80	Daunte	Culpepper	65	70	94	80
80	Charlie	Frye	72	70	85	86
79	Kerry	Collins	47	79	92	82
79	Trent	Edwards	63	65	90	87
79	Joe	Flacco	66	60	97	83
79	Rex	Grossman	57	66	95	84
79	Joey	Harrington	62	72	88	84
79	Shaun	Hill	64	70	87	87
79	Tarvaris	Jackson	86	58	94	78
79	J.P.	Losman	70	64	94	80
79	Josh	McCown	79	65	87	83
79	Matt	Moore	69	69	88	83

OFFENSIVE **PLAYER LIST**

Quarterback (QB) *CONTINUED*

OVR	FIRST NAME	LAST NAME	SPEED	AWARENESS	THROW POWER	THROW ACCURACY
79	Patrick	Ramsey	55	75	92	81
79	Sage	Rosenfels	60	74	87	86
79	Alex	Smith	72	67	89	83
78	Charlie	Batch	50	80	86	84
78	John	Beck	64	64	89	86
78	Kyle	Boller	69	69	92	78
78	Brodie	Croyle	55	66	93	85
78	Damon	Huard	57	75	86	86
78	Brad	Johnson	46	84	84	87
78	Kevin	Kolb	66	60	90	87
78	Tim	Rattay	52	74	86	87
77	John David	Booty	58	65	89	86
77	Mark	Brunell	60	76	85	82
77	Kellen	Clemens	66	62	93	82
77	Gus	Frerotte	52	78	86	84
77	Brian	Griese	53	73	87	86
77	Chad	Henne	60	63	95	82
77	Cleo	Lemon	65	70	84	85
77	Luke	McCown	78	66	87	80
77	J.T.	O'Sullivan	58	68	87	86
77	Chris	Simms	63	70	88	83
77	Drew	Stanton	66	61	90	85
76	Aaron	Brooks	72	62	92	78
76	David	Carr	68	60	89	84
76	Matt	Cassel	64	68	86	82
76	A.J.	Feeley	54	70	87	85
76	Quinn	Gray	71	66	90	78
76	Craig	Nall	60	68	88	84
76	Kyle	Orton	59	72	85	84
76	Andrew	Walter	54	62	92	86
75	Ryan	Fitzpatrick	60	66	86	84
75	Byron	Leftwich	54	65	95	80
75	Anthony	Wright	69	70	86	77

Right Guard (RG)

OVR	FIRST NAME	LAST NAME	RUN BLOCK STRENGTH	RUN BLOCK FOOTWORK	PASS BLOCK STRENGTH	PASS BLOCK FOOTWORK
97	Leonard	Davis	99	85	92	76
96	Shawn	Andrews	99	79	95	79
95	Chris	Snee	95	89	92	89
94	Stephen	Neal	88	89	93	94
93	Davin	Joseph	92	92	92	87

Right Guard (RG) *CONTINUED*

OVR	FIRST NAME	LAST NAME	RUN BLOCK STRENGTH	RUN BLOCK FOOTWORK	PASS BLOCK STRENGTH	PASS BLOCK FOOTWORK
92	Jake	Scott	84	94	91	93
92	Randy	Thomas	87	92	93	92
91	Maurice	Williams	94	87	91	82
90	Rex	Hadnot	90	85	88	75
88	Mike	Goff	92	78	88	75
88	Ben	Grubbs	93	92	90	82
88	Anthony	Herrera	93	82	87	72
88	Chris	Naeole	95	75	82	60
87	Brandon	Moore	88	85	87	82
87	Kendall	Simmons	91	87	89	75
87	Jason	Spitz	89	88	88	92
86	Cooper	Carlisle	82	92	87	88
86	Bobbie	Williams	90	76	87	79
85	Kynan	Forney	88	79	87	74
85	Roberto	Garza	86	84	85	84
84	David	Baas	87	85	87	74
84	Jahri	Evans	86	82	87	83
83	Brad	Butler	86	78	88	75
83	Jason	Fabini	88	80	86	79
82	Jeremy	Bridges	88	82	88	78
81	Richie	Incognito	87	78	85	68
81	Paul	McQuistan	85	70	89	65
80	Artis	Hicks	88	68	82	70
80	Max	Jean-Gilles	92	68	88	60
80	Stephen	Peterman	88	70	85	65
80	Rob	Sims	84	78	84	72
79	Montrae	Holland	90	65	86	62
79	Deuce	Lutui	90	86	86	80
79	Mike	McGlynn	90	77	90	76
78	Kevin	Boothe	88	69	83	65
78	Adrian	Jones	84	75	86	70
78	Mike	Pollak	87	84	86	82
78	Duke	Preston	84	83	86	82
78	John	Welbourn	84	70	84	70
78	Jeremy	Zuttah	92	80	90	70
77	Mike	Brisiel	87	85	88	80
77	Charlie	Johnson	82	65	84	75
77	Seth	McKinney	85	69	84	73
77	Steve	McKinney	83	65	82	80
76	Shawn	Murphy	85	75	84	70
76	Josh	Sitton	90	82	88	76
76	Herb	Taylor	80	85	85	85
76	Mansfield	Wrotto	88	68	85	65
75	Nick	Leckey	84	66	81	65
75	Roy	Schuening	91	72	87	68

ROSTER ATTRIBUTES

ROSTER ATTRIBUTES

Right Tackle (RT)

OVR	FIRST NAME	LAST NAME	RUN BLOCK STRENGTH	RUN BLOCK FOOTWORK	PASS BLOCK STRENGTH	PASS BLOCK FOOTWORK
94	Mark	Tauscher	93	89	96	90
93	Ryan	Diem	91	91	91	94
93	Kareem	McKenzie	93	88	96	80
92	Willie	Anderson	94	85	92	79
90	Jon	Jansen	93	79	90	78
90	Jon	Runyan	94	85	91	75
89	Kevin	Shaffer	90	87	90	92
88	Marc	Colombo	90	85	93	70
88	Jonas	Jennings	93	85	90	70
88	David	Stewart	94	85	93	79
88	Damien	Woody	92	82	93	79
87	Vernon	Carey	90	82	93	86
87	Ryan	Cook	93	86	91	74
87	Tony	Pashos	94	86	91	74
87	Jeremy	Trueblood	90	85	93	78
86	Nick	Kaczur	87	80	92	74
86	Sean	Locklear	86	84	91	80
86	Langston	Walker	92	78	91	72
85	Alex	Barron	90	87	92	86
85	Levi	Brown	93	87	91	82
85	Fred	Miller	90	89	88	76
85	John	Tait	90	80	90	74
84	Ryan	Tucker	91	82	89	78
84	Todd	Weiner	92	82	90	84
83	Willie	Colon	89	70	88	72
83	Cornell	Green	89	77	88	72
82	Jon	Stinchcomb	85	75	87	80
82	Eric	Winston	79	88	85	87
81	Shane	Olivea	90	85	87	78
81	Max	Starks	90	66	88	60
80	Jeromey	Clary	86	75	88	74
80	Damion	McIntosh	88	75	90	65
79	Gosder	Cherilus	92	77	90	65
79	Oliver	Ross	88	67	84	60
79	Marshal	Yanda	85	79	87	82
78	Ryan	Harris	84	75	89	75
78	Jeff	Otah	92	75	91	70
78	Todd	Wade	92	74	84	69
77	James	Marten	82	74	88	70
77	Ryan	O'Callaghan	90	64	90	58
76	John	Greco	91	82	88	80
76	Seth	Wand	85	70	84	70
75	Tyson	Clabo	85	85	85	85
75	Scott	Kooistra	86	69	85	66
75	L.J.	Shelton	91	78	86	78

Tight End (TE)

OVR	FIRST NAME	LAST NAME	SPEED	CATCH	RUN BLOCK	PASS BLOCK
99	Antonio	Gates	88	90	58	52
98	Tony	Gonzalez	86	94	55	50
97	Kellen	Winslow	85	87	58	53
97	Jason	Witten	84	85	59	52
95	Jeremy	Shockey	84	85	58	55
93	Dallas	Clark	88	91	52	54
92	Chris	Cooley	85	88	55	55
92	Heath	Miller	82	87	59	55
91	Todd	Heap	82	87	58	52
88	Owen	Daniels	85	85	55	52
87	Vernon	Davis	92	84	53	49
87	Benjamin	Watson	89	83	53	49
86	Desmond	Clark	79	86	60	55
86	Alge	Crumpler	78	82	60	50
86	Daniel	Graham	77	78	63	51
85	Greg	Olsen	87	85	55	53
85	L.J.	Smith	79	84	58	53
84	Marcedes	Lewis	82	82	59	55
84	Randy	McMichael	82	80	57	55
84	Tony	Scheffler	85	85	56	55
83	Donald	Lee	82	79	58	50
83	Zach	Miller	78	85	50	48
83	Alex	Smith	79	83	56	54
82	Anthony	Fasano	75	76	60	52
81	Reggie	Kelly	72	79	60	57
81	Bo	Scaife	83	85	54	50
81	Ben	Utecht	75	83	54	50
80	Chris	Baker	78	82	60	58
80	Martellus	Bennett	84	80	55	53
80	Kevin	Boss	79	82	58	52
80	Eric	Johnson	77	87	55	52
80	Dustin	Keller	89	82	48	44
80	Kris	Wilson	81	82	53	50
80	George	Wrighster	78	79	54	52
79	Kyle	Brady	66	65	70	58
79	John	Carlson	77	80	59	57
79	Michael	Gaines	78	77	60	53
79	Steve	Heiden	74	82	59	55
78	Bubba	Franks	64	72	60	50
78	Jeff	King	76	76	62	58
78	Jim	Kleinsasser	70	70	70	52
77	Jermichael	Finley	85	82	52	52
76	Troy	Bienemann	78	75	62	60
76	Brad	Cottam	85	78	54	52
75	Gary	Barnidge	86	82	52	48

OFFENSIVE **PLAYER LIST**

Wide Receivers (WR)

OVR	FIRST NAME	LAST NAME	SPEED	CATCH	CATCH IN TRAFFIC	ROUTE RUNNING
99	Randy	Moss	98	97	88	94
98	Terrell	Owens	96	89	97	96
98	Steve	Smith	97	95	95	93
97	Larry	Fitzgerald	93	95	95	96
97	Chad	Johnson	96	94	90	97
97	Reggie	Wayne	91	97	94	97
96	Plaxico	Burress	93	92	90	93
96	Andre	Johnson	95	90	92	94
95	Anquan	Boldin	91	93	99	92
95	Braylon	Edwards	93	89	88	93
95	T.J.	Houshmandzadeh	90	98	99	95
94	Marques	Colston	87	94	97	91
94	Marvin	Harrison	92	97	91	99
94	Torry	Holt	93	97	81	98
94	Wes	Welker	93	92	95	97
93	Greg	Jennings	96	90	88	92
93	Brandon	Marshall	92	89	90	88
92	Donald	Driver	93	90	90	93
92	Roy	Williams	92	92	86	87
91	Chris	Chambers	94	88	87	87
91	Laveranues	Coles	97	91	95	86
91	Lee	Evans	98	88	85	88
91	Calvin	Johnson	97	86	87	90
90	Dwayne	Bowe	93	86	90	88
90	Hines	Ward	87	93	97	90
89	Jerricho	Cotchery	89	93	94	85
89	Vincent	Jackson	93	89	88	82
89	Roddy	White	93	84	86	93
88	Joey	Galloway	97	88	82	85
87	Deion	Branch	92	86	85	92
87	Kevin	Curtis	96	87	84	88
87	Bobby	Engram	88	90	82	94
87	Derrick	Mason	88	93	84	88
87	Shaun	McDonald	94	89	84	90
87	Santana	Moss	97	86	81	88
87	Javon	Walker	91	87	87	88
86	Reggie	Brown	91	88	82	84
86	Terry	Glenn	92	94	78	85
86	D.J.	Hackett	89	88	84	89
86	Darrell	Jackson	89	88	82	90
86	Jerry	Porter	91	84	82	88
86	Amani	Toomer	88	88	88	87
85	Santonio	Holmes	96	82	78	86
85	Donte	Stallworth	97	84	74	84
84	Mike	Furrey	89	89	84	85

Wide Receivers (WR) *CONTINUED*

OVR	FIRST NAME	LAST NAME	SPEED	CATCH	CATCH IN TRAFFIC	ROUTE RUNNING
84	James	Jones	91	87	85	85
84	Muhsin	Muhammad	85	90	84	90
84	Brandon	Stokley	90	87	87	87
84	Ernest	Wilford	86	87	88	85
83	Nate	Burleson	92	81	81	85
83	Joe	Jurevicius	85	90	92	80
83	Eddie	Kennison	90	87	80	87
83	Reggie	Williams	90	82	82	86
82	Arnaz	Battle	89	88	78	79
82	Drew	Bennett	87	84	78	84
82	Marty	Booker	86	85	85	82
82	Patrick	Crayton	91	94	79	76
82	Ronald	Curry	89	86	74	82
82	Chris	Henry	93	84	77	82
82	Bryant	Johnson	92	87	80	82
81	Devin	Hester	100	83	70	80
80	Ike	Hilliard	87	86	76	84
80	Brandon	Jones	91	85	82	80
80	Eric	Moulds	86	84	84	84
80	Laurent	Robinson	92	84	80	84
80	Limas	Sweed	93	85	84	78
80	Devin	Thomas	94	83	84	76
80	Kevin	Walter	88	86	85	81
79	Earl	Bennett	93	85	79	86
79	Buster	Davis	93	82	82	79
79	Harry	Douglas	91	83	80	83
79	James	Hardy	93	82	83	81
79	Joe	Horn	86	82	78	84
79	Michael	Jenkins	89	86	70	77
79	Lance	Moore	93	83	72	80
79	Eric	Parker	90	84	84	82
79	Koren	Robinson	93	83	74	78
79	Maurice	Stovall	88	84	79	77
79	Roydell	Williams	90	83	79	79
78	Reche	Caldwell	90	85	70	80
78	Michael	Clayton	86	80	78	81
78	Andre	Davis	96	80	70	80
78	DeSean	Jackson	97	80	77	82
77	Josh	Reed	86	86	84	80
77	Eddie	Royal	97	80	76	79
77	Nate	Washington	94	79	77	79
76	Jeff	Webb	91	81	73	78
75	Devin	Aromashodu	92	80	70	76
75	Keenan	Burton	92	80	80	80
75	Jason	Carter	89	80	78	80

Cornerbacks (CB)

OVR	FIRST NAME	LAST NAME	SPEED	MAN COVER	ZONE COVER	PRESS
97	Champ	Bailey	97	95	95	93
96	Nnamdi	Asomugha	93	99	90	92
96	Asante	Samuel	93	94	97	90
95	Rashean	Mathis	94	95	92	88
95	Terence	Newman	97	96	90	80
94	Chris	McAlister	93	92	91	93
94	Marcus	Trufant	94	94	88	85
93	DeAngelo	Hall	99	93	90	76
93	Al	Harris	88	95	90	98
93	Quentin	Jammer	94	92	88	94
93	Terrence	McGee	94	95	94	78
93	Lito	Sheppard	94	94	90	82
92	Ronde	Barber	88	78	96	97
92	Nate	Clements	92	92	85	92
92	Antonio	Cromartie	97	87	92	84
92	Charles	Woodson	88	88	94	92
91	Sheldon	Brown	91	93	92	85
91	Charles	Tillman	88	93	89	94
91	Nathan	Vasher	92	90	89	83
91	Antoine	Winfield	90	88	90	94
90	Leigh	Bodden	90	93	87	88
89	Dre'	Bly	93	90	88	88
89	Mike	McKenzie	90	94	88	80
89	Carlos	Rogers	91	92	89	93
89	Patrick	Surtain	90	90	90	84
89	Ike	Taylor	94	93	85	92
89	Deshea	Townsend	88	93	90	90
88	Cortland	Finnegan	92	88	80	84
88	Chris	Gamble	92	90	90	75
88	Nick	Harper	88	85	90	82
88	Walt	Harris	88	91	91	82
88	Anthony	Henry	87	86	90	90
88	Kelly	Jennings	94	92	86	82
88	Ken	Lucas	93	90	87	88
88	Sam	Madison	87	92	88	92
88	Darrelle	Revis	93	90	85	85
88	Shawn	Springs	88	88	92	89
87	Fakhir	Brown	88	90	86	88
87	Kelvin	Hayden	92	82	88	77
87	Ellis	Hobbs	94	91	84	72
87	Marlin	Jackson	88	78	91	85
87	Dunta	Robinson	96	88	78	90
87	Fred	Smoot	92	92	88	82
86	Will	Allen	96	91	82	82
86	Tye	Hill	98	89	83	74

Cornerbacks (CB) CONTINUED

OVR	FIRST NAME	LAST NAME	SPEED	MAN COVER	ZONE COVER	PRESS
86	Roderick	Hood	90	90	85	78
86	Ty	Law	87	84	90	84
86	Aaron	Ross	92	88	85	88
85	Drayton	Florence	91	85	84	80
84	Bryant	McFadden	90	89	84	78
84	Eric	Wright	92	89	84	78
83	Fernando	Bryant	92	88	84	74
83	Kevin	Dockery	91	87	82	82
83	Eric	Green	89	85	82	82
83	Cedric	Griffin	89	86	85	78
83	Johnathan	Joseph	97	82	80	74
83	Richard	Marshall	92	87	84	78
82	Fred	Bennett	92	86	80	78
82	Phillip	Buchanon	96	83	83	68
82	Randall	Gay	89	88	85	72
82	Leodis	McKelvin	94	86	80	78
82	Dominique	R-Cromartie	97	82	82	77
80	Leon	Hall	91	80	82	78
80	Michael	Lehan	89	87	78	78
80	Stanford	Routt	97	84	77	75
80	Aqib	Talib	91	82	82	80
80	Corey	Webster	90	85	80	77
79	Jordan	Babineaux	90	80	82	77
79	Antoine	Cason	92	82	80	65
79	Shawntae	Spencer	91	79	83	61
78	Danieal	Manning	91	75	80	65
78	Trumaine	McBride	89	84	80	68
78	Keith	Smith	93	82	78	74
77	Ronald	Bartell	92	80	78	74
77	Charles	Gordon	90	83	78	72
77	Chevis	Jackson	89	79	80	80
77	Terrell	Thomas	92	78	79	80
77	Fabian	Washington	98	78	72	70
77	Terrence	Wheatley	94	80	83	65
77	Josh	Wilson	95	80	80	78
76	Jarrett	Bush	91	80	74	72
76	Andre	Dyson	93	80	75	70
76	Corey	Ivy	90	82	80	78
76	Pat	Lee	92	83	75	85
76	Ricky	Manning	88	78	80	76
76	Karl	Paymah	93	82	77	65
76	Tracy	Porter	94	79	78	76
76	Jack	Williams	94	78	80	70
75	David	Barrett	87	77	81	68
75	Reynaldo	Hill	89	80	82	62

DEFENSIVE **PLAYER LIST**

Defensive Tackles (DT)

OVR	FIRST NAME	LAST NAME	SPEED	STRENGTH	POWER MOVES	FINESSE MOVES
98	Albert	Haynesworth	64	98	98	77
98	Pat	Williams	56	99	99	69
97	Jamal	Williams	54	98	98	67
97	Kevin	Williams	71	92	95	94
96	Casey	Hampton	54	98	98	68
96	Tommie	Harris	77	90	93	93
95	John	Henderson	62	95	97	65
94	Shaun	Rogers	55	97	98	84
94	Marcus	Stroud	61	95	97	80
94	Vince	Wilfork	60	95	95	79
93	Darnell	Dockett	75	90	94	89
92	Kris	Jenkins	60	93	95	80
92	Amobi	Okoye	69	89	90	89
91	Tommy	Kelly	68	88	88	78
91	Cory	Redding	70	88	88	78
89	Adam	Carriker	76	92	91	84
88	Kelly	Gregg	56	88	88	60
88	Cornelius	Griffin	65	86	89	72
87	Rocky	Bernard	64	89	85	86
87	Jovan	Haye	70	89	86	79
87	Fred	Robbins	58	90	89	68
86	Tony	Brown	66	87	86	84
86	Ryan	Pickett	60	93	87	70
85	Barry	Cofield	68	89	86	74
85	Anthony	Montgomery	48	93	92	68
85	Brian	Young	67	85	82	60
84	Brodrick	Bunkley	65	95	89	80
84	Glenn	Dorsey	70	92	87	85
84	Sedrick	Ellis	66	93	89	83
84	Jason	Ferguson	55	90	88	54
84	La'Roi	Glover	64	82	82	86
84	Vonnie	Holliday	63	86	86	74
84	Chris	Hovan	66	86	80	86
84	Grady	Jackson	40	96	92	58
84	Mike	Patterson	63	89	82	84
84	Jay	Ratliff	67	84	83	78
84	Dewayne	Robertson	64	88	87	82
84	Kyle	Williams	59	88	86	78
83	Chuck	Darby	67	82	83	84
83	Ron	Edwards	62	88	82	66
83	Ethan	Kelley	56	90	86	60
83	Ma'ake	Kemoeatu	50	96	88	60
83	John	McCargo	66	87	88	78
83	Anthony	McFarland	62	89	88	76
83	Domata	Peko	61	92	88	74

Defensive Tackles (DT) *CONTINUED*

OVR	FIRST NAME	LAST NAME	SPEED	STRENGTH	POWER MOVES	FINESSE MOVES
83	Terdell	Sands	51	95	89	72
83	John	Thornton	62	86	86	58
83	Keith	Traylor	47	93	88	44
83	Marcus	Tubbs	60	92	88	67
82	Jonathan	Babineaux	69	85	84	77
82	Raheem	Brock	76	80	78	86
82	Chris	Hoke	59	88	86	60
82	Spencer	Johnson	65	88	85	68
82	Johnny	Jolly	66	89	86	69
81	Mike	Wright	58	87	78	79
80	Tank	Johnson	64	85	84	80
80	Brandon	Mebane	63	91	88	75
80	Hollis	Thomas	48	91	85	48
80	Larry	Tripplett	65	84	78	82
80	Gabe	Watson	58	93	89	64
79	Alan	Branch	62	94	90	67
79	Dusty	Dvoracek	68	88	85	72
79	Aubrayo	Franklin	55	91	87	66
79	Trevor	Laws	74	92	85	77
79	Ryan	Sims	62	89	84	74
79	Randy	Starks	64	88	84	76
79	Marcus	Thomas	65	87	87	83
79	Gerard	Warren	61	89	86	72
78	Anthony	Adams	61	87	83	66
78	Justin	Bannan	56	88	82	78
78	William	Joseph	64	87	82	79
78	Trey	Lewis	62	88	84	74
78	Alvin	McKinley	56	91	85	52
78	Montae	Reagor	65	79	80	75
78	Darrell	Reid	64	84	82	74
78	Tank	Tyler	64	96	87	72
78	Darwin	Walker	66	84	82	76
77	Derek	Landri	66	84	80	82
77	Damione	Lewis	64	86	79	77
77	Matt	Toeaina	66	92	86	70
76	Shaun	Cody	64	82	79	82
76	Colin	Cole	59	89	83	62
76	Travis	Johnson	65	84	81	85
76	LaJuan	Ramsey	60	88	83	76
76	Ian	Scott	62	85	82	74
76	Pat	Sims	72	88	85	78
76	Ellis	Wyms	65	85	78	75
76	Jeff	Zgonina	55	85	80	65
75	Jay	Alford	63	86	80	80
75	Joe	Cohen	60	91	86	73

ROSTER ATTRIBUTES

Free Safeties (FS)

OVR	FIRST NAME	LAST NAME	SPEED	MAN COVER	ZONE COVER	HIT POWER
98	Ed	Reed	93	75	90	85
93	Antoine	Bethea	90	65	85	79
92	Brian	Dawkins	88	60	85	94
92	Reggie	Nelson	93	65	85	84
90	O.J.	Atogwe	90	70	85	74
90	Ken	Hamlin	88	65	85	95
89	Antrel	Rolle	89	79	88	45
88	Michael	Griffin	92	75	85	82
88	Madieu	Williams	90	75	87	75
87	Mike	Brown	87	65	88	74
87	Deon	Grant	89	70	85	75
87	Michael	Huff	93	77	80	73
87	Tanard	Jackson	89	78	84	86
86	Nick	Collins	93	74	80	77
86	Brandon	Meriweather	92	75	84	70
86	James	Sanders	88	60	85	66
85	Clinton	Hart	87	70	80	72
85	Jarrad	Page	88	66	86	86
84	Gary	Baxter	85	80	80	62
83	Ryan	Clark	87	60	80	72
83	Ko	Simpson	89	78	85	55
83	George	Wilson	88	65	80	72
82	Daniel	Bullocks	87	70	85	42
82	James	Butler	87	60	75	68
82	Will	Demps	85	60	80	77
81	Josh	Bullocks	90	60	80	65
81	Kevin	Kaesviharn	84	60	80	58
80	Gerald	Alexander	90	75	80	62
80	Kenny	Phillips	93	72	82	86
79	Hamza	Abdullah	88	62	75	75
79	Mark	Roman	88	65	75	65
79	John	Wendling	89	70	80	60
78	Will	Allen	86	68	80	50
78	Abram	Elam	87	58	75	68
78	Aaron	Francisco	86	60	80	55
78	Vincent	Fuller	88	77	80	68
78	Lamont	Thompson	87	70	78	62
77	Jason	Allen	92	70	70	70
77	Greg	Wesley	84	60	74	89
77	Jimmy	Williams	92	75	75	68
76	Terrence	Holt	85	65	75	78
76	Jim	Leonhard	86	65	75	70
76	Stuart	Schweigert	90	55	75	84
76	Marvin	White	90	55	73	81
75	Mike	Adams	85	60	75	68

Left Defensive Ends (LE)

OVR	FIRST NAME	LAST NAME	SPEED	STRENGTH	POWER MOVES	FINESSE MOVES
97	Aaron	Kampman	79	86	95	90
95	Patrick	Kerney	78	84	93	86
95	Robert	Mathis	88	76	79	96
94	Aaron	Smith	70	88	94	80
94	Michael	Strahan	77	86	92	88
94	Justin	Tuck	78	88	93	88
93	Luis	Castillo	70	95	96	75
92	Derrick	Burgess	85	73	77	93
90	Trevor	Pryce	68	93	93	76
90	Ty	Warren	68	88	92	79
90	Corey	Williams	70	86	88	92
89	Adewale	Ogunleye	83	73	74	94
87	Charles	Grant	74	80	84	82
87	Leonard	Little	84	75	72	88
87	Juqua	Parker	79	74	79	88
87	Paul	Spicer	70	86	88	80
86	Marques	Douglas	70	85	87	78
86	Shaun	Ellis	69	87	90	75
85	Chris	Clemons	82	70	75	85
85	Shaun	Smith	64	94	88	74
84	Antwan	Odom	75	78	83	83
83	Jamaal	Anderson	80	72	82	88
83	Ray	Edwards	78	74	79	87
83	Chris	Kelsay	75	79	85	74
83	Antonio	Smith	74	79	84	78
83	Isaac	Sopoaga	58	95	87	76
82	Kevin	Carter	65	86	85	80
82	Jared	DeVries	74	80	82	78
81	Phillip	Merling	78	80	85	83
81	Jarvis	Moss	82	68	76	87
80	Tim	Crowder	84	82	80	84
80	Matt	Roth	73	84	83	79
80	Anthony	Weaver	67	84	85	74
79	Calais	Campbell	78	82	83	80
78	Charles	Johnson	77	78	77	85
78	Kenard	Lang	74	75	82	72
78	Renaldo	Wynn	70	85	80	68
77	Kenechi	Udeze	72	76	80	81
77	Jimmy	Wilkerson	74	80	72	82
76	Victor	Adeyanju	78	77	76	82
76	Brent	Hawkins	78	72	69	79
76	Israel	Idonije	72	80	78	84
76	Mike	Montgomery	80	76	74	79
75	Victor	Abiamiri	76	76	80	78
75	Travis	Kirschke	64	85	85	66

DEFENSIVE PLAYER LIST

Left Outside Linebackers (LOLB)

OVR	FIRST NAME	LAST NAME	SPEED	TACKLING	PURSUIT	PLAY RECOGNITION
93	Derrick	Johnson	87	90	95	85
92	Shaun	Phillips	87	96	95	75
91	Cato	June	84	88	93	85
90	Angelo	Crowell	82	92	92	85
89	Greg	Ellis	78	87	95	86
89	LeRoy	Hill	83	89	90	80
89	David	Thornton	77	92	94	84
89	Marcus	Washington	82	90	90	85
88	Mike	Vrabel	79	88	90	86
87	Michael	Boley	85	88	92	80
87	Thomas	Davis	87	85	90	74
87	Calvin	Pace	82	87	92	78
85	Manny	Lawson	90	86	91	69
85	Willie	McGinest	78	88	88	86
84	Scott	Fujita	82	85	90	85
84	Jarret	Johnson	76	86	90	80
84	Paris	Lenon	79	87	89	78
83	Justin	Durant	85	85	92	69
83	Mark	Simoneau	80	86	86	78
82	Boss	Bailey	87	82	90	62
82	Bertrand	Berry	80	85	90	78
82	Brady	Poppinga	79	87	90	78
81	Tyjuan	Hagler	86	82	92	70
81	Mathias	Kiwanuka	82	84	88	69
81	Ben	Leber	78	85	86	75
81	Rob	Morris	76	85	88	85
81	Nate	Webster	79	85	88	79
80	Brandon	Chillar	78	85	88	76
80	Warrick	Holdman	77	84	83	82
80	Anthony	Spencer	83	79	88	68
79	Chris	Draft	78	84	88	70
79	Hunter	Hillenmeyer	75	86	84	78
79	Lemar	Marshall	80	80	88	75
79	Bryan	Thomas	78	78	90	70
79	Robert	Thomas	83	84	86	69
79	LaMarr	Woodley	82	82	90	65
78	Clint	Ingram	84	83	86	60
78	Rashad	Jeanty	77	82	86	74
78	Antwan	Peek	82	82	88	69
78	Reggie	Torbor	82	84	82	66
78	Sam	Williams	81	83	84	68
76	Charlie	Anderson	80	82	85	65
76	Stephen	Nicholas	79	82	87	66
76	Carlos	Polk	77	82	86	65
75	Travis	LaBoy	77	80	88	72

Middle Linebackers (MLB)

OVR	FIRST NAME	LAST NAME	SPEED	TACKLING	PURSUIT	PLAYER RECOGNITION
98	Brian	Urlacher	88	93	97	95
97	Lofa	Tatupu	85	96	98	94
96	London	Fletcher-Baker	82	97	98	93
96	Patrick	Willis	91	96	98	85
95	Antonio	Pierce	85	94	95	92
95	DeMeco	Ryans	84	96	97	87
94	Nick	Barnett	84	94	95	87
94	Ray	Lewis	82	94	95	95
94	Zach	Thomas	76	97	95	97
93	Jon	Beason	85	94	97	84
93	Mike	Peterson	84	93	97	90
92	James	Farrior	78	93	96	93
92	E.J.	Henderson	78	95	95	88
92	Kirk	Morrison	80	95	96	90
92	Will	Witherspoon	88	93	98	85
91	Gary	Brackett	80	94	93	87
91	Jonathan	Vilma	85	91	95	89
90	David	Harris	82	94	95	84
90	Bart	Scott	82	91	92	86
89	Barrett	Ruud	82	93	94	86
87	Bradie	James	78	90	94	84
86	Tedy	Bruschi	75	89	90	94
86	Stephen	Cooper	79	90	93	79
86	Larry	Foote	80	88	91	82
86	Gerald	Hayes	75	88	94	85
85	Eric	Barton	78	88	93	86
84	Andra	Davis	77	90	90	84
84	Napoleon	Harris	85	87	90	77
83	Leon	Williams	84	90	95	78
83	Al	Wilson	84	88	89	78
82	Paul	Posluszny	82	84	93	79
82	Junior	Seau	72	88	88	93
81	Akin	Ayodele	82	86	85	76
81	Curtis	Lofton	82	86	93	69
80	Victor	Hobson	78	86	89	79
79	Stewart	Bradley	78	86	85	70
79	Ryan	Fowler	78	85	90	73
79	Stephen	Tulloch	80	85	90	69
78	Jordon	Dizon	82	83	90	75
78	Dhani	Jones	80	82	86	83
77	Dontarrious	Thomas	85	84	92	68
76	Dan	Connor	80	84	90	70
76	Brandon	Moore	79	82	85	72
75	Monty	Beisel	76	83	86	68
75	Abdul	Hodge	79	84	86	75

ROSTER ATTRIBUTES

Punters (P)

OVR	FIRST NAME	LAST NAME	AWARENESS	KICK POWER	KICK ACCURACY	TACKLING
97	Shane	Lechler	72	98	94	18
96	Andy	Lee	71	97	94	35
95	Mat	McBriar	71	97	93	10
94	Dustin	Colquitt	70	96	94	29
90	Donnie	Jones	72	96	90	23
89	Brian	Moorman	70	94	92	19
87	Hunter	Smith	80	91	92	14
86	Mike	Scifres	66	96	88	22
84	Josh	Bidwell	80	92	89	23
83	Scott	Player	85	88	92	22
83	Todd	Sauerbrun	72	92	89	26
82	Jason	Baker	72	92	88	14
82	Chris	Kluwe	68	93	88	20
82	Kyle	Larson	68	92	89	27
82	Brad	Maynard	90	88	90	12
81	Jeff	Feagles	96	83	94	19
81	Nick	Harris	70	92	88	13
81	Dave	Zastudil	69	92	88	12
80	Durant	Brooks	60	95	85	30
80	Sam	Koch	68	92	87	33
80	Jon	Ryan	62	96	84	31
79	Ben	Graham	60	92	88	39
79	Daniel	Sepulveda	66	92	87	55
78	Steve	Weatherford	74	91	86	23
77	Craig	Hentrich	80	90	85	12
77	Michael	Koenen	64	93	84	14
77	Matt	Turk	93	85	89	13
76	Derrick	Frost	78	89	86	10
75	Jeremy	Kapinos	65	91	85	25
75	Ryan	Plackemeier	64	92	84	40

Right Defensive Ends (RE)

OVR	FIRST NAME	LAST NAME	SPEED	STRENGTH	POWER MOVES	FINESSE MOVES
98	Jason	Taylor	85	77	75	96
97	Jared	Allen	84	76	88	96
97	Osi	Umenyiora	85	78	92	96
97	Mario	Williams	86	85	95	95
96	Julius	Peppers	87	80	84	97
96	Richard	Seymour	71	92	96	82
95	Dwight	Freeney	88	78	87	96
93	Trent	Cole	85	75	78	94
93	Kyle	Vanden Bosch	74	84	94	86
92	John	Abraham	80	77	82	92

Right Defensive Ends (RE) *CONTINUED*

OVR	FIRST NAME	LAST NAME	SPEED	STRENGTH	POWER MOVES	FINESSE MOVES
92	Cullen	Jenkins	74	88	92	86
92	Aaron	Schobel	74	82	92	80
91	Haloti	Ngata	66	95	96	76
90	Elvis	Dumervil	82	72	95	92
90	Will	Smith	82	80	85	93
89	Justin	Smith	75	82	88	79
88	Gaines	Adams	86	74	82	92
88	Andre	Carter	78	75	79	87
88	Kabeer	Gbaja Biamila	85	70	74	92
87	Kenyon	Coleman	75	78	78	82
87	Jarvis	Green	69	86	89	76
87	Robaire	Smith	65	87	88	78
86	Tamba	Hali	74	75	77	87
86	Reggie	Hayward	77	78	83	86
86	Igor	Olshansky	62	91	89	74
86	Dewayne	White	77	75	79	88
85	Alex	Brown	83	74	75	88
85	Greg	White	82	72	80	90
84	Mark	Anderson	85	76	79	90
84	Chris	Canty	72	82	84	82
84	Brett	Keisel	73	85	86	72
84	Chris	Long	80	84	84	83
83	Jacques	Cesaire	69	86	80	80
83	Robert	Geathers	77	77	74	88
83	Darryl	Tapp	82	74	74	86
82	Ebenezer	Ekuban	72	75	77	79
82	James	Hall	73	80	78	86
82	Brian	Robison	79	79	80	80
81	Greg	Spires	74	73	77	83
81	Josh	Thomas	76	78	80	86
80	Darren	Howard	73	80	82	80
80	Bobby	McCray	79	72	75	84
79	Quentin	Groves	87	74	74	82
79	Simeon	Rice	79	70	72	82
79	Corey	Smith	74	70	74	84
78	Patrick	Chukwurah	78	70	66	80
78	Lawrence	Jackson	79	83	86	77
76	Dan	Bazuin	77	80	75	77
76	Kroy	Biermann	77	80	80	70
76	Chauncey	Davis	76	66	70	82
76	Stanley	McClover	78	70	70	84
76	Joe	Tafoya	69	77	80	70
75	Chris	Ellis	82	72	75	80
75	Ray	McDonald	68	83	82	78
75	Bryan	Smith	84	68	70	82

DEFENSIVE **PLAYER LIST**

Right Outside Linebackers (ROLB)

OVR	FIRST NAME	LAST NAME	SPEED	TACKLING	PURSUIT	PLAY RECOGNIITION
98	DeMarcus	Ware	87	94	99	84
97	Keith	Bulluck	86	91	92	86
97	Shawne	Merriman	87	93	95	78
95	Lance	Briggs	80	92	94	85
95	Julian	Peterson	86	90	98	86
95	Adalius	Thomas	87	90	90	82
95	D.J.	Williams	86	92	90	82
94	A.J.	Hawk	87	92	94	80
94	Ernie	Sims	90	93	96	72
93	Derrick	Brooks	80	90	90	90
93	Donnie	Edwards	80	88	90	90
93	James	Harrison	83	90	97	82
92	Daryl	Smith	82	90	92	86
91	Thomas	Howard	88	86	91	74
89	Keith	Brooking	78	90	90	87
89	Morlon	Greenwood	85	89	91	81
88	Rocky	McIntosh	84	87	89	79
88	Joey	Porter	82	91	92	80
88	Terrell	Suggs	87	84	95	78
88	Kamerion	Wimbley	85	87	92	78
87	Omar	Gaither	82	87	92	80
87	Ian	Gold	85	86	91	84
87	Chad	Greenway	85	85	95	79
87	Freddie	Keiaho	86	86	94	70
87	Kawika	Mitchell	84	87	90	78
87	Takeo	Spikes	82	87	90	84
86	Rosevelt	Colvin	84	84	92	82
85	Clark	Haggans	77	89	90	78
85	Chike	Okeafor	79	88	88	78
85	Pisa	Tinoisamoa	87	84	92	70
84	Landon	Johnson	81	86	87	80
84	Demorrio	Williams	86	84	88	80
82	Vernon	Gholston	85	84	86	60
82	Keith	Rivers	89	84	88	66
80	Bobby	Carpenter	85	80	84	77
80	Na'il	Diggs	78	85	86	70
80	Scott	Shanle	78	85	90	76
79	Tully	Banta-Cain	78	82	86	78
79	Keith	Ellison	83	83	88	70
78	Danny	Clark	78	81	89	78
77	Gary	Stills	77	83	87	70
77	Gerris	Wilkinson	82	82	88	58
75	Bruce	Davis	84	81	91	54
75	Stanford	Keglar	84	78	86	55
75	Chaun	Thompson	85	84	82	60

Strong Safeties (FS)

OVR	FIRST NAME	LAST NAME	SPEED	MAN COVER	ZONE COVER	HIT POWER
99	Bob	Sanders	93	80	95	98
98	Troy	Polamalu	93	65	85	90
96	Kerry	Rhodes	88	60	90	80
96	Adrian	Wilson	89	65	85	84
94	Rodney	Harrison	84	45	75	97
93	LaRon	Landry	94	65	85	94
92	Chris	Hope	88	65	85	85
92	John	Lynch	85	50	65	94
92	Darren	Sharper	88	80	90	75
92	Donte	Whitner	92	75	86	88
88	Dawan	Landry	86	70	80	78
88	Jermaine	Phillips	87	65	75	92
88	Roy	Williams	86	40	65	98
87	Atari	Bigby	86	50	70	94
87	Sean	Jones	90	60	70	88
87	Michael	Lewis	87	60	80	85
87	Bernard	Pollard	86	62	77	90
87	Brian	Williams	88	80	85	60
87	Gibril	Wilson	88	65	85	80
86	Brian	Russell	85	65	85	84
86	Dwight	Smith	89	70	75	77
85	Chris	Harris	86	60	75	92
83	Yeremiah	Bell	86	65	75	84
83	Sammy	Knight	80	40	80	82
83	Marlon	McCree	84	55	70	86
83	Brandon	McGowan	87	60	75	82
83	Quintin	Mikell	85	70	80	80
82	Corey	Chavous	85	65	80	72
82	Donovin	Darius	84	40	60	95
80	Nedu	Ndukwe	90	60	75	80
79	Michael	Boulware	85	60	75	80
79	Mike	Doss	86	55	80	82
79	Glenn	Earl	86	62	83	80
79	Kenoy	Kennedy	84	45	70	89
79	Gerald	Sensabaugh	87	60	75	81
79	Eric	Weddle	89	65	78	74
78	C.C.	Brown	87	60	75	68
78	Sean	Considine	86	50	75	75
78	Tank	Williams	86	50	65	85
77	Eric	Smith	88	70	75	70
76	Tyrone	Carter	82	60	80	68
76	Matt	Giordano	94	55	75	60
76	Travares	Tillman	85	60	70	77
76	Pat	Watkins	89	70	80	66
75	Todd	Johnson	83	40	65	93

ROSTER ATTRIBUTES

Note: *The advanced strategies in this section of the guide were written on All Madden Hardcore level.*

▲ *Ward is the play's primary receiver*

▲ *Holmes is hot routed on a slant*

ADVANCED STRATEGY

GUN BUNCH WK CORNER STRIKE — *PITTSBURGH PLAYBOOK*

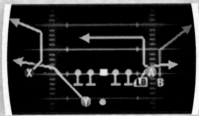

▲ *One of the better pass plays*

As we have already mentioned, finding bump-n-run man beaters is one of the most important things you will want to do before playing head-to-head against a human opponent, whether it be offline or online.

By spending time in the practice room, we found plenty of ways to beat bump-n-run man coverage with the use of motion. Motion allows us to get receivers off the line of scrimmage without being jammed. A bump-n-run man beater that we like to call from the Pittsburgh Steelers' playbook is the Gun Bunch Wk Corner Strike.

Here is a quick look at the pass routes by design of the play:

Flanker – Corner
Slot – Deep Dig
Tight End – Flat
Split End – Corner with inside release
Running Back – Flat

The only pre-snap route adjustment we make is to hot route split end Santonio Holmes on a slant route. We

▲ *Sweed lines up in the slot*

do this to give us another quick option on the backside.

Next, we take control of slot receiver Limas Sweed.

We then motion him out wide to the right and let him set.

▲ *Sweed lines up out wide*

We motion him back inside towards Hines Ward and Heath Miller.

▲ *Sweed in motion*

Once he gets in front of Ward, we snap the ball.

If the snap is timed right, Miller,

▲ *Sweed in front of Ward*

Sweed, and Ward will all get off the line of scrimmage without being jammed. The reason none of them get jammed is because the defenders that are covering them all switch.

▲ *All three receivers aren't jammed*

We like to move quarterback Ben Roethlisberger out to the right side. Notice in the screenshot that all three receivers are open.

▲ *Miller is the most open*

We throw the ball to Ward on the corner route once he breaks towards

the corner of the end zone. We achieve a bullet pass by pressing hard right on the Left Thumbstick.

▲ *Big Ben throws a rocket*

We take control of Ward and make the catch 12 yards down the field.

▲ *Ward has hands of glue*

QUICK TIPS ABOUT THE PLAY

Look to throw to Miller in the flat as your first option, then Ward on the corner, and then Sweed on a dig route.

If you see your opponent cheating his coverage towards the bunch side, consider throwing to Holmes running the slant on the back side. This will force your opponent to have to account for him.

▲ *Holmes is open on the slant*

▲ *Big Ben throws to Miller in the flat*

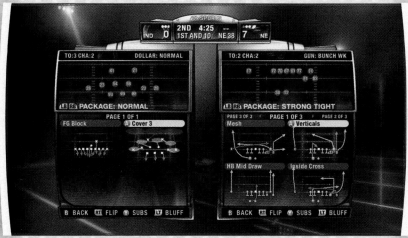

▲ *Gun Bunch Wk Vertical Concept*

▲ *Maroney lines up left of the quarterback*

ADVANCED ZONE COVERAGE BEATER

The Gun Bunch Wk Verticals Concept is best used to attack zone coverage, particularly Cover 2 and Cover 3. With four receivers running vertical routes, it stretches the defensive pass coverage.

In the play's default design, here is a quick look at each of the pass routes.

Flanker – Wheel
Slot – Deep Cross
Tight End – Wheel
Split End – Go
Running Back – Delayed Curl

VERSUS COVER 3 ZONE COVERAGE

▲ *Hot route Moss on a streak*

The play's primary receiver is the tight end running the wheel route. Notice in the screenshot that we have used the Strong Tight package to line up Randy Moss in the tight end position. We want to use his speed to get down the field quicker so he forces the deep defenders to drop back further.

As they drop further back in their deep coverage assignments, it will help get Wes Welker (running the wheel route on the outside) open underneath them.

Instead of having Moss run his default route, we want to hot route him on a streak.

▲ *Welker not open*

Once the ball is snapped, look at Welker first. If the coverage is Cover 3, he will be open for a quick pass in the flat.

▲ *Moss forces the RCB to cover him*

Notice that Moss has forced the left cornerback to turn inside to cover him.

Now, we throw to Welker running the wheel route. When making this throw, we want to press hard right on the Left Thumbstick. This will throw the ball outside and away from the left cornerback.

We take control of Welker and make the catch for a 20-yard pick-up.

If Welker is not open, look for Jabar

▲ *Throw the pass over the underneath coverage*

▲ *Brady zeros in on his target*

▲ *Gaffney makes the grab*

Gaffney on the deep cross or look for Laurence Maroney on the delayed curl route underneath.

VERSUS COVER 2 MAN

If man coverage is called, the same pass concept can be run. Instead of looking to throw to Welker on the wheel route, we look to throw to

Gaffney on the deep cross.

Moss and Gaffney will run straight down the field side by side for the first 10 yards.

▲ *Same pass routes are run*

Once they get to this point, Gaffney will cross underneath Moss. This will cause the defenders covering them both to switch.

Chad Jackson, who is running a go route on the left, will clear his man and free safety out, so that Gaffney will be

open underneath on his route. Once we see that he has a few yards of separation from his man, we throw him a hard bullet pass.

Once the ball is up in the air, we take control of Gaffney and make the catch for an 18-yard pick-up.

QUICK TIPS ABOUT THE PLAY

Not every quarterback can put the pass on the money like Tom Brady. If you use another team with the New England Patriots' playbook, check to see what your quarterback's throwing power and accuracy are. If the quarterback doesn't have the arm strength or accuracy, chances are that the ball cannot be delivered where it needs to be.

▲ *In Banjo defenders switch*

The higher the difficulty level, the smaller the passing window is going to be.

Most top players will scheme several offensive plays together to keep their opponent off-balance on defense. Many top players will mix one or two runs and three or four pass plays in their scheme. They will use the same set-up for each play. For instance, if their scheme involves sending the flanker in motion, then for each play they will send the flanker in motion to make the plays all look the same.

In *Madden NFL 09*, the Madden Playbook design team really stepped it up by adding plays within each formation with the same type of motion. This gives us the ability to create two, three, and four play schemes.

One of the four play schemes we like to run is out of the New York Jets' Playbook. The formation we use is the Weak Close.

The Weak Close formation has the flanker lined up tight on the right, and the split end lined up tight on the left. The tight end lines up on the right. The halfback lines up about 6 yards behind the quarterback. The fullback lines up offset to the quarterback's left side.

JETS PLAYBOOK SCHEME

There are four plays in the Jets' playbook out of the Weak Close that have the fullback going in auto motion to the right side:

Spacing (pass)
Flanker Drive (pass)
Power O (run)
PA Power O (play action)

▲ *Jets Play Combo*

Each one of these plays allows us to attack the defense in a different way.

PERSONNEL

By default, the personnel for the Weak Close has two receivers, one tight end, one halfback, and one fullback. We prefer to package out our fullback and package in a faster halfback. We use the Dual HB Swap package for this scheme. This moves our number one halfback to fullback and our number two halfback to the number one halfback spot.

SPACING

The Weak Close Spacing has Jones lined up at fullback. Once he is sent in

▲ *Baker runs a sit route*

auto motion, he will run a flat route to the left.

If man coverage is called, such as the 4-3 Normal 2 Man Under, he will be open for a quick bullet pass in the flat. Notice that before Jones is sent in auto motion, the right outside linebacker covers him in man coverage. The middle linebacker covers Washington.

▲ *A typical base defense*

Before we snap the ball, we hot route Baker and Coles on streaks. We do this so that the two defenders covering them will be further down the field once we make the throw to Jones in the flat. If we were to have them run their default routes, the two defenders covering them may be able to react quicker to Jones once he makes the catch. By sending Baker and Coles on streaks, both defenders will be too far down the field to make a tackle on

▲ *There are now three vertical routes*

Jones once the catch is made.

Jones is sent in auto motion to the right. At this point, the middle linebacker now covers Jones, while the right outside linebacker covers Washington.

Once the ball is snapped, the middle linebacker is already at a disadvantage because Jones has a few steps on him.

The middle linebacker must fight through the receivers running streaks and defenders covering them. As you can see in the screenshot, there is a lot of traffic for him to avoid while trying to cover Jones in the flat.

▲ *Washington stays in to pass block*

By the time the middle linebacker fights his way through, the ball is already thrown to Jones in the flat.

Once the catch is made, we take control of Jones and run straight up the field. Notice how much running room we have towards the sideline. This play is generally good for 8 or more yards against man coverage.

QUICK PLAY TIPS

Another option to look for is Cotchery on the deep post if Cover 2 Man coverage is called.

If you don't want to send Baker on a streak, consider hot routing him on a drag route. This will give you another underneath option to throw to if Jones isn't open in the flat.

FLANKER DRIVE

The second play we use in our four plays scheme out of the Jets Weak Close is the Flanker Drive. This play is designed to attack the opposite side of the field than the Spacing scheme attacks with the fullback.

The play's primary receiver is Coles, who runs a drag route from right to left. Jones is sent in auto motion to the right. Instead of him running a flat route, he runs a wheel route. Baker runs a crossing route and Cotchery runs a corner post. Washington runs a delayed curl route out of the backfield.

▲ 5 receivers run pass routes

Once the ball is snapped, we could look to throw to Jones before he breaks up the field.

If we don't throw to Jones, we then look for Coles on the drag route.

▲ Coles running a drag

With Coles's speed, he is able to get separation from the left cornerback covering him.

Once the catch is made, we take control of Coles and use his speed to pick up yardage after the catch.

QUICK PLAY TIPS

If you are playing against a human opponent who is sitting right next to you, try to act like you are hot routing the tight end and flanker. That way it makes it looks like you are sending them on streaks.

Baker is another option to look for running the crossing route from right to left.

POWER O

Of our four play Jet Weak Close scheme, the Power O is our only run play. The same auto motion is used with Jones. Keep in mind: we don't want to sub Jones out, even though he can't run

block as well as Tony Richardson. We want to make sure our opponent has no clue which play we are running.

Left guard Alan Faneca pulls to the right and becomes our lead blocker.

▲ A solid run play

Once Pennington hands the ball off to Washington, we take control of him and look to go outside.

Faneca makes a key block that allows us to spring Washington into the open field.

▲ Press down the sprint button

Once in the open field, we make a few moves and pick up 12 yards before finally being brought down.

PA POWER O

The PA Power O is the last play we want look at in our four play scheme. This play works best once the Power O has been established. Baker is the

play's primary receiver. He runs a corner route. Coles runs a go route. Cotchery runs a corner post. Jones is sent in auto motion. Once the ball is snapped, he runs a flat route.

▲ A good PA red zone play

Pennington play fakes to Washington. Watch to see if any defenders bite on the play fake.

As we already mentioned, the play's primary receiver is the tight end running the corner route. We don't normally look to throw to him first; instead, we look for Jones in the flat.

If Jones is not open, we then look for Baker on the corner route. In the screenshot, we throw a hard bullet pass to Baker by pressing right hard on the Left Thumbstick.

We take control of Baker and make the grab at the 1-yard line.

QUICK PLAY TIPS

Play action can be cancelled by hot routing the running back on a pass route or hot routing him to pass block.

This is a good red zone play to call.

▲ *A run commit banner drops down*

Now that we've discussed basic and intermediate tips on defending the run and pass, it's time to move to a few advanced tips to shut our opponents down.

RUN COMMIT

The Run Commit feature is a powerful tool to use to shut down your opponent's rushing attack. Many top players use this tool because they know what it can do and how effective it is.

By pressing the Right Thumbstick down shortly after the ball is snapped, defenders will react more quickly than normal to the ball carrier.

You will see the defense back off their coverage assignments and go aggressively after the ball carrier as soon as you activate Run Commit.

A common strategy is to bring the defense out in a strong pass defense formation like Dime or Quarters. This

▲ *The HB goes down in the backfield*

puts a lot of speed on the field.

If they see that a run has been called, they will quickly use the Run Commit to get after the ball carrier. This allows the defense to defend the running game from passing sets.

Flexibility is key. They can defend multiple receiver sets, yet at the same time stuff the run game and get their fastest players on the field to blitz."

PASS COMMIT

Pass commit is used in two different ways. To get pass commit to work, press up on the Right Thumbstick shortly after the ball is snapped.

DEEP COVERAGE

▲ *Both safeties quickly drop back*

The most common way to play deep coverage is to get the defenders playing in the deep zone to drop back quicker in pass coverage. Against speed receivers, this is an effective way of keeping the safeties from getting beat deep.

COUNTERING PLAY ACTION

▲ *The QB fakes the handoff to the HB*

Many players on offense like to use play action to go deep. It can be frustrat-

ing on defense when calling a blitz, and all the defenders go after the running back because they bite on the play fake. A great way to keep the defenders from biting on the play fake is to use pass commit. The defenders won't usually chase the running back; instead, they will go straight after the quarterback.

DELAYED BUMP-N-RUN MAN COVERAGE

▲ *Bump-n-run is called*

One last advanced pass defense tactic we want to discuss is delayed bump-n-run in man coverage. It's been in the game for some time now, but not everyone knows about it.

First, come out in man defense and then call bump-n-run man coverage. Next, reset the defense. Once the ball is snapped, the defenders will jam the receivers about 2 yards further down the field than if they were in normal bump-n-run man coverage. Why use this, you ask? First, it's a good way to disguise bump-n-run man coverage; secondly, it can throw the timing off between the receivers and quarterback.

▲ Bob Sanders is one the best defenders in the game

▲ Sprint Sanders towards the target

USER PICK

▲ Use the Sprint button if needed

There is nothing more satisfying than being able to take control of a defender and pick a pass off while in the air.

The key is taking control of the

▲ Sanders picks the pass off

defense and using the strafe to get him in between the ball and the intended receiver.

As the ball is coming down, hold the Strafe button down while pressing the Catch button.

If done correctly, the defender will pick the pass off and go the other way.

USER PICK TIPS

The best way to learn to user pick is to have a friend throw bombs. Don't worry about if he scores or not; just try to get the defender in position to pick the pass off.

Most players like to control safeties because it's the easiest way to defend the deep pass.

If you feel your user stick control skills aren't as good as you want them, only attempt to pick the pass off if

another defender is in the area. That way if you miss, you don't give up a deep pass.

USER SWAT

▲ Cut underneath Moss

The user swat is the safest way to defend the pass. If you don't feel like you can pick the pass off, use the user swat.

With the user swat, you don't have to use the Strafe button. Instead use the Sprint button to keep up with the receiver.

As the ball is coming down, press the Swat button to get the defender up in the air.

If timed correctly, the defender will swat the pass away from the receiver.

ADVANCED STRATEGY

Achievements are awarded after completing a specific in-game task as listed to the right —an "Achievement Unlocked" icon will appear when this occurs.

▲ *Slam Dunk Achievement*

▲ *Allen gets his 6th sack*

▲ *Hester returns his second punt*

DESCRIPTION	POINTS
Hold a rival opponent to under 20 points in a game	10
Rush for 300 yards in a game with the Jets	10
Kick a FG of over 50 yards in a Franchise game	15
Score 40 points against a rival in a Rivalry game	20
Complete a game without a fumble	25
Slam Dunk All-Star Dunk the ball over the goalpost (or at least attempt to) after a touchdown	30
Shine in the Spotlight Celebrate a touchdown in an end zone hot spot	30
Can you believe these seats Celebrate a touchdown in a wall hotspot	30
Steal Their Thunder Steal opponent's celebration	30
Score 60 points against a rival in a Rivalry game	30
Complete a game without throwing an interception	30
Midway Monster Create a legendary player from the past	50
Shut out a rival team in a Franchise game	50
Throw 7 TDs in a game with the Falcons	50
Throw for 550 yards in a game with the Titans	50
6 Sacks with one player in a game	50
Catch 10 passes with 1 receiver in a game	50
Hold a rival opponent to under 300 yards total offense in a game	50
Intercept 6 passes in a game	50
Maintain an 80 pct completion percentage for a game	50
Record 12 sacks in a game	50
Run for 6 TDs in a game with the Dolphins	50
Return 2 punts for a TD in a game	65
Return 2 kickoffs for a TD in a game	75